DÆMON
VOICES

www.davidficklingbooks.com

Dæmon Voices

IN OVER THIRTY ESSAYS, written over twenty years, one of the world's great storytellers meditates on storytelling. Warm, funny, generous, entertaining and, above all, deeply considered, they offer thoughts on a wide variety of topics, including the origin and composition of Philip Pullman's own stories, the craft of writing and the storytellers who have meant the most to him.

The art of storytelling is everywhere present in the essays themselves, in the instantly engaging tone, the vivid imagery and striking phrases, the resonant anecdotes, the humour and learnedness. Together, they are greater than the sum of their parts: a single, sustained engagement with story and storytelling.

Selected Works by Philip Pullman

***The Book of Dust* trilogy**	*La Belle Sauvage*
His Dark Materials trilogy	*Northern Lights* *The Subtle Knife* *The Amber Spyglass*
His Dark Materials **companion books**	*Lyra's Oxford* *Once Upon a Time in the North*
The Sally Lockhart quartet	*The Ruby in the Smoke* *The Shadow in the North* *The Tiger in the Well* *The Tin Princess*
Other books	*The Haunted Storm* *Galatea* *Count Karlstein* *How to be Cool* *Spring-Heeled Jack* *The Broken Bridge* *The Wonderful Story of Aladdin* *and the Enchanted Lamp* *Clockwork, or, All Wound Up* *The Firework-Maker's Daughter* *Mossycoat* *The Butterfly Tattoo* *I was a Rat! or The Scarlet Slippers* *Puss in Boots: The Adventures of That* *Most Enterprising Feline* *The Scarecrow and his Servant* *The Adventures of the New* *Cut Gang* *The Good Man Jesus and* *the Scoundrel Christ* *Grimm Tales: For Young and Old*
Graphic novels	*Count Karlstein* *The Adventures of John Blake*

PHILIP PULLMAN

—

DÆMON VOICES

ESSAYS ON STORYTELLING

edited by

SIMON MASON

David Fickling Books

31 Beaumont Street
Oxford OX1 2NP, UK

Dæmon Voices: Essays on Storytelling is
A DAVID FICKLING BOOK

First published in Great Britain in 2017 by
David Fickling Books,
31 Beaumont Street,
Oxford, OX1 2NP

Text © Philip Pullman, 2017
Introduction © Simon Mason, 2017
Cover illustration by John Lawrence
Cover based on an initial concept by Ness Wood
Design and Typography by Webb and Webb Design Ltd

978-1-910200-96-4
1 3 5 7 9 10 8 6 4 2

Papers used by David Fickling Books are from well-managed forests and other responsible sources.

MIX
Paper from
responsible sources
FSC® C018072

DAVID FICKLING BOOKS Reg. No. 8340307

A CIP catalogue record for this book is available from the British Library.
Typeset and designed by Webb & Webb Limited.
Printed and bound in Great Britain by Clays Limited, St. Ives plc.

To Michael and Clare

Contents

Topic Finder

Certain themes recur in more than one essay. The lists below identify some of those themes and group together the essays in which they are discussed.

On Children's Literature

Imaginary Friends (305)

Intention (113)

Children's Literature
　Without Borders (123)

On Education and Story

Let's Write it in Red (141)

Talents and Virtues (399)

Paradise Lost (53)

**On Folk Tales, Fairy
Tales and Epics**

Epics (165)

Folk Tales of Britain (169)

As Clear as Water (179)

Imaginary Friends (305)

Magic Carpets (7)

The Classical Tone (239)

On His Dark Materials

Dreaming of Spires (107)

God and Dust (423)

Heinrich von Kleist: On the
　Marionette Theatre (45)

Reading in the Borderland (259)

The Path through the Wood (85)

The Writing of Stories (23)

On My Other Books

As Clear as Water (179)

Intention (The Scarecrow and
　His Servant) (113)

Poco a Poco (Clockwork and
　I Was A Rat!) (205)

The Firework-Maker's Daughter
　on Stage (299)

The Path Through the Wood
　(I Was a Rat!) (85)

The Story of The Good Man Jesus
　and the Scoundrel Christ (357)

Introduction

As the author of some of the most popular stories of our time, Philip Pullman requires very little introduction; his books have been read by millions of eager readers the world over, not only the trilogy of *His Dark Materials*, but also the Sally Lockhart novels, his fairy tales, his retelling of Grimm's folk tales, the fable *The Good Man Jesus and the Scoundrel Christ*, and many others. He is recognised as one of the world's great storytellers.

During my work on his essays, we met several times, usually at his home. In person he is a striking presence, physically imposing but quiet in his manner. He typically dresses in casual, practical clothes with plenty of pockets that give him the air of a craftsman, an electrician perhaps, or a carpenter – which, in fact, he is. When we began our meetings he still had his famous ponytail, which he had vowed to keep until finishing the first volume of *The Book of Dust*. He reported that *The Bookseller* had said it made him look like a retired roadie. The ponytail came off a few months later, and he showed it to me in a transparent bag. 'I'm thinking of donating it to the Bodleian Library,' he said.

Humorous, formidably knowledgeable, sharply intelligent and firm in his opinions, he has absolutely no airs and graces, instinctively putting people at their ease. Each time I met him I was struck by his relaxed courtesy. (I was struck in a different way by his pair of hyperactive cockapoo puppies – Mixie and Coco – who flew at me from all angles, even, somehow, from above, while Philip calmly made coffee in the kitchen.) The low-ceilinged, open-fired room where we talked was filled with objects – musical instruments, pictures, books and wooden constructions, which he had made himself. The pleasure he takes in the well-made is evident, and I was often shown things he liked: a Doves Press edition of

Paradise Lost printed with the famous Doves type; a woodcut by John Lawrence; a life-size alethiometer made for him by an admiring reader. He nearly always had a story to tell about these objects. The Doves type, he told me, was once destroyed by their co-owner T. J. Cobden-Sanderson after a dispute with his business partner Emory Walker, by casting it, bit by bit, into the Thames from Hammersmith Bridge, a process which he undertook only on dark nights, and which took him five months to complete, beginning at the end of August 1916 and finishing in January 1917. (Nearly a hundred years later, it was retrieved by the Port of London Authority's Salvage diving team employed by a designer wishing to digitise the type.)

This instinct to tell stories is deep in Philip. For sheer storytelling excitement, his own stories are hard to beat. But their popularity is due also, I think, to their thoughtfulness, the way in which, with great curiosity and energy, they engage ideas and issues and ask interesting questions. Is the world conscious? What is our place and purpose here? What is evil? Where does religious belief come from? Can innocence be regained? His stories dramatise such questions in thrilling ways. And so do his essays.

The thirty-two here, selected from more than 120, were written over many years. The oldest is 'Let's Write it in Red', a fascinating – and fascinated – meditation on story writing considered as a game, dating from June 1997. The most recent is 'Soft Beulah's Night', from November 2014, an impassioned personal testament to the wisdom and originality of the poet William Blake who, arguably, has influenced Philip the most.

The essays are also very varied. Partly, this is because they were written in different circumstances, for different purposes: many were talks, delivered at conferences or symposia; others were articles in newspapers; yet others were commissioned pieces in journals, chapters in books, programme notes and promotional pieces. Mainly, though, it is because Philip's interests range so widely. Not for nothing is his personal dæmon the raven, that picker-up of bits and pieces here and there. Like most great writers, he is a great reader, and thinks about what he has picked up during a lifetime of passionate, engaged reading of the work of physicists, literary theorists, historians, film-makers, theologians, art historians, novelists and poets.

He is interested in the discoveries of science, ('intellectual daring and imaginative brilliance without parallel'), the freedoms of democracy (in particular 'the great democracy of reading and writing'), the evils of authoritarianism ('always reductive whether it's in power or not') and the pitfalls of education ('any education that neglects the experience of delight will be a dry and tasteless diet with no nourishment in it'). He is profoundly interested in religion, while remaining puzzled by aspects of it. 'The first thing to say about the Bishop's arguments in his book,' he writes in 'God and Dust', 'is that I agree with every word of them, except the words I don't understand; and that the words I don't understand are those such as *spirit, spiritual* and *God*.'

He is interested, above all, in human nature, how we live and love and fight and betray and console one another. How we explain ourselves to ourselves.

So there is great variety here. But all the essays relate, deliberately, to a single theme. Storytelling. It is what he knows best. His own stories, and his experience of writing them. Other people's stories, and his passionate appreciation of them. The techniques of writing stories. The pleasures of reading stories. The importance of stories in our culture.

To pick a few examples, at random. In 'Magic Carpets' he writes about the responsibilities of the storyteller – to his audience, to language, to his story and – not the least important thing – to his family's finances. In 'The Writing of Stories' he shares his thoughts on technical issues: tenses, perspective and other aspects of narration. In '*Oliver Twist*' and '*Paradise Lost*' he celebrates a few of the authors and books he particularly loves. In 'God and Dust' he writes about story and religion; and in

'The Origin of the Universe' about story and science. In 'Folk Tales of Britain' and 'As Clear as Water' he explains why he so loves the swift, clean tone of the oldest forms of storytelling. And in numerous essays he generously writes about his own work, including (in 'The Writing of Stories') his composition of the opening passages of *Northern Lights*, and (in 'The Path Through the Wood'), the thinking that led to the idea of the extraordinary wheeled creatures called *mulefa* who appear in *The Amber Spyglass*. 'Around this time,' he writes, 'my son Tom and I spent a morning walking around Lake Bled, in Slovenia, talking about the problem…' He has turned his account into a story, and it is all the more interesting for it.

Though they often deal with abstruse ideas, the essays are never in the least obscure; Philip's storytelling ('I realised some time ago that I belong at the vulgar end of the literary spectrum,' he remarks) is evident in the instantly engaging tone, the vivid imagery and striking phrases, the resonant anecdotes.

It is striking, though not surprising, how well the essays cohere, despite their diverse origins. As in a conversation, a favourite topic is explored in different ways, from different angles, raised in one essay, scrutinised at greater length in another, re-examined in a third, developed in a new context in a fourth, and transformed in a fifth. I think it is possible to read them, in fact, as a single, sustained engagement with story and storytelling by a great storyteller and, to my mind, the book takes its place naturally among Philip's others. I hope that it will give his readers the same excitement that it has given me in bringing them together.

I should say a word about the methodology of gathering and ordering them. As I mentioned, they were written over the years, for various purposes. Many were talks, delivered at a specific moment in time, at a particular place. Slight tweaks have been made here and there to eliminate instances of unnecessary outdatedness. A bigger issue was the occurrence of repetitions, as Philip returned over and again to favourite topics. Tweaks have been made here too – though not too many. As I say,

I felt that the return – the re-examination and development – of these ideas and themes are an important part of the overall story. Although Philip returns several times to, say, the gnostic myth or Kleist's essay 'On the Marionette Theatre', I have preserved these passages as much as possible, cutting out only word-for-word duplications.

The sense of an overall story also directed my ordering of the essays. I could have arranged them chronologically or thematically, but I found the former unenlightening and the latter too clunky. I toyed for a while with the idea of a random arrangement, but randomness can be dull and awkward as well as serendipitous, and in practice I doubted it would end up random at all. I opted for something else: a loose arrangement along a thread of connections and correspondences, which begins with the figure of the storyteller, proceeds through many different explorations of the writing of stories, broadens to take in the pleasures, purpose and nature of reading stories, and ends with a deeply felt statement of belief in the power and centrality of stories in our culture. If readers want to read the collection from the beginning, I hope they will find pleasure and interest in this order. But it is not intended to limit readers, who are of course free to dip in and out as they wish, find a congenial subject in the topic finder, or just choose an essay at random. After all, as Philip says, free and democratic reading is a vital part of the Republic of Heaven, and delight always an aspect of storytelling.

Simon Mason
Oxford, March 2017

Magic Carpets

THE WRITER'S RESPONSIBILITIES

On the various sorts of responsibility incumbent on an author: to himself and his family, to language, to his audience, to truth, and to his story itself

THANK YOU FOR INVITING ME TO TALK TO THIS CONFERENCE. I'VE BEEN racking my brains to think of a way of addressing your theme of magic carpets and international perspectives, because I think one should at least try, and I've come to the conclusion that although I'm not going to say anything directly about that, what I do have to say is as true as I can make it. I'm going to talk about responsibility.

And responsibility is a subject I've been thinking about a lot recently, because it has a bearing on the way the world is going, and on whether or not our profession, our art or craft, has anything to contribute to the continual struggle to make the world a better place; or whether what we do is, in the last analysis, trivial and irrelevant. Of course, there are several views about the relationship between art and the world, with at one end of the spectrum the Soviet idea that the writer is the engineer of human souls, that art has a social function and had better damn well produce what the state needs, and at the other end the declaration of Oscar Wilde that there is no such thing as a good book or a bad book; books are well written or badly written, that is all; and all art is quite useless. However, it's notable that the book in which he wrote those words as a preface, *The Picture of Dorian Gray*, is one of the most moral stories that was ever written, so even Saint Oscar admitted with part of himself that art does have a social and ethical function.

Anyway, I take it that art, literature, children's literature, do *not* exist

7

in an ivory tower; I take it that we're inextricably part of the world, the whole world; and that we have several kinds of responsibility that follow from that.

So that's what I'm going to talk about briefly this evening – the responsibility of the storyteller – and how far it extends, and what directions it extends in, and where it stops.

The first responsibility to talk about is a social and financial one: the sort of responsibility we share with many other citizens – the need to look after our families and those who depend on us. People of my age will probably remember that wonderfully terrifying advertisement they used to have for Pearl Assurance. It told a little story which I used to read all the way through every time I saw it. When many years later I learned the meaning of the word 'catharsis', I realised what it was that I'd been feeling as I read that little story: I had been purged by pity and terror.

The advertisement consisted of five drawings of a man's face. The first was labelled 'At age 25', and it showed a bright-eyed, healthy, optimistic young fellow, full of pep and vigour, with a speech balloon saying 'They tell me the job doesn't carry a pension.'

Each succeeding drawing showed him ten years older, and the speech balloons changed with each one. At forty-five, for example, he was looking sombre and lined and heavy with responsibility, and saying 'Unfortunately, the job is not pensionable.' It ended with him at sixty-five: wrinkled, haggard, wild-eyed, a broken-down old man staring into the very abyss of poverty and decrepitude, and saying, 'Without a pension *I really don't know what I shall do!'*

Well, I'm not going to sell you a pension. I'm just going to say that we should all insist that we're properly paid for what we do. We should sell our work for as much as we can decently get for it, and we shouldn't be embarrassed about it. Some tender and sentimental people – especially young people – are rather shocked when I tell them that I write books to make money, and I want to make a lot, if I can.

When we start writing books we're all poor; we all have to do another job in the daytime and write at night; and, frankly, it's not as romantic as it seems to those who aren't doing it. Worry – constant low-level unremitting anxiety about bank statements and mortgages and bills – is not a good state of mind to write in. I've done it. It drains your energy; it distracts you; it weakens your concentration. The only good thing about being poor and obscure is the obscurity – just as the only trouble with being rich and famous is the fame.

But if we find we can make money by writing books, by telling stories, we have the *responsibility* – the responsibility to our families, and those we look after – of doing it as well and as profitably as we can. Here's a useful piece of advice to young writers: cultivate a reputation – which need have no basis in reality – but cultivate a *reputation* of being very fond of money. If the people you have to deal with think that you like the folding stuff a great deal, they'll think twice before they offer you very small amounts of it. What's more, by expecting to get paid properly for the work we do, we're helping our fellow writers in their subsequent dealings with schools, or festivals, or prisons, or whatever. I feel not a flicker of shame about declaring that I want as much money for my work as I can get. But, of course, what that money is buying, what it's for, is security, and space, and peace and quiet, and time.

The next responsibility I want to talk about is the writer's, the story-teller's, responsibility towards language. Once we become conscious of the way language works, and our relationship to it, we can't pretend to be innocent about it; it's not just something that happens to us, and over which we have no influence. If human beings can affect the climate, we can certainly affect the language, and those of us who use it professionally are responsible for looking after it. This is the sort of taking-care-of-the-tools that any good worker tries to instil in an apprentice – keeping the blades sharp, oiling the bearings, cleaning the filters.

I don't have to tell any of you the importance of having a good dictionary, or preferably several. Every writer I know is fascinated by words, and developed the habit of looking things up at a very early age. Words change, they have a history as well as a contemporary meaning; it's worth knowing those things. We should acquire as many reference books as we have space for – old and out-of-date ones as well as new ones – and make a habit of using them, and take pride in getting things right. The internet also knows a thing or two, but I still prefer books. There's a pleasure in discharging this responsibility – of sensing that we're not sure of a particular point of grammar, for example, and in looking it up, and getting it to work properly.

Sometimes we come across people in our professional lives who think that this sort of thing doesn't matter very much, and it's silly to make a fuss about it. If only a few people recognise and object to a dangling participle, for example, and most readers don't notice and sort of get the sense anyway, why bother to get it right? Well, I discovered a very good answer to that, and it goes like this: if most people don't notice when we get it wrong, *they won't mind if we get it right*. And if we *do* get it right, we'll please the few who do know and care about these things, so everyone will be happy.

A simple example: the thing that annoys me most at the moment is the silly confusion between *may* and *might*. 'Without the code-breaking work at Bletchley Park, Britain may well have lost the Second World War,' you hear people say, as if they're not sure whether we did or not. What they mean is, 'Britain *might* well have lost the Second World War.' They should bloody well learn how to say it. Anyway, when I see someone getting that sort of thing right, I become just a little more sure that I can rely on the language they're using.

Of course, we can make our *characters* talk any way we like. It used to be one of the ways in which snobbish writers would mark the difference between characters who were to be admired and those who were to be condescended to. I think we've grown a little beyond that now; but when a present-day writer hears the difference between 'bored with' and 'bored of', and uses it with brilliant accuracy to mark not so much a class difference as a generational one, as Neil Gaiman does in his marvellous book *Coraline*, then he's being responsible to the language in just the way I'm talking about.

As well as taking care of the words, we should take care of the expressions, the idioms. We should become attuned to our own utterances; we should install a little mental bell that rings when we're using expressions that are second-hand or blurred through too much use. We should try always to use language to illuminate, reveal and clarify rather than obscure, mislead and conceal. The language should be safe in our hands – safer than it is in those of politicians, for example; at the least, people should be able to say that we haven't left it any poorer, or clumsier, or less precise.

The aim must always be clarity. It's tempting to feel that if a passage of writing is obscure, it must be very deep. But if the water is murky, the bottom might be only an inch below the surface – you just can't tell. It's much better to write in such a way that the readers can see all the way down; but that's not the end of it, because you then have to provide interesting things down there for them to look at. Telling a story involves thinking of some interesting events, putting them in the best order to bring out the connections between them, and telling about them as clearly as we can; and if we get the last part right, we won't be able to disguise any failure with the first – which is actually the most difficult, and the most important.

When it comes to imaginative language, to rich and inventive imagery, we have to beware. But what we have to beware of is too much caution. We must never say to ourselves: 'That's a good image – very clever; too clever for this book, though – save it up for something important.' Someone who never did that, someone who put the best of his imagination into everything he wrote, was the great Leon Garfield.

Here's a passage from one of my favourites among his books, *The Pleasure Garden* (1976):

> Mrs Bray was the proprietress of the Mulberry Garden...
> Although a widow for seven years, she still wore black, which
> lent her bulk a certain mystery; sometimes it was hard to see
> where she ended and the night began. Dr Dormann, stand-
> ing beside her, looked thinner than ever, really no more than
> a mere slice of a man who might have come off Mrs Bray in
> a carelessly slammed door.

There's fast-food language, and there's caviar language; one of the things we adults need to do for children is to introduce them to the pleasures of the subtle and the complex. One way to do that, of course, is to let them see us enjoying it, and then forbid them to touch it, on the grounds that it's too grown-up for them, their minds aren't ready to cope with it, it's too strong, it'll drive them mad with strange and uncontrollable desires. If that doesn't make them want to try it, nothing will.

Next in my list of responsibilities comes honesty – emotional honesty. We should never try to draw on emotional credit to which our story is not entitled. A few years ago, I read a novel – a pretty undistinguished family story – which, in an attempt to wring tears from the reader, quite gratuitously introduced a Holocaust theme. The theme had nothing to do with the story – it was there for one purpose only, which was to force a particular response and then graft it onto the book. An emotional response from the reader is a precious thing – it's the reader's gift to us, in a way; they should be able to trust the stimulus that provokes it. It's perfectly possible – difficult, but possible – to write an honest story about the Holocaust, or about slavery, or about any of the other terrible things that human beings have done to one another, but that was a dishonest one. Stories should earn their own tears and not pilfer them from elsewhere.

When it comes to the sheer craft of depicting things, describing them, saying what happened, the film director and playwright David Mamet said something very interesting. He said that the basic storytelling question is: 'Where do I put the camera?'

Thinking about that fascinating, that fathomlessly interesting, question is part of our responsibility towards the craft. Taking cinematography as a metaphor for storytelling, and realising that around every subject there are 360 degrees of space, and an infinity of positions from very close to very far, from very low to very high, at which you can put that camera – then it seems that the *great* director, the great storyteller, knows immediately and without thinking what the best position is, and goes there unhesitatingly. They seem to see it as clearly as we can see that leaves are green.

A good director will choose one of the half-dozen best positions. A bad director won't know, and will move the camera about, fidgeting with the angles, trying all sorts of tricky shots or fancy ways of telling the story, and forgetting that the function of the camera is not to draw attention to itself, but to show something else – the subject – with as much clarity as it can manage.

But actually, the truth is that great directors only *seem* as if they know the best place at once. The notebooks of great writers and composers are full of hesitations and mistakes and crossings-out; perhaps the real difference is that they *keep on* till they've found the best place to put the camera. The responsibility of those of us who are neither very good nor very bad is to imitate the best, to look closely at what they do and try to emulate it, to take the greatest as our models.

What I want to say next has to do with an attitude I suppose one could call tact. I mean that we who tell stories should be modest about the job, and not assume that just because the reader is interested in the story, they're interested in who's telling it. A storyteller should be invisible, as far as I'm concerned; and the best way to make sure of that is to make the story itself so interesting that the teller just… disappears. When

I was in the business of helping students to become teachers, I used to urge them to tell stories in the classroom – not read them from a book, but get out and tell them, face to face, with nothing to hide behind. The students were very nervous until they tried it. They thought that under the pressure of all those wide-open eyes, they'd melt into a puddle of self-consciousness. But the brave ones tried it, and they always came back next week and reported with amazement that it worked, they could do it. What was happening was that the children were gazing, not at the storyteller, but at the story she was telling. The teller had become invisible, and the story worked much more effectively as a result.

Of course, you have to find a good story in the first place, but we can all do that. There are thousands of good stories in the world, and it's perfectly possible for every young teacher to acquire three dozen or so and to know them well enough to tell them all, once a week, throughout a school year. Responsibility again: I salute all those who gather folk tales and give them back to us. Jane Yolen's marvellous *Favorite Folktales from Around the World* is a splendid example of this. So are the collections made by Alan Garner, by Kevin Crossley-Holland, by Neil Philip, by Katharine Briggs. The oral traditions of storytelling once seemed to be on the verge of dying out, but they didn't die; they're being kept alive by new generations of storytellers. And many of those who tell stories these days get their stories not from Granny or from Old Bob down in the Red Lion, but from books, because that's where they'll find them.

And there's nothing exclusive about stories, nothing snobbish, nothing stand-offish. They make themselves at home anywhere. Nowadays a storyteller in Ireland can learn Australian stories, an African storyteller can tell Indonesian stories, a storyteller in Poland can tell Inuit stories. Should we storytellers make sure we pass on the experience of our own culture? Yes, of course. It's one of our prime duties. But should we *only* tell stories that reflect our own background? Should we refrain from telling stories that originated elsewhere, on the grounds that we don't have the right to annex the experience of others? Absolutely not. A culture that never encounters any others becomes first inward-looking, and then stagnant, and then rotten. We are responsible – there's that word again – for bringing fresh streams of story into our own cultures from all over the world, and welcoming experience from every quarter, and offering our own experience in return.

And as I say, invisibility is important here. When it comes to actually putting the story across, the best storytellers are the tactful ones, those who don't burden the audience with their own self-consciousness, whether it's just plain nervousness at speaking in public or a complex intellectual post-modernist angst about the unreliability of signifiers and the slippery nature of the relationship between text and utterance. Whatever it is, we should put all that aside and try to say what happened, and who did what, and what happened next. That's all. The way to deal with feeling self-conscious is to pretend that we don't. Don't let's burden other people with our own embarrassment. That's what I mean by responsibility here: it's a form of tact. It helps us remember to be courteous to our readers and listeners.

And that leads me to the next thing I want to talk about, which is the matter of responsibility to the audience. Knowing that our readership includes children – notice, I don't say *consists of children*, because every children's book is also read by adults – but knowing that there are children reading us, what should our attitude be? Where does our responsibility lie?

Some commentators – not very well-informed ones, but they have quite loud voices – say that children's books shouldn't deal with matters like sex and drugs, with violence, or homosexuality, or abortion, or child abuse. Taboos do change over time: only a couple of generations ago, it was rare to find a children's book that confronted divorce. Against that, I've heard it said that children should be able to find in a children's book anything that they might realistically encounter in life. Children do know about these things: they talk about them, they ask questions about them, they meet some of them, sometimes, at home; shouldn't they be able to read about them in stories?

My feeling is that whatever we depict in our stories, we should show that actions have consequences. An example of this came up with Melvin Burgess's Carnegie Medal-winning novel *Junk* (1998). The predictable journalists said the predictable things, and the book created a storm of controversy. I defended Burgess on the grounds that in this book, he shows exactly the sort of responsibility that I'm talking about. It's a profoundly moral story, because it shows that temptation is truly tempting, and – as I said – that actions have consequences.

There are other kinds of responsibility to the audience too. Some writers feel that they shouldn't take too bleak a view of the world, that however dark and gloomy the story they're telling, they should always leave the reader with a glimpse of hope. I think that has something to be said for it, but we should remember that tragedy is uplifting too, if it shows the human spirit at its finest. 'The true aim of writing,' said Samuel Johnson, 'is to enable the reader better to enjoy life, or better to endure it.' Children need both those kinds of help, just as grown-ups do.

What's true about our responsibility towards depicting life in general is true of our responsibility when it comes to depicting people. There's a sentence I saw not long ago from Walter Savage Landor, which is the best definition of this sort of responsibility I've ever seen: 'We must not indulge in unfavourable views of mankind, since by doing it we make bad men believe that they are no worse than others, and we teach the good that they are good in vain.' Easy cynicism is no more truthful than easy optimism, though it seems to be so to the young.

So in depicting characters who struggle to do good, and do it, or who are tempted to be weak or greedy, but refrain, we the storytellers are providing our readers with friends whose own good behaviour, and whose high valuation of the courage or steadfastness or generosity of others, provides an image of how to behave well; and thus, we hope, we leave the world at least no worse than we found it.

But what about our responsibility to our readers in a more simple and basic sense? They write to us – many, many of them write. Should we respond to them all? I don't think there's any doubt in the mind of the writer who receives the first fan letter they've ever got. Of course they respond. It's wonderful! Someone out there loves me! But as you become better known, the number creeps up and creeps up, and you find yourself spending more and more time sending every individual child a reply. Should you carry on responding in the same sort of way, no matter how many of them write, no matter how much time it takes up?

It's difficult. The contact between the storyteller and the reader is a very close and personal one – more so from the reader's side, because they know both who they are and who I am, whereas I only know who I am. But there's no frustration quite as baffling as that felt by the writer who receives a wonderful letter from a child who's forgotten to enclose his or her address. They long for a reply – they deserve a reply – I *want* to reply – they'll think I'm mean and arrogant if I *don't* reply…

But what can we do about it? Well, not all that long ago, there was nothing we could do. But I had a delightful letter recently from a child somewhere in America who told me all about herself, how she loved my books, how she played the violin, and so on; but the publisher had forwarded it without including the envelope, and there was no address. My son suggested we try Google, so we typed in the child's name and presently there it was – I almost felt it should have been announced with the words 'Lo and behold' – a school in Pennsylvania was presenting a concert featuring a violin solo by… and there was her name. Amazing! So at least I could write to her, care of the school, and I did.

But it does take time, and as our books reach more and more readers, our time gets more and more eaten into. I don't mind spending a few minutes searching for things like that, while I can still manage to do so; but I'm less conscientious, shall we say, about the letters that say, 'I had to do this book report and we had to write to an author and I picked you because no one else did. You have to send me a reply or I will get a bad grade also can I have a photograph and a signed copy of your book *The Golden Spyglass* here are my questions. Where do you get your ideas from? What is your favourite colour? Do you have any pets? What is a spyglass?' And there was a good one recently from a boy who said, 'We have been studying obituaries in school and we have to write the obituary of someone famous and I would like to do you. Could you tell me how you would like to die and can you make it as dramatic as possible?' I told him that I would prefer to let nature take its course. They all do get a reply, eventually, but it takes time.

Almost the last in my list of responsibilities is this: we have to pay attention to what our imagination feels comfortable doing. In my own case, for reasons too deeply buried to be dug up, I have long felt that realism is a higher mode than fantasy; but when I try to write realistically, I move in boots of lead. However, as soon as the idea comes to me, for example, of little people with poison spurs who ride on dragonflies, the lead boots fall away and I feel wings at my heels. For many reasons (which, as I say, are beyond the reach of disinterment) I may regret this tendency of my imagination, but I can't deny it. Sometimes our nature speaks more wisely than our convictions, and we'll only work well if we listen to what it says.

But now I come to the most important responsibility of all. It's the one that's hardest to explain, but also the one I feel most strongly about. The last responsibility I want to look at is one that every storyteller has to acknowledge, and it's a responsibility that trumps every other. It's a responsibility to the story itself. I first became conscious of this when I noticed that I'd developed the habit of hunching my shoulders to protect my work from prying eyes. There are various equivalents of the hunched shoulder and the encircling arm: if we're working on the computer, for example, we tend to keep a lot of empty space at the foot of the piece, so that if anyone comes into the room we can immediately press that key that takes us to the end of the file, and show nothing but a blank screen. We're protecting it. There's something fragile there, something fugitive, which shows itself only to us, because it trusts us to maintain it in this half-resolved, half-unformed condition without exposing it to the harsh light of someone else's scrutiny, because a stranger's gaze would either make it flee altogether or fix it for good in a state that might not be what it wanted to become.

So we have a protective responsibility: the role of a guardian, almost a parent. It feels as if the story – before it's even taken the form of words, before it has any characters or any incidents clearly revealed, when it's just a thought, just the most evanescent little wisp of a thing – as if it's come to us and knocked at our door, or just been left on our doorstep. Of course we have to look after it. What else could we do?

What I seem to be saying here, rather against my will, is that stories come from somewhere else. It's hard to rationalise this, because I don't believe in a somewhere else; there ain't no elsewhere, is what I believe. *Here* is all there is. It certainly *feels* as if the story comes to me, but perhaps it comes *from* me, from my unconscious mind – I just don't know; and it wouldn't make any difference to the responsibility either way. I still have to look after it. I still have to protect it from interference while it becomes sure of itself and settles on the form it wants.

Yes, *it* wants. It knows very firmly what it wants to be, even though it isn't very articulate yet. It'll go easily in *this* direction and very firmly resist going in *that*, but I won't know why; I just have to shrug and say, 'OK – you're the boss.' And this is the point where responsibility takes the form of service. Not servitude; not shameful toil mercilessly exacted; but service, freely and fairly entered into. This service is a voluntary and honourable thing: when I say I am the servant of the story, I say it with pride.

And as the servant, I have to do what a good servant should. I have to be ready to attend to my work at regular hours. I have to anticipate where the story wants to go, and find out what can make the progress easier — by doing research, that is to say: by spending time in libraries, by going to talk to people, by finding things out. I have to keep myself sober during working hours; I have to stay in good health. I have to avoid taking on too many other engagements: no man can serve two masters. I have to keep the story's counsel: there are secrets between us, and it would be the grossest breach of confidence to give them away. (I sometimes think that the only way I could survive a creative writing class would be to write two stories — a fake one which I'd bring out to share with the class and be critiqued, and a real one which I'd work on in silence and keep to myself).

And I have to be prepared for a certain wilfulness and eccentricity in my employer — all the classic master-and-servant stories, after all, depict the master as the crazy one who's blown here and there by the winds of impulse or passion, and the servant as the matter-of-fact anchor of common sense; and I have too much regard for the classic stories to go against a pattern as successful as that. So, as I say, I have to expect a degree of craziness in the story.

'No, master! Those are windmills, not giants!'

'Windmills? Nonsense — they're giants, I tell you! But don't worry — I'll deal with them.'

'As you say, master — giants they are, by all means.'

No matter how foolish it seems, the story knows best.

And finally, as the faithful servant, I have to know when to let the story out of my hands; but I have to be very careful about the other hands I put it into. My stories have always been lucky in their editors — or perhaps, since I'm claiming responsibility here, they've been lucky they had me to guide them to the right ones. I suppose one's last and most responsible act as the servant of the story is to know when one can do no more, and when it's time to admit that someone else's eyes might see it more clearly.

To become so grand that you refuse to let your work be edited – and we can all think of a few writers who got to that point – is to be a bad servant, not a good one. Well, that's all I know about responsibility.

But I haven't quite finished, because I don't want anyone to think that responsibility is all there is to it. It would be a burdensome life, if the only relation we had with our work was one of duty and care. The fact is that I love my work. There is no joy comparable to the thrill that accompanies a new idea, one that we know is full of promise and possibility – unless it's the joy that comes when, after a long period of reflection and bafflement, of frustration and difficulty, we suddenly see the way through to the solution; or the delight when one of our characters suddenly says something far too witty for us to have thought of ourselves; or the slow, steady pleasure that comes from the regular accumulation of pages written; or the honest satisfaction that rewards work done well – a turn in the story deftly handled, a passage of dialogue that reveals character as well as advancing the story, a pattern of imagery that unobtrusively echoes and clarifies the theme of the whole book.

These joys are profound and long-lasting. And there is a joy too in responsibility itself – in the knowledge that what we're doing on earth, while we live, is being done to the best of our ability, and in the light of everything we know about what is good and true. Art, whatever kind of art it is, is like the mysterious music described in the words of the greatest writer of all, the 'sounds and sweet airs, that give delight and hurt not'. To bear the responsibility of giving delight and hurting not is one of the greatest privileges a human being can have, and I ask nothing more than the chance to go on being responsible for it till the end of my days.

THIS TALK WAS GIVEN AT THE SOCIETY OF AUTHORS CHILDREN'S WRITERS AND ILLUSTRATORS GROUP CONFERENCE, LEEDS, SEPTEMBER 2002.

There are other responsibilities, of course. In the years since I wrote this piece, the world of bookselling and publishing has changed enormously, and if I were giving this talk today I'd certainly say something about the need to preserve the best aspects of publishing (close editorial attention, the preservation of a midlist and a backlist, a mutual respect and understanding of common interest between author and publisher) and of bookselling (the knowledge and enthusiasm of individual booksellers, combined with the ability to exercise them free of overbearing commercial pressures towards the bland sameness of a narrow range of stock). The world of books is not a collection of random units of self-interest, but a living ecology. Or it used to be, and should be still. Whenever we can see something going on in any field where we can make a difference on the side of virtue, we have a responsibility to make it.

The Writing of Stories

MAKING IT UP AND WRITING IT DOWN

On the choices an author has to make as he tells a story, with special reference to points of view, time frames and story-patterns, using as an example the opening of Northern Lights *and other parts of* His Dark Materials

WHAT I'M GOING TO TALK ABOUT TODAY IS NOT THE READING OF literature, or of children's literature, but the writing of stories. I discovered thirty-five years ago in this university, if not in this room, that one thing I'm very bad at doing is literary criticism; but in the course of the subsequent thirty-five years I have learned something about the practical business of telling stories, so what I have to tell you today is actual hands-on stuff, what it's like to be in the middle of a story as you're telling it, and what considerations weigh with you, and what you can do when you're stuck, and that sort of thing.

I say *stories* rather than novels, because I think of my novels firstly as stories, and only then as books, and only then as novels. Besides, I have published some stories that aren't novels, and they're just as difficult and interesting to write – I mean fairy tales such as *Clockwork*, or *The Firework-Maker's Daughter*. As I say this, I seem to be implying a sort of distinction here between story and literature, if you like, or between the making-up part and the writing-down part, or the events and the sentences. It is a real distinction, and it's recognised in narratology, for example, which has found a number of terms to express this difference: substance and form, content and expression, story and discourse, *fabula* and *sjuzhet*, and so on.

And I suppose we could go on here to distinguish between the sort of

23

books that give prominence to one half of these opposed pairs, and the sort that favours the other; those where the story is more important than the words and those where the words are more important than the story; and you'd then have opposed pairs like genre fiction and literary fiction, popular art and high art – that sort of thing. G. K. Chesterton was thinking about this distinction when he said that literature was a luxury, but fiction was a necessity. Whether or not we agree with his conclusion, we can see the distinction he was making.

Well, no book is entirely the one or entirely the other – it couldn't be. And what many writers try to do, of course, is provide both at once. But your nature, the nature of your particular talent, is rarely as balanced as your intentions, and I realised some time ago that I belong at the vulgar end of the literary spectrum. I suppose it would be nice if you could send back your talents and ask for a different set, but you can't do that. You're stuck with the dæmon you've got, as Lyra learns. However, I'm reconciled to my limitations, because much as I enjoy the writing-down part, and hard as I try to do it as well as I can, I do find that the making-up part is where my heart lies.

So what I have to say today is mainly about that, but inevitably I'll be saying something about the writing-down part as well, and sometimes they'll be hard to tell apart.

I'm going to start with the first sentence of the first part of *His Dark Materials*.

> Lyra and her dæmon moved through the darkening Hall,
> taking care to keep to one side, out of sight of the kitchen.
> (*NL*, 3)

Stories have to *begin*. Out of the welter of events and ideas and pictures and characters and voices that you experience in your head, you the storyteller must choose one moment, the most suitable moment, and make that the start. You could begin anywhere in the chronology, of course; you could begin in the middle, *in medias res*, which is a soundly classical way to begin; but you do have to begin *some*where. One of your sentences is going to be the first.

So: where are you going to start, and what are you going to say?

There's an image here from science which I find useful when I think about this. Coleridge, apparently, used to go to scientific lectures to renew his stock of metaphors, and while I would never dream of saying that the main function of science is the production of metaphors for subsequent development in the arts, science *is* damned useful to steal from. The one I find helpful here is the idea of phase space – as far as I understand it, that is. Phase space is a term from dynamics, and it refers to the profound complexity of changing systems. It's the notional space that contains not just the actual consequences of the present moment, but all the possible consequences. The phase space of a game of noughts and crosses, for instance, would contain every possible outcome of every possible initial move, and the actual course of a game could be represented by a path starting from the one move that was actually made – a path winding past numbers of choices not made.

Robert Frost:

> Two roads diverged in a wood, and I –
> I took the one less travelled by.
> And that has made all the difference.

Of course, it does make all the difference. And we do have to choose: we can't go more ways than one. I am surely not the only writer who has the distinct sense that every sentence I write is surrounded by the ghosts of the sentences I could have written at that point, but chose not to. Those ghosts represent the phase space of what you could have said next. (One of the advantages of writing on paper and not on the screen is that some of those sentences remain and can be resurrected from the grave of the crossings-out.)

So the opening of your story brings with it a phase space. For example: 'It is a truth universally acknowledged that…'

Well, that *what*? The phase space implied by that opening is enormous. You can imagine Jane Austen saying to herself 'That's great! That's terrific! What an opening! Now, what can I say next?' She *could* have gone on to say, '…all happy families resemble one another, whereas each unhappy family is unhappy in its own way.' Jane Austen writing the first sentence of *Anna Karenina*: lost moments from the history of literature. She would have crossed it out at once and said: 'What nonsense! This will never do.'

Now this can be paralysing, if you're not careful. If you let the thought of all the things you *could* say get the upper hand, it becomes very hard to say anything. And if you're also aware that your audience is at least as clever as you are, and you know that they too are aware of all the things you could have said, you might begin to feel that they're raising their eyebrows at the one you do say – which makes you even more self-conscious, and the choice even more awkward.

The mind has plenty of ways of preventing you from writing, and paralysing self-consciousness is a good one. The only thing to do is ignore it, and remember what Vincent van Gogh said in one of his letters about the painter's fear of the blank canvas – the canvas, he said, is far more afraid of the painter.

So you begin. In this case I wanted to put my main character, Lyra, on the page as soon as possible. Her name is the first word in the story, as it is the last in the complete trilogy. You want to engage the reader's sympathy at once. Alfred Hitchcock said something interesting about this: he pointed out that if a film begins by following a burglar into an empty house, and watching him ransack the drawers, then when the lights of the owner's car show up outside the window, we think: hurry up! They're coming! We don't want them to catch him. We're on his side, because we started with him. I wanted the readers on Lyra's side from the start.

The next important thing is that Lyra, in this first sentence, is accompanied by her dæmon. I didn't actually think of dæmons at first. My first dozen or so attempts to write this opening chapter failed, because at that stage Lyra didn't have a dæmon; I didn't know that dæmons existed. She went into the Retiring Room at Jordan College on her own, and the story didn't work, because there was a sort of dynamic missing, and I wasn't sure what it was until the dæmon turned up. But then she could say, 'Let's go in there' and he could say, 'No, we're not supposed to' and she could say, 'Oh, don't be such a coward' and he could say, 'Well, only for a short time then' – and so on. You often need more than one person in a scene to make it work.

And the fact that it was a surprise to *me* helped, as well. Raymond Chandler knew what he was talking about when he said, 'When in doubt have a man come through a door with a gun in his hand.' The man with the gun might be anything – a postman with an important letter, a phone call asking the protagonist to contact her lawyer immediately, or, as here, an aspect of the protagonist's own character; the essential thing is that you, the storyteller, didn't know about it in advance. You didn't plan it. It takes you by surprise, and opens up new possibilities, and forces you to come up with solutions you wouldn't have had to think of otherwise.

Later sentences, or group of sentences, demonstrate something of that quality of the particular phase space that the first sentence opens up.

> That was Lyra's world and her delight. She was a coarse and greedy little savage, for the most part. But she always had a dim sense that it wasn't her whole world; that part of her also belonged in the grandeur and ritual of Jordan College; and somewhere in her life there was a connection with the high world of politics represented by Lord Asriel. All she did with

that knowledge was to give herself airs and lord it over the other urchins. It had never occurred to her to find out more. (*NL*, 37)

He looked at her carefully, but he was no match for the bland and vacuous docility Lyra could command when she wanted to; and finally he nodded and went back to his newspaper. (*TSK*, 86)

Some of the most interesting discussion about story and how it works (and remember, I'm talking practical hands-on stuff here) has come from the makers of films. In my experience film people talk a lot more about story than book people do, and I'm always interested to hear what they have to say. One comment that has struck me – as I've mentioned elsewhere – is by David Mamet. In his book *On Directing Film*, he says this: 'The main questions a director must answer are "Where do I put the camera?" and "What do I tell the actors?"'

The actors question doesn't apply to novelists, of course, but we do have to think very hard about the other one: 'Where do I put the camera?' I think that that's *the* basic storytelling question. Where do you see the scene from? What do you tell the reader about it? What's your stance towards the characters?

These are difficult problems to resolve – much more difficult than you might think if you haven't tried it. One way of avoiding the difficulty – and it's a way I can see increasingly taken by young novelists today, especially those who write for children – is to use a first-person and present-tense way of telling the story. I've used the present tense myself, but only rarely, because I always feel rather shifty and furtive about it. I know I'm doing it to *avoid* difficult choices, to avoid committing myself to this position or that, because the storytelling camera doesn't only see in space, it sees in time, and that's much harder to find the right place in. So

I'm not surprised when writers choose the present tense, because it helps them to feel neutral, uncommitted, objective, and to avoid making the wrong choice of camera position.

But you *do* make choices. You can't help it. That's the way narrative works. You privilege *this* over *that* by the mere fact of focusing on it. What you *give up* when you write in the present tense is a whole wide range of stuff that you *could* say, and which is available to you through the grammar – the rich field of time itself, continuing time, or intermittent time, or time that was and now is no longer, or time that might come one day. Think of that chapter in *Vanity Fair* – Chapter 32, *In Which Jos Takes Flight and the War is brought to a Close* – where the camera, or the narrator's attention, darts like a dragonfly not only here and there in Brussels and the nearby countryside but backwards and forwards along the stream of time, to what had happened before the chapter began, up high above the stream to look at the whole of a character's life and say, 'Jos seldom spent a half-hour in his life which cost him so much money', down close again to look at all the teeming life in the panic-stricken city, back in time to the youth of little Ensign Tom Stubble, brought in wounded and delirious and thinking of his father's parsonage, far forward in time to an imagined 'centuries hence, [when] we Frenchmen and Englishmen might be boasting and killing each other still ...'

It's the grammar of the language, the verbs in particular, and the temporal relations they embody so well, that allow you to do that. Reading a novel written entirely in the first person and the present tense seems to me like being in a room where they have those Venetian blinds that go up instead of across – you can only see out in vertical strips, and everything else is closed off to you.

But young novelists are often anxious about choosing the best *time* position for the camera, so they stick to the present tense, which seems to be safe. Unfortunately, what it conveys more often than not is a nervous self-consciousness.

Another aspect of the 'Where do I put the camera?' question is that of the narrator. Who is telling the story? Whose words do we read? Whose voice do we hear? There used to be a figure who was known to analysts of narrative – known to the police, if you like – as the omniscient narrator. This figure has been under suspicion for a long time – after all, everyone has an agenda, everyone is partial, no one knows everything, and so on. Like a solitary old man near a children's playground, the omniscient narrator must be up to no good.

But I'd like to say a word in his and her defence. Firstly, I can't think of any storyteller who ever claimed that the narrator *was* omniscient, and secondly, even if they're not omniscient, they still know a damn sight more than the characters Mr X or Ms Y, who are in the story themselves and can't see further than the things they know. To my mind, the most rich, surprising, subtle and mysterious character in the whole of literature, surpassing in these qualities even Hamlet or Falstaff, is *the narrator*. To impersonate this sprite-like, ageless, androgynous, amoral, wise, opinionated, understanding, sharp-eyed, partial, judicious, fond, credulous and cynical being is a privilege so great that we should happily pay to do it; and to avoid such impersonation, on the grounds that these days we're too sophisticated for that sort of simple-minded old-fashioned stuff, seems to me sometimes, regrettably, like a failure of nerve – or as Umberto Eco once put it, like the wish not to be mistaken for Barbara Cartland.

But as I said at the beginning of this lecture, I couldn't care less about being thought sophisticated. I'm quite happy to take my place among the vulgar storytellers – the Jeffrey Archers, the Danielle Steels – among the fluff under the bed of literature. So I'm quite happy for my narrator to have a distinctive point of view, and call Lyra a coarse and greedy little savage if she deserves it; and while the phrase 'bland and vacuous docility' probably wouldn't have occurred to her to describe the attitude she was presenting to the porter, it did occur to me, and I think the passage is the better for it. The narrator is with her, on her side, but not limited to her perception of herself; and that's where I like to put the camera.

Now then: most of what you're doing with the camera is stuff you're conscious of. But you're not conscious of everything. The next pair of sentences I quote exemplify something I wasn't conscious of at all until I read a book that drew my attention to it.

> It was such a strange tormenting feeling when your dæmon
> was pulling at the link between you; part physical pain deep
> in your chest, part intense sadness and love.
> (*NL*, 194)

> And she pushed him away, so that he crouched bitter and
> cold and frightened on the muddy ground.
> (*TAS*, 284)

This has to do with patterns – underlying structural shapes, and repetitions of them. To start by describing the dæmon: it's an aspect of your self which has a physical existence outside you, in the form of an animal. Your dæmon is often, but not always, of the opposite sex to you, to your body; and when you're a child, it can change shape. In adolescence it loses the power to change, and acquires one fixed animal form which it will keep for the rest of your life.

And the important thing about it as far as this passage is concerned is that you can't move away from it, from him or her. There's a space of a few feet or so around you in which the dæmon is free to move about, but if he or she tries to move beyond that, this is what happens: it hurts. You don't move away from your dæmon, or he from you, firstly because you don't want to – your dæmon is yourself, a self you can talk to and confide in, and so on – but secondly because it's physically painful. Everyone tries it, when they're young, to see what will happen, but they don't try it often.

Now then: with that in mind, here's a short passage from a book by a cognitive scientist called Mark Turner.

> How do we recognise objects, events, and stories? Part of the answer has to do with 'image schemas'… Image schemas are skeletal patterns that recur in our sensory and motor experience. Motion along a path, bounded interior, balance and symmetry are typical image schemas.

Turner is a professor of English as well as a cognitive scientist. His book is called *The Literary Mind*, and I picked it up expecting it to be about literature, but it isn't entirely; it *is* about stories, though, and how we understand them, how we recognise, predict, relate our experiences to them, and so on. I read it when I'd just finished writing *The Subtle Knife*, the second book in the trilogy, and was getting ready to begin the third, and as soon as I read his account of these image schemas, these little abstract patterns of experience, I felt a bell ring in my mind, because he was describing a pattern I was able to recognise in the story I was writing. I suddenly realised, two thirds of the way through, that over and over again the same pattern recurs: two things that were so closely bound together that they functioned as one are split apart, and function from then on as two. I suppose it's a form of binary fission. For example:

> Lyra and her home: she has to leave Jordan College
> Lyra and her best friend Roger: he's kidnapped,
> and vanishes
> Lyra's parents: Lord Asriel and Mrs Coulter come
> together for long enough to bring Lyra about, and then
> split up
> Serafina Pekkala the witch, and her lover the gyptian
> Farder Coram

Will's parents: his father vanishes

Will and his mother: loving her and wanting to protect
her, he nevertheless has to leave her and go off alone

...and so on. There are many others. The most dramatic, and many people have told me the most shocking, example of this pattern occurs when we discover that the children who have been kidnapped are being forcibly separated from their dæmons: they are severed from them in a sort of guillotine-like device.

The reason this is shocking is that I set it up to be – firstly, by establishing early on the tightness, the complete unity, of the dæmon-body pair, so that we come to think automatically that of course people are always with their dæmons, it's unthinkable that they should be without them; and secondly by throwing down a sort of false hint, a misdirection, with the word *severed*. Lyra hears people talking darkly about severed children without understanding what it means. But the word *severed* in our linguistic experience is often followed by *head*. That phrase is even the title of a novel by Iris Murdoch. It's inaccurate, of course, because it's the neck that's severed, not the head itself; but that's what we expect. So we're sort of looking in another direction when the surprise occurs and we learn that children are being severed from their dæmons. But it was another example of this pattern, this binary fission.

Now when I read Mark Turner on the way image schemas work in our experience of narrative, I realised that I could do what I wanted to do with the third book. Here was a pattern I hadn't been aware of; and now that I was aware of it, I could use it again, but consciously. And when Lyra and Will go into the world of the dead, she has to leave her dæmon, Pantalaimon, behind. I didn't know if I could write that – I don't mean emotionally: I didn't know if it would make sense in the story. But seeing this pattern helped me realise not only that it did make sense, but that it wouldn't make formal sense – pattern sense – if she didn't.

And there were two other things that helped here: very early, the Master of Jordan College makes a prediction that Lyra will be involved in a great betrayal, and that she herself will be the betrayer, and the experience will be terrible for her. When I wrote those words I thought that that betrayal would be her leading Roger to his death. She thinks she's rescuing him, but unwittingly she's leading him to the most dangerous place of all, and he dies. When, years later, I got to the world of the dead passage, I discovered that these words of the Master's could relate even more closely to Lyra's betrayal of Pantalaimon. And, of course, I thought how clever I was to have misdirected the readers again; they think that they've seen Lyra's great betrayal already, but here comes an even bigger one. Little did they know! Well, little did I know, actually.

The other thing that helped was the witches. One of the things that makes the witches seem uncanny to people like Lyra is that they alone can be seen without their dæmons. Witches' dæmons can leave them and wander far away, while still maintaining close mental and emotional contact. I didn't know how, or why; it was just a sort of picturesque detail that made the witches different and strange. When – again, much later – I thought about how I was going to bring Lyra and Pantalaimon together again, I remembered this, and retrospectively invented a sort of initiation that young witches undergo, when they have to go into the wilderness, to a place where dæmons can't enter, and they suffer the torments of separation voluntarily. But unlike severance, this results – after the suffering – in the witchy, witch-like power of being apart while still united; and I could grant this witch-like power to Lyra and to Will, as a sort of compensation for the suffering of having to leave their dæmons behind on the shores of the world of the dead. That's the value of leaving a lot of loose ends in a long narrative: when you get to the end it's very handy to have some lying around to tie up a bit of the story neatly.

And finally, on the subject of the image schema of binary fission, Lyra loses her power to read the alethiometer, and then comes the thing that causes the biggest pang of all for many young readers – Lyra and Will have to part. But it's a stronger ending than if they'd stayed together, and part of the reason for its superiority to the happier ending, I think, is that it's true to the formal pattern of the whole story: things splitting apart.

So Mark Turner and his image schemas came at the right moment; they helped me to see something I hadn't noticed and then to reinforce it. The next sentence brings me to what happens when you meet a critic at the wrong moment.

> She looked defiant as well as lost, Dame Hannah thought, and admired her for it; and the Master saw something else – he saw how the child's unconscious grace had gone, and how she was awkward in her growing body.
> (*TAS*, 518)

I don't know how other storytellers function, but in my case I never start with the theme of a story. My stories *are* about something, to be sure, but I never know what that is till I'm in the process of writing them. I have to start with pictures, images, scenes, moods – like bits of dreams, or fragments of half-forgotten films. That's how they all begin. In the case of this one I didn't realise what it could be about until after I'd discovered dæmons, which happened in the way I described just now. But more especially it was when I found that children's dæmons change and adults' dæmons don't; and I think that that idea and the theme must have leaped towards each other like a spark and a stream of gas. I don't really know which came first, but they took fire when they came together.

The theme of my story is the end of innocence. The whole thing – all 1,200 pages – is a sort of clumsy gloss on that marvellous essay by Heinrich von Kleist on the marionette theatre (which I go into in more detail later), which is itself a very elegant gloss on the third chapter of the Book of Genesis. It's also the subject of Rilke's *Eighth Duino Elegy*.

The story of Adam and Eve seems to me the fundamental myth of why we are as we are. Having eaten the fruit of the tree of knowledge, we are separate from nature because we have acquired the ability to reflect on it and on ourselves – we are expelled from the garden of Paradise. And we can't go back, because an angel with a fiery sword stands in the way; if we want to regain the bliss we felt when we were at one with things, we have to go not back but forward, says Kleist, all the way round the world in fact, and re-enter Paradise through the back door, as it were. In other words, we have to forget about innocence – it's gone; it's no use moping about our lost childhood, and becoming intoxicated by the sickly potency of our own nostalgia; we have to grow up. We have to leave the unself-conscious grace of childhood behind and go in search of another quality altogether, the quality of wisdom. And that involves engaging with every kind of human experience, making compromises, getting our hands dirty, suffering, toiling, learning.

Innocence is not wise; wisdom cannot be innocent. And it's very painful and it's very hard, but it's the only way forward, and in the end, if we keep on trying, we shall have acquired a deeper, fuller, richer understanding than we ever had before we tasted the fruit of the knowledge of good and evil.

That is the meaning of Lyra's losing the power to read the alethiometer. It came to her easily, like grace; it departs as if it had never been, leaving only a memory of the ease and swiftness and certainty she used to feel. But this is not a story about how wonderful it was to be a child, and its dominating principle is not nostalgia and regret. It's a story about how necessary it is to grow up, and its dominating principle is realism and hope.

Now I was going to tell you what happens when you encounter a critic at the wrong time. It came about because this focus on the Fall and all its meanings naturally led me to think about Gnosticism. Very fashionable thing, Gnosticism; there's a lot of it about these days. The original Gnostic myth tells of how this material world was brought into being by a false creator, a Demiurge, in order to imprison the sparks of true divinity which had fallen from the original God, the inconceivably distant true God, who is their home; and it's the task of those who know the truth – the Gnostics – to escape from this world altogether and find their way back.

Well, nowadays at the clever end of things we have the distinguished literary critic Harold Bloom writing about this in *Omens of Millennium*, and at the popular end we have *The X-Files* and *The Matrix* and *The Truman Show*, which are all pure Gnosticism. This world, they seem to be saying, this world we can see and touch, this world of power and politics and government and official pronouncements and large corporations, is a delusion and a fake, a vast conspiracy designed to trap us and keep us in ignorance. 'The truth is out there,' says Mulder in *The X-Files*.

The Gnostic myth is a very powerful story, because it's intensely dramatic, and it puts us and our predicament right at the centre of it, and it seems to explain why so many of us feel unhappy, ill at ease, alienated from the universe and from things like joy and purpose and meaning. We're not at home here, because the universe is not our home. But those who *know* can find their way out.

There's no time now to go further into this myth, which is full of psychological fascination, but the thing that was of obvious interest to me was its connection with the story of the Fall, because it's all about knowledge. There was no single body of official Gnostic doctrine, but some of the sects and cults whose influence wove in and out of early Christian thought (until they were finally rounded up and condemned as heretical) revered the Serpent, which helped Adam and Eve see the truth that had been concealed from them by the false creator-god.

So I was interested to read as much Gnosticism-related stuff from the clever end of the scale as I could find, as well as gaping at stuff from the popular end; and while I was in the middle of writing *The Amber Spyglass* a book came out by A. D. Nuttall called *The Alternative Trinity: Gnostic Heresy in Marlowe, Milton, and Blake*. It's full of connections and insights and information; I seized on it with delight and read it with fascination, and then found myself completely unable to proceed. I felt hypnotised into immobility. So interesting was Nuttall's argument, and so persuasive his examples, that I found myself thinking about my own story, 'Well, I've got this bit wrong… and surely I should be stressing the Ophite angle a bit more strongly… and he must be right about Milton saying such-and-such about Satan, so I'd better rethink what I say about so-and-so… and if Blake's attitude to the serpent was ambiguous, then maybe I'll be on dodgy ground when I write the next bit…'

In short, I was reduced to creeping around like a mouse in someone else's intellectual house, trying not to disturb things, or make too much noise, and not make any mistakes. All that had happened was that I'd met the book at the wrong time, you see, when my story was still partly in flux.

It was Blake who got me out of this perplexing state (as I describe in more detail in 'I Must Create a System'); I remembered his line 'I must create my own system, or be enslaved by another man's,' and with one bound I was free. I thought: actually, I can say anything I like. If I contradict Milton and Blake and A. D. Nuttall, so much the worse for them. There are times when the best attitude to adopt towards critics is that of P. G. Wodehouse's immortal character Bertie Wooster towards his spots. He was having a bath one day, and he noticed a rash on his chest. 'I should not advocate scratching, sir,' says Jeeves. 'I disagree' says Bertie. 'You have to take a firm line with these spots.' Sometimes I think you have to take a firm line with critics.

Actually, just to wind up the Gnostic motif, my system – my myth, if you like – is passionately anti-Gnostic in one vital respect: the story insists on the primacy, the absolute importance, of 'the physical world, which is our true home and always was,' as one of the ghosts says in the world of the dead. Lyra discovers this by accident when the ghosts beg her to tell them about the world, to remind them about the wind and the sunshine; and instead of telling them one of her Lyra-like fantasies, full of wild nonsense, she tells them about something that really happened, and tries with all her heart to evoke the smells and the sounds and the look, the sensuous texture and presence of the real world for them. She leaves fantasy behind, and becomes a realist. (As the whole story does, indeed – it's a movement away from fantasy and towards realism, which is why Lyra goes to school at the end of the book: a cruel disappointment to some critics, academics and teachers themselves, actually, who seem to have lost any sense of the nobility, the moral value, the sheer passionate excitement of education.)

Anyway, when that happens, when Lyra tells that true story, she sees to her astonishment that the harpies who guard and torment the ghosts in the world of the dead have stopped everything, and have been listening closely. This is what they have been hungering for all this time – the truth about the world, about life. So they make a bargain: if you go to the world of the dead with a story to tell – your story, the story of your engagement with life – then the harpies will guide your ghost out into the world again, where it can finally dissolve into the general world of life and physicality, and be free of the anguish and misery of immortality. So my heresy is to suggest that eternal life is not a reward, but the most cruel punishment, imposed on us by God for the sin of seeking to grow up and become wise.

And the implication is that if you spend your life doing nothing but watching television and playing computer games, you will have nothing to tell the harpies in the world of the dead, and there you will stay.

The final passage I want to comment on is a pretty straightforward piece of dialogue. Lyra is running away, and she stops at a coffee stall, where she attracts the attention of the man whose picture is reproduced here.

That's his dæmon on his shoulder – a lemur. If you imagine a sort of suave, upper-class Leslie Phillips voice for him you'll get his tone exactly right.

He begins a conversation with Lyra:

'Where are you going, all alone like this?'

'Going to meet my father.'

'And who's he?'

'He's a murderer.'

'He's what?'

'I told you, he's a murderer. It's his profession. He's doing a job tonight. I got his clean clothes in here, 'cause he's usually all covered in blood when he's finished a job.'

'Ah! You're joking.'

'I en't.'

The lemur uttered a soft mewing sound and clambered slowly up behind the man's head, to peer out at her. Lyra drank her coffee stolidly and ate the last of her sandwich.

'Good night,' she said. 'I can see my father coming now. He looks a bit angry.'

(*NL*, 101)

Illustration for Chapter 6 of
Northern Lights, by the author

The reason I put this in is to explain, just briefly, why dialogue is easier to write than narrative. Once you've got the characters established in your mind you can hear what they say to each other quite easily. And because they give you the words, you can write them down. You can also see what they do, of course, but that doesn't come in the form of words – it comes in the form of pictures, and you have to find the words, and that's not so easy. Do you say, 'She stopped at the coffee stall' or, 'Lyra saw the coffee stall and stopped' or, 'Seeing the coffee stall, Lyra decided to stop'…? There are a hundred ways of saying it, and with each variation you have to choose what to put in and what to leave out.

In fact, here I said:

> At a crossroads near the corner of a big department store, whose windows shone brilliantly over the wet pavement, there was a coffee stall: a little hut on wheels with a counter under the wooden flap that swung up like an awning. Yellow light glowed inside, and the fragrance of coffee drifted out. The white-coated owner was leaning on the counter talking to the two or three customers.
>
> It was tempting. Lyra had been walking for an hour now, and it was cold and damp.
>
> (*NL*, 100)

That's functional: you put in a few little visual details – the yellow light, the brilliance of the shop windows, the wet pavement; anyone who wanted to could visualise it without difficulty, but there's not so much that it gets in the way and holds the story up while you demonstrate your mastery of descriptive prose. But every phrase has to be thought about and alternatives rejected. And now I see this again, I realise that it would have been better to say of the wooden flap that it was suspended rather than that it swung up, because 'swung up' is active, it suggests movement, and of course it's not moving, it's still. That's the sort of thing you have to think about and often get wrong. It's just harder to do.

But when Lyra says, 'I told you, he's a murderer,' and so on, I didn't have to think about it in the same way. I did make one or two little changes; originally, after the words 'I can see my father', I began to write 'now', but stopped before I'd finished that word and changed it to 'coming now' instead – it's more vivid, he's not just standing there, he's getting closer; but that's all. Dialogue, for me, is very much easier than narrative.

And I don't think I'm alone in that. In fact, I know I'm not. I used to be a schoolteacher, teaching children roughly between the ages of ten and thirteen, and I noticed that when they wrote stories, many of them were much better at dialogue than at narrative. What they were doing in a number of cases was not actually writing a story at all, but writing a TV script without realising it, and without knowing how to make transitions between scenes or describe the things they were clearly seeing in their minds' eye – the stage directions, as it were. What they *could* do very well was put down the things they were hearing in their minds' ear, because those things were already words. Their difficulty with narrative, and their ease with dialogue, might be due to their lifelong experience of television and film, or it might just be that dialogue is intrinsically easier; I don't know.

The main task, though, is to keep it all – all these things I've been talking about today: the making-up part, the writing-down part, the formal patterns, the theme (once you know what that is), the right place to put the camera, the stance towards the characters, all that – to keep them all roughly in balance. In a novel, you never succeed, actually. If you want to write something perfect, go for a haiku. In a work of any length there are bound to be things that don't work, and passages where the emphasis is wrong, and places where the tone is too dark or too light, and a character or two who doesn't come to life; and when you read it back after a year or two, you see the faults all too clearly. But you just try to do better next time.

And when you're doing what I do, writing *story* rather than *literature*, you have to keep yourself out of the way. Readers – especially an audience that includes young readers – aren't in the least interested in you, and your self-conscious post-modernist anguish about all the things there are to be anguished *about* when it comes to text. They want to know what happened next.

So tell them.

And the way to do *that*, the way to tell a story, as I've said before, is to think of some interesting events, put them in the right order to make clear the connections between them, and recount them as clearly as you can. And while you're doing that, if you also give the reader enough visual clues for them to know where a scene is taking place, and who's present, and what time of day it is, and where the light's coming from; if you make it clear who's speaking and what they're saying; if you put the camera in the best place, and don't move it till you need to; if you get all those things more or less right, then, with a bit of luck, the readers will stay with you till the end of the story, and go and buy your next book when that comes out.

There – I think I've said enough. Thank you for listening, and if you have any questions, I'll try to answer them; and if I don't know the answers, I'll make them up.

THIS LECTURE WAS GIVEN AT ST CROSS BUILDING, OXFORD, 21 MAY 2002.

It's always struck me as curious how much film people talk about story, and how little book people do. No doubt it's because film is a much more collaborative business, and because so much money is involved, and because those who put up the money are so much more anxious about getting their investment back. Naturally they're all passionately interested in making the story watertight.

But it's also the fact that a book is a solitary enterprise. We don't have to talk about it before it's finished, and in fact it's better not to. I can't possibly talk about a novel I'm writing, because everything beyond the sentence I'm writing at the moment is provisional, and I'm not even sure how I'm going to end the sentence.

Heinrich von Kleist:
On the Marionette Theatre

GRACE LOST AND REGAINED

*On an essay of extraordinary insight and power
– and its influence on* His Dark Materials

SOMETIMES, BY CHANCE OR FATE OR THE WORKINGS OF AN INSCRUTABLE Providence, we meet exactly the right work of art at exactly the right time to have the maximum impact on us. We raise the steel-framed umbrella just as the thunderbolt gathers in the cloud.

For me, this happened one day in 1978, when I came across an essay in the *Times Literary Supplement* by an author I'd never heard of: Heinrich von Kleist. It was called *On the Marionette Theatre*, and it was translated and introduced by Idris Parry. When he wrote the essay, in 1810, Kleist was thirty-three years old. A year later he was dead.

It had the force of a revelation on me. It is an unusual essay, very short and very simple on the surface. It has the form of a little story, a dialogue, an encounter between two friends – both thoughtful and intelligent men – who talk in a leisured, thoughtful way about puppets, and about grace, and about consciousness… And about that mysterious moment when we become self-conscious, a moment that occurs in every human life at around the age of adolescence, as in this wonderful little story:

'About three years ago, I happened to be at the baths with a young man who was then remarkably graceful in every respect. He was about fifteen, and one could see in him faintly the first traces of vanity, a product of the favour

45

shown by women. It so happened that just before that, we'd seen in Paris the figure of the boy pulling the thorn out of his foot. The cast of the statue is well known; you can find it in most German collections. He was reminded of this when he looked into a tall mirror just as he was putting his foot on a stool to dry it. He smiled and told me what he had discovered.

'In fact I'd noticed it too at the same moment, but... I don't know if it was to test the quality of his apparent grace or to provide a salutary counter to his vanity... I laughed and said he must be imagining things. He blushed and raised his foot a second time, to show me, but the attempt failed, as anybody could have foreseen. In some confusion he raised his foot a third time, a fourth time, he must have tried it ten times, but in vain; he was quite incapable of reproducing the same movement. What am I saying? The movements he did make were so comical that it was only with difficulty that I managed to keep from laughing.

'From that day, from that very moment, an extraordinary change came over this boy. He began to stand all day in front of the mirror. One by one, his attractions slipped away from him. An invisible and incomprehensible power seemed to settle like a steel net over the free play of his gestures, and after a year nothing remained of the lovely grace which had given pleasure to all who had seen him. I can tell you about a man, still alive, who was a witness to that strange and unfortunate event. He can confirm it word for word, just as I have described it.'

The theme interested me firstly because I loved and revered William Blake's *Songs of Innocence and of Experience*, which as Blake said were written to show those contrary states of the human soul; and secondly because my own childhood and adolescence were still painful and fresh in my mind, though I'd left them behind over fifteen years before; and thirdly because in 1978 I was a schoolteacher, and my pupils were at the age when they were going through precisely the sort of change described by Kleist.

Every teacher of young children knows the wonderful freedom and expressiveness – the natural grace – they bring to such things as painting, for instance; they'll spread the paint around with no hesitation or doubt or uncertainty, without any self-consciousness. But something happens to them as they grow up; they become aware of the difference between what they can do and what accomplished artists can do; they realise that their pictures look clumsy, ill-coordinated, naïve, in a word childish; and they lose the confidence to work as freely as they used to. A sort of cramp seizes their hands. They say, 'Oh, I can't draw at all, I was never any good at it.' And they stop drawing.

And so the freedom they once had vanishes like smoke. In Kleist's words, 'an invisible and incomprehensible power seems to settle like a steel net over the free play of their gestures'.

This self-consciousness is also bound up with the coming of sexual awareness, of course. This is a time when our bodies are beginning to change visibly; when hormones we've never experienced begin to flood through our bloodstream; when the greatest social difficulty we have to deal with on a daily basis is sheer embarrassment.

Anyway, I used to notice this effect, this steel net settling over the children I was teaching, this transition; and I remembered my own adolescence, and the curious double sense I had, of the awful embarrassment of physical things combined with the opening out of mental ones. It was a time when I discovered poetry and painting. It was like discovering a new continent – new forms of knowledge, new ways of understanding, immense vistas of possibility.

And then I realised why Kleist links these two most unlikely things — the marionettes in the marketplace, and the story of the Temptation and Fall in the Garden of Eden. Eve was tempted not by wealth or love but by knowledge. Eat this fruit, says the serpent, and you shall be as gods, knowing good and evil. So, tempted by that prospect, the dizzying prospect of knowledge, they ate the fruit that had been forbidden to them.

And the first result of their eating the fruit was embarrassment. They knew they were naked; it hadn't occurred to them before. Knowledge comes with a cost. Like the bear that appears later in von Kleist's essay who effortlessly parries a sword-thrust, because his mind wasn't troubled by knowledge; like the puppets who swing with effortless grace on their strings, because they have no minds at all; like the beautiful young boy who fell without thinking about it into the attitude of a beautiful work of art, Adam and Eve in their first state were full of grace and innocence. But once they had eaten the fruit, consciousness was open to them, and with consciousness came self-consciousness, awkwardness, embarrassment, sorrow, grief and pain.

As I say, this happens every day, and it happens in every life. Every young child is born into the Garden of Eden, and every child is eventually expelled from it. And you can't go back. As Kleist points out, we can't regain innocence once we have lost it. An angel with a fiery sword guards the way back into Paradise. The only way is forward, through life, deep into life, deep into the difficulties and the compromises and the betrayals and the disappointments that we inevitably encounter.

But it isn't all gloom. There is a prize, and it's a great one. In Kleist's terms, we might eventually re-enter Paradise from the back, as it were, by going all the way round the world. This grace that we lost by acquiring knowledge has two forms: that of the puppet, with no consciousness at all, and that of the god, whose consciousness is infinite. Innocence at one end of the spectrum: wisdom at the other. But if we want the wisdom that comes with experience, we have to leave the innocence behind.

I thought about Kleist's essay and everything it implied for a long time, but I didn't think of writing anything about it. There was nothing I could add to what was already perfect. It became part of the way I thought about everything.

Then one day I found myself beginning to write a long story of a sort I hadn't tried before, a sort I could only call fantasy. There was another world, and there were landscapes of Arctic wildness and Gothic complexity; there were gigantic figures of moral darkness and light engaging in a conflict whose causes and outcome were invisible to me. And it began with a little girl going into a room where she shouldn't go, and having to hide when someone comes in, and then overhearing a conversation whose meaning she doesn't fully understand, but which fills her with a sense of excitement and dread...

I daresay some writers begin with a theme they want to write about, and then find a story to fit it, and characters to embody the various arguments within it, and so on. I never do. It would feel mechanical, contrived. I don't know what my theme is until the story is already well under way.

And it wasn't until this story was advanced enough for me to have written a dozen or more versions of the first chapter, and to have discovered that Lyra had a dæmon called Pantalaimon who could change shape and who was a part of her very self, that I discovered what the theme of this book was. I discovered it in the same moment that I realised that children's dæmons could change shape, but adult dæmons couldn't.

I knew enough about storytelling by that time to know that if something doesn't help, it'll hinder. If a shape-changing dæmon were something that every character had as a matter of course, the reader would get fed up with it, and so would I, because it would mean nothing. It would be a silly bit of decoration that had no purpose or significance.

But if the difference between children and adults were this visible and dramatic...

And if the theme of the whole story were this very change from innocence to experience...

Then all kinds of possibilities opened up, including the possibility, after a dozen years or more, of doing something like justice to the matters touched on so lightly, so gracefully, in that essay on the marionette theatre by Kleist. If we want wisdom, we have to leave the innocence behind...

That's what it means when Lyra, at the end of *His Dark Materials*, loses the power to read the alethiometer. She's leaving her innocence behind. Where I disagree with a number of writers from the so-called golden age of children's literature is precisely here, in their view of innocence. Too many of them seemed to feel that childhood was a golden age and its loss is tragic, something to be looked back on forever with nostalgia and regret.

Well, that's a view I don't share. That view would have left Lyra perpetually bereft, able only to lament the loss of her power, stuck in a lifelong mourning for the death of her childhood. I think we can be more positive than that about growing up; I think we can find some reason for welcoming it, some reason for hope. And Kleist's wonderful essay gave me a clue as to how.

One of the two friends who have this conversation about puppets is himself a dancer. He has learned to dance. By toil and effort and discipline, he has worked his way through the pain and disappointment and setback until he has begun to achieve a mastery of his art. He has left the puppet behind; he is on his way to becoming a god. It seemed to me there was a clue here for Lyra. The adults who read the alethiometer do so with the aid of books of reference – of conscious awareness, in other words. They have to look things up and make the connections consciously, unlike the young Lyra, who does it with the grace and speed of an animal or a bird. To her, the conscious way of reading the alethiometer must seem terribly clumsy and slow and pedestrian and earthbound.

But as she is told, eventually, after great study and toil, her reading of the instrument will be better, deeper, truer, more aware, in every way richer than the one she could achieve when she was a child. There is a great deal of work, and not a little suffering, and many setbacks, before she will reach that goal; but there *is* a goal, and it can be reached.

That's where the hope comes in. It's the hope of every human life, in fact; the hope that we can learn something true, and pass it on.

My debt to Kleist doesn't quite end with adopting his theme. There is a bear in his essay, and there happens to be a bear in my story as well, and at one point I stole an incident involving Kleist's bear and gave it to mine. I hope I shall be forgiven for that, because after all I can hardly own up to it without drawing attention to that essay in the first place. My story is much longer than the essay, but that is because I am much less of a genius than Kleist was; he managed to say in 2,500 words or so what I could only cram into 1,200 pages. Nevertheless, I think there are some incidents in the story that might divert the reader, and a character or two who might engage the interest and affection.

I hope so, anyway. It is my way of thanking Providence, or chance, or fate, for that original and unforgettable thunderbolt.

THIS ESSAY WAS ORIGINALLY DELIVERED AS TWO SEPARATE PIECES: A PLATFORM SPEECH AT THE NATIONAL THEATRE FOR A PERFORMANCE IN 2004 OF *ON THE MARIONETTE THEATRE*, AND AS A PART OF THE INTRODUCTION TO THE FOLIO SOCIETY EDITION OF *HIS DARK MATERIALS* (2008).

As I say, I first came across Kleist's essay in 1978, when information still had a physical form. That being the case, the only way I could keep it by me was to cut it out of the TLS and look after it, which I did, with the help of much Sellotape as it got more and more worn and frayed. But that was in the very old days, when we were only a step away from having to copy things out by hand if we wanted to preserve them. Practically medieval. By the time I was able to pay tribute to Kleist in the Afterword to The Amber Spyglass, *the internet had arrived, and anyone who was interested in his essay only had to enter the title in a search box, and up it came within seconds. Of course that's a great gain, and I wouldn't be without it, but I do remember treasuring that tattered page of newsprint with its precious cargo of words, and I still have it.*

Paradise Lost

AN INTRODUCTION

On the poetry, story, mood of Milton's great epic,
and its influence on His Dark Materials

THERE IS AN OLD STORY ABOUT A BIBULOUS, SEMI-LITERATE, AGING country squire sometime in the eighteenth century, sitting by his fireside listening to *Paradise Lost* being read aloud. He's never read it himself; he doesn't know the story at all; but as he sits there, perhaps with a pint of port at his side and with a gouty foot propped up on a stool, he finds himself transfixed.

Suddenly he bangs the arm of his chair, and exclaims, 'By God! I know not what the outcome may be, but this Lucifer is a damned fine fellow, and I hope he may win!'

Which are my sentiments exactly.

I'm conscious, as I write this introduction to the poem, that I have hardly any more pretensions to scholarship than that old gentleman. Many of my comparisons will be drawn from popular literature and film rather than from anything more refined. Learned critics have analysed *Paradise Lost* and found in it things I could never see, and related it to other work I have never read, and demonstrated the truth of this or that assertion about Milton and his poem that it would never have occurred to me to make, or, having made, to think that I could prove it.

But this is how I read this great work, and all I can do is describe that way of reading.

The story as a poem

So I begin with sound. I read *Paradise Lost* not only with my eyes, but also with my mouth.

From Book II, line 636:

> As when far off at sea a fleet descried
> Hangs in the clouds, by equinoctial winds
> Close sailing from Bengala, or the isles
> Of Ternate and Tidore, whence merchants bring
> Their spicy drugs: they on the trading flood
> Through the wide Ethiopian to the Cape
> Ply stemming nightly toward the pole. So seemed
> Far off the flying fiend...

I was lucky enough to study Books I and II for A level, and to do so in a small class whose teacher, Miss Enid Jones, had the clear-eyed and old-fashioned idea that we would get a good sense of the poem if, before we did anything else to it, we read it aloud. So we took it in turns, in that little sixth-form classroom in Ysgol Ardudwy, on the flat land below the great rock of Harlech Castle, to stumble and mutter and gabble our way through it all, while Miss Jones sat with arms comfortably folded on her desk, patiently helping us with pronunciation, but not encumbering us with meaning.

I can't remember whether the passage above was one of the ones I read when it was my turn, but I do know that it stayed with me for years, and still has the power to thrill me. *Ply stemming nightly toward the pole* – in those words I could hear the creak of wood and rope, the never-ceasing dash of water against the bows, the moan of the wind in the rigging; I could see the dim phosphorescence in the creaming wake, the dark waves against the restless horizon, the constant stars in the velvet sky; and

I saw the vigilant helmsman, the only man awake, guiding his sleeping shipmates and their precious freight across the wilderness of the night.

To see these things and hear them most vividly, I found that I had to take the lines in my mouth and utter it aloud. A whisper will do; you don't have to bellow it, and annoy the neighbours; but air has to pass across your tongue and through your lips. Your body has to be involved.

> Through many a dark and dreary vale
> They passed, and many a region dolorous,
> O'er many a frozen, many a fiery alp,
> Rocks, caves, lakes, fens, bogs, dens, and shades of death,
> A universe of death, which God by curse
> Created evil, for evil only good,
> Where all life dies, death lives, and nature breeds
> Perverse, all monstrous, all prodigious things,
> Abominable, inutterable, and worse
> Than fables yet have feigned, or fear conceived,
> Gorgons, and Hydras, and Chimeras dire.
> [*Book II, lines 618-628*]

The experience of reading poetry aloud when you don't fully understand it is a curious and complicated one. It's like suddenly discovering that you can play the organ. Rolling swells and peals of sound, powerful rhythms and rich harmonies are at your command; and as you utter them you begin to realise that the sound you're releasing from the words as you speak is part of the reason they're there. The *sound* is part of the *meaning*, and that part only comes alive when you speak it. So at this stage it doesn't matter that you don't fully understand everything: you're already far closer to the poem than someone who sits there in silence looking up meanings and references and making assiduous notes.

By the way, someone who does that while listening to music through earphones will never understand it at all.

We need to remind ourselves of this especially if we have anything to do with education. I have come across teachers and student teachers whose job was to teach poetry, but who thought that poetry was only a fancy way of dressing up simple statements to make them look complicated, and that their task was to help their pupils translate the stuff into ordinary English. When they'd translated it, when they'd 'understood' it, the job was done. It had the effect of turning the classroom into a torture chamber, in which everything that made the poem a living thing had been killed and butchered. No one had told such people that poetry is in fact enchantment; that it has the form it does because that very form casts a spell; and that when they thought they were bothered and bewildered, they were in fact being bewitched, and if they let themselves accept the enchantment and enjoy it, they would eventually understand much more about the poem.

But if they never learn this truth themselves, they can't possibly transmit it to anyone else. Instead, in an atmosphere of suspicion, resentment and hostility, many poems are interrogated until they confess, and what they confess is usually worthless, as the results of torture always are: broken little scraps of information, platitudes, banalities. Never mind! The work has been done according to the instructions, and the result of the interrogation is measured and recorded and tabulated in line with government targets; and this is the process we call education.

However, as I say, I was lucky enough to learn to love *Paradise Lost* before I had to explain it. Once you do love something, the attempt to understand it becomes a pleasure rather than a chore, and what you find when you begin to explore *Paradise Lost* in that way is how rich it is in thought and argument. You could make a prose paraphrase of it that would still be a work of the most profound and commanding intellectual power. But the poetry – its incantatory quality – is what makes it the great work of art it is. I found, in that classroom so long ago, that it had the power to stir a physical response: my heart beat faster, the hair on my head stirred, my skin bristled. Ever since then, that has been my test for poetry, just as it was for A. E. Housman, who dared not think of a line of poetry while he was shaving, in case he cut himself.

The poem as a story

The question 'Where should my story begin?' is, as every storyteller knows, both immensely important and immensely difficult to answer.

'Once upon a time', as the fairy-tale formula has it; but once upon a time there was – what? The opening governs the way you tell everything that follows, not only in terms of the organisation of the events, but also in terms of the tone of voice that does the telling; and not least, it enlists the reader's sympathy in *this* cause rather than *that*.

So when the story of *Paradise Lost* begins, after the invocation to the 'heavenly muse', we find ourselves in hell, with the fallen angels groaning on the burning lake. And from then on, part of our awareness is always affected by that. This is a story about devils. It's not a story about God. The fallen angels and their leader are our protagonists, and the unfallen angels, and God the Father and the Son, and Adam and Eve, are all supporting players. And we begin *in medias res*, in the middle of the action, with the first great battle lost, and the rebel angels just beginning to recover their senses after their vertiginous fall. What an opening! And what scenery!

Satan first looks around at:

> The dismal situation waste and wild,
> A dungeon horrible, on all sides round
> As one great furnace flamed, yet from those flames
> No light, but rather darkness visible
> Served only to discover sights of woe,
> Regions of sorrow, doleful shades, where peace

And rest can never dwell, hope never comes
That comes to all: but torture without end
Still urges, and a fiery deluge, fed
With ever-burning sulphur unconsumed...

C. S. Lewis remarks that for many readers, it's not just the events of the story that matter: it's the world the story conjures up. In his own case, he loved the Leatherstocking tales of James Fenimore Cooper not just for 'the momentary suspense but that whole world to which it belonged – the snow and the snow-shoes, beavers and canoes, war-paths and wigwams, and Hiawatha names'.

The same thing is true for some writers of stories. They are drawn to a particular atmosphere, a particular kind of landscape; they want to wander about in it and relish its special tastes and sounds, even before they know what story they're going to tell. Whether Milton worked like that I don't know, but it's easy to see that his imagination delighted in the scenery of hell, and we see that from the very beginning, with Satan surveying his 'dungeon horrible'.

Books I and II are full of these magnificent and terrifying landscapes, and when the tale reaches Paradise itself, in Book IV, the descriptions reach a peak of sensuous delight that we can almost taste.

But landscapes and atmospheres aren't enough for a story; something has to happen. And it helps the tightness and propulsion of the story enormously if it's the protagonist himself who sets the action going, who takes the initiative. It also encourages our interest in the protagonist to develop into admiration. That is exactly what happens here, as the fallen angels, who are devils now, gather themselves after their great fall, and begin to plot their revenge.

Revenge is one of the great story themes, of course, and it's inspired storytellers of every rank and in every age, from Homer and Aeschylus and Shakespeare to Jeffrey Archer. The interest here is in how Milton handles the narrative. How well does he tell the story?

I think it could hardly be told any better. After their first struggle on the burning lake, the fallen angels hold a great debate in Pandemonium, where the characters of their leaders are vividly revealed: Moloch, the fearless, savage warrior; Belial, graceful, false, and hollow, counselling 'ignoble ease and peaceful sloth'; Mammon, intent only on gold and riches; and then Beelzebub, 'majestic though in ruin', who sums up all the preceding arguments and then points the way to another world altogether, 'the happy seat Of some new race called Man', and suggests that they make that the target of their vengeance. We can see and hear the plan taking shape, we can feel the surge of determination and energy it brings, and inevitably that makes us curious to know how they'll bring it off. There is a sort of curiosity that isn't short-circuited by our knowledge of how things did, in fact, turn out: Frederick Forsyth's *The Day of the Jackal* demonstrated that although we know full well that General de Gaulle was not assassinated, we are still eager to read about how he might have been.

And Milton is careful to remind us that it was Satan himself who first thought of this plan, and it's Satan who sets out across the wastes of hell to find his way to the new world. The hero is firmly in charge.

If the opening of a story is important, the closing of one part of it – a chapter, a canto – is important in a different way. The purpose here is to charge the forthcoming pause with tension and expectation. Popular storytellers have always had a firm grasp of this principle; it's exactly what Conan Doyle does, for example, at the end of the first episode of *The Hound of the Baskervilles*, in the *Strand Magazine* for August 1901. Dr Mortimer has just been describing the mysterious death of Sir Charles Baskerville, and mentions the footprints nearby. 'A man's or a woman's?' asks Holmes, and Dr Mortimer replies, 'Mr Holmes, they were the footprints of a gigantic hound!'

There the episode ends. There was no shortage of eager buyers for the September issue.

Storytelling principles hold true, whatever the subject, whatever the medium. Time the pause right, and the audience will be eager for what follows. The break after the end of the second book of *Paradise Lost* is powerfully charged with tension because it obeys that principle. After his journey to the gates of hell, and his encounter with Sin and Death, Satan sees the distant vastness of heaven:

And fast by hanging in a golden chain
This pendant world, in bigness as a star
Of smallest magnitude close by the moon.
Thither full fraught with mischievous revenge,
Accursed, and in a cursed hour he hies.

And there Book II ends, and we pause with that image in our minds. This newly created world, suspended in its golden chain, so beautiful and fresh, knows nothing of what is coming towards it. But we know. To cite Alfred Hitchcock again, who knew more about suspense than most other storytellers, you can depict four men sitting around a table calmly playing cards, and the audience will be on the edge of their seats with tension – as long as the audience knows what the card-players don't, namely that there is a bomb under the table about to go off. Milton knew that too.

There are examples of his great storytelling power all the way through – far too many to mention here. But one we should look at is the very end of the poem. Like the beginning, the end of a story is such an important place that it has a traditional formulaic tag, but 'and they lived happily ever after' certainly won't do in this case. Adam and Eve have chosen to disobey the explicit command of God, and the consequences of this have been laid out for them not only by their own experience of guilt and shame, but by the narrative of the future they've heard from the angel Michael. They must leave Eden: Paradise is now irrecoverably lost. This is a part of the story that has often been illustrated, and in a picture the scene is indeed intensely dramatic, with the man and woman in tears, and the angel with the fiery sword expelling them – just as it is in Medina's illustration.

But the story closes on a mood, a tender emotional harmony, that is both crystal-clear and profoundly complex. Part of its complexity depends on the interplay between the past and the future, between regret and hope, and this is the very thing that's so difficult to convey in a picture, where the only tense is the present.

The best way to experience the full richness of this mood is to read the last lines of the poem aloud, as I've suggested earlier, and succumb to the enchantment, because at this point poetry and storytelling come together perfectly.

> High in front advanced,
> The brandished sword of God before them blazed,
> Fierce as a comet; which with torrid heat,
> And vapour as the Libyan air adust,
> Began to parch that temperate clime; whereat
> In either hand the hastening Angel caught
> Our lingering parents, and to the eastern gate
> Led them direct, and down the cliff as fast
> To the subjected plain; then disappeared.
> They, looking back, all the eastern side beheld
> Of Paradise, so late their happy seat,
> Waved over by that flaming brand; the gate
> With dreadful faces thronged, and fiery arms:
> Some natural tears they dropt, but wiped them soon;
> The world was all before them, where to choose
> Their place of rest, and Providence their guide:
> They, hand in hand, with wandering steps and slow,
> Through Eden took their solitary way.

Michael Burgesse after John Baptist Medina, for Book XII of *Paradise Lost*

'The world was all before them' implies not only an end but a new beginning. There are many more stories to come.

Paradise Lost *and its influence*

A poem is not a lecture; a story is not an argument. The way poems and stories work on our minds is not by logic, but by their capacity to enchant, to excite, to move, to inspire. To be sure, a sound intellectual underpinning helps the work to stand up under intellectual questioning, as *Paradise Lost* certainly does; but its primary influence is on the imagination.

So it was, for instance, with the greatest of Milton's interpreters, William Blake, for whom the author of *Paradise Lost* was a lifelong inspiration. 'Milton lovd me in childhood and shewd me his face,' he claimed, and in *The Marriage of Heaven and Hell* he wrote what is probably the most perceptive, and certainly the most succinct, criticism of *Paradise Lost*: 'The reason Milton wrote in fetters when he wrote of Angels & God, and at liberty when of Devils and Hell, is that he was a true Poet, and of the Devil's party without knowing it.' And Blake's continuing and passionate interest in Milton resulted in a long (and, frankly, difficult) poem named after the poet, as well as a series of illustrations to *Paradise Lost* which are some of the most beautiful and delicate watercolours he ever did.

Other poets at the same period felt the influence of Milton, Wordsworth in particular, who began one of his sonnets with the words:

> Milton! Thou shouldst be living at this hour:
> England hath need of thee:

And very near the beginning of his own great long poem, *The Prelude*, Wordsworth deliberately echoes the phrase in the closing lines of *Paradise Lost*:

The earth is all before me ...

– as if he's taking hold of a torch passed to him by Milton.

Today, nearly three and a half centuries after *Paradise Lost* was first published, it is more influential than ever. New dramatic adaptations appear on the stage, new illustrated editions are published. It will not go away.

In my own case, the trilogy I called *His Dark Materials* (stealing that very phrase from Book II, line 916, with due acknowledgement in the epigraph) began partly with my memories of reading the poem aloud at school so many years before. As I talked to my publisher, I discovered that he too remembered studying it in the sixth form, and we sat at the lunch table swapping our favourite lines; and by the time we'd finished, I seemed to have agreed to write a long fantasy for young readers, which would at least partly, we hoped, evoke something of the atmosphere we both loved in *Paradise Lost*.

So it was the landscape, the atmosphere, that was my starting point. But as the narrative began to form itself on the page, I found that – perhaps drawn by the gravitational attraction of a much greater mass – I was beginning to tell the same story too. I wasn't worried about that, because I was well aware that there are many ways of telling the same story, and that this story was a very good one in the first place, and could take a great deal of re-telling.

Inevitably, the storyteller's own preoccupations become visible in the emphasis and the colouring they give to this or that aspect of the tale. In my case, I found that my interest was most vividly caught by the meaning of the temptation-and-fall theme. Suppose that the prohibition on the knowledge of good and evil were an expression of jealous cruelty, and that the gaining of such knowledge were an act of virtue? Suppose the Fall should be celebrated and not deplored? As I played with it, my story resolved itself into an account of the necessity of growing up, and a refusal to lament the loss of innocence. The true end of human life, I found myself saying, was not redemption by a non-existent Son of God, but the gaining and transmission of wisdom, and if we are going to do any good in the world, we have to leave childhood behind.

That is how one modern writer told this great story. It will certainly be told many times again, and each time differently. I think it is the central story of our lives, the story that more than any other tells us what it means to be human. But however many times it is told in the future, and however many different interpretations are made of it, I don't think that the version created by Milton, blind and aging, out of political favour, dictating it day by day to his daughter, will ever be surpassed.

Introductions to the Twelve Books of Paradise Lost

Book I

I love the audacity of this opening – the sheer *nerve* of Milton's declaring that he's going to pursue 'Things unattempted yet in prose or rhyme', to 'justify the ways of God to men'. How could anyone fail to thrill to a story that begins like this? How could any reader not warm to a poet who dares to say it?

As the story begins, we meet the rebel angels as they lie stunned and vanquished on the burning lake in hell. Surely there's no way out for them? But when we read the great description of Satan calling his legions together, with his shield hanging on his shoulders like the moon and his spear mightier than the tallest pine, we realise that the story is in safe hands. The rebels raise the palace of Pandemonium, with its monstrous grandeur, and gather to decide what they should do. They haven't been destroyed: 'war Open or understood must be resolved.'

Book II

The leaders of the rebel angels debate their next course of action, and decide to take their revenge by seducing the 'new race called Man' to their party.

Satan sets off alone to undertake this great task, and the rest of the book concerns his journey to the gates of hell and out into the chaos beyond, and ends with a glimpse of the distant new world hanging in a golden chain, no bigger than a star beside the moon, beautiful and ignorant of the malice moving towards it.

Apart from that magical cliffhanger of an ending, what never fails to thrill me in Book II is the sensuous power of the language, from the opening 'where the gorgeous East with richest hand Showers on her kings barbaric pearl and gold', through the savage wilderness that Satan traverses with such labour and determination: 'O'er bog or steep, through straight, rough, dense, or rare, With head, hands, wings, or feet pursues his way, And swims or sinks, or wades, or creeps, or flies'. No one, not even Shakespeare, surpasses Milton in his command of the sound, the music, the weight and taste and texture of English words.

Book III

We open with an invocation to light, and a reminder of the poet's own blindness; but with magnificent confidence, Milton evokes the names of blind poets and prophets of classical antiquity, including no less a name than Homer (Maeonides), and calmly, despite his tactful disavowal ('were I equalled with them in renown') assumes his right to be counted in their company.

In this Book we meet God the Father, and begin to see what Blake meant; for almost the first thing God does is to forecast the Fall of man, and immediately go on to say, 'Whose fault? Whose but his own?' in that unattractive whine we hear from children who, caught at a scene of mischief, seek at once to put the blame on someone else.

Satan, meanwhile, lands in our world, deceiving the angel Uriel, 'For neither man nor angel can discern Hypocrisy, the only evil that walks Invisible' – another indication that Milton is concerned in this story with psychological truth as much as any other kind.

Book IV

The psychological theme continues, as Book IV opens with Satan's savage self-examination: 'Which way I fly is hell; my self am hell', and his resolution, 'Evil be thou my good'. This great speech functions exactly like a Shakespearian soliloquy, both advancing the story and plumbing the depths of self-exploration. It's a reminder, perhaps, that Milton originally thought of making this story into a drama. However, no scenery for the stage of Milton's time could ever have depicted the landscape of Paradise – the breadth of it, and all its myriad details – as richly as his verse does here.

The setting established, Milton brings on Adam and Eve, 'with native honour clad In naked majesty': something else, perhaps, that would have been difficult to show on the stage at that period, essential as it is to the story. As Satan watches their innocent loveliness and delight in the physical world, his self-torment turns to self-delusion, and he advances political reasons – 'public reason just... compels me now To do what else though damned I should abhor' – to justify his action.

The angels under the command of Gabriel, uneasy and watchful, discover Satan in the form of a toad whispering in the ear of the sleeping Eve, and he confronts them in a scene that both expresses his romantic defiance of their authority and reveals his psychological complexity: 'abashed the devil stood, And felt how awful goodness is, and saw Virtue in her shape how lovely, saw, and pined His loss'. Stage or no stage, Milton's storytelling is intensely dramatic.

Book V

Unease: that is the tone that begins Book V. Satan's whispers have brought Eve disturbing dreams. Satan himself is absent from this Book in a direct way, as he is from the next three, although his actions have set everything in motion, and the talk is of no one but him; there is no doubt who is dominating the narrative.

Adam and Eve pray, and God sends the angel Raphael to warn them of the danger lurking nearby, and to make sure, by telling them clearly, that they won't be able to plead ignorance later on. Again, something in

Milton leads him to show a petty and legalistic side of God the Father, which is quite different from his view of the Son. When Raphael is welcomed by Adam and Eve, there is a curious passage where Milton becomes unnecessarily (it seems to me) literal about whether angels can eat, and if so, what, and what happens to the food once eaten. That's the sort of thing that happens when a storyteller takes his eye off the impulse of the story for a moment.

The rest of the Book is Raphael's account of the origins of the war in heaven: of how God's announcement that he had begotten the Son provoked the envy of Satan and some other angels, and of how they withdrew to the north to plot their rebellion, and of how one among them, Abdiel – 'Among the faithless, faithful only he' – defied them and set off back to the armies of God.

Book VI

Raphael continues his account of the war: he tells of how Abdiel, a champion of God now, challenged Satan and stuck him a mighty blow, and how Michael gave the order for the heavenly hosts to engage the enemy, and himself dealt Satan a grievous wound, which humbled his pride.

Raphael's account goes on to tell of how the rebel angels, in that first night of the war, dug mines, extracted metal, mingled 'sulphurous and nitrous foam' to make gunpowder, and made great guns. The description of their effect is very powerful: their roar 'Embowelled with outrageous noise the air, And all her entails tore, disgorging foul Their devilish glut, chained thunderbolts and hail Of iron globes'. At first thrown back by these weapons of mass destruction, Michael and his forces retreated in confusion, but soon rallied; and so another day of battle passed.

On the third day, as God the Father had ordained, the Son triumphed, and hurled the rebels down into hell, which is where we found Satan and his hosts at the beginning of Book I.

Once again, for this reader at least, it's difficult to warm to a God who watches complacently while his forces suffer terrible punishment, deliberately waiting before letting the Son rout the enemy so as to make his triumph seem more splendid: 'that the glory may be thine Of ending this great war'. That's not divinity: it's public relations. We don't have to think that this was a deliberate strategy on Milton's part; it's not uncommon for writers to be unaware of exactly what effect their portrayal of this character or that is having on the reader. Blake's point was that Milton was of the devil's party *without knowing it*.

Book VII

Milton invokes the aid of Urania, once known as the Muse of Astronomy, but then immediately denies that she is one of the classical nine: this is some other muse, the sister of Wisdom. Astronomy would have been appropriate, because this Book contains Raphael's account of God's creation of the world – not just our earth, but the whole universe, 'Of amplitude almost immense, with stars Numerous, and every star perhaps a world Of destined habitation'.

Once again Satan is offstage, and the chief interest of this Book is in the glorious description of the emerging natural world: 'last Rose as in dance the stately trees, and spread Their branches hung with copious fruit'. And it is in the invocation to Urania that Milton speaks of his own difficult, almost desperate situation, 'fallen on evil days, On evil days though fallen, and evil tongues; In darkness, and with dangers compassed round, And solitude'. But he is comforted by the thought that Urania will govern his song, and (in a phrase that has sustained many a solitary writer) will 'fit audience find, though few'.

Book VIII

The four central Books of *Paradise Lost*, ending with this one, function as a sort of flashback in the main story. Strictly speaking, they're not, because the main framing narrative continues to move forward in time, but we experience them as a flashback, because all that the main narrative shows us is characters who tell each other what happened at an earlier stage.

Here in Book VIII Adam and Raphael continue to talk about the origins of things, and Adam manifests that curiosity that is already a dominating human characteristic. Raphael's advice about that is to curb it: 'Solicit not thy thoughts with matters hid… be lowly wise'. Easier said than done, we might think. And Raphael himself displays some of this quality when he asks Adam to tell him about his own creation, which happened when Raphael was elsewhere; so Adam tells of his awakening, his wish for a companion, and the creation of Eve. Again comes a warning from Raphael, who advises Adam not to be intoxicated by her beauty, which is 'worthy well Thy cherishing, thy honouring, and thy love, Not thy subjection'. However, when Adam asks whether angels themselves express their love in a physical way, Raphael blushes: not only do angels eat, as we saw in Book V, it seems that they can experience a gaseous kind of sexual intercourse. And with that, the long digression comes to an end.

Book IX

This is the longest Book in the poem, and in some ways the most astonishing. Milton's powers as a dramatic storyteller come to their highest point as he deals with the encounter between Satan and Eve. His account of the psychological and moral progression of the seduction scene itself, as well as of the ensuing reactions of Adam and Eve and their mutual recrimination, are unsurpassed in any novel or drama I know.

Once again we see how much more *interesting*, as a character, Satan is than God: for instance, when he gazes at Eve's innocent beauty, and finds that:

> her every air
> Of gesture or least action overawed
> His malice, and with rapine sweet bereaved
> His fierceness of the fierce intent it brought:
> That space the evil one abstracted stood
> From his own evil, and for the time remained
> Stupidly good.

And all the imagery of which Milton is a master is fully deployed: Satan moves towards Eve

> with tract oblique
> At first, as one who sought access, but feared
> To interrupt, sidelong he works his way.
> As when a ship by skilful steersman wrought
> Nigh river's mouth or foreland, where the wind
> Veers oft, as oft so steers, and shifts her sail.

Their encounter is the point towards which all the rest of the story has moved. I imagine Milton looking forward to this great scene from the moment he first conceived it; I imagine him measuring his powers against it, and finding them equal to the magnitude of the task, and working with a fierce and sober joy.

Book X

And now all the sorry consequences begin to unfold. God has seen every-thing, and forgives the angels who were set to guard Paradise, because they could not have prevented Satan's deed. The Father sends the alto-gether more sympathetic Son to judge the fallen pair, and he pronounces a curse on the serpent.

Apart from the continuing psychological interest of the course of guilt and repentance in the minds of Adam and Eve, and their saddened under-standing of the new state of things, all of which is very subtly conveyed, we see how the whole framework of nature is unsettled by their action; because God commands the angels to tilt the axis of the earth so as to cause the seasons, and bring 'pinching cold and scorching heat' where previously a perpetual spring 'smiled on earth with vernant flowers'.

Furthermore, Sin and Death have been building a stupendous bridge between this universe and hell, and they enter the world and begin to sow discord among the animals: 'Beast now with beast gan war, and fowl with fowl, And fish with fish; to graze the herb all leaving, Devoured each other'.

In this Book we see the last of Satan, who returns to hell, as he thinks, in triumph, only to hear his speech greeted with 'A dismal universal hiss, the sound Of public scorn'. He and all the devils find themselves changed into serpents, and are tormented further by the appearance of a tree exactly like the Tree of Knowledge in Paradise, whose fruit, to them, tastes like nothing but ashes. This medieval comic-grotesque scene of degradation is a pitiful comedown for a great romantic hero. From now on, all the interest in the poem belongs to humanity, and to history.

Book XI

God decrees that Adam and Eve shall leave Paradise, and sends the angel Michael to drive them out. But before they go, Michael shows Adam a vision of all that is to come, and reveals everything that will happen to his descendants up to the time of the Flood. This may or may not be fascinating to a modern reader; what remains absorbing to me is the growing humanity of Adam and Eve, and the subtle play of emotions – fear leavened by hope, sorrow tempered by resolution – that characterises their new and fallen state.

Book XII

Michael continues his foretelling of history up to the life and death of Christ, and beyond, including a severely Protestant view of the development of the church: 'Wolves shall succeed for teacher, grievous wolves. Who all the sacred mysteries of heaven To their own vile advantages shall turn Of lucre and ambition'. However, finally after long ages all shall be well: 'New heavens, new earth, ages of endless date Founded in righteousness and peace and love To bring forth fruits joy and eternal bliss'. Eve, who has been sleeping, wakes to tell of a comforting dream: 'By me the promised seed shall all restore'.

And then come the final twenty-five lines of this great poem, which we can only read and wonder at. 'Some natural tears they dropped, but wiped them soon' is so simple, so truthful, and so generous that it reminds us that no work can be truly great if it is not about ourselves, and unless it tells us what it is like to be alive.

Afterword

There are many ways to read this poem, but if you fall under its spell you will want to understand it as well as you can; and that means, at the very least, seeing all the patterns of imagery, discovering the meanings of all the classical references, untangling the occasionally complicated cosmology, and understanding the structures of rhetoric that shape the whole work.

In a reading like this one, ten thousand jewels have had to lie untouched.

Sparse notes are better than none, if they are accurate. But in my own reading I have found no better and fuller guide than Alastair Fowler's annotated edition in the *Longman* series. Fowler's notes are rich, complete and unfailingly helpful; they are a model of what annotations should be, and of the luminous understanding that a critical intelligence can reach.

These introductions were first published by Oxford University Press in their World's Classics edition of *Paradise Lost* (2005).

The classroom as a torture chamber, interrogating poetry until it confesses: I stand by that image.

The Origin of the Universe

THE STORYTELLING OF SCIENCE AND RELIGION:
A RESPONSE TO A LECTURE BY STEPHEN HAWKING

On origin myths and origin accounts, the excitement of science,
the misreadings of fundamentalists, and our responsibilities

STEPHEN HAWKING'S ACCOUNT OF THE ORIGIN OF THE UNIVERSE TOLD a story of great brilliance and clarity. The questions 'Why are we here?' and 'Where did we come from?' are very good ones, and we all find ourselves asking them on the day we begin to grow up. When we're children, other questions occupy us; we want to know why we can't have more ice cream, and why we have to go to bed right now, and why nothing is fair; but on the day we begin to grow up, which is usually in our early adolescence, we find Professor Hawking's questions becoming more and more interesting. Of course, some people stop growing up, and then they stop asking those questions. They ask other questions instead, such as 'What's on TV tonight?' or 'Where can I get the best return for my investments?'.

Professor Hawking's lecture began with an account of the great god Bumba and his digestive problems, which I hadn't heard about before. According to the myths of the Boshongo people, Bumba had a belly-ache and vomited up the sun, the moon, the stars and various animals including the first human beings. This ingenious piece of gastro-theology provides a very good account of why we're here and where we came from, with only the slight disadvantage of being untrue. Or at least unlikely. As I understand the theoretical physicist Richard Feynman's sum over histories, the great god Bumba may be busily at work somewhere, but probably not in this suburb of the universe.

As the lecture progressed, I was struck by how much more interesting Professor Hawking's account was than that of the Boshongo people. I don't only mean more likely, more persuasive, better argued, though it was all of those; I mean more interesting. It was better storytelling; I always wanted to hear what was going to happen next, and why. It was full of more interesting characters and settings. The Steady State, for example, which I couldn't help picturing as a sort of 1950s advertisement, with a pipe-smoking father sitting comfortably in his living room, next to the radiogram, with a wife knitting submissively in the background and a small boy playing with Meccano on the carpet. The father would remove his pipe and twinkle knowledgeably as he said, 'Of course, I'm with Steady State Insurance,' and a caption underneath would say 'You Know Where You Are With a STEADY STATE Policy'.

Then there were other fascinating characters, such as the General Theory of Relativity, and the microwave radiation from the very early universe that turns up on your television screen, and the spontaneous quantum creation of little bubbles that grow, or don't grow, into universes.

Another reason that the story we heard from Professor Hawking was different from that of the Boshongo people has to do with the relationship we have with the story itself. It's to do with the way we – the audience at an academic lecture, the congregation in a church, the jury in a courtroom, the listeners around the cooking fire in the darkness of the savanna – the way we regard the stories we're hearing. Different kinds of stories *expect* different kinds of audience and certain kinds of attitude from that audience. I don't mean an attitude of liking or respect, though every storyteller would like those; what I mean is there's something in the circumstances of the telling that says 'This story is to be taken literally', or 'This is a metaphor. One thing stands for another'.

Because in the normal course of life, we depend on knowing which attitude it's appropriate to take to the stories we hear. A witness in court might be telling the truth, or telling a lie, and the jury might believe him or not; but they don't think that he's talking in metaphor. If the prosecuting counsel says, 'Tell the court what you saw the accused do,' and the witness says, 'He stuck a knife in the victim's heart,' the jury isn't expected to understand this as meaning, 'I saw him write a savage review of the victim's latest book.' The jury is there to decide whether or not the statement is true, but not what kind of statement it is. It's supposed to be a literal one.

Now we don't know whether the first people who listened to the Bumba story thought it was literally true. Maybe they did. But I think that if people have evolved to the point where they can tell stories at all, they've already got a fairly sophisticated mental world in place, in which they know the difference between what's literal and what's figurative. After all, every one of the Boshongo people must at some point have eaten a piece of dead wildebeest or something that didn't agree with them, and the consequences of that would have looked nothing like the sun, the moon, the stars and the animals and so on. So they were capable of thinking that Bumba's belly-ache and its results were like theirs in some ways but unlike them in others: they were capable of thinking in analogy or metaphor.

As long as that mental capacity persists, human beings are able to think about their world and describe it in more ways than one, and a very great gift that is. At the high point of what we might call the Bumba tendency, we find the sublime poetry of Milton's account of the Creation in *Paradise Lost*. Milton pictures the angel Raphael talking to Adam and Eve and telling them what happened before they themselves were created, and does it in words that celebrate the sensuous physical beauty of the world so vividly that it's impossible, for this atheist at least, to withhold a rush of imaginative empathy. I know it isn't literally true, and yet I can enjoy it to the full. Most of us are capable of that sort of mental double vision, and that capacity can't only have evolved last week. I think it's as ancient as language and as humanity itself.

The trouble comes when the fundamentalists insist that there is no such thing as analogy or metaphor, or else that they are wicked or Satanic, and that there must only be a literal understanding of stories. The Bible is literally true. The world was created in six days. The Kansas Board of Education says so. The worshippers of Bumba, as far as we know, haven't developed this modern perversion, this modern limitation on the meaning of narrative; it's only the worshippers of Yahweh and Allah who are as silly as that.

The delight for me in the account Professor Hawking has given us in his lecture and in his marvellous book *A Brief History of Time*, is that we can both listen to it with wonder *and* take it literally. It's a tale of heroic endeavour, of intellectual daring and imaginative brilliance without parallel, and those people like me who are in the business of playing variations on the Bumba story, and trying to get as close to the Milton end of the spectrum as our talent will let us, can only take off our hats and salute the storytelling of those like Professor Hawking – those who not only tell the story, but who themselves played a part in the events: who uncovered a corner of the mystery, who shone a light into the darkness and revealed something that no one had ever seen before.

The sort of story that these great heroes (and I'm using the word carefully and accurately) – that these great heroes of modern science tell does have one thing in common, and I mean in a technical, structural sense, with stories of the Bumba sort. And that has to do with how they *end*. Most stories that we read in novels or fairy tales, or see in films and plays, are shaped with a conclusion in mind. The events are all arranged to lead up to 'And they lived happily ever after'. Or 'Reader, I married him'.

Or the last sentence of George Orwell's *Animal Farm*:

The creatures outside looked from pig to man, and from man to pig, and from pig to man again; but already it was impossible to say which was which.

Stories of that kind take us on a journey through harmonies and tensions and releases and discords and finally we come to a resolution. The story's done; all the ends are tied up; there's no more to be said.

But the stories that both religion and science tell us about our origins don't do that. There isn't that sense of cadence and finality that we have at the end of a play or novel, or the aesthetic and moral closure we feel at the end of one of the classic fairy tales. Stories about origins don't have that sort of determined ending. The religious kind of origin-story might tell us that we were brought forth by a great father in the sky, or in the case of Bumba by a great gurgitator, and they usually go on to put us in some kind of relationship with our creator. We are his children. We owe him gratitude and worship and obedience. The other kind of origin-story, the scientific kind, tells us about the development of matter from the first moments of the universe, the formation of atoms, the way atoms join with other atoms to form more complex structures that eventually give rise to life, and how life itself evolves by means of natural selection.

We are the children of the sky-god, or we are made of the same material as the stars.

Either way, stories like this tell us how we got here: but then they say, in effect, 'The story continues, and the rest is up to you.'

And whether or not we know this, whether or not we like it, that puts us in a moral relationship with the thing we came from too, whether that's God or whether it's nature. The God stories go on to make this quite explicit: *do this, believe that.* The stories of science have moral consequences too, but they convey them more subtly, by implication; we might say more democratically. They depend on our contribution, on our making the effort to understand and concur.

The implication is that true stories are worth telling, and worth getting right, and we have to behave honestly towards them and to the process of doing science in the first place. It's only through honesty and courage that science can work at all. The Ptolemaic understanding of the solar system was undermined and corrected by the constant pressure of more and more honest reporting: 'Yes, we know the planets are supposed to go round the earth in perfect circles, but really, if you look, you don't see that. You see *this* instead. Now why do you think that could be? What's actually going on up there?'

So we have the courage of such as Galileo and the other victims of persecution and fearful closed-mindedness. I was very glad to hear that Professor Hawking escaped the clutches of the Inquisition during his visit to the Vatican; four hundred years ago, he would not have done, and in the context of the time scales we've been hearing about tonight, four hundred years is the merest flicker of an instant. We sometimes forget how lucky we are to live in this little bubble of time which is still warmed, you could say, by the background radiation from the Enlightenment. We're privileged to be able to hear the words of Professor Hawking without having to meet in secret, without having to depend on passwords and disguises, without the danger of betrayal and arrest and torture; and that is not only because of the intellectual brilliance of the great heroes of science, both past and present, but because of their valour too.

Professor Hawking ended his lecture with a survey of the current state of cosmology, and the prediction that we are getting close to answering the age-old questions, 'Why are we here? Where did we come from?' Some people are rather afraid of thinking that there might be a final answer to those questions; they think it will take all the mystery and delight out of the universe. I think they could hardly be more wrong. The more we discover, the more wondrous the universe seems to be, and if we are here to observe it and wonder at it, then we are very much part of what it is. And there is no shortage of important questions. Once we know where we come from, we might find that our attention turns to questions like, 'Where are we going? What shall we do?'

The story continues, and the rest is up to us. I'm immensely grateful to science, and to Stephen Hawking in particular, for illuminating our path to the present day with such brilliant clarity, such intellectual daring, and such wit.

THIS ARTICLE FIRST APPEARED IN *EXON*, THE EXETER COLLEGE MAGAZINE, AUTUMN 2006, WRITTEN IN RESPONSE TO THE DENNIS SCIAMA MEMORIAL LECTURE DELIVERED BY STEPHEN HAWKING, MARCH 2006.

The Path through the Wood

HOW STORIES WORK

On the 'phase space' of the story world and the path a writer makes through it, with comments on Cinderella *and an account of how I came to imagine the wheeled mulefa in* The Amber Spyglass

THANK YOU VERY MUCH FOR INVITING ME HERE. THIS IS THE SECOND time my body has been in Finland, but my imagination has come here often. I'm honoured by your wish to hear me speak, and I hope I can find something interesting to say.

But I can only talk about what I know. When I was adding up what I know before coming here, I discovered that to tell you all I know would take me about forty-five minutes, which is a useful coincidence, because that's about the amount of time I've got. You're welcome to ask me questions at the end, but if you ask me something I don't know I shall have to make up the answer on the spot.

So I'm not going to say much about science fiction, because I don't know much about it. Nor do I know much about fantasy. I know nothing at all about the interactive multimedia narrative experiences made possible by computer games and so on. The thing I know about is printed on paper, and was created in the first place by a single mind. It has a beginning, a middle and an end – though not necessarily, as somebody said, in that order; or, as Philip Larkin said, 'a beginning, a muddle, and an end'. The interactive multilayered multimedia experience may well be superior, it may well be the future, it may be destined to brush the novel aside and populate the earth with its progeny; but I am talking about the novel.

And in doing so I'm going to bring in my own experience as a novelist, though I have to enter a warning here too. I have friends who write books, and it always surprises me how differently we work. One will make a detailed plan and submit that to a publisher for his comments and then alter the plan and make an even more detailed scenario and then finally write the finished thing. Another will begin to write with not the faintest idea what she's going to finish up with. I have my own method which is like neither of those. The only thing we have in common is that we all end up with finished books, and that we are each convinced that our method is the only sensible one. So when I describe my own way of going about it, please remember that I'm not recommending it as the only way, or the best way, or an infallible way. It's none of those things; it's only my way.

Now here I want to come to the title of my talk, 'The Path through the Wood'. Some of you might know that Robert Frost poem. 'The Road Not Taken', which I think was used as the title of a book not long ago. He talks about coming to a fork in the road through a wood, and having to choose which way to go, and the poem ends:

> Two roads diverged in a wood, and I –
> I took the one less travelled by,
> And that has made all the difference.

So here we have two ideas: the wood and the path. The wood, or the forest if you like, is a wild space. It's an unstructured space. It's a space full of possibilities. It's a space where anything can happen (and it frequently does, in the words of the song from that great movie *Hellzapoppin*). There are monsters in the wood. There are life forms unlike any others. There are quarks and neutrinos and virtual particles; it's full of charm and strangeness. It's non-linear. It just grew.

The path, on the other hand, is a structure. And it has a function: it leads from here to there, or from A to B. It's extremely linear; even when it doubles back and crosses itself it does so with an air of purpose. It says:

'I know where I'm going, even if you don't.' It was made.

I expect you can see where this is going. Each novel or story is a path (because it's linear, because it begins on page one and goes on steadily through all the pages in the usual order until it gets to the end) that goes through a wood. The wood is the world in which the characters live and have their being; it's the realm of all the things that could possibly happen to them; it's the notional space where their histories exist, and where their future lives are going to continue after the story reaches the last page.

(This is the point where practitioners of literary theory will throw up their hands in disgust. Characters don't have histories, they would say; the only life they have is that in the words on the page; they are not real people, they are only literary constructions; to mistake the characters in a novel for characters in real life is to make a fundamental category error; it's naïve to the point of stupidity – etc, etc. To these ladies and gentlemen of theory I say, *Thank you very much; now go away until you can tell me something useful*).

So the wood, or the forest, is the sum of all possibilities, and, as I have mentioned elsewhere, I found a nicely scientific-sounding term for it in a book about elementary physics. The term is *phase space*. I could sort of grasp the edge of it, and get a vague idea of the meaning of the whole, but I couldn't understand the explanation, and when my seventeen-year-old son tried to explain the explanation to me, I got even more confused, so I won't try to explain it to you; but no doubt some of you are already familiar with the idea. It's something like the sum of all the consequences that could follow from a given origin.

And each story we can tell has its own phase space, its own forest, which is different from the forests of every other story. I can illustrate what I mean by the story which in English we call *Cinderella*, and which in French is *Cendrillon*, and which in the great collection by the Brothers Grimm is called *Aschputtel*, and which no doubt has a different name in every language in the world. It's one of the most familiar stories of all, which is why I can use it here.

The Cinderella-world contains many, many things. It contains a young girl who's bullied by her sisters. It contains a palace with a charming young prince. It contains rats and pumpkins and a fairy godmother. It contains an invitation to a ball... and so on. Those are the things we know about from the story.

But by extending what we know just a little, it's possible to see some other things that the world contains – things that lie off to the side of the path which is the story we know. We know there was a ball – so there must have been musicians to play there. There must have been an orchestra. We know Cinderella did all the dirty work in the kitchen, and she got her name from the ashes – so they didn't have a gas-fired boiler and central heating in that house; they must have had an old-fashioned stove with a chimney. Chimneys have to be swept. There must have been a chimney sweep who called regularly.

We can see the Cinderella-world, the Cinderella-forest, getting a bit deeper as we look at it. We can imagine more, even further from the path: what about the town they all lived in? Was there a mayor and a town council, was there a police force, was there a department for dealing with pests – for getting rid of rats, for example?

It would be possible to invent a million facts about Cinderella's world, each consistent with every other, each something that Cinderella could have known about or experienced. The world or the wood can be as detailed and rich as we like.

But the path, which is Cinderella's own story, goes from here to there, going through this part and that part. Always. And the business of the storyteller, or the novelist, it seems to me, is with the path and not the wood.

It doesn't have to be Cinderella's path, though. My book *I was a Rat!* begins with an old couple called Bob and Joan. He's a shoemaker and she's a washerwoman, and they never had any children, though they would have liked to. One evening, as they're sitting quietly in their kitchen, they hear a knock at the door. Standing there is a little boy in a ragged pageboy costume, all dirty and torn, and all he can say is, 'I was a rat'. He doesn't have a name, he can't remember where he comes from, he says he's three weeks old, though he looks about nine years.

Well, they take him in, and the story begins. The story of the boy who had been a rat is another path through Cinderella's wood, and one that touches her life, Cinderella's life, at two points, though it only touches her story once. It touches her story at the point where the fairy godmother turns the rats and the lizards and the pumpkin into a coach and horses and coachmen. There's a young rat that Cinderella used to play with and give crumbs to, and the fairy godmother turns him into a pageboy to open the coach door and let down the steps and so on.

Well, they go to the ball, but he gets up to mischief in the palace, and he doesn't make it back to the coach; so there he is, stuck as a boy for ever. And he has a great deal of trouble as a result.

Meanwhile, Cinderella's story is going on elsewhere in the wood, and coming to a triumphant end with her marriage. That's the end of her story – the Cinderella path – but it's not the end of her life, which is just as well, because the poor little rat-boy ends up in desperate need of a *dea ex machina* in order to save him from the terrible fate towards which the path of his story seems to be taking him. And who better than a beautiful young princess to fill that role? Why, it's almost life-like.

That's what I mean by the wood and the path, anyway. It's the difference between the story-world and the story-line. And I want to stress again that the business of the storyteller is with the story-line, with the path. You can make your story-wood, your invented world, as rich and full as you like, but be very, very careful not to be tempted off the path. Another path in another wood: remember the wicked wolf tempting Little Red Riding Hood to stray off the path and pick the pretty flowers? Don't do it! Don't be weak! Don't give in! Stick to the path. Admire them by all means, and slow down a little if you must, but don't leave the path.

The reason for this is simple: if you leave the path, the readers put down the book. Suddenly they remember that phone call they had to make; they look in the paper to see what's on TV; they think a cup of coffee would be nice, and when they're in the kitchen they look out the window and see that hedge they meant to trim yesterday, or they switch on the radio to hear the football commentary, or when they get the milk out the fridge they remember they had to get some cheese for supper, and there's just time to go and get it...

And meanwhile the book is lying there forgotten. Because you left the path. Because you became more interested in the wood, in elaborating all the richness and invention of the world you're making up. Never leave the path.

However, that's when you're telling the story. When you're *talking* about telling the story, as I am now, you are allowed to leave the path and wander through the wood as much as you like. And I know that many science fiction fans, and fantasy fans, enjoy exploring the woods and the forests and the worlds that writers have dreamed up. I've been contacted by people in Canada and elsewhere who have been playing a game that they based on the world I made up for *The Golden Compass* (*Northern Lights*, in the UK). It looks like an odd kind of activity to me, but they seemed to be enjoying it. However, I've never been a games player of any kind – computer games and card games and chess and Monopoly have never had the slightest attraction for me – so maybe it's the games-playing cast of mind that you need and I haven't got. I'm quite willing to go into someone else's fictional world and follow the path they lead me on, but I don't want to leave their path and fool about among the trees; I'd rather make up my own wood and fool about in that. However, if I see something in their wood worth stealing, I'll pick it up and take it away without hesitation. If they didn't want me to steal from their story, they shouldn't have invited me into it – that's my view.

Anyway, I'm going to tell you something about the world I made up for the third book in the trilogy called *His Dark Materials*, which began with *The Golden Compass* and continued with *The Subtle Knife*, and which is completed with a book called *The Amber Spyglass*. When you begin by calling your first book *The Something Something*, and call the second *The Something-else Something-else*, you really have to give the third one a similar name. Eric Rohmann, the American illustrator who designed the covers, suggested *The Sophisticated Monkey-Wrench*, but I thought that wasn't a good idea.

The whole trilogy is based on the notion of parallel worlds. We know that there must be other universes parallel to ours, because (as I understand it) an experiment which has been a cornerstone of twentieth-century physics leaves us with no alternative as an explanation. According to the physicist David Deutsch, the famous demonstration of the dual nature of light as both wave and particle – the double-slit experiment, where single photons are interfered with by something that we cannot observe, which makes them behave as if they are part of a wave – indicates clearly that the universe we see and touch must be surrounded by vast numbers of other universes.

That's good enough for me. I don't understand why, but I wouldn't dream of arguing with him. The only problem is how to get from one universe to another.

In a sense, this is a basic problem of science fiction: how to get from *here*, where we live, to *there*, where the strange things happen. And there are as many ways of solving it as there are novelists. One of my favourite ways occurs in that great, mysterious, powerful, odd and inimitable novel, David Lindsay's *A Voyage to Arcturus*, which was published in 1920. Here is the hero, Maskull, examining some small torpedo-shaped bottles containing a colourless liquid, and possessing queer-looking nozzle-like stoppers. I quote:

He now made out on the larger bottle the words 'Solar Back-Rays'; and on the other one, after some doubt, he thought that he could distinguish something like 'Arcturian Back-rays'.

He looked up, to stare curiously at his friend. 'What are back-rays?'

'Light which goes back to its source,' muttered Night-spore.

'And what kind of light may that be?'

Nightspore seemed unwilling to answer, but finding Maskull's eyes still fixed on him he brought out – 'Unless light pulled, as well as pushed, how would flowers contrive to twist their heads round after the sun?'

How indeed. To fly to Arcturus, all they have to do is get into a space-ship fuelled by Arcturian Back-rays, which will suck them up to the star in nineteen hours – light goes even faster backwards than forwards, apparently.

Absolute nonsense, of course, and it doesn't matter a bit. The real point is not how they get there, but what they do when they arrive: not the wood, but the path. So when I needed a way of getting from one universe to another, I didn't waste time inventing anything fancy: I just cut a hole. In the second book in my trilogy, the young boy Will has acquired a knife, known as the subtle knife, which is sharp enough to cut even between the molecules of the air, and he's now learning how to use it. I quote:

The second time it was easier. Having felt it once, he knew what to search for again, and he felt the curious little snag after less than a minute. It was like delicately searching out the gap between one stitch and the next with the point of a scalpel. He touched, withdrew, touched again to make sure, and then did as the old man said, and cut sideways with the silver edge.

It was a good thing that Giacomo Paradisi had reminded him not to be surprised. He kept careful hold of the knife and put it down on the table before giving in to his astonishment. Lyra was on her feet already, speechless, because there in the middle of the dusty little room was a gap in mid-air through which they could see another world.
(*TSK*, 193)

And so on. Once you have the subtle knife, you can open the way to any other world, and the problem of travel is dealt with at once.

In the third and final book, *The Amber Spyglass*, I needed a new world altogether to which Lyra and Will must travel. If anyone here has read *The Subtle Knife*, they might remember the scientist Dr Mary Malone, who leaves her world – ours – because she's told she has an important task to fulfil somewhere else. Part of *The Amber Spyglass* deals with her journey there, and with the making of the instrument named in the title. She goes there to prepare the way for Will and Lyra, though she doesn't know why.

This world itself is peopled by creatures with wheels, and I want to say a little about how I developed them. (And here my ignorance of science fiction comes into play: it may well be that every science fiction novel which I have not read has dealt with this question, and done it far more neatly and cleverly than I have. However, you have to put up with the fact that I can only tell you what I know, so here goes).

At first I didn't know why these creatures had wheels: it was just a puzzle and I was interested in solving it. How could a living creature have wheels? The wheel is almost the prototypical human invention: the first big technological idea. The main problem, of course, is that to revolve at all, a wheel has to be detachable: it has to have no communication with the axle apart from the bearing on which it revolves. It can't be part of it.

Around this time my son Tom and I spent a morning walking around Lake Bled, in Slovenia, talking about the problem. He was fifteen then. I don't usually talk about my books till they're finished, but this wasn't the path, it was the wood. That's all right; I can talk about that.

We decided that either there had to be a connection or there had to be no connection: either they could take the wheels off, or they were part of them and they had to leave them on. If they were connected, if the wheels themselves were living tissue, they would need oxygen and nutrition and so forth; so how would that be supplied?

There could have been some sort of infinitely extensible and flexible material to make the blood vessels from, which could wind round and round the axle as the wheel revolved but didn't take up any room – but that was such a clumsy idea that we didn't like it at all. We could have gone for a different idea, where the blood or the equivalent material passed directly into an open chamber in the hub of the wheel through an open chamber on the axle, the edges being sealed in the same way as a tubeless tyre is sealed on to a car wheel: pressure, basically.

But I felt another idea coming, and I wanted to go for detachable wheels. Were they made, or were they natural? There were a lot of trees around us as we walked along the lake side, and the idea of seed-pods almost fell on my head: very large ones – flat and perfectly circular – very hard – with a soft place in the centre through which a claw could be inserted for an axle. I liked the idea of symbiosis: the creatures depending on the trees that produced the seed-pods, the trees depending on the creatures to spread their seeds for them. Eventually, after much hard riding, the pods would break open, and more trees would grow. And there was that other idea hovering somewhere just out of reach…

What shape should the creatures be? Like us, vertebrate with a central spine and four limbs, a wheel at each corner like a car? I didn't like that. I saw them as moving swiftly and with great freedom, and if each limb had a wheel on it, how could they propel themselves? There was no reason to limit them to four limbs, of course; they could have as many as I liked. But four is neat.

However, they didn't have to be disposed like ours. If they were like motorcycles, with one wheel in front of the other, they could move quickly and balance easily and be in every way more mobile; and if there were two lateral limbs, then they could scoot along by using them to push with. But how could that arrangement work with a skeleton based on a central spine? It couldn't. I needed a different structure altogether: a diamond-shaped skeletal frame, with a limb at each corner. Almost there. (And that other idea was pressing at me more and more.)

But before we went any further, Tom reminded me of something very important. Wheels are so successful in our world because we've made plenty of smooth surfaces for them to run on; it would be no good having creatures with wheels in a world full of rocks and bogs and quicksands and covered in thick undergrowth. Where could they use their wheels? We stopped to think about that. Should they have artificial roads, or should they be something that developed naturally?

Well, the creatures might adapt and improve them later, but to start with, they had to be natural: they had to be there to allow evolution time enough to bring the creatures and the seed-pods together. Suppose there had been many volcanoes in that world, and suppose that the lava they produced contained the right combination of minerals to flow across the landscape like rivers, and suppose that the ambient temperature was such as to let them cool at just the right rate to solidify as flat surfaces and not break up into crystalline columns, as the basalt pillars of the Giant's Causeway in Ireland did.

We decided we could suppose that, so we did. That was the roads taken care of. I could have consulted geologists, no doubt (one advantage of living where I do, in the city of Oxford, is that there are experts on everything under the sun just a phone call and a bicycle ride away) – and I could have persuaded someone to come up with the exact combination of minerals and temperature that would give a result like that... But I haven't yet. Maybe I will, and maybe I won't. Is it the path, or is it the wood? If it's the path, I will, and if it's the wood, I won't.

Similarly, I could have gone into the evolution of the diamond-frame skeleton. It wouldn't have been too hard: a moment of luck at the time of the Burgess Shale, for example, and our own earth might never have given rise to vertebrates at all. We and our ancestors and our present-day cousins might all have walked about on seven pairs of legs and lived inside a shell made of intricate plates of silica.

So it would have been quite easy, had I wanted to, to invent a series of chances and contingencies that would have favoured the development of a skeleton based on a frame rather than a flexible spine. Actually, the diamond-frame is a pretty versatile thing as the basis of an animal structure: there's a large seagoing bird in that world which has two lateral legs for swimming with and two long wings, fore and aft, which it extends upwards and uses as sails. It can skim before the wind, or tack against it, and the legs give it great manoeuvrability and speed. And there could be all sorts of other variations on the diamond-frame skeleton, if anyone wanted to make them up. They're all there in the phase space, somewhere off in the wood.

Mind you, not all creatures in that world have diamond-frame skeletons, any more than all the creatures in our world are vertebrates. It's just that the diamond-frame is successful, and predominates. There are vertebrates there too: they have snakes, for example, of which more later.

But just to finish describing the main creatures, the ones with the wheels. In order to reach the level of sophistication and technology I wanted them to get to, they had to have something to make and hold tools with: the equivalent of the opposable thumb. But if all four limbs are busy with transportation, what could that be? Well, there's a ready-made structure in the animal kingdom of our own world that would do: the tip of an elephant's trunk is packed with muscles and nerves and very strong and almost infinitely flexible and sensitive. Very well: give them trunks.

And at this point that other idea that I've been mentioning all the way through kept on coming closer and closer until I was able to look at it directly. In fact, I couldn't ignore it any longer.

It had to do with the matter I've been talking about all through: the path and the wood. Making up creatures like this was good fun as I walked around a lake in Slovenia with my son, but what did it have to do with the story I was writing? What was the *point*? Did the wheels add to the story or only decorate it? Were they part of the wood, or could they be part of the path?

Well, of course, they had to be part of the path, or I wouldn't have wanted to waste my time with them. In other words, the wheels had to advance the story. The story had to concern the wheels. If they're just picturesque, if they're just part of the wood, the book gets put down.

Well now: one of the themes of the story from the very beginning was

Mulefa visualization by Eric Dubois

97

this substance which I called Dust, with a capital D. To Dr Mary Malone, the scientist, it seems to be what we in this universe call *dark matter*, the subject of her research. But in Lyra's universe, Dust is a source of great anxiety to the authorities, and since her world is more or less a theocracy, the authority is the church. Dust, they think, is the physical evidence of original sin; Dust comes to us when we grow up and become corrupted by the wickedness of the world, of knowledge. In their version of the Book of Genesis, the serpent is responsible for bringing Dust into the world by tempting Eve to taste the fruit of the knowledge of good and evil. Dust is something to be hated and feared.

However, Lyra comes to a different point of view, which by a strange coincidence is also mine: that Dust is a positive good. This does not mean embracing evil instead of good: it means understanding that since the loss of innocence is inevitable, we should welcome it and embrace the next stage of our development instead of hiding our eyes from it. Knowing about good and evil is not the same as embracing evil, though it might look like that to a church that likes to think it has all the answers.

Anyway, since Dust and the puzzle of what it is and how we come to terms with it is such a large part of the theme, it was only sensible to see whether I could use my wheeled creatures to illuminate it. Like that, we'd be on the path, where we should be, and not in the wood, getting lost. How, then, could wheels and Dust come together?

Well, my creatures are conscious, self-conscious, as we are. Otherwise they wouldn't be interesting. They are subject to Dust. They have an affinity to it, as we do. In religious or mythical terms, our affinity to Dust is due to the Temptation and Fall, and it's something we have to be redeemed from by the intercession of a Saviour, who can cleanse us from the consequences of knowledge. In evolutionary terms, it is probably due to language, or to the increased capacity of our brains to reflect on their own experience.

My creatures' affinity to Dust might have a mythical origin too. But in physical terms, suppose their affinity had a physical origin. Suppose that something happened when the creatures and the wheels came together: a moral and mental symbiosis as well as a physical one? But because I'm keen to get right away from mysticism and because I loathe the idea of a spirit-matter dualism, and because I want to ground everything firmly in the physical world, I thought not about good and evil and conscience and guilt but about axles and bearings and lubrication.

Because of course you can't have a wheel turning on an axle without some kind of bearing. What helps a wheel turn smoothly is a ball-race, or a cage of needle-roller bearings, or something of that sort. If there's a hole in the middle of the seed-pod, could there be something similar inside it? Could the seeds themselves act as ball bearings? That seemed a bit fiddly. I didn't like it. What about a smooth surface, though? If the inside of the hub and the lower edge of the creature's claw, the edge that took the weight as it rested inside the hub, fitted each other perfectly and were as smooth and hard as Teflon, we wouldn't need ball bearings; and the seed-pod itself could contain a kind of oil, like *lignum vitae* wood, which would lubricate the surface to make it even smoother.

Aha! Couldn't this oil be the vehicle for Dust? Couldn't it combine with a similar oil expressed from the creatures' claws and thus pass into their bloodstream and... Now I was getting somewhere. And now I saw why I wanted symbiosis, and what that other idea was: the creatures become fully conscious and grown-up and adult and responsible when they get their wheels. When they're young, they're too small: the wheels are too big for them. They are like human children, innocent. Free of Dust. Dust, or full grown-up consciousness, or the knowledge of good and evil, comes when they begin to interact with the world: it comes from them and the tree together. They need the seed-pods to become fully what they are. We too can't be fully ourselves if we don't engage with the world.

And I saw another thing: their trunks and what that meant for cooperation and interdependence. They have a technology based not on metal, but on wood. They are marvels at growing and breeding trees of every kind; they use vegetable products to make everything they need, including the ropes and nets they fish with. To make a net you need to tie knots; you can't tie knots easily with one hand, or one trunk; you need two. So two of them would stand face to face, their trunks moving swiftly together, tying knots. Everything they do is based on cooperation.

When Mary Malone turns up, with a central spine and two free hands, and ties knots all by herself, they are both impressed and horrified by her self-sufficiency; just as Lyra is horrified when she first meets Will, the boy from our world, because unlike her he hasn't got a dæmon, and seems to be less than human.

But dæmons are another part of the path, because I use them too to say something about Dust; but before I've finished with my wheeled creatures I'd like to read you a short passage that explains the meaning of the title, *The Amber Spyglass*.

To introduce it: Mary Malone has been researching a previously unknown kind of elementary particle, which she calls *Shadows*. They may or may not be what is known as dark matter, but they are linked in some way with human consciousness. She finds herself after many adventures in this pastoral world occupied by these creatures with wheels. Mary manages to communicate with them – it doesn't matter how. One day she discovers that they know about Shadows, about these particles of Mary's, about Dust. Her friend Atal is talking:

> Atal surprised her by saying, *Yes, we know what you mean – we call it...* and then she used what sounded like their word for *light.*
>
> Mary said, *Light?* And Atal said, *Not light, but... like the light on water when it makes small ripples, at sunset, and the light comes off in bright flakes, we call it that, but it is a make-like.*

Make-like was their term for metaphor.

… Atal said, *All the mulefa have this. You have too. That is how we knew you were like us and not like the grazers, who don't have it. Even though you look so bizarre and horrible, you are like us, because you have* – and again came that word that Mary couldn't hear quite clearly enough to say: something *sraf.*

Mary said to Atal: *How long have there been mulefa?*

And Atal said, *Thirty-three thousand years… Ever since we have had the sraf, we have had memory and wakefulness. Before that, we knew nothing.*

What happened to give you the sraf?

We discovered how to use the wheels. One day a creature with no name discovered a seed-pod and began to play, and as she played… she saw a snake coiling itself through the hole in a seed-pod, and the snake said —

The snake spoke to her?

No, no! It is a make-like… The snake said What do you know? What do you remember? What do you see ahead? And she said Nothing, nothing, nothing. So the snake said Put your foot through the hole in the seed-pod where I was playing, and you will become wise. So she put a foot where the snake had been, and the oil entered her foot and made her see more clearly than before, and the first thing she saw was the sraf. It was so strange and pleasant that she wanted to share it at once with all her kindred. So she and her mate took the first ones and they discovered that they knew who they were… They gave each other names. They named themselves mulefa. They named the seed-tree, and all the creatures and plants.

Because now they were different, said Mary.

Yes, they were. And so were their children… and being wise because of the Sraf, they saw that they should had to plant more

seed-pod trees for the sake of the oil, their children and their children's children, but the pods were so hard that they very seldom germinated. And the first mulefa saw what they must do to help the trees, which was to ride on the wheels and break them, so mulefa and seed-pod trees have always lived together, which was to do what we have done ever since, and ride on them.
(*TAS*, 222)

Well, that's a familiar story to Mary, of course, for more than one reason. So she decides to try and see the sraf, the Shadows, the Dust. What Atal says about its appearance – like reflected light – makes her think it might be polarised, so she sets about making a kind of glass to see them through.

As I said earlier, the mulefa have got a technology based not on metal but on wood and cord, on bark and sap, on bone and horn. Using the materials to hand, Mary makes a glass to look through – a spyglass – of sap-lacquer. It is as flat as the finest mirror, and the most delicate brown-yellow like amber: the amber spyglass.

But when she looks through it, although she can see many different and surprising optical effects, she can't see Shadows.

Atal, her friend, comes along to look, but she's not really interested; what she really wants is for Mary to groom her claws. The mulefa do this every day, grooming each other's claws, maintaining their wheels.

I read again:

> Mary put down the two pieces of lacquer and ran her hands over the astonishing smoothness of Atal's claws, that surface smoother and slicker than Teflon that rested on the lower rim of the central hole and served as a bearing when the wheel turned. The contours of the claw and the wheel matched exactly, of course, and as Mary ran her hands around the inside of the wheel she could feel no difference in

texture: it was as if the mulefa and the seed-pod really were one creature which by a miracle could disassemble itself and put itself together again.

She was happy to clean the wheel-holes of all the dust and grime that accumulated there, and smooth the fragrant oil gently over her friend's claws while Atal's trunk lifted and straightened Mary's hair.

When Atal had had enough, she set herself on the wheels again and moved away to help with the evening meal. Mary turned back to her lacquer, and almost at once she made her discovery.

Something had happened. As she looked through, she saw a swarm of golden sparkles surrounding the form of Atal. They were only visible through one small part of the lacquer... at that point she had touched the surface of it with her oily fingers.

'Atal!' she called. 'Quick! Come back!'

Atal turned and wheeled back.

'Let me take a little oil,' Mary said. 'Just enough to put on the lacquer.'

Atal willingly let her run her fingers around the wheel-holes again, and watched curiously as Mary coated one of the pieces with a film of the clear sweet substance.

Then she pressed the plates together and moved them around to spread the oil evenly, and held them a hand-span apart once more.

And when she looked through, everything was changed. Everywhere she looked she could see gold, just as Atal had described it: sparkles of light, floating and drifting and sometimes moving with a current of purpose. Wherever she saw a conscious being, one of the mulefa, the light was thicker and more full of movement.

I didn't know it was beautiful, Mary said to Atal.

Why, of course it is, her friend replied. *It is strange to think that you couldn't see it. Look at the little one…*

She indicated one of the small children playing in the long grass, leaping clumsily after grasshoppers, suddenly stopping to examine a leaf, falling over, scrambling up again to rush and tell his mother something, being distracted again by a piece of stick, trying to pick it up, finding ants on his trunk and hooting with agitation… There was a golden haze around him as there was around the shelters, the fishing-nets, the evening fire… it was full of little swirling currents of intention, that eddied and broke off and drifted about, to disappear as new ones were born.

Around his mother, on the other hand, the golden sparkles were much stronger and the currents they moved in more settled and powerful. She was preparing food, spreading flour on a flat stone to make the thin bread like tortillas or chapattis, watching her child at the same time, and the Shadows or the sraf or the Dust that bathed her looked like the very image of responsibility and wise care.

So at last you can see, said Atal. *Well, now you must come with me.*

Mary looked at her friend in puzzlement. Atal's tone was strange: it was as if she were saying *Finally you're ready; we've been waiting; now things must change.*

And others were appearing, from over the brow of the hill, from out of their shelters, from along the river: members of the group, but strangers too, who looked curiously towards where she was standing. The sound of their wheels on the hard-packed earth was low and steady.

Where must I go? Mary said. *Why are they all coming here?*
Don't worry, said Atal, *come with me, we shall not hurt you.*
(TAS, 229)

So that's how Dr Malone discovers how to see Dust, and that's why the book is called *The Amber Spyglass*. And that is why the creatures with their wheels are part of the path, not just part of the wood: part of the story-line, not just part of the story-world. Apart from anything else, it's just more interesting for *me* when that happens. Stories are not only a sequence of things that happen, they are also – or they can be – *patterns* as well. The shape of the story-line can weave in and out in a shape which is attractive in an abstract way, which is aesthetically pleasing no matter what it means.

And the fun of making patterns like that is one of the reasons why I write stories. There are many other reasons, such as making money, and becoming famous enough to be invited to Finland, and because I was never much good at doing anything else; but certainly one of the reasons for making art of any sort is the making of those patterns. Some story-patterns are very ancient and based on traditional folklore, such as having things happening in threes: three wishes, three brothers, three gifts and so on.

Others are basic to our understanding of the world at all, for example the fascinating work done on narrative and cognitive science by the American critic Mark Turner, who in his book *The Literary Mind* explains the function of what he calls 'image schemas' in our processing of mental events. Not to go into too much detail, an image schema is a skeletal pattern of some simple perceptual structure such as *motion along a path*, or *pouring something into a container*, or *emerging*, or *being underneath something*.

What happens when we understand things is that we project our familiarity with these tiny little narratives on to the details and events of the world itself, on to the flux of sense impressions, so that instead of seeing chaos, we perceive bits of story that we can assimilate into larger ones.

But the whole business of image schemas is not only another path, it's another wood. My point here is simply that patterns are pretty, and that you can have fun in weaving them. So, for instance, it gave me great pleasure when I saw how I could tie up the very end of this long story of mine with a thread that began at the very beginning, three books ago. But since to tell you what that was I would have to read to you all the 1,200 pages that come between.

So that's what I mean by the path, and that's what I mean by the wood. Thank you for listening.

THIS TALK WAS GIVEN AT FINNCON SCIENCE-FICTION CONVENTION AT THE UNIVERSITY OF TURKU, IN AUGUST 1999.

Science fiction and fantasy conventions have been generous enough to invite me to speak, from time to time, and although they've always made me welcome I never feel quite at home at such gatherings. The fact is, I'm not a fan of anything in particular, though I like a good many things. The sheer knowledge on display at fantasy or science fiction conventions is awe-inspiring, though it's occasionally made me wonder whether gathering it leaves much time for anything else. Another reason for my slight feeling of dissociation is that I seem to be regarded, while there, as a writer of fantasy, whereas I've always maintained that His Dark Materials *is a work of stark realism. There: I was glad to have the chance to say that again.*

Dreaming of Spires

OXFORDS, REAL AND IMAGINARY

On the unlikeliness of Oxford and its effects on the imagination,
with particular reference to the colleges of Exeter and Jordan

A COUPLE OF YEARS AGO I FINISHED THE LAST IN A TRILOGY OF NOVELS (*The Amber Spyglass*, part three of *His Dark Materials*) set partly in an alternative universe, which contains an imaginary Oxford. Perhaps a great deal of Oxford is imaginary anyway. In Oxford, likelihood evaporates. At about the time the book was published, the Fellows of All Souls announced that they had just spent an evening parading around their college following a wooden duck on a stick. That was obviously a very sensible thing to do, and I wish I had thought of it first.

However, it is better to ease your readers in without startling them too much, so the Fellows of Jordan College, in my imaginary Oxford, eat dinner in Hall and then retire elsewhere to drink coffee, almost as if it were real life; and that is the point at which the story begins.

Jordan College occupies the same physical space in Lyra's Oxford (Lyra is the young heroine of my story) as Exeter College occupies in real life, though rather more of it. Exeter was where I was an undergraduate many years ago, and I didn't see why I shouldn't make my college the grandest of all. Jordan, where Lyra grows up, has developed in a haphazard, piecemeal way, and for all its wealth some part of it is always about to fall down and is consequently covered in scaffolding; it has an air of jumbled and squalid grandeur. And furthermore:

What was above ground was only a small fraction of the whole. Like some enormous fungus whose root-system extended over acres, Jordan (finding itself jostling for space above ground with St Michael's College on one side, Gabriel College on the other, and the University Library behind) had begun, sometime in the Middle Age, to spread below the surface. Tunnels, shafts, vaults, cellars, staircases had so hollowed out the earth below Jordan and for several hundred yards around it that there was almost as much air below ground as above; Jordan College stood on a sort of froth of stone.

(*NL*, 48)

I don't know whether that is true of Exeter, but I can locate the origin of that bit of fantasy. When I was up (1965–68) I had a group of idle friends who occupied their time and mine betting on horses, getting drunk, and sprawling about telling creepy tales. One of the stories we frightened ourselves with concerned the Bodleian Library, which, we assured one another, had been intended to be Hitler's Chancellery when he had conquered Britain. Beneath the library, apparently, the stacks extended for untold miles in every direction, and each of the levels, named with letters of the alphabet, was more secret than the one above. The lowest, Level L, was profoundly sinister. It was occupied by a race of sub-human creatures, the secret of whose existence was only divulged to the vice-chancellor on his accession.

However, there were forgotten shafts and lost passages through every part of the ground between the Clarendon Building and Palmer's Tower in Exeter College, and sometimes the creatures got out. You could hear them howling and scrabbling if you pressed your ear to the cellar wall under staircase 9. I did, and you can.

When she's not exploring underground, Lyra spends a good deal of time on the college roof, spitting plum-stones on the heads of passing scholars or hooting like an owl outside a window where a tutorial is going on. That too is based on something I remember from Exeter. In my second year I occupied the rooms at the top of staircase 8, next to the lodge tower, and a friend, Jim Taylor, discovered that you could get out of the window and crawl along a very useful gutter behind the parapet. From there you could climb in through another window further along. I gave Lyra a better head for heights than I have, but I did the gutter crawl a number of times, usually when there was a party on the next staircase.

One of the pleasures of writing fiction is that you can sit at your desk and just make up what you are too lazy to go and find out. But sometimes I do stir myself to look for things, and when I find something interesting but irrelevant to my immediate purpose, I save it up for a later book, and invent a context to fit it. In the Retiring Room at Jordan, for example, after the dinner that takes place in the first chapter:

> The Master lit the spirit-lamp under the little silver chaf-
> ing-dish and heated some butter before cutting open half a
> dozen poppy-heads and tossing them in. Poppy was always
> served after a Feast: it clarified the mind and stimulated the
> tongue, and made for rich conversation. It was traditional
> for the Master to cook it himself.
> (*NL*, 19)

Heaven forfend that the rector of Exeter should feel obliged to serve opium after dinner, but this is an alternative universe, after all. I lifted that dainty detail from the diary of an English lady living in India before the Mutiny, which I'd come across ten years before while I was looking for something else entirely. I knew I could use it somewhere.

The way a novelist 'researches' – this one, anyway – is quite different from the coherent, focused, disciplined sort of reading which I imagine you need to do if you want an academic career. Despite my three years at Oxford, I never mastered that sort of grown-up reading: I couldn't do it then, and I don't do it now. Instead, intrigued by this patch of colour or that scent, beguiled by a pretty shape or blown sideways by a wayward breeze, I flit from book to book, subject to subject, place to place; and it is only later, in solitude and silence, that I begin the laborious process of changing it all into something else.

Fiction, of course, allows you to change things into other things as much as you like. The part of Oxford known as Jericho (whose name, by the way, suggested that of Jordan) is, in real life, thoroughly respectable: terraces of small Victorian houses built for labourers, now occupied by young professionals and their families; the campanile of St Barnabas, the embodiment of Victorian high church Romanesque; and, of course, the great building of the university press, sometimes apparently mistaken for a rather distinguished college, not only by tourists. (I have known editors who had the same impression.) However, the area has always struck me as having a hidden character, more raffish and jaunty altogether, with an air of horse-trading, minor crime, and a sort of fairground bohemianism. That is the Jericho I describe in the story.

A similar sort of opportunistic transformation went to work on the highly respectable road called Linkside, north of Sunderland Avenue and its strange, artificial-looking hornbeam trees. Behind the neat houses is a pretty little lake which used to be a brickworks, apparently. I was describing Lyra's life among the other children of Oxford:

> … the rich seething stew of alliances and enmities and feuds and treaties… The children (young servants, and the children of servants, and Lyra) of one college waged war on those of another. But this enmity was swept aside when the town children attacked a colleger: then all the colleges banded together and went into battle against the townies. This rivalry was hundreds of years old, and very deep and satisfying.

But even this was forgotten when the other enemies threatened. One enemy was perennial: the brick-burners' children, who lived by the Claybeds and were despised by collegers and townies alike. Last year Lyra and some townies had made a temporary truce and raided the Claybeds, pelting the brick-burners' children with lumps of heavy clay and tipping over the soggy castle they'd built, before rolling them over and over in the clinging substance they lived by until victors and vanquished alike resembled a flock of shrieking golems.

(*NL*, 36)

That idea came to me the moment I began the paragraph, and not a second before. I needed to describe an enemy for Lyra who would make a contrast with the slippery, light-fingered, here-today-and-gone-tomorrow enemy I was going to describe in the following paragraph, the Jericho enemy, and since I live only ten minutes' walk from the lake in question, I suppose I just thought of it. This enemy had to be different, so the thought process went: dull - slow - heavy - mud - clay - bricks - ah! Linkside! Got it! The battle in the Claybeds would turn out to be very useful 1,034 pages later, but I certainly didn't know that when I was writing Chapter Three of the first book.

The commonest question writers get asked is: where do you get your ideas from? The truthful answer is: I dunno. They just turn up. But when you are wandering about with your mouth open and your eyes glazed waiting for them to do so, there are few better places to wander about in than Oxford, as many novelists have discovered. I put it down to the mists from the river, which have a solvent effect on reality. A city where South Parade is in the north and North Parade is in the south, where Paradise is lost under a car park, where the Magdalen gargoyles climb down at night and fight with those from New College, is a place where, as I began by saying, likelihood evaporates.

I shall always be grateful to Exeter College for letting me in and allowing me to discover the fact. If it is, in fact, a fact.

THIS ARTICLE FIRST APPEARED IN THE *GUARDIAN*, 27 JULY 2002.

And my tuition was free, and furthermore I had a local authority grant to cover my living expenses. But we've done away with all that sort of thing. It felt rather like civilization.

Intention

WHAT DO YOU MEAN?

On the sorts of questions authors are most frequently asked,
with reference to The Scarecrow and his Servant

'What was your intention when writing this book?'
'What did you mean by the passage on page 108?'
'What did you want the reader to feel at the end?'
'What message did you intend the book to deliver?'

Authors of novels, especially novels for children, know that questions such as these are not uncommon. This might be surprising, in view of the fact that more than sixty years have gone by since Wimsatt and Beardsley published their famous essay 'The Intentional Fallacy' (in the *Sewanee Review*, 1946), except that somehow it isn't surprising at all to find that lengthy and passionate discussion among literary critics has not the slightest influence on the way most readers read most books. Clearly, for many readers, the author's intention still does matter, and getting it right, or not reading against this supposed intention, is an important part of the satisfaction, or perhaps the relief from anxiety, they hope to feel.

Recently I answered online a number of questions from readers of *His Dark Materials*, including this one: 'Is a reader "allowed" to have a Christian/religious reading of a text that is supposed to be atheistic?'

What seems to be going on here is the feeling that reading is a sort of test, which the reader passes or fails according to how closely the interpretation matches the one the author intended. It would be easy to criticise or mock this feeling, but it is genuine. It comes from the same source as the indignation readers feel when a text they believed was a truthful memoir turns out to be fiction, and it's almost certainly related to the anger felt by a child who learns what the rest of the family has known for years, namely that he is adopted. It's the desire not to be made a fool of: the wish not to be shown up as ignorant of a truth that everyone else knows.

In fact, it's a natural human feeling. People think there really is an answer. I should probably qualify that by saying that it's young readers, or unsophisticated readers, who seem to be most anxious to know the author's intention. English Literature graduates will have all the arguments about the intentional fallacy at their fingertips, and a dozen other fallacies besides. But do we expect all readers to have that sort of knowledge? It would be absurd. There are plenty of other things for people to be interested in. The question is how we deal with this one.

What I want to examine here is what part intention really plays in the writing of a book, and whether it really helps readers to know what that intention is. Unfortunately, writers are not always trustworthy when they tell us about their intentions. Firstly, they might not remember; secondly, they might not want to reveal their true intentions anyway; thirdly, the context of the question sometimes determines the sort of answer it gets. Questions like this tend to be asked at events such as literary festivals, where the task in hand is that of entertaining an audience rather than revealing deep and complex truths, and faced with that task, the story-teller's instinct in front of an audience takes over and shapes a few scraps of half-remembered fact and a sprinkle of invention into a coherent and interesting narrative: a story about their intentions.

But they – *they*? I mean *we*. I mean *I*. I, we, and they do that with most questions, especially the old favourite: 'Where do you get your ideas from?'

We do it because it's necessary. One of the occupational hazards the modern writer has to negotiate is the book tour, and it's in the course of such a tour that we have most need of such instant stories about telling a story, because the same questions come up in every interview, at every bookstore, with every audience, twenty, fifty, a hundred times; and in sheer self-defence we develop a performance, with a set of neat anecdotes and one-liners and pat answers. And one of the consequences of this anti-madness strategy is that our audiences, which consist for the most part of people who like reading but don't necessarily follow the convolutions of literary theory, come to believe – or are confirmed in an existing belief – that there really is a simple answer to such questions as 'What did you intend when you wrote this book?', and that that answer matters to their reading of it.

But here, I hope, I can abandon the pat answers and tell a little more, or as much as I know, anyway, of the truth about my intentions when I wrote one of my books, *The Scarecrow and his Servant.*

This tells the story of a scarecrow who miraculously comes to life, engages a young boy called Jack as his servant, and wanders about a land which seems to be a sort of fairy-tale Italy. After several adventures, during that they are followed without their knowledge by a lawyer representing the obviously villainous Buffaloni Corporation, they discover that the Scarecrow, thanks to the will that his maker had hidden in his stuffing, is the real owner of a farm in a place called Spring Valley. The Buffaloni Corporation, which had illegally taken possession of the land, is foiled and evicted, and the Scarecrow and his servant live happily ever after.

The story forms a book 240 pages in length, and is illustrated with delicate pen-and-ink drawings by Peter Bailey. I mention that because it was part of my intention to write a story with pictures, and because Peter Bailey had done such delightful illustrations for some of my previous books. So I had his talent in mind from the start, and I intended to write a story that would suit his light and fantastical style.

But as I write those words I know that 'intended' should really have been 'hoped'. And this is perhaps the first thing to say about writing and intention: intending to write a particular kind of story is not the same sort of thing as intending to rake up the leaves on the lawn, or telephone

one's cousin, or buy a present for one's grandchild. We know we can do those things. We don't know we can write a story that will be funny, or moving, or exciting, though we hope we can. All we can honestly intend to do is try.

Then there is the matter of the subject, the characters, and the setting. This is also difficult to explain in terms of intention. I can recall the moment the notion of this story first came to me: it was during a performance of Leonard Bernstein's *Candide* at the National Theatre in London in 1999. I found the relationship between Candide and his servant Cacambo intriguing, and wondered about other such simple master/ clever servant pairs, such as Bertie Wooster and Jeeves. I liked the inbuilt dynamics of the relationship. Did that mean that I *intended* to write a story about such a pair? Not yet, but the possibility was there. However, the observation struck me with a particular resonance, which I've learned means that I probably *am* going to write about it.

There were two other sources that I was conscious of. One was a book of reproductions of the younger Tiepolo's lively and brilliant drawings in pen and brown wash of Punchinello. Punchinello, or Pulcinella, was one of the characters in the *commedia dell'arte*, and whereas the Scarecrow is not Pulcinella, he has this in common with him as well as with the other *commedia* characters, that he is flat and not round. I had found that an absence of psychology in my protagonists was a positive advantage in writing fairy tales of the sort this was going to be, and the sort of intense vivid character embodied in the *commedia* mask – its reactions instant and predictable and its attempts at subtlety absurdly obvious – was exactly the sort of personality I could already sense developing when I thought of the Scarecrow. Again, it's impossible to separate what is *intention* here from what is something else – hope, as I've suggested, or simple fascination: here's a new character to play with. And, of course, the *commedia* background suggested Italy, and that soon became inseparable from the rest of the idea.

The second source I was aware of was a book of vivid watercolour sketches sent me by a friend, a poet and painter living in Japan, who had become intrigued by the scarecrows Japanese farmers made for their fields. Anything will do: a pink plastic Wellington boot, a toy plane on a string, a doll trailing scores of coloured ribbons. They are a riot of improvisation. My friend had sketched dozens of these, and the infinite transmutability of the Japanese scarecrows certainly played a part in one important development of the plot, when the lawyer for the Buffalonis is trying to prove that the Scarecrow in the witness box is not the Scarecrow mentioned in the will, since every single part of him has now been replaced by something else.

But at what point did I intend to make that idea a part of the plot? From the beginning? I don't think so. I seem to remember I found it with a start of pleasure as I was writing the court scene, but all that might indicate is that my mind had been preparing the way without my being aware of it: that my intention had been unconscious. However, once I had become aware, I could go back and prepare the way by making sure that in the course of each adventure the Scarecrow lost a leg, or an arm, or his clothes, and his servant Jack found a replacement. I definitely remember intending to do that.

In fact, it may be that the major decisions are out of our control, and the intentions we're conscious of are concerned with matters of detail. That certainly goes for what we're going to write in the first place. I learned a long time ago that it was a mistake to intend, in a calm and rational way, having looked at a range of options and considered their relative merits and drawbacks, to write a certain book rather than another. The part of me that intended to write that particular book wasn't capable of it, and the part of me that was capable of writing books didn't want to write that one.

Among those major decisions, the ones that are made for me, is the one about voice and point of view. I couldn't truthfully say that I 'intend' to write in the third person, though I almost invariably do write like that. Nor did I 'intend' to make the voice that tells *His Dark Materials* different in tone from the voice that tells the Sally Lockhart novels, or both of them different from the voice that tells *The Scarecrow and his Servant* and my other fairy tales, though they are. The voice I found, in each case, seemed to be what the story wanted. And although I think those voices are different, I dare say that if anyone were to perform a stylistic analysis by computer of all my various stories, it would show that I have certain habits and mannerisms that would always give me away, no matter which 'voice' I was using; but as I don't know what they are, I can't say that I intend anything very much in connection with them.

The aspect of the author's intention that readers are perhaps most concerned about is the one about 'message'. After the first and second volumes of *His Dark Materials* had been published, but before the third, I was asked many times which of the characters were supposed to be good, and which bad; whom should the readers cheer for, and whom should they boo? They were clearly frustrated by the lack of a clear signal from the author, or the book itself, or the publisher via the blurb, and they felt unmoored, so to speak. The answer I gave was, in effect, 'I'm not going to tell you, but the story isn't over yet. Wait till you've read it all, and then decide for yourself. But what are you going to think when someone you've taken for a bad character does something good? Or when a good character does something bad? It's probably better to think about good or bad actions rather than good or bad characters. People are complicated.'

Audiences seemed satisfied with that, and the question faded away; it was seldom asked in that form after the final book was published. But anxiety about religion and morality is particularly sharp in the present age, so variants of that question turn up still, such as the one I quoted earlier: is it all right to think X, when the book is apparently intended to say Y? What's the correct view? What's the right answer? People clearly feel that intention matters a great deal, and that they can trust the author to tell them about it.

The final aspect of 'intention' I shall look at here is to do with audience. 'What age of reader is this book written for?' is a question that different authors feel differently about. Some are quite happy to say, 'It's for sixth and seventh graders', or, 'It's for thirteen and upwards.' Others are decidedly not. In 2008 most publishers of children's books in the UK announced that in an attempt to increase sales they were going to put an age-figure on the cover of every book, of the form 5+, 7+, 9+, and so on, to help adult purchasers in non-specialist bookstores decide whether a particular book would make a suitable present for a particular child. They met a passionate and determined resistance from many authors, who felt that their efforts to write books that would welcome readers of a wide age-range were being undermined by their own publishers, and that the age-figure would actively discourage many children from reading books they might otherwise enjoy. The argument continues, but again it shows the problematic nature of 'intention'. Does age-guidance of any sort imply that the book is intended for a particular kind of reader? My own view is that the only appropriate verb to use is, again, *hope* rather than *intend*. We have no right to expect any audience at all; the idea of sorting our readers out before they've even seen the first sentence seems to me presumptuous in the extreme.

To conclude: a writer's intention with regard to a book is a compli-cated and elusive matter, and explaining each case truthfully and in full is not always possible. Would a reader want to know that complicated and elusive truth in any case? Would it be any use to them? Possibly, if they were genuinely interested in the process of composition, and prepared for ambiguities and contradictions and uncertainties; probably not, if their desire was for a simple answer that would end their anxiety about whether they'd really understood what the book was saying.

But it would be frivolous to maintain that a writer's intention doesn't matter at all. In other spheres of activity it matters a great deal. If we accidentally dislodge a flowerpot from a sixth-floor balcony on to somebody's head, it's unfortunate; if we intend to do so, it's murder. The courts certainly recognise the difference. There is also the related question of responsibility. If a writer produces a story that has the effect of inflaming (for example) racial hatred, can he or she disclaim responsibility by saying that whatever intention they had, it wasn't that, and that in any case their intention is irrelevant? To disclaim intention and responsibility altogether seems to me to regard the author as little more than an elaborate piece of voice-recognition software, taking down dictation from an unseen source. Of course our intentions matter to some extent: it's just rather difficult to say what they are.

In practice, the way we answer questions depends as always on what we judge to be the needs, the age, the maturity and the intellectual ability of the questioner, and the situation in which the question is posed. If we're lucky enough to have a long line of young customers waiting for us to sign their newly purchased books, we can't spend much time on any of our answers; with a small group of well-prepared university students in a seminar room, the case is different.

But I think that I would try – that I do try – to explain that what I *intended* to do was make up as good a story as I could invent, and write it as well as I could manage. And I try to explain something about the democratic nature of reading. I say that whatever my intention might have been when I wrote the book, the meaning doesn't consist only of my intention. The meaning is what emerges from the interaction between the words I put on the page and the readers' own minds as they read them. If they're puzzled, the best thing to do is talk about the book with someone else who's read it, and let meanings emerge from the conversation, democratically. I'm willing to take part in such conversations, because I too have read the book, and if I'm asked about my intentions, then any answer I give will be part of the conversation too; but it's hard to persuade readers that my reading has no more final authority than theirs.

In that way, I may not clarify much for people who want to know about my intentions, but I do introduce the idea of reader response theory, which is probably more helpful.

THIS ESSAY WAS FIRST PUBLISHED IN *KEY WORDS IN CHILDREN'S LITERATURE*, EDITED BY PHILIP NELL AND LISSA PAUL (NEW YORK UNIVERSITY PRESS, 2011).

Beginning in 1986 I was lucky enough to work for a while at Westminster College, which is now part of Oxford Brookes University, with a man called Gordon Dennis. I learned a great deal from him, including the notion that you could say interesting things about children's books just as much as you could about books that only adults would want to read. The growth of children's literature as an academic subject is something I welcome warmly, despite the fact that I feel rather shifty about my own ability to talk academically, as I explain in the essay that follows.

Children's Literature Without Borders

STORIES SHOULDN'T NEED PASSPORTS

On storytelling, children and adults

THIS TALK IS GOING TO BE PARTLY AT LEAST ABOUT CHILDREN'S literature, or so it says in the programme. I should say at the outset that I'm not going to treat the subject in an academic way, even if I could; I find it hard to think about anything for very long, or at all deeply, unless I can get some practical grasp of it. My qualifications for saying anything about books that children read are strictly limited to the fact that I write them. So these reflections are those of someone who makes up stories and thinks about how he does it, rather than those of a scholar who has studied the subject from an academic point of view.

I thought I should begin by trying to say what children's literature is; but that's not as easy as it seems. We *think* we know what it is – there are books about it, you can be a professor of it – but it still seems to me rather a slippery term. It's not quite like any other category of literature.

For example, if we go into a large bookshop we find many different ways of dividing up the stock. We find books separated by genre, for example horror, crime, science fiction; but children's books – children's literature – isn't a genre in that sense.

However, we also find shelves labelled women's literature, black literature, gay and lesbian literature. Is children's literature like that?

No, it isn't like that either, because books of those kinds are written by members of the named groups as well as being about them and for them. After all, those categories, those bookshelf labels, came into being because people felt they needed a voice, not just an ear. They didn't say, 'Write more stuff for us!' They said, 'We *are* writing, and we want to be read.'

But children's literature isn't produced by children. It's written, edited, designed, published, printed, marketed, publicised, sold, reviewed, read, taught at every level from nursery school to post-graduate, and very often bought by adults. A novel written by a child is a very rare thing. Whereas we accept the idea of the child prodigy in the fields of music or chess or mathematics, those activities depend on abstract pattern-recognition more than on the sort of stuff that novels are made of, namely experience of life. A ten-year-old child writing something like *A Dance to the Music of Time*, say, or *Pride and Prejudice*, or *Tom's Midnight Garden*, would be not a prodigy but a monster.

I'm talking about novels, not poetry: poems, at least to the extent to which they are patterns themselves, seem to be more within the reach of a young mind, and we've seen remarkable poems produced by young children under the guidance of good teachers such as Jill Pirrie (author of *On Common Ground: A Programme for Teaching Poetry*, Hodder, 1987) – though when I was teaching young children I was occasionally reminded of that observation by the pre-Socratic philosopher Ion of Chios: 'Luck,' he said, 'which is very different from art, sometimes produces things which are like it.' I'm perpetually conscious of the part that luck plays in my own work; it would be odd if it played no part in the work of others. We need to give children plenty of opportunity to be lucky.

So children's literature isn't like women's literature or black literature; but there's another difference as well. Membership of those other groups I mentioned is presumably a permanent condition: I have always been male, and white, and heterosexual, and while we can never be completely sure what'll happen tomorrow, I'm fairly safe in saying that I always will be. But I was once a child, and so were all the other adults who produce children's literature; and those who read it – the children – will one day be adults. So surely there isn't a complete and unbridgeable gap between them, the children, and us, the grown-ups; or between their books and ours. There must be some sort of continuity here; surely we should all be interested in books for every age, since our experience includes them all.

Or so you'd think. But it doesn't seem to work like that. To look at the reception of children's literature today, you'd think that it was a separate thing entirely, almost a separate country, because there are important people like literary editors and critics, who decide what should go where, and why. People who act like guards on an important frontier, and who walk up and down very importantly carrying their lists and inspecting papers and sorting things out. You go there – you stay here. There was an example recently in the *Times Literary Supplement* An eminent critic and poet was reviewing a novel that appeared on its publisher's adult list. The critic called it 'too simple by a mile', placed much of it on the abysmal level of Kipling's *Thy Servant a Dog*, said, 'The glossary of Australian slang terms is over-literal and out-of-date', and laid into it heartily for being sentimental.

However, he added, 'as a children's book, it might make its mark.'

So children's books, apparently, are like bad books for grown-ups. If you write a book that isn't very good, we'll put it over there, among the stuff that children read.

That's not a view that's unique to this country, and nor is it confined to the books themselves. Their authors are not very good, either. A year or two ago I saw a piece by Robert Stone in the *New York Review of Books*. He was writing about Philip Roth's latest novel. Stone opened by praising Roth for his great achievements in the past thirty years, the authority of his voice, his energy, his manic but modulated virtuosity, and so forth. Then he went on to say that Roth was – these are his words – 'an author so serious he makes most of his contemporaries seem like children's writers.'

Well, that put me in my place. You can imagine how embarrassed I felt at not being serious, and having a voice with no authority, not to mention a virtuosity that was sober and unmodulated.

The model of growth that seems to lie behind that attitude – the idea that such critics have of what it's like to grow up – must be a linear one; they must think that we grow up by moving along a sort of timeline, like a monkey climbing a stick. It makes more sense to me to think of the movement from childhood to adulthood not as a movement *along* but as a movement *outwards*, to include more things. C. S. Lewis, who when he wasn't writing novels had some very sensible things to say about books and reading, made the same point when he said in his essay *On Three Ways of Writing for Children*: 'I now like hock, which I am sure I should not have liked as a child. But I still like lemon-squash. I call this growth or development because I have been enriched: where I formerly had only one pleasure, I now have two.'

But the guards on the border won't have any of that. They are very fierce and stern. They strut up and down with a fine contempt, curling their lips and consulting their clipboards and snapping out orders. They've got a lot to do, because at the moment this is an area of great international tension. These days a lot of adults are *talking* about children's books. Sometimes they do so in order to deplore the fact that so many other adults are reading them, and are obviously becoming infantilised, because of course children's books – I quote from a recent article in the *Independent* – 'cannot hope to come close to truths about moral, sexual, social or political' matters. Whereas in even the 'flimsiest of science fiction or the nastiest of horror stories… there is an understanding of complex human psychologies', 'there is no such psychological understanding in children's novels,' and furthermore 'there are nice clean white lines painted between the good guys and the evil ones.' (wrote Jonathan Myerson in the *Independent*, 14 November 2001).

Consequently any adult reading such stuff is running away from reality, and should feel profoundly ashamed.

In the same week, however, we had a well-known journalist and social commentator saying that children's books *are* worth reading, because:

'People are desperate for stories… Yet in our postmodern, deconstructed, too-clever-by-half culture, narrative is despised and a cracking read is as hard to find as a moth in the dark.' (Melanie Phillips, *Sunday Times*, 11 November 2001).

So there's a lot of tension along this border – a lot of pride and suspicion and harsh words and dangerous incidents. It might flare up at any minute, we feel.

But when we step away from the border post, when we go round the back of the guards and look about us, we see something rather odd. The guards have entirely failed to notice that all around them people are walking happily across this border in both directions. You'd think there wasn't a border there at all. Adults are happily reading children's books; and what's more, children are reading adults' books. A thirteen-year-old boy of my acquaintance was a passionate reader of Kazuo Ishiguro's *The Unconsoled*; and only the other day I spoke to some children in the public library in Oxford, none of them older than thirteen, and found that they were reading, among other things, Dorothy L. Sayers, Agatha Christie, Ruth Rendell, Ian Rankin, Stephen King, David Eddings, Helen Fielding – much of it genre fiction, to be sure, but all of it firmly on the adult side of the border.

And I well remember my own childhood reading consisting among other things of Aldous Huxley and Lawrence Durrell as well as Superman and Batman, Arthur Ransome and Tove Jansson at the same time as Joseph Conrad and P. G. Wodehouse, Captain Pugwash overlapping with James Bond – a whole mixture of things, both apparently grown-up and apparently not. Furthermore, a book that made a great impression on me and my young schoolfriends was *Lady Chatterley's Lover*. So highly did we think of its qualities that we used to pass it around from hand to hand; in fact, like many copies of that book, it used to fall open at the passages most keenly admired.

Now it's quite common to criticise this kind of cross-border reading on the grounds that it's reading *for the wrong reasons*. Adults today are reading *Harry Potter*, apparently, in order to be in the fashion, or to retreat into a state of childish irresponsibility; the teacher who confiscated our copy of *Lady Chatterley's Lover* did so because he thought it wasn't the literature we were after, but the sociology. At least, I think that's what he said; he said it in Welsh.

Reading for the wrong reasons is something that the guards on the border never do, but which other people do all the time, unless they're supervised. Well, my view about that is that even if there *are* right and wrong reasons for reading, I don't know what they are when *I'm* doing it, never mind anybody else. What's more, it's none of my business, and to make it still harder, everything is more complicated than we think. An ignoble reason for doing something can turn into a worthy one; as well as being intrigued by the sociology that was going on in *Lady Chatterley's Lover*, I do remember being fascinated by the way Lawrence put words together.

This sort of mixing-up happens all the time, and in other fields as well as literature. One minute we're admiring the way Degas puts his pastel marks on the paper, the next we're wondering what it might be like to kiss the model. But then we notice something intriguing in the diagonals of the composition, and that sets us thinking about the Japanese print in the painting by Van Gogh on the other wall of the gallery, and while we're thinking about Japanese art we remember that very sociological woodblock print involving the fisherman's wife and the octopus; and that reminds us that it's time for lunch. But on the way out, we look again at Degas, and think that his way with pastel really is exquisite. He puts *this* colour against *that* one, and something quite different happens. Could I do that with words? we think. How would it work?

And so on. Which are the wrong reasons there, and which are the right ones? They're all mixed up together inextricably. And no one else can possibly know whether to condemn us for the ignoble, or praise us for the worthy. So I don't believe for a second in criticising anyone for reading for the wrong reasons. We're much better off minding our own business.

In a similar way, I don't think it makes any sense for someone else to decide who should read this book or that. How can they possibly know? Much better not to decide at all, and just let things happen. One of the questions I'm addressing this evening is that of what children's and adult literature have got in common: one thing they have in common, plainly, is that both literatures, whatever they are, are read by both groups, whatever *they* are. But as I began by saying, I'm thinking in a practical way of what will help me write; and one thing that helps me do that is the vision of a marketplace.

I like to imagine the literary marketplace as if it were precisely that, a place where a market is being held, a busy open space with a lot of people buying and selling, and eating and drinking, and stopping for a gossip, and walking through on their way to somewhere else, or just running up and down and playing; and in this corner there's someone playing the fiddle, and over there is a juggler, and here's a storyteller on his square of carpet with his hat in front of him, telling a story.

And some people have gathered to listen.

They've got heavy shopping bags in their hands, and they probably can't stay for long, but still, they're intrigued, they want to know what's going to happen next, so they stay a minute more, and then another, just to see how it turns out; and there's an old man leaning on a stick, and here's a child sucking a lollipop, and they're both listening hard; faces looking over shoulders or peering between taller bodies, pressed together, crammed close, all listening. And some other people go past and listen for a moment and decide it's not for them, so they go on somewhere else; and others walk past entirely oblivious, chatting together without noticing the story at all; and once in a while someone who has to leave and catch a bus sees a friend and says, 'There's a good story going on over there, you ought to go and listen.'

And when the story's over, some coins fall in the hat. The storyteller catches his breath and stretches his legs and then sits down to start another tale.

That's a picture of storytelling in an imaginary state of nature, so to speak: one storyteller, one tale, one audience, and no borders between anyone or anything. It's imaginary, because for one thing I'm deliberately ignoring the differences which I know exist between writing and telling, between reading a story and listening to it; but this is an abstraction, and I'm ignoring those differences for a particular purpose, which I'll come to in a minute.

In the real world, the literary marketplace is nowhere near so simple as the one I've just described. We haven't got just the storyteller and the audience any more; there are other people in the business too.

For example, there are some who go to the storyteller and say, 'I happen to have the lease of that prime site under the trees, next to the fountain, where a lot of people pass by. I can guarantee you a big audience if you split the money in the hat with me – as a matter of fact, I can offer you an advance on your takings.'

There are others who go to the storyteller and say, 'That's all very well, but what's the split they're asking for? *What?* Let me handle the deal and I'll guarantee you a better return than that. I'll only take ten per cent.'

There are some who say to the storyteller, 'Look, you're attracting a big crowd, but half of them are leaving without paying. Let me sell tickets — that way we can be sure of making a decent amount. Did I say we? I meant *you*, of course, but I'll need to cover my expenses.'

And then there are those who, noticing the number of people looking for a good story and the number of storytellers in business, set up an advisory service. 'I've listened to all these storytellers,' they say, 'and for a very small consideration I can point out the good ones. There's a cracking yarn going on just now by the flower stall – bright young talent, well worth a visit. As for old so-and-so next to the bus stop, he's been recycling the same stuff for days now, you've heard it all before – frankly, I wouldn't bother.'

And in recent years, storytellers have had a new sort of service offered to them. 'It's no good just telling your story these days – you need to attract attention to *yourself*. Pay me, and I can guarantee to get you talked about. I can't buy your story a good report from the advisory service, but I can promise lots of interest in *you*. By the way, you need to get your hair cut – and wear something blue tomorrow.'

Now most of those other people who come between the storyteller and the audience do so for the best of reasons, and few of us in the real world would want to be without the services that publishers and book-sellers and literary agents and critics provide. I'm glad they're there. But among the other intermediaries in this imaginary marketplace are the security guards. They are another branch of the same service that watches the border. They're interested in the audience more than the stories. They make it their business to say, 'This story is only for women.' Or, 'This story is intended especially for very clever people.' Or, 'The only people who will enjoy this story are those under ten.'

They sort out the audience, and chivvy some this way, some that way, and if they could, they'd make them stand in lines and keep quiet. Some of them even want to give the audience a test on the story afterwards – but I shall say no more about our current educational system.

The result is that instead of that audience I described earlier, all mixed up together, old and young, men and women, educated and not edu-cated, black and white, rich and poor, busy and leisured – instead of that democratic mix, we have segregation: segregation by sex, by sexual preference, by ethnicity, by education, by economic circumstances, and above all, segregation by age.

But, as I pointed out, the trouble is that no one can tell what is going on in a mind that's reading or listening to a story; no one can know whether we're reading for the right reasons or the wrong reasons, or what's right and what's wrong anyway; no one can tell who's ready and who isn't, who's clever and who isn't, who'll like it and who won't.

Not only that; do we really believe that men have nothing to learn from stories by and about women? That white people already know all they need to know about the experience of black people? Segregation always shuts out more than it lets in. When we say, 'This book is for such-and-such a group', what we seem to be saying, what we're *heard* as saying, is: 'This book is not for anyone else.' It would be nice to think that normal human curiosity would let us open our minds to experience from every quarter, to listen to every storyteller in the marketplace. It would be nice too, occasionally, to read a review of an adult book that said, 'This book is so interesting, and so clearly and beautifully written, that children would enjoy it as well.'

But that doesn't seem likely in the near future.

Can we ever have a state of things free from labelling and segregating, though? And if we can't, what's the use of imagining this democratic open-to-all marketplace which doesn't really exist?

Well, my reason for thinking about it is strictly practical. Storytellers can do exactly what they like. Those who want to speak only to adults may do so with perfect freedom, and I shall be there in the audience. Those who want to speak only to children may do so too, and if what they say has nothing to interest me, I'll pass on and leave them to it.

But as a storyteller myself, and one who depends on the contents of the hat to pay the mortgage and buy the groceries and save up for my old age, I don't want my audience to be selected for me; I want it to be as large as possible. I want everyone to be able to listen. The larger the crowd, the more goes in the hat.

Besides, it's more *interesting*. The work you do to keep a mixed audience listening is technically intriguing.

So, for purely practical reasons, I turn to this imaginary and abstract vision because I find that it brings about, in the field of storytelling, something not unlike the 'original position' in John Rawls's *A Theory of*

Justice. According to Rawls, the 'original position' is the state in which we are to imagine ourselves behind a veil of ignorance, without knowing what position in society we actually occupy. In this original position we can work out what principles should govern a society that would be just and fair to all, given that we might find ourselves anywhere in it. In real life, we know what position we occupy, and we're influenced by all sorts of considerations – not only selfish ones – to favour that position over others; when we're distracted by the knowledge of where we really are, it becomes much harder to see the way to bring about justice for all.

Similarly with the storyteller in the marketplace. I find that there are certain practical ways in which this 'original position' idea – the picture of the storyteller and the mixed audience, whose attention I have to keep, but whose reasons for listening, right or wrong, are none of my business – does help me to think about what I'm doing when I tell a story, and what a story is, and how I could tell it most effectively.

For example: if you're going to keep people listening, you need to know your story very well. You need to think about it and go over it and clarify it so that you know the line of the story as well as you know the journey from your front door to the bus stop. By 'the line of the story' I mean the connection between this event and that one. The world in which Little Red Riding Hood meets the wolf contains all sorts of events and facts and histories, and we could make them up if we had time, but the story we know as *Little Red Riding Hood* ruthlessly ignores most of them. It goes in a line from one event to the next, and in a good telling those events will be in the most effective order and follow swiftly and cleanly one after another; everything that's important will be there, and everything that's irrelevant will be left out.

The same, of course, is true of any great novel. Given the events that take place in and around the town of Middlemarch, the book that's named after it *tells their story* about as well as it could be told. It does many other things besides, but that is one thing it does do.

The advantage of thinking yourself into the original position here is that it helps you concentrate on getting the story as clear as possible. Without taking anything into consideration but the audience-that-includes-children-but-doesn't-entirely-consist-of-them, you can work at the story like a craftsman, calmly and quietly going about the task without imposing your own concerns or your own personality on it. If you're going to keep them all listening, you have to subdue everything that you think makes *you* interesting.

As a matter of fact, you the intelligent, well-read, educated storyteller and your post-modernist doubts about narrative and fictionality, your anguish about *jouissance*, are *never* going to be as interesting, to this mixed audience, as the people and the events in the story you're telling. Realising this is a great help when it comes to overcoming the tormenting self-consciousness that many writers of stories feel and have felt for a century now, and which I fully understand, and which I used to share: because when you tell a story to an audience that includes children, you actually become invisible. You don't matter any more. You can be impersonal about it.

This impersonality brings me to the second consideration, which is the matter of style. How do you put the words together? What kind of voice are you hearing in your head? What kind of voice does the story want?

This is partly a matter of taste. But a limpid clarity is a great virtue. If you get that right, the story you tell will not seem to anyone as if it's intended for someone else. No one is shut out. There are no special codes you have to master before you can follow what's going on. Of course, this sort of thing has been said many times before; W. H. Auden and George Orwell both compared good prose to a clear windowpane: something we look through, not at.

Which naturally brings me to the next question: what are you inviting your audience to look at, through the window of your telling? What are you showing them?

If you want your mixed crowd to be interested, you have to *make up interesting things*. Here's an interesting scene. In a little inn, a country doctor is talking calmly over a pipe and a glass, and in another corner of the parlour, a drunken sea-captain is singing loudly.

> The captain... at last flapped his hand upon the table in a way we all knew to mean – silence. The voices stopped at once, all but Dr Livesey's; he went on as before, speaking clear and kind, and drawing briskly at his pipe between every word or two. The captain glared at him for a while, flapped his hand again, glared still harder, and at last broke out with a villainous, low oath: 'Silence, there; between decks!'
>
> 'Were you addressing me, sir?' says the doctor; and when the ruffian had told him, with another oath, that this was so,
>
> 'I have only one thing to say to you, sir,' replies the doctor, 'that if you keep on drinking rum, the world will soon be rid of a very dirty scoundrel!'
>
> The old fellow's fury was awful. He sprang to his feet, drew and opened a sailor's clasp- knife, and, balancing it open on the palm of his hand, threatened to pin the doctor to the wall.
>
> The doctor never so much as moved. He spoke to him, as before, over his shoulder, and in the same tone of voice; rather high, so that all the room might hear, but perfectly calm and steady: 'If you do not put that knife this instant in your pocket, I promise, upon my honour, you shall hang at next assizes.'
>
> Then followed a battle of looks between them; but the captain soon knuckled under, put up his weapon, and resumed his seat, grumbling like a beaten dog.
>
> 'And now, sir,' continued the doctor, 'since I now know

there's such a fellow in my district, you may count I'll have
an eye upon you day and night. I'm not a doctor only; I'm
a magistrate; and if I catch a breath of complaint against
you, if it's only for a piece of incivility like tonight's, I'll take
effectual means to have you hunted down and routed out of
this. Let that suffice.'

Soon after Dr Livesey's horse came to the door, and he
rode away; but the captain held his peace that evening, and
for many evenings to come.

Treasure Island, of course. Another scene that's interesting in a similar
way is the return of Odysseus to Ithaca, stringing the great bow that none
of the suitors can manage.

So they mocked, but Odysseus, mastermind in action,
once he'd handled the great bow and scanned every inch,
then, like an expert singer skilled at lyre and song –
who strains a string to a new peg with ease,
making the pliant sheep-gut fast at either end
so with his virtuoso ease Odysseus strung his mighty bow.
Quickly his right hand plucked the string to test its pitch
and under his touch it sang out clear and sharp as a swallow's cry.
(Homer's *The Odyssey*, from book 21: 451–458, translated by Robert Fagles, Penguin Classics)

I was once telling that story to my five-year-old son, and he was so
tense and excited that at the point when the string sang out clear and
sharp as a swallow's cry, he bit clean through the glass he was drinking
from. You can hardly get more interested than that.

Scenes like these never fail, because they involve danger and tension
and courage and resolution, circumstances and qualities which listeners

or readers of every age respond to. Not every story has to involve high adventure, by any means; but no successful storyteller is afraid of the *obvious* – of conflict and resolution, faithfulness and treachery, passion and fulfilment. If your narrative shies away from a situation because you think it will seem hackneyed, if you wince fastidiously and refuse to follow your characters where they want to go, on the grounds that you don't want to be mistaken for the other writers, less good than you are, who have gone there before, then the audience will go away and find another storyteller with more vigour and less self-importance.

Another very important thing we can discover in this original position is that of *stance* – not quite the same as voice, not quite the same as *point of view*; it's a mixture of where the camera is, so to speak, and where the sympathy lies. I recently re-read some of Richmal Crompton's William stories, and found her particular stance more interesting than I remembered. The story in which William and the Outlaws first encounter Violet Elizabeth Bott ends with them pretending to rescue her and being rewarded, but the money is small consolation for the shame they've had to endure at being manipulated by her all morning.

> They tramped homewards by the road.
>
> 'Well, it's turned out all right,' said Ginger lugubriously, but fingering the ten-shilling note in his pocket, 'but it might not have. 'Cept for the money it jolly well spoilt the morning.'
>
> 'Girls always do,' said William. 'I'm not going to have anything to do with any ole girl ever again.'
>
> ''S all very well sayin' that,' said Douglas who had been deeply impressed that morning by the inevitableness and deadly persistence of the sex, ''s all very well saying that. It's them what has to do with you.'
>
> 'An' I'm never going to marry any ole girl,' said William.

'S all very well sayin' *that*,' said Douglas again gloomily, 'but some ole girl'll probably marry you.'

There's a very subtle and fluid mixture here of sympathy and satire, of affection and mockery, of cool knowledge and the memory of what it is not to have it; it's a matter of being *with* the characters but not entirely *of* them, and it's a stance that works very well with this mixed audience.

Courtesy comes into it too: an attitude to the audience that doesn't assume either that they're simple and need to have things made easy for them, or that, since only clever people read books, you can make jokes about how dull everyone else is. A recent writer of books that children read who embodied that kind of courtesy perfectly was Henrietta Branford, whose early death robbed us of someone who, in my view, might have become the best of us all.

The last point I want to make is that in a good telling – the sort one tries to emulate, or bring off oneself – the events are not interpreted, but simply related. 'Events themselves,' as Isaac Bashevis Singer said, 'are wiser than any commentary on them.' Don't tell the audience what your story means. Given that no one knows what's going on in someone else's head, you can't possibly tell them what it means in any case.

Meanings are for the reader to find, not for the storyteller to impose. The sort of story we all hope we can write is one that will resonate like a musical note with all kinds of overtones and harmonics, some of which will be heard more clearly by this person's ear, others by that one's; and some of which may not be heard at all by the storyteller. What's more, as the listeners grow older, so some of the overtones will fade while others become more clearly audible. This is what happens with the great fairy tales. What you think *Little Red Riding Hood* is about when you're six is not what you think it's about when you're forty. The way to tell a story is to say what happened, and then shut up.

When I first started thinking about children's literature for this talk

I found myself surrounded by images of gardens. *Alice in Wonderland* is full of gardens, and so is *Through the Looking Glass*; Humphrey Carpenter called his study of children's literature of the so-called golden age *Secret Gardens*, after the novel by Frances Hodgson Burnett. Nursery rhymes sing about them: it was in a garden where the unfortunate maid lost her nose to the blackbird, and *Mary, Mary, quite contrary* was describing a garden makeover of which Alan Titchmarsh would have been proud.

A garden is a safe place, a pretty place, after all; you'd be happy to let your children play in the garden. And it suggests ideas of growing and cultivation and training, of bringing things up, of nurturing them in the greenhouse to the point where they're hardy enough to stay outside; and also of keeping them in order, of making sure they look tidy, and so on. There are all kinds of reasons to associate children and their literature with gardens.

So when I was asked to speak about children's literature I looked for a garden metaphor to start me off, but I couldn't make it work; because what kept coming to mind was the crazy disordered garden in that little scrap of genius, *The Great Panjandrum*:

> So she went into the garden to cut a cabbage leaf to make an apple pie; and at the same time a great she-bear, coming up the street, pops its head into the shop. 'What? no soap?' So he died, and she very imprudently married the barber: and there were present the Picninnies, and the Joblillies, and the Garyulies, and the great Panjandrum himself, with the little round button at top; and they all fell to playing the game of catch-as-catch-can, till the gunpowder ran out at the heels of their boots.
> (*Samuel Foote, 1755*)

Well, there was my garden metaphor. What could I do with it? This isn't one of those safe gardens, where all the plants behave predictably; if you want an apple pie here, you have to pick a cabbage leaf. And people can die suddenly – from shock, one presumes. What's more, danger-ous and explosive substances are casually sprinkled around the floor. It shouldn't be allowed. Someone should stop it.

But of course someone's trying to: the great she-bear is demanding cleanliness and trying to keep order. She's obviously one of those security guards in disguise, or perhaps a school inspector, and the only effect she has is to cause the death of an innocent bystander.

But the consolation is that nobody takes any notice at all, and the wedding goes ahead, imprudent or not, and the game of catch-as-catch-can is still going on, as far as I can tell. When I find it, I shall join in.

THIS TALK WAS DELIVERED AT THE ROYAL SOCIETY OF LITERATURE, 6 DECEMBER 2001.

The idea of borders, and frontiers, and guards, and customs regulations, and all the paraphernalia of passports and visas and 'letters of transit' (the imaginary papers required by the protagonists of the film Casablanca *before they could leave for Lisbon and safety), is full of metaphorical implication. And in these days of Brexit and the politically induced paranoia about hordes of refugees who are all probably terrorists, the desire to 'regain control of our borders' seems to flourish. The point I'd still like to make is that all that apparatus of suspicion doesn't help us to get on together. In some parts of the world, it's becoming harder and harder for writers to publish their work without the threat of imprisonment or worse, which isn't a metaphor at all.*

Let's Write it in Red

THE PRACTICE OF WRITING

On writing as a game with rules, including rules for the beginnings
and endings, the making-up parts and the writing-down parts –
and how not everything should be written in red

I AM VERY HONOURED TO HAVE BEEN ASKED TO GIVE THE PATRICK HARDY Lecture. I never knew Patrick Hardy, but as a reader of *Signal* I've been aware of the quality of the previous lectures and of the many merits of those who gave them, all of them distinguished and unfailingly interesting commentators on this large world of ours, the world of children's books. And I say 'large world' without the slightest irony: I have said before that children's books, for various reasons, at this time in our literary history, open out on a wideness and amplitude – a moral and mental spaciousness – that adult literary fiction seems to have turned its back on. But I'm not going to rehearse that argument again tonight; instead I'm going to start with a story, continue with a look at some principles of storytelling, and end with a confession.

The story is a true one, and it happened to me – or rather I witnessed it – about a year ago. (And that sentence itself illustrates part of the fascinating difficulty of talking about story. The story, of course, didn't happen: the events happened. The story happened later, when I picked out certain of the events and told them. And I've told them several times since, because I think they're fascinating, but tonight I'm going to think about the implications of them in a more coherent way.)

I was on a train going from Oxford to Newcastle. The carriage was crowded, and sitting near me was a young woman who had six children to look after. I don't think they were all her own: I think some of them were cousins, so she was both mum and auntie. There was a baby who was being fed, and there was a four-year-old with a huge bag of crisps, so they were happily occupied; and there were two boys of roughly eleven who were swapping football stickers, so they were all right; and there were two girls, I guess about eight or nine, who didn't have anything to do, and who were a bit restless.

So the mother gave them some coloured pencils and a pad of paper and said, 'Why don't you write a story?'

My eyes were firmly fixed on what I was reading, namely the papers concerning the Centre for the Children's Book (now known as Seven Stories), which was what I was going to Newcastle for; but the magpie who sits in every storyteller's head turned his beady-eyed attention at once to what the girls were doing. 'What can we steal from this?' he said. 'What can we copy? What can we use?'

(Actually, the roosting space in my head is shared between the magpie and another bird: that dusty, broken-down, out-of-date old owl who used to be a teacher. And he opened an eye too, and cocked an ear, if owls can do that, to see what these girls had been taught.)

They began by deciding what their heroine should be called, and where she should live, and the names of her friends, and what school she went to, and all that. And then they got down to writing the opening of the story, and then one of the little girls said to the other, 'Are we allowed to write that she can do magic?'

That's exactly what she said: not, 'Let's write that she can do magic' but, 'Are we *allowed*?'

The owl opened both eyes. The magpie cocked his head even more intently.

Anyway, they decided that their heroine could do magic, and they wrote a page or so, agreeing what should happen as they went along. The owl was pleased to see that they wrote neatly and punctuated appropriately, and they could even do paragraphs. The magpie was trying to read upside down.

Then the second girl said, 'I know! When we come to an exciting bit, let's write it in red!'

And at this point the magpie and the owl turned to each other in awe. I think I'll put the bird metaphor to sleep now, because both those parts of me were fully joined with all the rest, and my respect for these great eight- or nine-year-old artists was such that I would have asked for their autographs, if I had dared; but they got out at the next stop, and I never had the chance to hear any more.

Now you can see what I'm going to derive from this story. The girls' comments embody two great principles of storytelling, and I'm going to expand on those and then add a third principle which I think was already implicit in their activity, if not their words.

The first principle is this: there are rules.

Because this was an activity freely engaged in, something to pass the time, a game, fun. It wasn't homework. It wasn't a task set by a teacher in order to satisfy some requirement of that great blight in Britain, that educational murrain, the National Curriculum for schools. They could do with it exactly what they liked. And yet she said, 'Are we allowed to write such-and-such?' No one would have chastised her, or given her poor marks, if she had done what was not allowed; she wanted to know what *was* allowed, not so that she could avoid punishment, but so that she could do it. She wanted to play the game properly.

We need to be a little careful with this analogy between storytelling and games, because in most games you're playing against an opponent, and the object of the game is to beat them. That isn't the case with storytelling, unless we consider every storyteller to be an avatar of Scheherazade, the opponent being the Sultan (or the listener or reader in general, or the critic) and the object of the game being to stop them killing you (or putting the book down, or giving you a bad review). That's one way of looking at it. Another is that storyteller and audience collaborate in a game of let's-pretend. But let's-pretend has rules as well: you can't pretend a new thing without telling the others, for instance.

And as we know about all games, it's much more satisfying to play with rules than without them. If we're going to enjoy a game of football in the playground, we need to know where the touchline is, and agree on what we're going to regard as the goalposts. Then we can get on with playing, because the complete freedom of our play is held together and protected by this armature of rules. The first and last and only discovery that the victims of anarchy can make is: no rules, no freedom.

So here are some of the rules of story, as I understand and try to follow them. They're only in a rough order, and this list isn't by any means complete – I don't suppose any such list ever could be, because it would shade off into the fatuous at one end and the numinous at the other – but these are the rules I myself have found most helpful.

My first rule is that stories must *begin*. Out of the welter of events and ideas and pictures and characters and voices that you experience in your head, you the storyteller must choose one moment, the best moment, and make that the start. You could begin anywhere in the chronology, of course; you could begin in the middle, *in medias res*, as Homer does; you could begin at the end of it if you wanted to, as J. G. Ballard does in one of his short stories, with the character's death, and work towards his birth. But unless you are writing one of those rather dated experimental loose-leaf collections of pages to be shuffled and read in any order, one of your pages is going to be the first page, and one of your sentences is going to be the first sentence. So: where are you going to start, and what are you going to say?

At this point I'm going to introduce a notion from the world of science which I've mentioned on other occasions. I read more about science than I understand, but I've always thought that one of its many great gifts to us is the cornucopia of metaphor it provides for discussing the arts. The notion I want to metaphorise is phase space. Phase space is a term from dynamics. It's the notional space which contains not just the actual consequences of the present moment, but all the possible consequences. The phase space of a game of noughts and crosses, for instance, would contain every possible outcome of every possible initial move, and the actual course of a game could be represented by a path starting from the one move that was actually made first.

So the opening of your story brings with it a phase space. For example:

> Alice was beginning to get very tired of sitting by her sister
> on the bank, and of having nothing to do: once or twice she
> had peeped into the book her sister was reading, but it had
> no pictures or conversations in it, 'and what is the use of a
> book,' thought Alice, 'without pictures or conversation?'

You have to make the first mark somewhere. You have to open a story at some point. The first sentence of *Alice's Adventures in Wonderland*, by taking up the position it does towards Alice, by letting us know her firm, decided, no-nonsense view of what kind of book is no use, opens up many possibilities and closes many others. It establishes the fact that we are going to know her thoughts; that doesn't mean we won't know other characters' thoughts, but it does mean that that first privilege won't be withdrawn. We are with Alice: our stance is sympathetic.

(I have a personal rule that's a variation of this: I never start a story with a pronoun. '*She stood at the window, gazing down at the ...*' If I read a story like that, I'm irritated before I begin. *Who* stood at the window? What's her name? How am I supposed to know who *she* is?)

The next rule I want to talk about concerns consistency. When my colleague on the train said, 'Are we allowed to write that she can do magic?' what she meant was, 'Within the game of this particular story, is such-and-such a move permitted?' Putting it another way, would such-and-such a move violate a unity or destroy a mood or contradict a proposition?

Notice, this isn't a warning against subverting expectations. It's more to do with having a sense of what sort of story it is that you're telling, and being true to the vision of it, and not sticking something in from another kind of story altogether because it makes it easier.

This unity is part of what we look for and enjoy in, for example, Arthur Ransome. We know perfectly well that in *Swallows and Amazons* there's going to be no fairy dust on Wild Cat Island. He is very firmly *not* allowed to write that Captain Nancy can do magic. And what authority is it that grants or withholds the permission? Simply the rest of the story, the authority of the context, and especially the storyteller's sense of it. Ransome's awareness of what he's doing is so secure that even if the notion of a little bit of magic to get him out of a hole (and we know from his letters that he frequently lamented the difficulty of getting his plots to move satisfactorily) – even if the notion fluttered like a moth at the very edge of his attention, his storyteller's sense of what was proper would swat it away without his even beginning to consider it consciously.

Another requirement is consistency of tone. For example, open Leon Garfield where you like, you won't find a page of sober dullness anywhere. Fantastical gloom, yes; grimness illuminated by shafts of grotesque humour, certainly; a darkness as profound and velvety as the black of an old mezzotint, by all means; but nothing sober, nothing drab, nothing workaday. The exuberance is all of a piece: even a first paragraph that begins like a travel guide twirls upwards into a rococo curlicue of imagery:

> Eastward in Clerkenwell lies the Mulberry Pleasure Garden... lamps hang glimmering in the trees and scores of moths flap and totter in the shadowy green, imagining themselves star-drunk ...

The Pleasure Garden (Viking, 1976). There, by the way, is a book that ought never to be unavailable. The way to celebrate children's literature is not to print postage stamps showing Noddy and Big Ears but to spend a little money to keep books by great writers in print. A smaller, poorer country than ours would do it. So should we.

Garfield knew what he was doing, and that's the rule I mean: have a sense of the kind of story you're telling, and then you'll know whether or not you're allowed to write that she can do magic. And part of this sense is a sense of what you yourself, as a storyteller, are good at. You'll discover, if you think about what you're doing, whether you're good at the funny stuff or the thrilling stuff or the six-handkerchief stuff. Cultivate your own abilities first, become certain of your command in one field, and then you can begin to extend your range.

Now here's a very important rule. It's so important I've written it on a piece of paper and stuck it above my desk. It says: 'Don't be afraid of the obvious.'

Because it's very tempting, once you've begun to tell stories seriously, to over-complicate. Part of the reason for this, I think, is the natural wish of everyone who aspires to be a good writer not to be mistaken for a bad one. You don't want them to think you're writing trash, so you try to avoid the stock situations, the stereotyped characters, the second-hand plot devices, all the obvious things that trashy books are full of. But the habit of resistance has to be supervised and kept in check. Your 'built-in, shockproof bullshit detector', as Hemingway called it, is a good servant but a bad master. It should warn, not decide. If you rely too much on it, your main concern will no longer be to tell a story but instead to make it perfectly clear that you're too exquisite and fastidious to be taken in by any trite, common little idea. One result of this wish to avoid the obvious is the sort of wincing mannered affectation that, for me, disfigures far too much fiction by people who are praised for how clever their fiction is: picking up your story with a pair of tongs, as I once put it. 'Oh dear, yes,' as E. M. Forster said: 'the novel tells a story.'

If I can briefly quote an example from my own work where I stopped myself from avoiding the obvious: in *Northern Lights* there's a bear. I knew from the start he would have to be even more formidable than a real polar bear, so he's an armoured bear, but I didn't know how formidable he'd be till he turned up and began to speak. And as soon as he did, the idea came: why not make him not just any bear but the king of the bears? And in exile? Because then I could have him fight to regain his throne. And Lyra the heroine could help, and that in turn would strengthen her own story – and so on.

And almost at once that voice at my shoulder said, 'No! Don't be silly. That's far too obvious. Everyone'll predict that. It's been done a hundred times. No – what you want is to give it a twist. Let him pretend to help her, but really let her down. Let him seem to be a brave bear, but in fact be a coward. Don't go for the obvious.'

But fortunately I know how to resist that voice now, and I looked at my piece of paper, and I did the obvious thing, and I think the story is better for it. The same impulse came to me with Lyra's parents: Lord Asriel and Mrs Coulter are her father and mother, but that's obvious, isn't it? Much cleverer to make her think they are and then reveal that they're not, or something. But I resisted that too. We shouldn't be afraid of the obvious, because stories are about life, and life is full of obvious things like food and sleep and love and courage which you don't stop needing just because you're a good reader.

There are many other rules, which I could spend a lot of time on, such as the one that says *Whatever doesn't add, subtracts*, and the one that says *The pluperfect is not the right tense to tell stories in*, and the three very interesting laws of the Quest: *the protagonist's task must be hard to do, it must be easy to understand, and a great deal must hang on the outcome*... But I'll just mention one more. It has to do with what I call 'the path through the wood', the line taken by the story through the world it exists in. And a path is a path *to*: it has a destination.

For every story has to have an ending. Sometimes you know what the ending is before you begin. Well and good. Sometimes you don't, and then you have to wander about through the events until you manage to see the natural destination. But once you know where it is, you must make for it, and then go back and clear the path and make sure that every twist and turn is there because you want it to be: because this one shows a better view of the landscape to come, or that one illustrates the fate of someone analogous to our protagonist, or another because it reveals a deep romantic chasm just at the moment when you need to introduce a note of sublimity… And all of them because they lead to the end. In other words you must design the path so that it leads to the destination most surely, and with the maximum effect.

And you mustn't fudge it when you get there. One of the best endings in modern children's fiction is the last page of Janni Howker's *The Nature of the Beast* (Julia MacRae, 1985). This marvellous book, to my mind the best picture of the 1980s we've yet seen in adults' or children's fiction, ends with young Bill Coward, his life in ruins, speaking these words:

> The Haverston Beast is dead. I saw him die. I wish he was still alive. I wish he'd come padding along High Street!
>
> The Haverston Beast is dead, or so they think.
>
> I'll not be there next Tuesday.
>
> I've got my air-rifle. I've packed a bag. If they want me, they'll have to come and get me. They'll have to hunt me down.
>
> Don't tell them, but I'm going up Hardale. The Haverston Beast is dead.
>
> They've not seen nothing yet.
>
> I'm going to take over where the Beast left off.
>
> They've not seen nothing yet!

The rhythm of that is outstanding in its power and effect. And what a perfect ending: this is the destination of the path which we have followed through every twist. Every single element in Bill's life, his grandfather's drinking, his father's violence, the closing of the mill, everything in the world he knows has combined to bring him to this point, armed, with red-hot hatred in his heart. This is the end. This is where the story had to come.

Well, enough about rules. I'm going to look now at what the other writer on the train said; you remember, partway through the story she said, 'I know! When we come to an exciting bit, let's write it in red!' (And I seemed to imagine a busy actor four hundred plus years ago scribbling away at something of his own behind the scenes while someone else's bombastic verse-drama occupies the stage. He dips his quill in the ink – a thought strikes him – 'Ah! When I come to a funny bit, I'll write it in prose!')

This is about form, and my colleague's perception that it's different from content, and that it's not arbitrary, it's expressive. It's not something tacked on at random. There was an ice-skating commentator a few years ago who used to amuse me because he would talk about Torvill and Dean, for instance, adding interpretation to their performance. But a good performance, of course, *is* interpretation. You can't have added interpretation – or if you do, it's false, it's an affectation. In the same way, if the form doesn't express the content, it's no use; it'll get in the way.

But there is a duality here which is important, and for which narratology has found many pairs of similarly opposed terms: substance and form, content and expression, story and discourse, *fabula* and *sjuzhet*, and so on. In short, there are the events, and there is what you tell about the events. There is the wood and there is the path. The making-up part is different from the writing-down part, but (let's write it in red) the writing-down part can express a great deal of the meaning.

Now a lot of the time, of course, making-up and writing-down happen more or less simultaneously. You think of an idea and it comes with the words already attached. I used to think that this was the entire process: that stories were literature, and literature was made out of language, and, in the approved style of the time, that there was nothing *de hors-texte*. But one day, when I was still a teacher, I invited a small theatre company who were performing in the city to come to my school for an afternoon and do a show. They were called *Théâtre de Complicité*, and they still are, but these days you wouldn't find them at Marston Middle School on a Thursday afternoon. What I saw that day astounded me, enslaved as I was to the idea that stories were made out of language. Because here was a complete story – funny, moving, frightening, absurd, thought-provoking – presented to an audience who could understand every nuance without a single word being uttered.

My reaction could best be expressed in cartoon form, with a think bubble containing only an exclamation mark.

To tell a story, I realised, you don't need words at all. There is a great deal *de hors-texte*. Stories aren't made of language: they're made of something else. A little earlier I said that stories were about life; perhaps they're made of life.

So now I do the making-up and the writing-down with more of a consciousness that there is a difference. I'm not sure that writers talk to one another enough about the making-up part, by the way. Some of the best conversation about it comes not from novelists but from film-makers. You can find examples of this in *Who the Devil Made It* edited by Peter Bogdanovich (Knopf 1997).

Here's one from Allan Dwan, who learned his trade in the silent days:

> Everything I did was triangles with me. If I constructed a
> story and it had four characters in it, I'd put them down as
> dots and if they didn't hook up into triangles, if any of them

were left dangling out there without a sufficient relationship to any of the rest, I knew I had to discard them because there'd be a distraction. And you're only related to people through triangles or lines. If I'm related to a third person and you're not, there's something wrong in our relationship together. One of us is dangling. So I say, 'How do I tie that person to you? How do I complete that line?'

Once you've noticed that, it's a useful principle. Whether you draw dots on a page or keep it in your head, or as I do use those little yellow Post-it stickers to move ideas and characters and scenes around on a big piece of paper till they're in the best order, some kind of diagrammatic abstract of the relationships in the story does help to clarify and strengthen it. In other words: I know! When we want to work out who's who, let's draw a picture.

And here's Fritz Lang in the same collection:

I honestly believe that any camera movement must have a reason. In my opinion, to move a camera just to move it is wrong: to make a 300-degree pan for no reason is a technical feat, but that's all. Camera movement must express something.

Form is expressive. In other words: if you've got nothing exciting to say, don't use the red pencil.

But content and expression, or substance and form, don't always come to you simultaneously, or in the same sequence. Sometimes one can suggest the other, and sometimes the other can suggest the one. I'm diffident about quoting my own work again, but I suppose, after all, you've asked me to give this lecture because my experience as a maker of stories might have given me something to say; so here goes.

It concerns my story *Clockwork, or All Wound Up* (Doubleday, 1996). The first notion I had of that was of... a thing like a piece of clockwork. I like looking at how things work. I stood in the Science Museum for a long time one day memorising all the connections in one of those big old iron clocks from a church tower, and I loved the way that *this* bit moving in *this* direction made *that* bit move in *that* direction. It didn't *mean* anything, because what a clock means is the time, and I wasn't looking at it to tell the time, after all. It was just technical.

And I thought, suppose I tried to tell a story like that – how might it work? If I had this bit folded inside that bit, and yet connected to this other bit somewhere else – how could I make them all join up? And how could I make them all move when the first bit moved?

That's how I started: just fitting the bits together. Purely formal. It didn't mean anything.

Only later, after several attempts, did I get the connections to work. And only then, when I saw the gears enmesh smoothly and this bit begin to turn that bit, did I see what it might mean. I realised I could use the story to say something about the inexorable nature of responsibility. If you have a child, you should look after him. If you make a promise, you should keep it. If you start a task, you should finish it. If you begin telling a story, and people are listening, you should take it to its end and not run out halfway through. (In *Clockwork*, my storyteller, Fritz, is irresponsible, because he thinks he can perform a story without rehearsing it. If he'd rehearsed it he'd never have had any trouble.)

So having seen the kind of idea the form of my tale could express, I was able to go back and help it do it. But the form came first. In other words: Look – here's a red pencil! What can I write in red?

To my mind, the most effective form is always that which displays the story most clearly.

Here's Howard Hawks, another film-maker:

The best thing to do is tell a story as though you're seeing it… Just tell it normally. Most of the time, my camera stays on eye level now. Once in a while, I'll move the camera as if a man were walking and seeing something. And it pulls back or it moves in for emphasis when you don't want to make a cut. But outside of that, I just use the simplest camera in the world.

Easy to say, and very hard to do. It throws much more emphasis on the making-up part, which is actually where the life is, than on the writing-down part. How nice it would be to tell the story in an unfamiliar way! How relaxing to spend one's time arranging *the camera angles*, and not have to wrestle with *the truth*!

I noticed something just the other day that had a bearing on this. I go to a life-drawing class once a week, where we sit in a circle with the model in the centre, and during the two-hour session she – usually a she – takes up half a dozen poses, so that each session you draw the figure from a number of different angles. And I am often pleased when I find myself confronted with an angle that's unfamiliar, for example if the model is lying with her head towards me so that I see only a head of hair and maybe the back of a hand, and beyond that some anonymous undulations that might be hips or shoulders or anything. I like drawing from an unusual perspective, and the other day it occurred to me why this was so: the reason is an ignoble one – it's simply that it's harder to tell from the finished drawing whether I've done it well or not. 'Gosh, how clever to draw her from that angle!' Not a bit of it: it's really, 'Gosh, how much easier to draw when no one can tell whether or not it's a poor drawing.'

So when the figure is standing or sitting, in full face or in profile, in what you might call a simple, classic pose, there's no doubt in the viewer's eye about whether or not you've got the knees in the right place, or whether the arms are too long: there's nowhere to hide them. And similarly, if a story is told from an unusual angle, or in something fancy like the second person, or with alternative openings and unclosed endings, or larded through and through with flashbacks and flash-forwards and flashbacks within flashbacks, then you can't see so easily that it's poorly constructed out of thin materials. Tell it plainly, and if it still stands up, it works. The real challenge for the draughtsman is the straightforward classical pose; the real challenge for the storyteller is the tale told simply.

In other words: if you can't draw (or write) with the lead pencil, you won't be able to draw with the red one.

(Of course. I'm not saying anything original here. Dr Johnson, quoting his college tutor: 'Read over your compositions, and where ever you meet with a passage which you think is particularly fine, strike it out.')

Now if the story is a path, then to follow it you have to ignore quite ruthlessly all the things that tempt you away from it. Your business as a storyteller is with the path, not the wood. But the wood is full of fascination, and it is so tempting to try and convey some of the richness of it, of all that phase space, by using a first-person stream of consciousness, or a number of differently situated narrators, and even more so by making those narrators unreliable, their knowledge partial, their different agendas out there conflicting in the text... So tempting. But *resist* it.

One small example of a temptation that I try to resist – as I have said elsewhere – is the present tense. I say *I* try to resist it: I know that many fine writers have written many admirable books in the present tense. But I can't make it work. As I've said before, the present tense is like those Venetian blinds that, instead of having horizontal slats, have vertical ones. I don't like being in a room that has those blinds because you can only look up and down. But life isn't vertical, life is horizontal. Friends and neighbours and cats and dogs and cars and the postman come along the road, not down from the sky. The present tense is like that: what it gives you is a vertical slice across a horizontal life. Use it sparingly. In other words: just because you have a red pencil, don't write everything in red.

Another formal discovery, a discovery about form that storytellers make is that you can sometimes leave things out and thereby create a stronger impression. There's a lovely parallel between Quentin Tarantino and Anthony Trollope that makes this very clear. One of Tarantino's most celebrated effects comes in the scene in *Reservoir Dogs* when Mr Blond, or Mr White (I can't remember his colour), cuts off the policeman's ear. We see the build-up – we know just what's coming – and then at the critical moment the camera swings away and very consciously shows us the wall, to swing back again when the deed is done.

Precisely the same effect (even down to the drawing attention to it) comes in *Barchester Towers*. Trollope has just shown us Bishop Proudie, urged on by Mr Slope, gathering up his courage to defy Mrs Proudie. But now comes the evening. Mr Slope isn't there to help him any more, and Mrs Proudie is in the bedroom, waiting to deal with the Bishop's ear, curiously enough.

> ... As the clock on the chimney piece warned him that the stilly hours of night were drawing on, as he looked at his chamber candlestick and knew that he must use it, his heart sank within him again... He took a couple of glasses of sherry, and mounted the stairs. Far be it from us to follow him thither. There are some things which no novelist, no historian, should attempt; some few scenes in life's drama which even no poet should dare to paint. Let that which passed between Dr Proudie and his wife on this night be understood to be among them.
>
> He came down the following morning a sad and thoughtful man. He was attenuated in appearance; one might almost say emaciated... At any rate he had aged materially.

Reservoir Clerics, perhaps? In other words: sometimes a scene will be even redder if we use no pencil at all.

There are plenty more things to be said about the red pencil, but I want to move on to my third principle of storytelling. This is the one I said was implicit in what the girls on the train were doing in the first place. I mean *knowledge*. They thought there were things to know about storytelling, that it was an activity which was discussable, learn-able, practisable – if such a word exists. That's what I think too.

But they were very young, and I don't think that they had yet become sophisticated enough for the knowledge they were acquiring to trip them up. There's an analogy here between our sort of activity and what I take to be the central myth of Judaeo-Christian culture, the story of Adam and Eve and the Fall in Chapter 3 of Genesis. In his extraordinary essay of 1810, *On the Marionette Theatre*, Heinrich von Kleist reveals this analogy in a brilliant light by means of his comments on puppets and dance.

In brief, he points out that the first consequence of knowledge is self-consciousness. The puppet is not self-conscious in the least, and that allows it to dance with perfect freedom and grace. A puppet can never be guilty of affectation, because affectation appears when the soul, or moving force, appears at some point other than the centre of gravity of the movement. The human dancer, on the other hand, is plagued by self-consciousness:

> Just look at that girl who dances Daphne. Pursued by Apollo, she turns to look at him. At this moment her soul appears to be in the small of her back. As she bends she looks as if she's going to break… Or take that young fellow who dances Paris when he's standing among the three goddesses and offering the apple to Venus. His soul is in fact located (and it's a frightful thing to see) in his elbow.

When you become self-conscious about the act of storytelling, it's very easy for your soul to wander into your elbow, so to speak. But the way to become unself-conscious again is not to try and go backwards into innocence (the way is barred by an angel with a fiery sword) but to become more interested in your subject-matter than in the way you appear to others to be dealing with it. And there's so much to be interested *in*.

For example, there's the fascinating business of such devices as surprise. It really does help to know that surprise is the precise opposite of suspense, for example. Surprise is when something happens that you don't expect: suspense is when something doesn't happen that you do expect. Surprise is when you open a cupboard and a body falls out. Suspense is when you know there's a body in the cupboard – but not which cupboard. So you open the first door and… no, not that one. And up goes the suspense a notch.

And then there's the matter of variation. Given a theme, what variations are possible on it? The pianist and critic Charles Rosen, in a review of *Bach and the Patterns of Invention* (1996) by Laurence Dreyfus, has some very interesting things to say about this.

> Several of [Bach's] contemporaries testified to his ability, when given two different themes, to see at once all the different ways that they could be played together, with all the possible contrapuntal combinations. He knew immediately what could be done with a single theme: his son, Carl Philipp Emmanuel, showed him a fugue he had been writing and asked if any other variations were possible; after a moment's glance, he replied firmly, 'None.'

That sort of knowledge is what we (and by *we* I mean not just writers but editors and critics and teachers too) should aim at in our understanding of storytelling. Given the bare notion of one particular character in relation to another (or to two others in the form of a triangle), we ought to be able to look at them and see all the implications and possibilities and outcomes. This little thicket of relationships grows into the wood through which we must trace the path of our story.

But it helps immensely to see what can grow from what. A simple example: does the female protagonist whose dim outline we can see in our mind's eye have the silhouette of Little Red Riding Hood or Cinderella? Because Little Red Riding Hood's phase space is quite different from Cinderella's. And if Cinderella, then which variation? The sweet and put-upon Two-Eyes, from the story 'One-Eye, Two-Eyes, and Three-Eyes', or the cool and sassy Mossycoat?

Then there's the matter of the making-up part itself.

Charles Rosen again:

> 'Invention' was a key word for Bach, as it was for many con-temporary German musicians. What was most important for a young student to learn, Bach himself insisted, was how to have 'good inventions'. The word is sometimes taken to mean the initial theme, motif, or melody, but Dreyfus shows that a much larger sense must be assumed. 'Invention' in a fugue covers not merely the opening motif, but also all the interesting things that can be done with it: Can it be inverted (with all the intervals that went up now going down and vice versa), augmented (played twice as slow), diminished (twice as fast), and played in *stretto* (where a second voice plays the theme before the first voice has finished, so that the theme is performed by two or more voices but out of phase)? Can it be played in *stretto* in its original and inverted forms together? Can the augmented form be played in *stretto* with the original one? 'Good inventions' means, of course, that all of this must be done

while producing a beautiful harmony, and without infring-
ing the simple rules of counterpoint. 'Invention' is what
makes the fugue interesting. Dreyfus, following some eighteenth-century writers on music, distinguishes invention
from decoration and disposition (or ordering): they make
the work agreeable and acceptable – the fascination must
come from the invention.

As I've been saying.

So part of the knowledge I'm arguing for is a knowledge of stories.
I have been lucky: I was able to earn a living as a teacher here in Britain
before the National Curriculum sifted into the land like the Red Death
in the Edgar Allan Poe story. No Key Stage or Component or Unit
prevented me from telling my class the stories I wanted to tell. I was able
to tell and learn and get to know dozens and dozens of myths and folk
tales. It was the making of me as a storyteller. (I don't know where the
next generation of children's authors is going to come from, by the way,
but I predict that they won't come out of the ranks of the teachers. Young
teachers today have too many other stupid things to do to have time or
energy left at the end of the day to sit down and write, and the National
Curriculum forbids them to do what I used to do, and simply tell stories
for the love of it when they want to.)

We need to know stories, dozens of them. The best source, of
course, is myth and folk tale. Such anthologies as those of Kevin
Crossley-Holland, Alan Garner, and Neil Philip should be treated in
two ways: firstly, they should be bound in gold and brought out on
ceremonial occasions as national treasures; and secondly, they should be
printed at the public expense in the hundreds of thousands and given
away free to every young teacher.

We need to keep those old stories burnished and bright and new by
telling them over and over again, and if we do we'll find that curiously

enough we never get tired of them. Tell them to children. Tell them to friends. If you haven't got any friends, go for a long walk and tell them to the dog. Don't *read* them: get them in your head and tell them. Ted Hughes is advising us now to learn poems: excellent idea. Well, we can learn stories too.

I've stressed the importance of the making-up part, but we need to know a good deal about the writing-down part as well.

Fritz Lang again:

> You have to tell a story with the camera. Therefore, you have to *know* the camera and what you can make the camera do. You have to know the instruments with which you tell the story.

The instrument for those of us who tell stories in books is language. I've said stories aren't made only of language, but those of us who do use it should know it as well as we can. And we should look after it. The world out there is careless with language.

Take the word they use in Britain now on the railways for people like us: they call us customers. They do this in order to stress the commercial nature of the transaction, and disguise any other. But when you pay money to a hotel, they call you a guest. When you pay money to a lawyer, he calls you a client. When I pay money to my dentist she calls me a patient. It isn't difficult to use these words, and we all understand them; and it was never difficult to understand that when you paid to go on the railway, you were a passenger. To obliterate that word, to use a vaguer word for an ideological purpose, is to try and turn the richness of the living language into a monoculture.

We can't stop them doing it, but we can stop ourselves. My favourite image for language itself is a great forest: it's a living thing, and it's bigger than we are, and we're born into the middle of it and we gradually get to know more and more about it as we grow ourselves. It provides us with shelter and food and pleasure. (The forest is the phase space of all we can possibly say.) But parts of it are being burned down, and other parts are struggling to find light and nourishment, and the terrible thing is that now we're conscious, the nature of the forest itself has changed.

As Wallace Stevens puts it in the poem 'Narrative of the Jar':

> I placed a jar in Tennessee,
> And round it was, upon a hill.
> It made the slovenly wilderness
> Surround that hill.

The presence of the jar – of art, of consciousness – changes the nature of the wilderness. In the poet's words, 'It took dominion everywhere.' We can't pretend to be innocent in the face of language, any more than in the face of knowledge of any sort: we are conscious, and so we are responsible. Whether we like it or not, the forest of language is not wild virgin forest any more; it's being managed, and some of it is being managed badly.

And we're responsible, we the story people, the poetry people, the book people. In our parts of the forest, we are in charge. There's no one else who'll clear out the dead undergrowth of cliché, or provide a habitat for a rich variety of living words and expressions, and make sure no single plant or creature drives out all the others in a monoculture where everyone is a customer and no one can be anything else, if we don't.

Anyway, I'm going to end with a confession, as I promised, but it's not the sort that would interest the *News of the World*, I'm afraid.

I go into schools occasionally to talk to children about my work. And when I do, I try to bear in mind that my mission is to inform and educate and enlighten. But in truth that's a secondary motive. My primary motive is the one I mentioned earlier, namely Scheherazade's: I want to stop them from killing me. And I use her method.

So I tell them a story about telling stories. And as with any other story, this one has to begin at the right point and take in some interesting views and last about fifty minutes. It has to be shaped, in other words. Consequently, there are things I don't tell them about, such as the brutal nature of the toil, and the boredom that occupies much of the time, and the savage melancholy that comes after the end of a book, and the financial calculations that sometimes determine whether you can write this book or that one, and so on. What I tell them, in short, isn't fully true in a law-court sense. It's a story. Other writers, I'm sure, will know just what I mean.

And in telling you this story tonight I've done something similar. So now I'm going to come clean and tell the law-court truth. This narrator is going to become reliable. Those little girls on the train: well, they did almost everything I said they did. They did write a story, and the first one did say, 'Are we allowed to write that she can do magic?'

But the second little girl didn't say, 'Let's write it in red.' What she actually said was, 'Let's write it in blue.' They didn't have a red pencil.

However, when I was thinking about it afterwards, I did a bit of editing. Blue makes the point, but red makes it better; red is a better story. And now this story – red, blue, black and white – has come to the end, and I hope we all live happily ever after.

This talk was delivered as the Patrick Hardy Lecture at a meeting of the Children's Book Circle on 3 November 1997 at the English-Speaking Union in London, and later appeared in *Signal* no. 85, January 1998.

The News of the World *no longer exists. How nice to realise that even the most offensive things will eventually require a footnote to explain what they were.*

Epics

BIG STORIES ABOUT BIG THINGS

On the style, purpose, value and figures of epic literature

ABOVE ALL, AN EPIC IS BIG. IT'S ABOUT BIG THINGS – DEATH, COURAGE, honour, war, shame, vengeance. It's about large and public matters – the fate of a nation, the return of a king, the success of an army, the origin of a people. Its protagonists are larger than human beings, and perhaps simpler too: they are heroes. The preservation of an epic is a matter not of private dilettantism, but of national importance. It is less precious than literature, but more valuable.

An epic is independent of the identity of its author. Oh, someone eventually transcribes the often-told tale, sometimes in a highly wrought style, sometimes as a masterpiece of poetry, sometimes in a rough and clumsy version full of repetitions or jumbled with contradictions or riddled with gaps; and sometimes there's a name attached to it, and sometimes that name is like Homer, meaningless, because who composed the *Iliad*? Homer. Who was Homer? He who composed the *Iliad*. Perhaps. And sometimes there's no name at all: *Gilgamesh* does not even have a Homer.

These days, the author is everything: the book tours, the media profiles, the online interviews, the literary festivals, the signing sessions, the panel discussions promoted by cultural organisations – they could all take place just as happily in the absence of the literary work altogether, because the author as celebrity is all that matters. But with a great tale of the epic kind, all we need to do is accept the work of the scribe with gratitude, and edit the scattered remains as well as we can; and the absence of an author and all the attendant personal appearances and lifestyle features and PR ballyhoo is wonderfully clarifying, like the wind from the desert that smells of nothing.

Perhaps the epic is in some ways the very opposite of the novel, which began on the page and which really came into its own in the era of printing, as a domestic romance that was enjoyed most happily in solitude and in silence. The oldest epics have something of the declamatory about them: they are more suitably experienced through the ear, perhaps, and in company, than through the eye and in private. Like the theatre, the epic is an arena for the hero. Great heroes are uncomfortable in the novel, whose point of view is too close, too familiar, whose lens has exactly the right focal length to pick up the little flaws, the 'spots of commonness', in George Eliot's famous phrase. No man is a hero to his novelist. An epic hero has flaws, to be sure, but they are not on a domestic scale. To see heroes in the frame that best fits the greatness of their nature and their actions, we need to be at some distance from them.

Epic heroes, in fact, seem to be at some distance from themselves. This realisation lies behind the crazy and yet tantalisingly rich idea of Julian Jaynes, whose book *The Origin of Consciousness in the Breakdown of the Bicameral Mind* (Allen Lane, 1976) puts forward the bizarre suggestion that human beings only became conscious in the modern sense during the past 4,000 years; that until then, they heard the promptings of conscience, or temptation, or inspiration, as the voices of gods, coming apparently from elsewhere, with no sense that their own minds were responsible. He instances Achilles in the *Iliad*, experiencing his own reluctance to strike Agamemnon as the goddess Athena seizing his golden hair and pulling him back.

Similarly Jane Smiley, in talking of the Icelandic sagas, points out that:

> ... they seem far removed from modern literary subjectivity,
> and yet, the gossip and the comments of other characters

supply a practical and readily understandable psychological context. Characters speak up, they say what they want and what their intentions are. Other characters disagree with them and judge them. The saga writer sometimes remarks upon public opinion concerning them. The result is that the sagas are psychologically complex and yet economical in their analysis.

(*Jane Smiley, introduction to* The Sagas of Icelanders, *Viking, 2000*).

The human interactions in epic stories are out in the open, where all can see them, with the fresh air blowing through them; there is nothing enclosed, nothing stale, nothing stuffy.

Finally, the epic vision is a tragic one. Jasper Griffin, discussing a translation of *Gilgamesh* in *The New York Review of Books*, remarked, 'There is no happy ending, even for mighty heroes who are close to the gods... This is the true epic vision... An older wisdom, and a truer poetry, sees that the highest nobility and the deepest truth are inseparable, in the end, from failure – however heroic – from defeat, and from death.' (*NYRB*, 9 March, 2006).

So Beowulf dies in the moment of his triumph against the dragon, and King Arthur and his knights of the Round Table go down to defeat in their final battle, and as Hjalti says in *Sagas and Myths of the Norsemen* in this collection, 'It is not possible to bend fate, nor can one stand against nature.' Odysseus, safely returned home at last after his twenty years of battle and wandering, will not stay in his cleansed and peaceful palace for good; a time will come when he'll want to move on yet again, though he knows that, as Tennyson has him say, 'Death closes all.' And even Sindbad, that peerless traveller in the realms of wonder, has to succumb in the end, when 'there came to him the Spoiler of worldly mansions, the Dark Steward of the graveyard; the Shadow which dissolves the bonds of friendship and ends alike all joys and all sorrows.'

The epic is not a place where anyone lives happily ever after; it obeys a mightier realism than that.

First published as an introduction to a box set of twenty epics by Penguin Books, 2006.

Folk Tales of Britain

STREAMS OF STORIES DOWN THROUGH THE YEARS

On Katharine M. Briggs's great three-volume collection of British folk tales, and the tradition of oral storytelling in the British Isles

FOLK TALES OF BRITAIN IS ONE OF THE GREAT BOOKS OF THE COUNTRY. Every nation needs its own collection of folk tales, and this is the fullest and the most authoritative we have. To open it anywhere is to sink a shaft into the memory of a people and all that they know, from sheep-shit to sputniks, from wicked uncles to clever tailors, from a Professor of Signs to a secret agent in Wales. Katharine M. Briggs, who gathered these marvels together, should have a statue in every town square in Britain, but alas: we in Britain are no longer sure of who we are or what we should remember, and her name is too little known. Perhaps this edition of her great work will remind us.

Katharine Briggs was born in 1898 into a mine-owning family whose wealth meant that she never had to earn a living, and was free to devote herself to learning. She studied at Oxford, gaining a BA in 1922, and being awarded a doctorate for a thesis on folklore in seventeenth-century literature. Folklore was a lifelong interest: her father, an amateur artist and folklorist, had sparked her enthusiasm for it by telling tales to her and her sisters. They had a passionate interest in amateur dramatics too, and writing and producing plays became a lifelong activity. In later life Katharine Briggs devoted her scholarly attention entirely to folklore, going on to become President of the Folklore Society, which honours her memory with an annual prize. She died in 1980.

Her knowledge of the subject was profound, and of the sort that seems to be carried as lightly as a sack of thistledown. Her book on *The Fairies in Tradition and Literature* has the air of personal acquaintance as well as deep scholarship, and her *Dictionary of Fairies* is the last word on the subject. She also wrote two novels for children, *Hobberdy Dick* and *Kate Crackernuts*, which take their subjects from folklore but locate the events in a realistic historical background, and above all relish the telling of a story.

And *story* is what we're given in full measure in this book. The collection in these volumes is grouped roughly into five sections, but within those fairly loose and accommodating divisions, the stories are arranged according to the system used by Ted Hughes and Seamus Heaney in their great anthology *The Rattle Bag*: in alphabetical order of title. This is a very good system, because it ensures a democratic arbitrariness. You never know what'll come next.

It also means you can open the books at random, as if performing the *sortes Virgilianae*, the old custom of bibliomancy, and read whatever you come to. That's the method I myself prefer; there is no doubt, for example, that reading the final section consisting of Jocular Tales from beginning to end quite soon induces a mood that is far from jocular. On the other hand, a random search produces the story of 'Old John and Young John', a sturdy old yarn that has done duty in ancient Rome, in Germany, in China, in Ireland, and no doubt in many other countries besides, and in the context of 'high' literature as well as 'low' folk tale. And that in turn reminds us that every tale has a rich and complex history, and some tales have travelled very far from wherever their land of origin was.

And just looking at this tale and its surroundings we can see the depth of scholarship that Briggs brought to her massive work. The notes tell us where she found it, and that it's a tale of Type 1510, which we can look up in the Index of Tale-Types in the first volume (did we know there were that many tale-types? I didn't) and that it contains two motifs, which are given formidable-looking numbers. The numbers refer to the entries in a truly fascinating work called *Motif-Index of Folk-Literature: a Classification of Narrative Elements in Folktales, Ballads, Myths, Fables, Mediaeval Romances, Exempla, Fabliaux, Jest-Books and Local Legends*. This is the expansion and development, by the American Stith Thompson in 1955–8, of a list first drawn up by the Finnish folklorist Antti Aarne in 1910. A massive work in six dense volumes, it contains every imaginable motif or tale-element, all ranked in order with the most scrupulous care and attention. It's now available in its entirety online. (If *Folk Tales of Britain* is like Ali Baba's cave filled with treasures, the Aarne-Thompson *Index* is rather like the same cave after the robbers had found poor Cassim there and hung his body up in several pieces).

Will we need to look at all this apparatus of notes every time we read a story? Of course not. Most of us will skip over the notes without a second glance. But what excellent book-making, to put the notes right there at the end of the story and not tucked away out of sight hundreds of pages away at the back of the book! Then, if we want them, there they are at once.

And the principle of serendipity can come into play, and our eyes can be caught by the notes for the tale that comes before 'Old John and Young John'. That tale, 'The Old Farmer and his Wives', was taken down from the telling of someone called Eva Gray in 1915, and Katharine Briggs is rather severe about it. 'This tale was made up by Eva Gray,' she says. 'The second half does not match the first in mood or plot.' She's right; it's a rotten story. Not a patch on 'Old John and Young John'. Nevertheless, there it is, and poor Eva Gray has her moment of immortality, if only as an example of how not to tell a story.

However, the same Eva Gray turns up elsewhere in the collection, and redeems herself entirely with a tale that goes under the magnificent title of 'The Cellar of Blood'. Who could resist that? The tale is told in note form, more or less, as if the transcriber had trouble keeping up with Eva Gray's hectic imaginings. At a particularly dramatic point occurs the passage 'Rang up Scotland Yard. Detectives came disguised as farmers. Girl disguised as young man. All to tell their dreams. Girl last.'

That story was collected in 1914. It's interesting to see Scotland Yard appearing in a tale of the ancient and widespread Robber Bridegroom type; no doubt Eva Gray's imagination had been fed by penny dreadfuls and other popular literature, and this example shows how folk tales develop naturally from whatever streams of story flow around them.

One thing that strikes the reader-at-random quite soon is the wide variety of voices in the book. Some tales were transcribed exactly as they were told, dialect and all, with interpolated clarifications:

> There wiz aince a man traivllin in a hill, and he gede will [lost his way], an he gede an he gede [went] till he saw a bonnie clear lichtie, and he gede till he cam till't.
>
> ('The Lion, the Leper and the Tod').

> Wonce when I was sittin' i'front o' th' Pywipe, doon by river at Lincoln, a man cum'd up wi' won o' them theare barges an' sets hissen' doon, an' efter a bit we gets to talkin', an' has a pot o' beer together.
>
> ('Th' Lad 'at Went Oot to Look fer Fools').

The transcriptions are meticulous and scholarly, and the tales recorded in this way preserve dialect forms and words that might otherwise have no record at all.

But there's no denying that some of them are difficult to read. I find the way to engage with them is to get them into my mouth, and take them slowly. They belong in the mouth and the ear as well as the eye, and to read a splendid tale like 'De Little Fox' without the use of the vocal nerves and muscles is to make it more difficult than it need be. No one need be ashamed to be caught reading this book while moving their lips:

it's sometimes the best way to do it.

And these tales are, after all, performances. Katharine Briggs herself was a fine storyteller, and I envy those who had the chance to hear her. Margaret Hodges, in the journal *Children's Literature in Education*, tells of 'her sense of fun, her wit, her histrionic ability and the remarkable memory that made her a brilliant exponent of the almost lost art of storytelling… My first memory of Katharine goes back to the Domus Academicus in Helsinki at the 1974 meeting of the International Folk-lore Congress. I sat at the very back of the big auditorium, but her voice, low and beautifully modulated, trained by early experience in the theatre, reached us all with full impact.'

She goes on to describe how Briggs told the tale 'Kate Crackernuts', ending with the words: 'And they lived happy and died happy, and never drank from a dry cappie.' Then she added a personal note: 'This homely rhyme at the end sums up the traditional earthy quality of the whole tale, with the little kingdom where the Queen consorts with the henwife and the Princess is sent out to ask for eggs… and above all with its wild, true, loving little heroine.' (Margaret Hodges, *Children's Literature in Education*, December 1981).

Some of the tales here read like notes that an experienced storyteller would use as the basis of a new performance, full of improvised detail and flourishes. Such a one is 'Fairest of all Others', taken down from the telling of Taimi Boswell, a gypsy, in 1915. It's a strange little tale – only a paragraph in this version – involving such familiar motifs as a heroine cast away to sea in a box and a ring thrown into the sea which returns inside a fish, but it's easy to see how good storytellers would build on this skeleton, cover it with living flesh, and make it their own.

As it happens, we have a good example of this sort of imaginative detail-building from Taimi Boswell in person, in one of the finest of all folk tales, the great 'Mossycoat'. This transcription is a miracle of re-creation: it lets us hear the very voice of Taimi Boswell, phrase by

melodious phrase, playing over the skeleton of the events as a jazz musician – an Art Tatum, a Charlie Parker, a Coleman Hawkins – impro-
vises over the sequence of chords in a song, stepping lightly, seeming
to spin away so far that they lose touch with the structure altogether,
only to land with total precision on the right note which is also the
least expected one, and the one that makes us laugh with delight. So
here, when Mossycoat turns out to be the one girl whose foot fits the
slipper (yes, it's a variant of 'Cinderella'), and the young master, who's
been sick with love for the beautiful girl at the ball, reaches to take her
in his arms –

> 'Stop', she says, and runs off; but afore long, she's back agen
> in her satin dress wid gowld sprigs, her gowld crown, and
> both her silver slippers.
>
> De young master is jus' a-going to tek her in his arms.
> 'Stop,' she says, and agen she runs off. Dis time she comes
> back in her silk dress de colour of all de birds o' de air. She
> don't stop him dis time, and as de saying used to be, he
> nearly eats her.

Taimi Boswell was clearly a marvellously funny and inventive storyteller, and this version of the tale is a classic, just as much as Coleman
Hawkins's 'Body and Soul', and for some of the same reasons. A mastery
of *timing*, whether it's that indefinable essence of rhythm called swing or
the placing of a joke, is common to both storytellers and jazz players, and
in Taimi Boswell's 'Mossycoat' we can see another example of brilliant
timing in the delicate way we switch between past tense for the quiet
background passages:

> So it was settled as she was to be under-cook. And after
> when de lady'd showed her up to her bedroom, she took her

to the kitchen and interdoosed her to de t'other sarvants.
and present tense for the vivid moments of drama:

> She's in de ballroom now, Mossycoat is. De young master
> bin waiting and watching for her. As soon as he sees her, he
> exes his father to send for de fastest horse in his stable...

The switch of tenses feels natural and unforced, almost impalpable, as if the story just grew like that. In fact, it's great craftsmanship. Those present-day novelists who limit their narratives to the present tense have a lot to learn from an artist like Taimi Boswell.

'Mossycoat' has been a favourite of many subsequent folk tale editors – Alan Garner and Kevin Crossley-Holland have both included it in their excellent collections – and I've had a go at it myself. But this is the gold standard.

Another great storyteller is more familiar: Charles Dickens tells the shocking tale of 'Captain Murderer' (another of those superb penny-dreadful titles) with all the relish we might expect. Apparently he had a nursemaid who terrified him with this story when he was a child. It might have been the same nursemaid who gave him the tale of 'Chips and the Devil', a rare example of a story in which the Devil comes out on top. I'm sorry for the young Dickens; being scared when you're young is not a nice experience; but good for the nursemaid, say I. Are children still told stories that frighten them, or do they watch horror DVDs instead?

A good tense creepy tale for telling aloud is 'The Robbers and the Housekeeper'. If I were teaching a course in storytelling I'd get my students to study this example, because for most of the story it's full of tension and drama, but for some reason it falls a little flat at the end. What's gone wrong? And can we mend it?

Because we are allowed to make changes and improvements when we tell stories. In fact – and this is very important to remember – we *have* to if we want them to live. Italo Calvino, in the introduction to his great collection *Italian Folk Tales*, quotes an old Tuscan proverb: 'The story is not beautiful unless something is added to it.' We all have our own way of telling stories, and our own strengths and weaknesses; some of us can make our listeners laugh, while others can make them shudder, and others again can bring them to tears, and the best of us can do all three. But we do it by making the stories our own – by adding, taking away, twisting, decorating, bringing up to date. The printed version is a starting point, not a destination.

I began by saying that this was one of the great books of Britain, and I meant Britain and not just England. And I'm writing at a time when there is a lot of confusion about national identity: is being Scottish different now that there's a parliament in Edinburgh? Can you be seen as English if your skin is black, or do you have to say you're British? And what connection can a Muslim child born and living in inner-city Birmingham feel with these stories about boys called Jack and farmers going home drunk from a fair?

The only thing that has preserved these tales for us is dedicated scholarship and profound knowledge, and we should celebrate that and praise the name of Katharine Briggs and every collector who sat by the side of a storyteller or painstakingly transcribed a tape recording.

But being put in a book has its drawbacks. It gives a fixed quality to things. It seems to imply that all that scholarship and learning should be respected in the way we respect ancient monuments, by preserving them exactly as they are, by walking around them carefully and speaking quietly and not disturbing anything. It seems to imply that nothing should change.

And that is the greatest danger for stories such as these: if they remain undisturbed, they will die of neglect. They should be taken out and made to dance. A superb example of the sort of thing I mean is Benjamin Zephaniah's dub poetry version of the strange old tale 'Tam Lin', set in a world of clubs and DJs and sex in the back of a car and immigrants without official papers. It makes something new out of something old, and the old is still there beside the new, to inspire another telling another day.

In short, this book is a treasure-house, the greatest source we have in our language for these funny, coarse, uncanny, beautiful, earthy, tender, cruel, shrewd and mysterious old stories. But treasure should not be hoarded. This is for spending. And the strangest thing of all about this sort of treasure is that the more you give away, the more you have left.

THIS ESSAY WAS ORIGINALLY PUBLISHED AS THE FOREWORD TO *FOLK TALES OF BRITAIN: NARRATIVES I, II AND III* (EDITED BY KATHARINE M. BRIGGS, FOLIO SOCIETY, 2011).

The task of writing this piece and the next were the most enjoyable commissions I ever had.

As Clear as Water

MAKING A NEW VERSION OF THE BROTHERS GRIMM

On the brothers, their collection of tales,
and the nature of folk tales in general

> Fed
> Up so long and variously by
> Our age's fancy narrative concoctions,
> I yearned for the kind of unseasoned telling found
> In legends, fairy tales, a tone licked clean
> Over the centuries by mild old tongues,
> Grandam to cub, serene, anonymous.
> ... So my narrative
> Wanted to be limpid, unfragmented;
> My characters, conventional stock figures
> Afflicted to a minimal degree
> With personality and past experience –
> A witch, a hermit, innocent young lovers,
> The kinds of being we recall from Grimm,
> Jung, Verdi, and the commedia dell'arte.

So writes the American poet James Merrill at the opening of 'The Book of Ephraim', the first part of his extraordinary long poem *The Changing Light at Sandover* (1982). Discussing the way in which he hopes to tell a story of his own, he singles out two of the most important characteristics of the fairy tale, as he sees it: the 'serene, anonymous' voice in which it's told, and the 'conventional, stock figures' who inhabit it.

When Merrill mentions 'Grimm', he needs to say no more: we all know what he means. For most western readers and writers in the past two hundred years, the *Kinder- und Hausmärchen* (*Children's and Household Tales*) of the Brothers Grimm has been the fountain and origin of the western fairy tale, the greatest collection, the most widely distributed in the largest number of languages, the home of all we feel to be unique in that kind of story.

But if the Grimm brothers hadn't collected all those tales, no doubt someone else would have done. Others were already doing something similar, in fact. The early nineteenth century was a time of great intellectual excitement in Germany, a time when scholars of law, of history, of language were examining and arguing about what it meant to be German in the first place, when there was no Germany as such but instead three hundred or so independent states – kingdoms, principalities, grand duchies, duchies, landgraviates, margraviates, electorates, bishoprics and so on, the fragmented detritus of the Holy Roman empire.

The facts of the Grimm brothers' lives are not remarkable. Jacob (1785–1863) and Wilhelm (1786–1859) were the eldest surviving sons of Philipp Wilhelm Grimm, a prosperous lawyer of Hanau in the principality of Hesse, and his wife Dorothea. They received a classical education and were brought up in the Reformed Calvinist Church. Clever, diligent and serious-minded, they aimed to follow their father into the legal profession, in which they would no doubt have distinguished themselves; but his sudden death in 1796 meant that the family, which now included six children, had to depend on the support of their mother's relatives. Their aunt, Henriette Zimmer, a lady-in-waiting at the prince's court in Kassel, helped Jacob and Wilhelm to find places at the *Lyzeum* or high school, where they each graduated at the head of their class. But there was little money, and when they attended the University of Marburg they had to live very frugally.

At Marburg they fell under the influence of Professor Friedrich Carl von Savigny, whose idea that law grew naturally out of the language and history of a people and should not be arbitrarily applied from above turned the Grimms to the study of philology. Through von Savigny and his wife Kunigunde Brentano, they also made the acquaintance of the circle around her brother Clemens Brentano and Achim von Arnim, who married Brentano's other sister, the writer Bettina. One of the preoccupations of this group was German folklore. Their enthusiasm for this subject resulted in von Arnim and Brentano's *Des Knaben Wunderhorn* (*The Youth's Magic Horn*), a collection of folk songs and folk poetry of all kinds, the first volume of which appeared in 1805 and immediately became popular.

The Grimm brothers were naturally interested in this, but not uncritically: Jacob wrote in a letter to Wilhelm in May 1809 of his disapproval of the way in which Brentano and Von Arnim had treated their material, cutting and adding and modernising and rewriting as they thought fit. Later, the Grimms (and Wilhelm in particular) would be criticised on much the same grounds for the way they treated their source material for the *Kinder- und Hausmärchen*.

At all events, the decision by the Grimm brothers to collect and publish fairy tales was not an isolated phenomenon, but part of a widespread preoccupation of the time.

The sources they depended on were both oral and literary. Some of their tales were taken directly from literary sources; two of the finest, 'The Fisherman and His Wife' and 'The Juniper Tree', were sent to them in written form by the painter Philipp Otto Runge, and reproduced by the Grimms in the Low German dialect Runge wrote them in. Much of the rest came in oral form from people at various levels of the middle class, including family friends, one of whom – Dortchen Wild, the daughter of a pharmacist – Wilhelm Grimm eventually married. After two hundred years, it's impossible to say how exact their transcriptions were, but the same is true of any collection of folk tales or songs before the age of tape recording. What matters is the vigour and zest of the versions they published.

The Grimm brothers went on to make great and lasting contributions to philology. Grimm's Law, formulated by Jacob, describes certain sound-changes in the history of Germanic languages; and the brothers together worked on the first great German dictionary. In 1837 came what was probably the most dramatic incident in their lives; together with five other university colleagues, they refused to take an oath of allegiance to the new king of Hanover, Ernst August, because he had illegally dissolved the constitution. As a result they were dismissed from their university posts, and had to take up appointments at the University of Berlin.

But it was the *Kinder- und Hausmärchen* for which their names are mostly remembered. Their first edition was published in 1812, and the collection went through six further editions (Wilhelm, by this stage, doing most of the editorial work) till the seventh and final one of 1857, by which time it was immensely popular. It shares its eminence with *The Arabian Nights*: the two of them are the most important and influential collections of folk tales ever published. Not only did the collection grow bigger, the tales themselves changed as the nineteenth century went past, becoming in Wilhelm's hands a little longer, in some cases more elaborate, occasionally more prudish, certainly more pious than they were to begin with.

Scholars of literature and folklore, of cultural and political history, theorists of a Freudian, Jungian, Christian, Marxist, structuralist, post-structuralist, feminist, postmodernist and every other kind of tendency have found immense riches for study in these 210 tales. But my interest has always been in how the tales worked *as stories*. So I decided to retell the best and most interesting of them, clearing out of the way anything that would prevent them from running freely. I didn't want to put them in modern settings, or produce personal interpretations, or compose poetic variations on the originals; I just wanted to produce a version that was as clear as water. My guiding question has been: 'How would I tell this story myself, if I'd heard it told by someone else and wanted to pass it on?'

There is no psychology in a fairy tale. The characters have little interior life; their motives are clear and obvious. If people are good, they are good, and if bad, they're bad. Even when the princess in 'The Three Snake Leaves' inexplicably and ungratefully turns against her husband, we know about it from the moment it happens. Nothing of that sort is concealed. The tremors and mysteries of human awareness, the whispers of memory, the promptings of half-understood regret or doubt or desire that are so much part of the subject matter of the modern novel are absent entirely. One might almost say that the characters in a fairy tale are not actually conscious.

They seldom have names of their own. More often than not they're known by their occupation or their social position, or by a quirk of their dress: the miller, the princess, the captain, Bearskin, Little Red Riding Hood. When they do have a name it's usually Hans, just as Jack is the hero of every British fairy tale.

The most fitting pictorial representation of fairy-tale characters seems to me to be found not in any of the beautifully illustrated editions of Grimm that have been published over the years, but in the little cardboard cut-out figures that come with a toy theatre. They are flat, not round. Only one side of them is visible to the audience, but that is the only side we need – the other side is blank. They are depicted in poses of intense activity or passion, so that their part in the drama can be easily read from a distance.

Some of the characters in fairy tales come in sets of multiples. The twelve brothers in the story of that name, the twelve princesses in 'The Shoes that were Danced to Pieces', the seven dwarfs in the story of 'Snow White' – there is little, if anything, to distinguish one from another. James Merrill's reference to the *commedia dell'arte* is apposite here: the *commedia* character Pulcinella was the subject of a famous set of drawings by Giandomenico Tiepolo (1727–1804), depicting him not as a single character but as a swarm of identical nitwits. In one drawing there may be a dozen or more Pulcinellas all trying to make soup at the same time, or gazing in astonishment at an ostrich. Realism cannot cope with the notion of multiples; the twelve princesses who all go out every night and dance their shoes to pieces, the seven dwarfs all asleep in their beds side by side, exist in another realm altogether, between the uncanny and the absurd.

Swiftness is a great virtue in the fairy tale. A good tale moves with a dreamlike speed from event to event, pausing only to say as much as is needed and no more. The best tales are perfect examples of what you do need and what you don't: in Rudyard Kipling's image, fires that blaze brightly because all the ashes have been raked out.

The opening of a tale, for example. All we need is the word 'Once...' and we're off:

> Once there was a poor man who couldn't support his only
> son any more. When the son realised this, he said, 'Father,
> it's no use my staying here. I'm just a burden to you. I'm
> going to leave home and see if I can earn a living.'
> ('The Three Snake Leaves')

A few paragraphs later, he's already married a king's daughter. Or this:

> Once there was a farmer who had all the money and land he
> wanted, but despite his wealth there was one thing missing
> from his life. He and his wife had never had any children.
> When he met other farmers in town or at the market, they

would often make fun of him and ask why he and his wife had never managed to do what their cattle did regularly. Didn't they know how to do it? In the end he lost his temper, and when he got back home, he swore and said, 'I will have a child, even if it's a hedgehog.'

('Hans-my-Hedgehog')

The speed is exhilarating. You can only go that fast, however, if you're travelling light; so none of the information you'd look for in a modern work of fiction – names, appearances, background, social context, etc. – is present. And that, of course, is part of the explanation for the flatness of the characters. The tale is far more interested in what happens to them, or in what they make happen, than in their individuality.

When composing a tale of this sort, it's not always easy to be sure about which events are necessary and which are superfluous. Anyone who wants to know how to tell a tale could do much worse than study 'The Musicians of Bremen', both a nonsensical little yarn and a masterpiece, in which the narrative carries not one unnecessary ounce. Every paragraph advances the story.

There is no imagery in fairy tales apart from the most obvious. As white as snow, as red as blood: that's about it. Nor is there any close description of the natural world or of individuals. A forest is deep, the princess is beautiful, her hair is golden; there's no need to say more. When what you want to know is what happens next, beautiful descriptive wordplay can only irritate.

In one story, however, there is a passage that successfully combines beautiful description with the relation of events in such a way that one would not work without the other. The story is 'The Juniper Tree', and the passage I mean comes after the wife has made her wish for a child as red as blood and as white as snow. It links her pregnancy with the passing seasons:

One month went by, and the snow vanished.

Two months went by, and the world turned green.

Three months went by, and flowers bloomed out of the earth.

Four months went by, and all the twigs on all the trees in the forest grew stronger and pressed themselves together, and the birds sang so loud that the woods resounded, and the blossom fell from the trees.

Five months went by, and the woman stood under the juniper tree. It smelled so sweet that her heart leaped in her breast, and she fell to her knees with joy.

Six months went by, and the fruit grew firm and heavy, and the woman fell still.

When seven months had gone by, she plucked the juniper berries and ate so many that she felt sick and sorrowful.

After the eighth month had gone, she called her husband and said to him, weeping, 'If I die, bury me under the juniper tree.'

This is wonderful, but it's wonderful in a curious way: there's little any teller of this tale can do to improve it. It has to be rendered exactly as it is here, or at least the different months have to be given equally different characteristics, and carefully linked in equally meaningful ways with the growth of the child in his mother's womb, and that growth with the juniper tree that will be instrumental in his later resurrection.

However, that is a great and rare exception. In most of these tales, just as the characters are flat, description is absent. In the later editions, it is true, Wilhelm's telling became a little more florid and inventive, but the real interest of the tale continues to be in what happened, and what happened next. The formulas are so common, the lack of interest in the particularity of things so widespread, that it comes as a real shock to read a sentence like this in 'Jorinda and Joringel':

> It was a lovely evening; the sun shone warmly on the tree trunks against the dark green of the deep woods, and turtle-doves cooed mournfully in the old beech trees.

Suddenly that story stops sounding like a fairy tale and begins to sound like something composed in a literary way by a Romantic writer such as Novalis or Jean Paul. The serene, anonymous relation of events has given way, for the space of a sentence, to an individual sensibility: a *single mind* has felt this impression of nature, has seen these details in the mind's eye and written them down. A writer's command of imagery and gift for description is one of the things that make him or her unique, but fairy tales don't come whole and unaltered from the minds of individual writers, after all; uniqueness and originality are of no interest to them.

William Wordsworth's *The Prelude*, or James Joyce's *Ulysses*, or any other literary work, exists as a text first of all. The words on the page are what it is. It's the job of an editor or a literary critic to pay attention to what exactly those words are, and to clarify places where there are divergent readings in different editions, to make sure that the reader can encounter exactly the text that the work consists of.

But a fairy tale is not a text of that sort. It's a transcription made on one or more occasions of the words spoken by one of many people who have told this tale. And all sorts of things, of course, affect the words that are finally written down. A storyteller might tell the tale more richly, more extravagantly, one day than the next, when he's tired or not in the mood. A transcriber might find her own equipment failing: a cold in the head might make hearing more difficult, or cause the writing-down to be interrupted by sneezes or coughs. Another accident might affect it too:

a good tale might find itself in the mouth of a less than adequate teller.

That matters a great deal, because tellers vary in their talents, their techniques, their attitudes to the process. The Grimms were highly impressed by the ability of one of their sources, Dorothea Viehmann, to tell a tale a second time in the same words as she'd used before, making it easy to transcribe; and the tales that come from her are typically structured with marvellous care and precision. I was equally impressed when working on her tales for this book.

Similarly, this teller might have a talent for comedy, that one for suspense and drama, another for pathos and sentiment. Naturally they will each choose tales that make the most of their talents. When X the great comedian tells a tale, he will invent ridiculous details or funny episodes that will be remembered and passed on, so the tale will be altered a little by his telling; and when Y the mistress of suspense tells a tale of terror, she will invent in like manner, and her inventions and changes will become part of the tradition of telling that tale, until they're forgotten, or embellished, or improved on in their turn. The fairy tale is in a perpetual state of becoming and alteration. To keep to one version or one translation alone is to put a robin redbreast in a cage. A fairy tale is not a text.

Can the writer of any version of a fairy tale ever come near to James Merrill's ideal tone, 'serene, anonymous'? Of course, the writer might not wish to. There have been many, and there will be many more, versions of these tales that are brimful of their author's own dark obsessions, or brilliant personality, or political passions. The tales can stand it. But even if we want to be serene and anonymous, I think it's probably impossible to achieve it completely, and that our personal stylistic fingerprints lie impressed on every paragraph without our knowing it.

The only thing to do, it seems to me, is to try for clarity, and stop worrying about it. Telling these stories is a delight it would be a pity to spoil by anxiety. An enormous relief and pleasure, like the mild air that refreshes the young count when he lies down to rest in 'The Goose Girl at the Spring', comes over the writer who realises that it's not necessary to *invent*: the substance of the tale is there already, just as the sequence of chords in a song is there ready for the jazz musician, and our task is to step from chord to chord, from event to event, with all the lightness and swing we can. Like jazz, storytelling is an art of performance, and writing is performance too.

Finally, I'd say to anyone who wants to tell these tales, don't be afraid to be superstitious. If you have a lucky pen, use it. If you speak with more force and wit when wearing one red sock and one blue one, dress like that. When I'm at work I'm highly superstitious. My own superstition has to do with the voice in which the story comes out. I believe that every story is attended by its own sprite, whose voice we embody when we tell the tale, and that we tell it more successfully if we approach the sprite with a certain degree of respect and courtesy. These sprites are both old and young, male and female, sentimental and cynical, sceptical and credulous, and so on, and what's more, they're completely amoral: like the air-spirits who helped Strong Hans escape from the cave, the story-sprites are willing to serve whoever has the ring, whoever is telling the tale. To the accusation that this is nonsense, that all you need to tell a story is a human imagination, I reply, 'Of course, and this is the way my imagination works.'

But we may do our best by these tales, and find that it's still not enough. I suspect that the finest of them have the quality that the great pianist Artur Schnabel attributed to the sonatas of Mozart: they are too easy for children and too difficult for adults.

And the fifty tales I chose to tell are, I think, the cream of the *Kinder- und Hausmarchen*. I have done my best for the sprites who attend each one, as did Dorothea Viehmann, Philipp Otto Runge, Dortchen Wild, and all the other tellers whose work was preserved by the great Brothers Grimm. And I hope we all, tellers and listeners alike, live happily ever after.

THIS ESSAY WAS FIRST PUBLISHED AS THE INTRODUCTION TO PHILIP PULLMAN'S RETELLING OF GRIMM'S FAIRY TALES, *GRIMM TALES* (PENGUIN, 2012).

The one regret I have about the Grimm tales is that I didn't encounter them properly until I'd left the business of classroom teaching behind. I told the Iliad *and the* Odyssey *many times to children of twelve or thirteen; if I were going into teaching now, I'd be sure to add some of the best Grimm tales to the mix. Except, of course, that I'd be forbidden to do it, because there's no provision for simple enjoyment in the curriculum that schools now have to follow.*

A Bar at the Folies-Bergère

MODERNISM AND STORYTELLING

On the puzzles in Manet's great painting

A Bar at the Folies-Bergère by Édouard Manet (*see also colour section*)

THIS IS A PAINTING COMPLETED BY ÉDOUARD MANET IN THE LAST TWO years of his life, when he was already suffering badly from the effects of the disease that would kill him, at the age of fifty-one, in 1883. The condition was a result of an untreated syphilis infection. Apparently one early owner of this painting was the composer Emmanuel Chabrier.

That is all the biographical information I'll go into; from now on we'll concentrate on the picture. We might end up anywhere, but at least if we start by looking closely at what's there, we'll be starting from the right place.

The painting itself does what the title says it does: it depicts a bar at the music hall, or the theatre (it's hard to find a precise English equivalent) known as the Folies-Bergère. We, or the spectator's eye, the owner of the point of view, seem to be standing in front of the counter in the position of a customer about to order a drink. In front of us there is a marble counter with various bottles arranged on it, together with a glass bowl containing oranges or mandarins and a glass with two flowers standing in water.

Behind the counter, with her hands resting on the edge, stands a young woman wearing a grey skirt, a dark velvet jacket fastened by a line of buttons and with a low-cut lacy collar. Her blonde hair is cut in a fringe in front and gathered behind. There is a large gold locket on a black ribbon around her neck. She has a gold bangle on her right forearm, two small earrings, and a corsage of pink flowers at her breast.

Everything we see is painted in a style of dash and brilliance, with textures such as the velvet of the barmaid's jacket, the waxy skin of the oranges, and the crinkled gold foil on the champagne bottles rendered beautifully. The reflections in the various glass surfaces are especially vivid and convincing.

Behind the barmaid is a large mirror, the lower edge of whose golden frame can be seen just above the marble counter, running along the whole width of the painting parallel to the counter and only, apparently, a few inches behind the barmaid. She hasn't got much space to move in. Most of the picture-plane is occupied by what is reflected in the mirror... and here the puzzles begin.

Because whereas it's possible to describe what's in front of the mirror, that's to say on *our* side of the mirror, reasonably objectively, as I've just done, what's behind the mirror or within it is much less easy to pin down. *Is* it a mirror at all? In some ways it behaves like a mirror – in other ways it doesn't. Let's assume that it is, and look at what it reflects.

Reading upwards from the gold frame, then, we see the reflection of the marble counter, and we see the left-hand end of it, which isn't visible in the space on our side of the mirror. We can see that the marble is an inch or so thick, and the corner is slightly rounded. On it there stands a group of bottles including one that looks like the bottle of Bass on the counter in front, a bottle of some reddish wine or liqueur, and some bottles of champagne which are mostly behind her arm. But the ones in the mirror are not where they ought to be: in front, the red liqueur and the beer are level with each other, in the mirror the beer is considerably nearer to us.

On the right-hand side of the picture, behind the dish of mandarins, the gold frame of the mirror is visible again. But here too things begin to go awry, because the line of the frame on that side is an inch or two lower than the one on the left, and in fact is tilted downwards slightly from right to left. If the barmaid weren't there, we could see that the two parts of the frame wouldn't join up. (As a matter of fact, that part of the frame is tilted exactly as much from the horizontal as the barmaid's head is tilted from the vertical). Above the line of the frame there's the back of a young woman – the barmaid's reflection is how it's usually described – who, unlike the young woman who's facing us and standing upright, seems to be leaning slightly forward, engaged in some transaction with the man in the top hat, most of whom is out of the picture altogether, and whose face is sketchily painted very close to hers. I'll come back to her in a minute.

Behind the reflection of the immediate foreground, the bottles and the counter, we see a reflection of the interior of the theatre, with spectators behind a gilded balcony front across on the other side, chandeliers, glowing lights on the columns, what looks like a cloud of tobacco smoke between the barmaid's head and the reflection of her head, and high up in the top left-hand corner, a trapeze with the feet of the artiste at the far end of her swing poised above the crowd in the balcony and about to swing back towards us.

There are many puzzles here, but to make sense of the space, we need to know how the Folies-Bergère was arranged. The auditorium was horse-shoe-shaped, with a balcony running all the way around, supported on columns. At the back of the balcony was a promenade with bars like this one spaced along it, and behind each of the bars was a large mirror. The spaces between the large columns in the area at the back apparently represent the mirrors on the far side.

However...

If we, the spectators, the looking eye, the owner of the point of view, if we are standing on a balcony like the one we can see on the far side, then where is it? If we look at the reflection of the counter again, we can see nothing supporting it. It seems to be floating in mid-air above the crowd below, and so must we be too, if we are standing in front of it. Certainly, if this side of the balcony has a front like the one the women in the background are resting their elbows on, it's invisible. It should be there beyond the reflection of the counter, and so should the reflection of the spectators who must be sitting at this side like the ones across the way.

Then there's the reflection of the barmaid, which I mentioned a minute ago. If the mirror is parallel with the plane of the picture surface, then her reflection should be directly behind the barmaid and invisible to us. And yet it's some way to one side; and where on our side is the man whose face is so close to hers, and whose reflection we see on that side? Those two figures, the man and the reflected barmaid, are seen as they would be if firstly there *were* a man in front of her, and secondly if the mirror were swung away from us, the right-hand side close and the left further away; but the slight tilt in the frame at the bottom, which I mentioned before, implies that if it's swung at all, it's swung the other way.

All very puzzling, if we take it literally, if we think of a painting as a window into a space. This space doesn't seem to make sense.

Now, in the Walker Art Gallery in Liverpool is a painting – one of their most popular exhibits – which is probably much better known for

'And When Did You Last See Your Father?' by William Frederick Yeames (*see also colour section*)

its title than for the name of the artist who painted it. It's by Frederick William Yeames, and it's called *'And When Did You Last See Your Father?'* You probably know it. It's a narrative painting, showing a scene from the English Civil War, and it depicts a little boy of about six years old being interrogated by Roundhead officers.

The scene's taking place in the comfortable parlour of a large manor house, and the little boy is dressed in bright blue satin, his golden hair neatly brushed, his hands politely folded behind him as he stands on a little stool to give his evidence. His trembling mother and sisters are waiting in the background hoping that the honest little chap won't betray his father. The Roundheads – there are seven of them, each clearly characterised – are behaving strictly, and efficiently, but not brutally; indeed the Roundhead sergeant seems to be comforting the little boy's older sister, who's weeping.

It's effectively composed, as if an experienced stage director had blocked out the scene; and the draughtsmanship is secure; and the handling of the paint is immaculate; and everything works, from the perspective of the room in which they're standing to the shine on the sergeant's steel helmet to the little boy's pale profile against the dark oak panelling.

Yeames was only a year or two younger than Manet, and *'And When*

Did You Last See Your Father?' was painted in 1878, only a year or two before Manet painted *A Bar at the Folies-Bergère*. They were exact contemporaries, and their paintings embody two utterly different conceptions of art – they almost belong to two different worlds.

I think the main difference between them goes right to the heart of what we call modernism in all the arts, not just in painting. It has to do with what the subject is – what they're about. The Yeames is, of course, about the figures, the personages, the individuals in their historical-dramatic situation. It's a literal sort of painting, in that it depicts the space with a one-to-one easy-to-read correspondence between the image and the actuality, but it's also a very *literary* painting: it looks like the illustration to a historical novel. And that, I think, is how it was read and enjoyed by its first public, and by the probably millions of people who have seen and enjoyed it since in reproduction.

But here's a thought-experiment. Let's imagine a full description of that Civil War scene in words – we haven't got time to do it now, but let's imagine it done. It would be perfectly possible. There are no puzzles about mirrors and reflections and things in the wrong place: everything is easily and immediately readable.

Then let's imagine we give that description to another artist, of equivalent skill in draughtsmanship and composition and the handling of paint, one whose ability to convey character through facial expression was the equal of Yeames's, and let him or her paint a picture on a canvas of the same size and shape. It would be a different painting, but would it differ substantially in ways that are important to the way the painting works? I don't think so. Effectively, functionally, it would be the same picture. It would move a spectator in the same way. What there is in Yeames's painting that excites admiration for the skill of the artist or arouses compassion or empathy for the people in the picture would do just the same in this one.

Now imagine the same experiment carried out with the Manet.

Well, would that be possible at all? We could describe what's in front of the mirror more or less unambiguously, but as for what's beyond it – we've already seen how difficult that is. There are too many passages that are ambiguous: for example, what's that patch of lighter pigment under the marble counter in the reflection, between the barmaid's right arm and the champagne bottles? Is it a leg for the counter to stand on, or is it something happening down on the lower level among the spectators? No, it can't be that, because if we look closer it seems to be *in front* of the marble in the mirror, not below it. It's an effect of the light on the glass. And then there is the appearance of the painted surface, which is so important a part of our experience of the picture – and which we can only see when we're looking at the painting itself, and not at a reproduction: the way the paint is scumbled in the handling of the flowers in the barmaid's corsage, and in the great chandelier, and in the massing of the spectators on the balcony. It's Manet's particular touch, his hand, his brushstrokes, that matter in passages like these. I don't think we could describe this picture in words with anything like the clarity and accuracy with which we can describe *'And When Did You Last See Your Father?'*.

So the thought-experiment that worked with the Yeames fails at the very first hurdle when it comes to the Manet. Long before we get to the difficulty of *painting* an equivalent picture by reading a description of this one, we can't even find the words to say exactly what's there and write the description.

The important things about the Yeames can be put into words: the important things about the Manet cannot.

That's why I can stand in front of this one and describe the Yeames, and the important things about it come through, but I couldn't stand in the Walker Art Gallery and describe the Manet and hope the important things would come through. Yeames's picture is a window on something behind it, which is the subject, the important thing about the picture: the surface isn't really important, provided it does its job of *representing* without confusing or being ambiguous. In Manet's picture, the painted surface itself is as important as the subject. If Manet had wanted to paint a window, he'd have been perfectly able to; and if he had, the things that puzzle us in the depiction of space would all be solved and clear and readable. But he wasn't interested in windows.

And this is the difference I mentioned before – the great chasm that divides modernism from what it was reacting against. The modernists in painting, from the Impressionists through Cezanne to Picasso and beyond, were interested not only in the things that painting depicted – they were interested in the very nature of depiction itself. Painting became self-conscious in their hands.

The modernists in literature – James Joyce, Virginia Woolf – show narrative becoming self-conscious in the same way. It was no longer necessary to find a grand, noble, dramatic, historical, religious *subject* for your work of art or literature to be taken seriously: the thoughts passing through the mind of an ordinary man during an ordinary day in Dublin, or an ordinary woman on her way to buy flowers in London, or the way light flickers and divides in a mirror, or the way the sun glows as it sinks behind the smoke of a railway station – the substance of daily life, especially modern life with all its glitter and variety, was more than enough material for the new self-conscious consciousness to work on.

A little later, Picasso's most profound and revolutionary explorations of the nature of seeing and representation were conducted on the most ordinary and everyday subjects: a pipe, a bottle, a newspaper on a table.

And that's why the only thing in this painting that's anything like a story, the transaction on the right-hand side of the picture between the man and the barmaid, is depicted so briskly and so casually. If Yeames, or his colleagues among the Victorian narrative painters, had depicted a bar at the Folies-Bergère, you can bet that this transaction would have been at the very centre of the painting, and the picture would be called something like *Temptation*, and we'd be invited to wonder about whether the barmaid was tempting the man to drink, or whether he was tempting her to come away with him and lose whatever remained of her virtue. For Manet, it was no more important than the oranges.

But I still haven't mentioned the greatest mystery of all, an enigma so profound that even if we solved the difficulty of how to describe the rest of the painting in words, we'd still have to throw up our hands in despair at the impossibility of resolving it, and it's this: what does the barmaid's expression mean? What is she thinking about? How on earth do we describe it? It is the most unreadable expression I know in any painting. It is far more mysterious and enigmatic than that smirking Florentine we know as the Mona Lisa.

At the heart of this scene of pleasure, of glittering light and the sensuous richness of a dozen different textures, with the promise of delicious things to eat and drink, with music (you can almost hear the band) and conversation and laughter and applause as the trapeze artiste swings fearlessly across the auditorium, with the hint of sexual bargaining as well (the Folies-Bergère was well known for that) – at the very centre of this world of brilliant surfaces, at the very point to which our attention is led by the line of her arms and the buttons on her jacket, there is this pretty young face expressing that profound, inexplicable... What is it? Sadness? Regret? Unease? Alienation? Her face is flushed; it might be simply that she's warm under all those lights; it might be the flush that suffuses the cheeks of a young child kept too long from her bed. She's by no means a child, but for all the corseted fullness of her figure, she *does* look young; she looks innocent; at the same time, we wouldn't be surprised to learn that the conversation in the mirror between her reflection and the man in the top hat concerns her availability for quite other purposes than pouring glasses of wine and selling oranges.

But perhaps there's a clue in that. Which is the real girl, this one, or the one in the mirror? The reflection is displaced: is she displaced in another way as well – made strange, made different, a Mr Hyde to a Dr Jekyll (which Stevenson wrote, incidentally, only a year or two after this picture was painted)? Is she two people, one whose character is as shallow as that of the man in the hat, as shallow as everything else in the mirror, only as deep as the glass itself, no more truly *there* than anything else in that glittering surface, because it's *all* surface – and the other who is as complex and profound as the expression on her face, a look that defies all description?

I said that *'And When Did You Last See Your Father?'* could be the illustration to a novel, but *A Bar at the Folies-Bergère* is nothing like an illustration. It's more like a novel itself, compressed into a single image. Nothing shorter than a novel, anyway, would begin to plumb the depths of the character who seems to be standing patiently, thinking of something else, in a dream, abstracted, miles away – all those expressions that mean *not there*. The one in the mirror is not really there, and the one who is really there is not there either. She's somewhere else, thinking of her lover, or her debts, or her parents in the village she comes from, who haven't heard from her for months; or her little sister who has consumption… or thinking of nothing. And of course she can't think really, she's not real at all – she's a painted surface, just like the reflection that isn't a reflection.

But these reflections on reality (we can't get away from *reflections*) are right at the heart of modernism, that astonishing movement in all the arts that was fertilised by Baudelaire, germinated with the Impressionists, and grew throughout the latter part of the nineteenth century to burst into a brilliant and fertile flowering with Picasso and Braque, with Stravinsky, with Joyce.

In Wallace Stevens's great poem about modernism, *The Man With the Blue Guitar*, he has the guitarist faced with the accusation that he does not play things as they are.

> The man replied, 'Things as they are
> Are changed upon the blue guitar.'

And they said then, 'But play, you must,
A tune beyond us, yet ourselves,

A tune upon the blue guitar
Of things exactly as they are.'

They wanted *And When Did You Last See Your Father?'* But what they got was *A Bar at the Folies-Bergère*, and Cézanne's *Grandes Baigneuses*, and Picasso's *Les Demoiselles d'Avignon* – and *The Rite of Spring*, and *Ulysses*, and *The Waste Land* – and jazz, and the cinema, and the whole great twentieth-century cornucopia of beauty and strangeness and truth, and a new kind of artistic consciousness, which was really a re-working of an *old* consciousness, a making explicit something that true artists of every period have always known: that the work of art is not only about the things it depicts, it is about itself as well.

As Wallace Stevens says later in the same poem:

Poetry is the subject of the poem,
From this the poem issues and
To this returns.

This is how art is different from science. Science *progresses*: it proceeds by falsifying what came before, by providing better and truer explanations. Later science is better than earlier science.

But in art, there is no progression. Later art is not better than earlier art. Revolutions in art – such as Impressionism, and Cubism, and the whole enterprise of modernism – are all, at bottom, attempts to get *back* to something that had been lost sight of.

The tomb-painters of ancient Egypt were interested not only in depicting everyday life – fowling in the marshes, hunting with a chariot, dancing – they were also interested in making beautiful patterns on a flat surface.

In the early sixteenth century, Leonardo da Vinci was concerned not only to paint a likeness of that woman I was so rude about a few minutes ago – he was just as concerned with the fascination of applying paint so as to suggest the way air casts a soft veil over the rocks in the distance.

In the middle of the seventeenth century, Vermeer was deeply interested in representing the appearance of a young girl with a pearl earring and her mouth slightly open – and he was equally interested in the way he could represent her three-dimensionalness by painting the highlight in her left eye in a very slightly different place from the one in her right.

The Chinese artist of the Ching dynasty who painted a branch of bamboo on a porcelain pot was trying not only to make it look like bamboo, but also to dispose the line of the branch and the leaves across the curved surface in a way that would be beautiful even if it meant nothing.

The marks in soft black crayon that Seurat made on rough paper in 1884 look just like the figure of a woman that he intended them to, but we can also see the sensuous pleasure he took in the application of the pigment, the way the light seems to soften and gather around the edges where the pigment catches only the high parts of the paper and lets the tiny depressions remain white.

The unknown, the immensely ancient geniuses who painted the bison, the horses, the lions on the cave walls of Lascaux and Chauvet 20,000, 30,000 years ago, took the greatest of care to represent them accurately, but that wasn't their only motivation: we can also see a delight in the rhythmic arrangement of the figures, an awareness of the contours of the cave and how they could be used to add liveliness and movement to the shapes they outlined with ochre and carbon.

All those great artists are contemporaries, not only of one another but of us too. Art does not progress by *improving* what came before, by doing to it what chemistry did to alchemy: art does not progress in that sense at all. Great art has always had this double character, this ability to look at the world and to look at itself at the same time, and the greatest art is perhaps where we see the two things in perfect balance.

That's the real difference between *A Bar at the Folies-Bergère* and *'And When Did You Last See Your Father?'* Yeames and all the other Victorian narrative painters were only interested in half of what there was to be interested about. Manet was interested in *all* of it. *A Bar at the Folies-Bergère* is about a bar at the Folies-Bergère; it's about the mystery of that unfathomable expression on this ordinary young woman's face; it's about those legs suspended at the very end of the acrobat's swing; it's about champagne and oranges and tobacco smoke and chandeliers and fashionable dress; but it's also about seeing, and about recording the way the light glistens on those oranges, and the way things in a mirror are different from things in front of our eyes; it's about the sensation of sight and the mysteries of representation; it's about painting itself.

THIS ESSAY WAS ORIGINALLY PUBLISHED IN *WHAT MAKES A MASTERPIECE: ENCOUNTERS WITH GREAT WORKS OF ART*, EDITED BY CHRISTOPHER DELL, 2010.

In a book of reproductions of famous paintings, we can see the pictures with marvellous clarity, thanks to modern printing techniques. And when we look at paintings online, on the websites of the great museums and galleries, the sense of light shining through them makes them even more vivid than being printed. What we don't get from such experiences is a sense of scale. Part of the physical experience of seeing on a gallery wall (for instance) Salvador Dali's The Persistence of Memory *with its famous melting clock is seeing, with a slight shock, how small it is; and an encounter with Jackson Pollock's* Autumn Rhythm *is incomplete without seeing it both from halfway across the gallery and from very close up, to examine how intricately the skeins of dripped paint are interwoven. In a book, every picture, like every other one, is a size that will fit on the page.*

Poco a Poco

THE FUNDAMENTAL PARTICLES OF NARRATIVE

On one such particle traced through many different stories

First of all, I want to thank Trinity College for inviting me to join the distinguished list of writers who've given the Richard Hillary Lecture. My predecessors seem to have covered a great deal of ground, but I think there are a few more things to say. In any case what I'm going to talk about this evening is not a settled authoritative statement of anything, but more in the nature of a report of discovery in progress. Every so often I see something new about the craft of storytelling, and when I do I like to stop and rearrange my ideas; so, as I say, this is not a final pronouncement on the art, but the latest stage of my research, as it were.

Now lectures, like the language they're given in, are sequential and not instantaneous, and whenever we have something to say, we come up against the problem of what order to put our remarks in. Order them *this* way, and they tell one story; order them differently, and they tell another one. 'What story do I want to tell?' is the question we have to ask ourselves.

Well, today I want to tell a story about fundamental particles: the fundamental particles of narrative. We're going to look at what they are and how they work, what they're made of and what sort of charge they can carry; we're going from Fairyland to Babylon, from the river Jordan to the slopes of Parnassus, and we're going to finish with a cup of tea.

So the first thing I'll do is read two very short extracts from books of mine. I'll be coming back to them later in the talk, but if I get them out of the way now it won't interrupt the argument when I do.

The first comes from a fairy tale called *Clockwork*. Karl, the bitter young clockmaker's apprentice, and a sinister stranger are talking in the inn.

'Bring a glass for my companion,' said Dr Kalmenius, 'and then you may leave us.'

The landlord put the bottle and another glass on the counter. Only five minutes before, the parlour had been full to bursting; but now Dr Kalmenius and Karl were alone, and the inn was so quiet that Karl could hear the whisper of flames in the stove, and the ticking of the old clock in the corner, even over the beating of his own heart.

Dr Kalmenius poured some brandy, and pushed the glass along the bar. Karl said nothing. He bore the stranger's stare for nearly a minute, and then he banged his fist on the counter and cried:

'God damn you, what do you want?'

The second comes from *I Was A Rat!* Roger, the little pageboy who says he used to be a rat, has been taken in by old Bob and Joan. They give him some bread and milk, and he tries to eat it by putting his face down to the bowl.

'What you doing?' said Joan. 'Dear oh dear! You don't eat like that. Use the spoon!'

The boy looked up, milk in his eyebrows, bread up his nose, his chin dripping.

'He doesn't know anything, poor little thing,' said Joan. 'Come to the sink, my love, and we'll wash you. Grubby hands and all. Look at you!'

The boy tried to look at himself, but he was reluctant to leave the bowl of bread and milk.

'That's nice,' he said. 'I like that…'

'It'll still be here when you come back,' said Bob. 'I've had my supper already, I'll look after it for you.'

The boy looked wonder-struck at this idea. He watched over his shoulder as Joan led him to the kitchen sink and tipped in some water from the kettle, and while she was washing him he kept twisting his wet face round to look from Bob to the bowl and back again.

'That's better,' said Joan, rubbing him dry. 'Now you be a good boy and eat with the spoon. I'm surprised they didn't teach you manners when you was a pageboy.'

'I was a rat,' he said.

Now as I said a minute ago, I want to look at some fundamental particles and their associated forces – what they are and what they do. The search for the fundamental particles of *matter*, of course, is an enthralling one, with each discovery supplanting the one before it: everything is made of water, said Thales; no, everything is made of fire, said Heraclitus; no, there are four elements – fire, water, and earth, and air; no, the fundamental particle is the atom, whose very name means that it cannot be cut or divided any further; no, atoms themselves are made up of smaller particles, electrons and protons and neutrons; no, we can go smaller still, and discover all kinds of exotic little bits down there in the very small, quarks and neutrinos and the like, with properties so strange that we can't even imagine them; and one of the latest theories maintains that the very smallest things are not particles at all but loops of vibrating string… The search for what matter is made of still continues, because I gather that the string theory itself is now beginning to be questioned.

But what are *stories* made of? Are they made of words? It would be easy to think that they are, because so many stories come to us in the form of words, whether printed or spoken. Words do tell stories, but pictures aren't bad at it, and even ballet can manage to convey what happens and then what happens next, in a broad sort of way. The reason language is so good at transmitting stories is that stories happen in time – one thing is succeeded by another, and was prepared for by something that happened earlier – and the sequential nature of language fits that temporal aspect of their nature. Besides, time is built into the very grammar: we have a variety of tenses that allows us to notate with great precision the order of events in time, and how long they go on for, and so on.

But stories are not made of language. I don't think they're made of any of the media in which they may happen to be transmitted. I'm going to say straight out that I think stories are made of events, and that the fundamental particles of story are the smallest events we can find. So small, in fact, that they are more or less abstract. The scale on which we live, with our bodies and our normal everyday consciousness, is round about the middle scale of size between the cosmic level and the quantum level, and one of the characteristics of this middle scale is *individual difference*, every person, every face, every story, being recognisably itself and different from everything else; some novels are very similar to others, to be sure, but when we discover a novel that's exactly the same as another one, we call it plagiarism. But what we find when we think our way down to the scale of the very small is that everything down there is the same. Abstract, neutral, devoid of inflection or emotional colouring of any kind; rather like a parallelogram or a mathematical equation. An abstract narrative particle.

I'm going to focus on just one of these little abstract narrative particles tonight, which is this one –

A little story about pouring something out of a container. That's all it is. The liquid is in here, and we pour it out into there.

Now one reason I find these fundamental particles so interesting is that they explain something that's otherwise very difficult to understand. It's this: there is *so much information* coming at us every second, especially

The Milkmaid by Johannes Vermeer

through our eyes, and yet somehow we effortlessly extract the essential narrative heart of it without even realising what we're doing. Every square millimetre in our entire visual field is occupied. The point is firstly that there is an overwhelming Niagara Falls of information pouring into our eyes, and, secondly, that we are *not* overwhelmed by it.

We're not overwhelmed, because our unconscious mind does so much sorting out and interpreting for us that we take it for granted that things just sort themselves out. We're in the position of immensely rich monarchs in the grandest period of royalty such as Louis XIV, for whom every routine activity is done by a thousand servants whose job is to work perfectly and remain invisible. Each of us has a staff of diligent butlers, footmen, housekeepers, kitchen maids, gardeners, secretaries, clerks, all working away night and day, sorting everything out for us. Something deeper than our conscious mind selects the essential from the inessential in the constantly changing colours and shapes we see, and lets us understand without the slightest effort what's happening – and thanks partly to our experience of this fundamental particle of narrative, we map the little abstract story we're familiar with on to the welter of sense-impressions, and we realise that someone is watering the hanging basket.

And in fact every experience we have of, for example, pouring milk into a bowl of cornflakes, or pouring coffee from a cafetière into a mug, or everything we read in a story about Sherlock Holmes letting drops of a chemical fall into a solution in a test tube, or Jeeves pouring a cocktail for Bertie Wooster, or see in a play-within-a-play about a murderer pouring poison into his victim's ear – our understanding of all these processes is underpinned by our familiarity with the basic little story about pouring something out of a container. Our knowledge of the pattern lets us see different parts of those other stories in their proper relation to the whole, and not get snagged on the details instead of getting the main point. Furthermore – and this is where it gets really interesting – these little patterns, many of them based on spatial experience, can be used to make sense of things that are not spatial at all. We'll come back to that later on.

But the little original skeletal story, the fundamental particle itself, grows directly out of the experience of our bodies: our acquired knowledge of how things behave relative to one another in space, and how our limbs and our senses interact with them.

Fundamental particles like the pouring-from-a-container idea are sometimes known as *image schemas*. My interest in this was sparked by the work of George Lakoff and Mark Turner and Mark Thompson and other cognitive linguists, but in my butterfly way I've cheerfully taken what I want from their work and carried it away to do something else with it. You remember what Muhammad Ali said: he said his method was to float like a butterfly, sting like a bee. My variation is that I read like a butterfly, and write like a bee. So, fluttering lightly from place to place like a Camberwell beauty in a wayward summer breeze, I'm going to follow this little bit of narrative about and see what turns up, and first of all we'll take it literally: pictures and stories about pouring something out of a container.

So here are a few examples of the sort of thing we can do with this little pattern, this fundamental particle of story.

One way we make meaning out of an action is to read it in a context. Here is a detail from the *New Yorker*:

"Poor little girl—to think you've never had anyone to protect you."

Cartoon for the *New Yorker* by Wallace Morgan

This is a scene in a crowded and fashionable restaurant, perhaps, or a club. The actual joke isn't great… But we might just wonder why the gentleman at the table in the background isn't ordering a drink from the waiter. Why is he using a hip flask? Well, the date is 1926, and therefore the drink he's pouring out is certainly bootleg liquor. Perhaps the club is a speakeasy, and it'll be raided by the police any moment. The pouring-out story isn't at the centre of the action here, it's at the edge, it's part of the scenery. It's just a little throwaway detail at the middle of the artwork, its function being to wink at us, as it were, and say, 'You know where we are.'

Here's another cartoon from the *New Yorker*, this time by the great Charles Addams (*see facing page*).

Because of the way we integrate this little pouring-something-out story into what goes on around it, by means of the effortless work (effortless to our conscious minds) done by all those neuronal secretaries and filing clerks and so on, we can look at a picture and see beyond the moment that's being depicted. We can see what's going to happen next, and what has led up to it.

And in order to understand this cartoon, which we all effortlessly do, we instantaneously call on our memories not only of what we've seen happen when you tip over a container of liquid, but of such things as carol singing – we know why there is a group of people standing in the snow, and what they're doing, and we contrast the innocent purity of their intentions with the wicked mischief being planned by Morticia, Gomez and the rest of the Addams family on the roof; and we understand graphic imagery too – we interpret the wispy trail of white leading from the container as meaning that this isn't just cold water, it's hot. It's probably boiling oil. And all this resides in a subtle framework of ironical understanding that lets us laugh instead of recoiling in horror. This is a cartoon. It's not real. It's situated in a tradition of mock-Gothickry with which the very name Charles Addams is synonymous. What's more, in this cartoon, unlike the first one, the act of pouring isn't just scenery, it is the very joke itself.

Christmas Carollers by Charles Addams

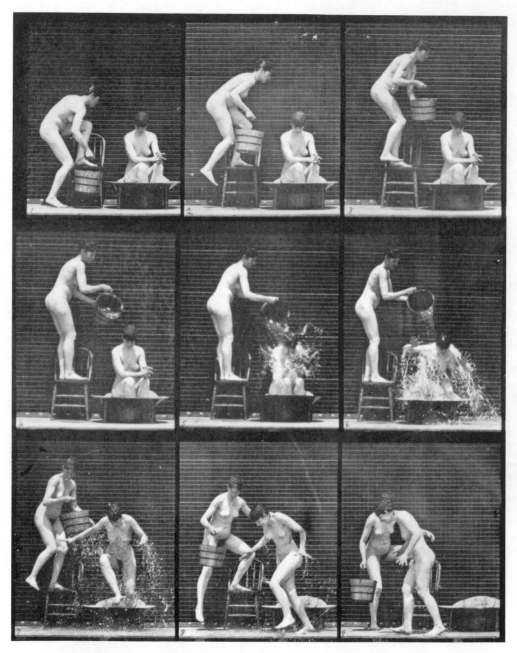

A sequence of photographs showing movement by Eadweard Muybridge

And look how important it is to get the timing right. This split-second is the funny one; a split-second earlier or later would not be.

The action of pouring something out of a container, the fundamental particle itself, is emotionally neutral, as I said. It can take any tone, any emotional colouring.

This next one is a light-hearted one, from a sequence of pictures from the immense collection of Eadweard Muybridge (*see facing page*), whose research into the photography of motion was a precursor of the movies.

His pictures of horses galloping established once and for all something that every painter of horses had wondered about and none had been able to know for certain – that there does come a moment when all four of the horse's feet are off the ground at once. His studies of *The Human Figure in Motion* showed men and women running, jumping, throwing things, walking, standing up and sitting down, with photographs taken a fraction of a second apart – a great and previously unavailable resource for artists concerned with the human figure. I'm not sure that any artist in previous centuries had ever really wondered what it would look like when you tipped a bucket of water over a young lady in the bath, but just in case, here is the evidence.

This little sequence, and all the others in Muybridge's great work, are actually hugely significant in the history of storytelling. I mentioned the business of *time* and language earlier on: in Muybridge's studies, and in the work a little later of the Lumière brothers which were the real beginnings of cinema, it became possible for the first time ever for pictures to show time passing without the intervention of language. A sequence of pictures could embody and depict time itself, without any words being used. You could make sequences of pictures before then, of course, but people seldom did, because it was so laborious: you had to draw every one separately. This, by comparison, was effortless. And among all the hundreds and thousands of photographs that Muybridge made of living creatures in motion, there was room for a splash.

Belshazzar's Feast by Rembrandt (*see also colour section*)

The next picture (*above*) is by Rembrandt and it shows the moment when King Belshazzar sees the writing on the wall foretelling that he will be killed and his great city sacked and ruined.

Here the little story of ours, our fundamental particle, plays a different part in the drama. In his alarm at seeing the mysterious writing appear, the king turns around hastily and knocks over a golden vessel, spilling the wine. Actually there are two inadvertent spillings going on: the woman in the right foreground is also losing the wine in her goblet.

Unlike the pouring-out in the Charles Addams cartoon, these accidents are not the central action of the picture. They're part of the scenery here, like the hip flask in the first *New Yorker* cartoon, but there's a difference: here they function as metaphors as well as scenery. These are the very vessels of gold and silver that Belshazzar's father Nebuchadnezzar had taken from the temple at Jerusalem, and their presence in the picture,

216

and the spilling of the wine, can be read as standing for excess, for the loss of control and order and temperance: they foretell the spilling of blood that will happen later that very night.

Now this is the point at which the real power of the pouring-out story begins to become apparent. Because like all the other fundamental particles of this sort, it doesn't only mean what it seems to mean; it can mean something else as well. Some of the fundamental particles of matter carry an electrical charge. Fundamental particles of story, like this one, can carry a metaphorical charge. We'll come back to that more fully in a minute.

Another painting (*see overleaf*), this time by Goya; and unlike the Rembrandt, where everything is clear and every reference legible (provided we know the Bible story), this is mysterious and obscure. A man who might be a priest is pouring what must be oil into a lamp held by a demonic figure, in a setting that seems to teem with darkness and supernatural threat. He's got his hand over his mouth as he looks at us, as if to say that he knows he's taking part in some forbidden ritual, or making some evil bargain, and wants us to keep silent about it. The picture is full of that eerie witchiness, that grim and enigmatic sense of supernatural dread that Goya was so good at evoking. It could be a scene in the progress of a damnation. And once again the pouring-out is not mere scenery here, it's the subject of the whole picture. This is all about the filling of the lamp from the jug of oil.

The difference between this and the Rembrandt is that although the pouring of the oil into the lamp is rich with significance, we don't know what it means. It's enigmatic and paradoxical. Light is proverbially symbolic of good, and filling a lamp symbolic of care and prudence; we think of the wise virgins, who had enough oil for their lamps, and the foolish ones who didn't, and who missed the wedding feast. Filling a lamp, bringing light, is a good act, and yet here it seems to be haunted by guilt and fear. Is this lamp going to light the way to evil, or to show us

A scene from 'The Forcibly Bewitched' by Francisco Goya

things better left unseen? Is that what it means? The metaphorical charge is clearly working, it's clearly doing something; but what is it?

Our experience of looking at this picture – mine, anyway – is a useful reminder that these days most people must feel similarly puzzled in front of the Rembrandt. People of my generation, in whose background the Bible figured largely, are at home with Belshazzar; we know what's going on. But for many people Rembrandt's painting must be as weird and enigmatic as the Goya – until they read the caption on the wall beside it, or in the book under the reproduction. And when we read the caption to this painting, we learn that in fact it illustrates a scene from a comedy, a play by Antonio de Zamora called *The Forcibly Bewitched*, and it shows the foolish and timorous Don Claudio replenishing the lamp on which he's been led to believe his life depends. He's a dupe, he's a gull. It's a debatable point whether the explanation diminishes the impact of the picture; for my money, it does. There are some stories that are more rich and powerful unexplained.

Earlier on I mentioned the neutrality, the uninflected tone of the fundamental particle itself, which enables it to lend itself to any emotional purpose. We've seen it being funny, we've seen it being dramatic, and here it's different again; when we see the whole of this picture, we can tell that the atmosphere is clearly solemn and reverent. I wonder what the intelligent but uninformed spectator would make of Piero della Francesca's *The Baptism of Christ* (*see overleaf*). Whatever is happening here, no one could mistake the fact that it is of profound importance; our fundamental particle here is about as central as any pictorial element could be in a picture, and because of the surrounding activity, the air of ritual and the calm and dignified purpose of all the participants, the pouring-out here carries a charge of great gravity. Whatever the man is doing as he pours out the water, it isn't a trivial business.

As a matter of fact, here we see the fundamental particle acting in a way we haven't seen before. Early Christians, and Eastern Orthodox

The Baptism of Christ by Piero della Francesca
(see also colour section)

Christians still, believe that only total immersion counts as valid baptism: 'If the person to be baptised is so ill that immersion would endanger his life, then it is sufficient to pour water over his forehead; but otherwise immersion must not be omitted,' says Timothy Ware in his book *The Orthodox Church*. The Western churches – or most of them – are content to let the pouring-out, the fundamental particle, act metonymically, so to speak, to be one part standing for the whole. And here the meaning of the picture resides not just in what it depicts, but in what that signifies.

So we need to know what things signify, but we can have too much explanation. Next in this little picture gallery is an engraving from George Wither's *A Collection of Emblemes*, from 1635 (*see facing page*).

The vogue for emblem-books was a century old by that time, but the appetite for these little pictorial-poetical devices was undiminished. Typically each page shows a picture whose symbolism is then explained at exhaustive length in the accompanying verse. As with the Goya, I sometimes think they're better unexplained: what's sometimes the infinitely suggestive mystery of the pictures is sometimes reduced to the bleeding obvious by the verse. But at least here it does show us another use for our fundamental particle. The idea is that there are some things it's better to do gradually – *poco a poco* – than to rush at:

Embleme for the Month of May by George Wither

When, thou shalt visit, in the Month of May,
A costly Garden, in her best array;
And, view the well-grown Trees, the wel-trimm'd Bowers,
The Beds of Herbs, the knots of pleasant flowers,
With all the deckings, and the fine devices,
Perteyning to those earthly Paradises,
Thou canst not well suppose, one day, or two,
Did finish all, which had been, there to doe…

And so on, and so on.

Well, if you had nothing better to do in 1635 I suppose you could spend a improving hour or so pondering the truth of that, and then advise your friends about it sententiously for weeks. Everybody seemed to have so much more time in those days.

At almost exactly the same date, the French painter Laurent de La Hyre was commissioned to decorate a room with personifications of the Seven Liberal Arts. This one (*see facing page*) is Grammar.

The view of Grammar depicted here is not the one currently held by the British Department for Education, which is that grammar is a set of facts about which children must be drilled and tested so that their school can be ranked in order in a league table. This is a more humane proposition, which happens to be expressed in terms of the metaphor of watering something to make it grow: 'Like young plants, young brains need watering, and it is the duty of Grammar to undertake this.' So said Cesare Ripa's *Iconologia*, the source book for countless allegorical paintings and poems.

When I was training to be a teacher, we were told that in the old days children used to be thought of as empty vessels and it was the teacher's job to fill them with knowledge. 'But of course we don't think that any more,' we were told very firmly. I can't remember what metaphor they brought in to replace it. I'm pretty certain it wasn't this one – watering plants – but I like this. There's life in it.

So our little narrative particle has moved from the realm of the literal, where there is a physical container with something physical in it, water or bootleg hooch, and you pour it out, and there it is, in a story or a picture – into another realm, which is the metaphorical. We project that idea on to activities that are not in any way concerned with literal pots and literal jugs, literal water or literal wine.

But there's no hard-and-fast division between one kind of picture, or story, and another. We've seen that some of the literal pouring-out can be read metaphorically as well, and as the great scholar of symbols and

Allegory of Grammar by Laurent de La Hyre

iconography Ernst Gombrich says, 'Our language favours this twilight region between the literal and the metaphorical. Who can always tell where the one begins and the other ends?'

This fluidity, this twilight region, is the medium through which these fundamental particles lend themselves to metaphor. To take the pouring-out one, consider these expressions, some of which we scarcely recognise as metaphors:

> Pouring oil on troubled waters
> Pour cold water on something
> She's poured money into the venture

A drop in the ocean
The accountant poured scorn on the idea
She poured her heart out
He's feeling absolutely drained
Her cup is running over

And then there's this idea: The Spring, *La Source* (*see p. 225*).

And this is the point at which the full reach of this particular fundamental particle is revealed, in the metaphor of the source, the spring, the fountain, *fons et origo*. Two other ideas arrive at once: a nursing mother, her breasts full of milk, and the image of Christ's blood: 'This is my blood of the New Testament, which is shed for you and for many for the remission of sins; do this, as oft as ye shall drink it, in remembrance of me.' The essence of the source, the spring, is *something good coming out of something else* – liquid that is useful, fertilising, refreshing, nourishing, life-giving.

Because it would be of no value, it would have no meaning, if it were poured out where it was not needed. It comes as a gift, something not paid for, something given freely, from a fullness to an emptiness – from an ever-replenished abundance to a scarcity – life to the lifeless, drink to the thirsty, water to the parched earth.

How often the image of dryness stands for emotional or spiritual death. T. S. Eliot is full of it:

> thoughts of a dry brain in a dry season;

and

> where the sun beats,
> And the dead tree gives no shelter, the cricket no relief,
> And the dry stone no sound of water …

A Bar at the Folies-Bergère by Édouard Manet (*see also p. 191*)

'And When Did You Last See Your Father?' by William Frederick Yeames (*see also p. 195*)

Belshazzar's Feast by Rembrandt (*see also p. 216*)

The Baptism of Christ by Piero della Francesca (*see also p. 220*)

Cover of *The Pleasure Garden*, illustration by Fritz Wegner (*see also p. 266*)

The Convalescent by Gwen John (*see also p. 260*)

Lyra by Peter Bailey for the Folio Society (*see also p. 279*)

Lyra making sense of the alethiometer by Peter Bailey for the Folio Society (*see also p. 279*)

RUPERT BOWS TO THE KING

At last, the old man comes to tell,
" My king, him wish to say farewell."

" I hope he means to let us go ! "
Sam whispers, as the friends bow low.

The aged man escorts the chums,
And bids them board the boat that comes.

" I'm still not sure they'll let us leave ! "
Sam whispers, clutching Rupert's sleeve.

The meal is over at last. " Now I wonder how we're going to get home again," says Sailor Sam. Seeing his guest wishes to speak, the king sends for his aged interpreter. " Ah, my king realise it time you return to your country," says the old man. " So now he make farewell, yes ? " And Rupert and Sam bow low while the little king waves and chatters as cheerfully as ever. " I hope he's not asking us to come and see him again," murmurs Sam under his breath. " I've s̲e̲ ̲ ̲ ̲

enough of these parts ! " The soldiers and servants of the king do not delay. Rupert and Sam are marched outside to the long causeway over the sea. The great gong is banged and a boat heads rapidly for them with its odd rattling noise. " Here, I say. I hope those men have had the right orders," says Sam, as they are hustled aboard. " This is the same sort of boat that took me to that sea-prison." However, it swings away from the prisons and towards the distant water city.

Rupert Bows to the King from *Rupert* by Alfred Bestall (*see also p. 274*)

La Source by Jean Auguste Dominique Ingres

And one place where we see this pouring-out of refreshing, life-giving blessedness in action is the situation of the artist, the painter, composer, poet, novelist, in need of, and seeking, and sometimes gaining, the favour of the Muse. Work without inspiration is possible, of course. The only way to become a professional artist of any sort is to learn how to work efficiently when you're not feeling inspired in the least.

But there are periods of dryness, of deadness, of despair, which are not like the usual drudgery. Then we need something more. We need the waters of the spring struck by the hoof of Pegasus from the flanks of Mount Helicon. That wasn't the only spring that did the trick, of course; there were several. There was the spring Aganippe, also on Mount Helicon, that brought inspiration to those who drank from it. There was the Pierian spring on the slopes of Mount Olympus that did the same: 'A little learning is a dangerous thing,' said Pope; 'Drink deep, or taste not the Pierian spring.' There was the Castalian spring on Mount Parnassus, sacred to Apollo.

Now as a principle of life I'm perfectly happy to be both sceptical and credulous simultaneously, and here I'm credulous. The business of inspiration is a subject I'm a little superstitious about. Perhaps it's dangerous to talk about it; perhaps the spring will dry up if you make it too public. But I know people are curious about the process of composition, because the question I and other writers get asked more than any other is: 'Where do you get your ideas from?' Another question from the same centre of feeling is 'How can I become inspired?'

And like many other writers, because I don't know the answer to these questions I tend to be unhelpful or evasive about my answers. 'Where do you get your ideas from?' they ask, and I say, 'I don't know where they come *from*, but I know where they come *to*: they come to my desk, and if I'm not there, they go away again.' Which may not be helpful, but it is true. The capacity to sit and be bored and frustrated for very long stretches of time is essential, but nowhere near as glamorous as the inspiration idea, and people don't like to hear about that so much.

Let me try and describe briefly what it's like to feel inspired in the way that I think people mean when they talk about inspiration. I actually talk about it very rarely, and I don't think I've ever had a conversation with another writer on the subject. But this is what it feels like to me. It feels like *discovery*, not *invention*. It feels as if the story I'm writing already exists, in some Platonic way, and that I'm privileged from time to time to gain access to it. The curtain twitches aside for a while; the moon comes out from behind a cloud, and illuminates a landscape that was previously invisible; something like that.

Something happens, and there's a moment or so of clarity in which I see all kinds of possibilities and connections and patterns and correspondences that I never suspected were there in the great clumsy bundle of darkness and confusion that is the story I'm trying to write. I see the way out of a narrative cul-de-sac. I see what I must do in order to bring these two people together. I see a way of resolving the problem of the ending at the same time as making use of one of those loose ends. I see a perfection of form that makes it worth continuing to struggle with the intractable material I have to shape it out of.

It doesn't last very long, this feeling of inspiration, or whatever we want to call it, but it doesn't really have to; all you need to do is see the possibilities, and that cheers you up, and you go back to work with a will.

And it does – I don't want to get all spiritual about this – but it does feel like a blessing, precisely like the sense you get when you're walking in a mountainous bit of country on a hot day and your bottle is empty, and you come across a spring of fresh water. A little poem from the *Greek Anthology* by Leonidas of Tarentum perfectly expresses this sense of refreshment, gratitude, blessedness:

> Traveller, don't drink here; the water's warm
> And muddy from the torrent. Climb the hill
> There where the heifers graze, go on a step or two,

And by the shepherds' pine you'll find a spring,
A fountain bubbling through the generous rock,
Its waters colder than the northern snow.

I have to tell the truth about what I feel, and that is the truth about
it. That's what it feels like. And as I say, it's always accompanied by a
sense that *there's more where that came from* – that somewhere there's an
inexhaustible source of strength, truth, meaning, encouragement, blessedness. It feels like being blessed. Something has come from somewhere
else to refresh and strengthen me. And it's not given parsimoniously;
I'm not offered just a drop or two, and told that's all I can have because
they're running short, and other people need it too, and I have to make
it last, and I can't expect any more in this financial year. There's never
that implication; there's always enough. And that feeling itself is a great
source of hope and strength. A *source*, you see: the image enters the language. There's the fundamental particle again, almost too hard to see,
except when we look.

The image of inspiration as a spring, and its connection with storytelling, is vividly present in Samuel Taylor Coleridge's two great poems
'The Rime of the Ancient Mariner' and 'Kubla Khan'. 'Kubla Khan' is
structured around the image of a river, the sacred river Alph, which runs
'Through caverns measureless to man / Down to a sunless sea'.

In the central section of the poem Coleridge describes the 'deep
romantic chasm' which is 'a savage place! As holy and enchanted / As e'er
beneath a waning moon was haunted / By woman wailing for her demon-
lover'. Now the woman wailing for her demon lover appears just once,
and out of nowhere, and is never more than a figure for comparison. She's
not a character in the poem – she's the sort of person you might see in
a place like that, so that's the sort of place it was. There is an old Scots
ballad called 'The Demon Lover', which Coleridge must have known (he
was well read in the Scots ballads), though in that, the situation between

the woman and her demon lover is quite different from the one in 'Kubla Khan'. But the woman here, who is the sort of person you might well see in a deep romantic chasm, is a figure from a story (something must have led her to this; something will follow in consequence) even if it's a story we don't know. And it's right in this story-haunted place that the river bursts out of the earth:

> And from this chasm, with ceaseless turmoil seething,
> As if this earth in fast thick pants were breathing,
> A mighty fountain momently was forced…

The river makes its way from the fountain where it emerges, 'Five miles meandering with a mazy motion', to the cave where it sinks again. Halfway between them Kubla built his pleasure-dome, 'Where was heard the mingled measure / From the fountain and the caves.' The river itself is bountiful, life-bringing: along its course

> … there were gardens bright with sinuous rills
> Where blossomed many an incense-bearing tree.

When the river has run its five-mile course, and reaches the caverns measureless to man, it 'sinks in tumult to a lifeless ocean', but as it pours down it evokes yet more stories, this time stories of the future: 'And 'mid this tumult Kubla heard from far / Ancestral voices prophesying war!'

The poet's own description of inspiration in the final section of the poem owes nothing to springs or fountains. He describes how he once had a vision of an Abyssinian damsel singing and playing a dulcimer, and says

> Could I revive within me
> Her symphony and song,

To such a deep delight 'twould win me
That with music loud and long,
I would build that dome in air…

In other words, I would speak about it in such a way that my words alone would bring it into being:

That sunny dome! Those caves of ice!
And all who heard should see them there,
And all should cry, Beware! Beware!
His flashing eyes, his floating hair!
Weave a circle round him thrice,
And close your eyes with holy dread,
For he on honey-dew hath fed,
And drunk the milk of Paradise.

So there are two different images for inspiration here: one consists of hearing music from a vision, and the other of consuming something magical or sacred. (I wonder about that milk of Paradise, though: where does milk emerge from? Whose breasts are there in Paradise to give this milk? Whose udders? Is there a sacred cow of Paradise?)

But the image he most wants to evoke, the one he says he would evoke if he were inspired, is that of the sunny dome and the caves of ice, from which, it was possible to hear both the fountain and the caves: the river emerging and disappearing again; the woman wailing for her demon lover and the ancestral voices, the stories from both directions.

In 'The Rime of the Ancient Mariner', where of course we are at sea for most of the poem – 'Water, water everywhere, / Nor any drop to drink' – the spring appears at the very moment of the mariner's greatest torment, and it brings a blessing, literally. The mariner is alone on the still ship, alone with the albatross around his neck, tormented by his guilt and his anguish among the bodies of the dead sailors, and unable to pray for forgiveness. The moon shines on the still sea, and

> Where the ship's huge shadow lay
> The charmèd water burnt alway
> A still and awful red.

And in the shadow he watches the water-snakes:

> Within the shadow of the ship
> I watched their rich attire:
> Blue, glossy green, and velvet black,
> They coiled and swam; and every track
> Was a flash of golden fire.

> Oh happy living things! no tongue
> Their beauty might declare:
> A spring of love gushed from my heart,
> And I blessed them unaware:
> Sure my kind saint took pity on me,
> And I blessed them unaware.

> The self-same moment I could pray;
> And from my neck so free
> The Albatross fell off, and sank
> Like lead into the sea.

Love comes as a spring, and makes his redemption possible. He finds his way home and visits the hermit good who lives in the wood, who hears his story and gives him absolution; but ever afterwards he has to tell the story again.

I pass, like night, from land to land;
I have strange power of speech;
The moment that his face I see,
I know the man that must hear me:
To him my tale I teach.

As if his story, as if all stories, were something contained, something carried carefully from here to there, like a vessel full of precious liquid; you don't want to spill any of it, you don't want to let it leak away or evaporate fruitlessly, and then when you've found the right place you release it in a controlled flow: he poured out his story. I found myself using this image once quite instinctively to someone who wanted me to interrupt my work and go to America to speak at a conference or something: here I am, I said, with this story, this bowl brim-full that I have to carry precariously through a field strewn with obstacles, and you throw more rocks in my path...

Well, we've come a long way, but I said we'd end with a cup of tea, and we're nearly at the end, which is back where we started. I read a few paragraphs from two stories, and what I'm going to look at finally is the way in which this little action, our fundamental particle, the pouring-something-out story, can take on different meanings in a written tale depending on the context, and furthermore can set up patterns – actions and repetitions of actions – that themselves reinforce the meaning and the emotional colouring of the story they occur in.

And also, of course, it makes a great difference what it is that's being poured out.

In the first story, *Clockwork*, the mysterious clockmaker Dr Kalmenius is in the bar of the inn with the troubled young apprentice Karl, and he pours him a glass of brandy. The pouring of brandy might have a number of different connotations, hospitality for one; but in this case it serves to reinforce the sinister power of the older man. Power belongs to those who bestow, not to those who receive. And as for what he's offering, what he's pouring out, you give strong drink to a much younger person if you want to befuddle or trick or dominate them. The pouring of the drink here is emblematic of danger, intoxication, confusion, perhaps even oblivion.

And the action of pouring brandy turns up once more near the end of *Clockwork*, and the pattern reinforces the meaning that was established first time. The little girl Gretl has found her way through the night to the room where the hapless young storyteller is packing a bag in desperation. It was the story he began to tell in the inn, earlier that night, that set all the strange events in motion. Gretl has gone to beg him to finish the story properly.

> 'You've got to listen to me!' she said. 'Something dreadful's going to happen, and I don't know what it is because you didn't finish the story properly. What happens next?'
>
> 'I don't know!' he groaned. 'I dreamed the first part of it, and it was so strange and horrible that I couldn't resist writing it down and pretending it was mine... But when the door opened and the old man came in, I must have panicked... Oh, I wish I'd never begun! I'll never tell a story again!'
>
> 'You must tell the end of this one, though,' said Gretl, 'or something bad will happen. You've got to!'
>
> 'Impossible,' he said. 'I can't control it any more. I wash my hands of it. I'm off – as far away as I can get!'
>
> And he poured himself another glass of plum brandy and swallowed it all in one go.

So these little actions, the pouring of a glass of brandy once near the beginning and once near the end of the story, set up and reinforce a pattern of feelings to do with desperation and loss of control.

If you remember, the other story concerned the way in which Roger the ex-rat, who doesn't know how to eat with a spoon, makes a mess of his bread and milk; and how Joan takes him to the kitchen sink, where she tips in some water from the kettle.

The kettle, because we're in a world where modern things like hot-water taps would be out of place. In the fairy-tale world, we know what kettles do: they sit on kitchen ranges quietly steaming away, or at the edge of a fire in the hearth. They suggest warmth, cosiness, domesticity, nourishment: 'Polly put the kettle on.' So at the beginning of that story Joan pours the hot water into the sink in order to wash the little boy, not only the milky face he's acquired in the kitchen but the grubby hands he came in with as well. The kettle is a vessel of cleanliness and order, of domestic harmony, in contrast to the wild outside, where rats live among the dirt.

And at the very end of the story, after all Roger's adventures, after we've seen him brought almost to the point of death by the greed and fear and ignorance of those outside, only to be rescued by a princess and restored to his new-found family, the three of them are in the kitchen once more. Roger is telling Bob and Joan what he's learned about the difference between rats and people.

> 'You have less trouble being a rat,' he says, 'except for being sterminated. I wouldn't want that. It's hard being a person, but it's not so hard if they think you *are* a person. If they think you ain't a person, then it's too hard for me. I think I'll stick to cobbling.'
>
> 'That's a wise decision,' said Bob. 'There's always a demand for good craftsmanship. If I hadn't made them slippers, well, I don't like to think what would have happened.'
>
> The kettle came to the boil, so Joan made them all a cup of

tea, and Bob toasted some cheese, and they all sat down comfortably around the hearth. The world outside was a difficult place, but toasted cheese and love and craftsmanship would do to keep them safe.

And once again the image recurring makes a pattern that reinforces the feeling. The kettle, and what you do with it, what you pour out of it, is a signifier of all that safety and warmth and nurturing domestic happiness.

To sum up, then, we've followed this little narrative pattern, this fundamental particle, through various appearances and transformations and contexts, and seen some of the ways in which it works. There are many other such fundamental particles, such as the journey – the idea of a task as a journey along a path from here to there; or the one about balance, with equilibrium being disturbed or restored; or the one about repetition and echoing; or the one in the form of a cycle, moving around and coming back to where you started. I sort of did that with this talk this evening. For those who know *His Dark Materials*, you can find yet another fundamental particle underlying that long story, and that's the one in which two things that are closely bound together split apart and go their separate ways. That little pattern turns up over and over again in the story – quite without my intending it to; I only saw it there when the story was finished.

And finally I should explain why I've found these little fundamental particles of narrative so rich and rewarding to think about. It's because of their groundedness in physical experience, in the actions and sensations of our bodies as we interact with the world – as we pour water out of a jug, or as we walk along a path, or as we open a door and go into a room: simple basic physical experiences that underlie so many metaphors and so much understanding. If I could name one idea I'd like readers of *His Dark Materials* to retain when they finish the book, it would be the emphasis the story puts on the value and centrality of bodily experience.

Detail of *The Milkmaid* by Johannes Vermeer

The angels envy the vivid and intense sensations that we have through our nerves and senses. As Will says at the end of *The Amber Spyglass*: 'Angels wish they had bodies. They told me that angels can't understand why we don't enjoy the world more. It would be sort of ecstasy for them to have our flesh and our senses.'

We need to remember that we are not a ghost in a machine; we don't sit in our heads like an astronaut in a command module. We are our bodies. Body and mind are one. Or as William Blake put it, 'Man has no Body distinct from his Soul; for that call'd Body is a portion of Soul discern'd by the five Senses.'

As I say, there are many fundamental particles of this kind, and it would be possible to say a great deal about each one of them; but I thought it better this evening just to focus on one. Thank you for inviting me to give this lecture, and thank you for listening.

POCO A POCO

This talk was delivered as the Richard Hillary Lecture at Trinity College, Oxford, February 2007.

Some more of these abstract fundamental particles of narrative:
Going out of somewhere / Going in to somewhere
Moving upwards / Moving downwards
Getting larger / Getting smaller
Carrying something
Striking something
Handing something to someone else
Assembling something / Taking something apart
… and so on.

The Classical Tone

NARRATIVE TACT AND OTHER CLASSICAL VIRTUES

On the narrator – a very unusual character – time and viewpoint in relation to Philippa Pearce's Tom's Midnight Garden

Time present and time past
Are both perhaps present in time future
And time future contained in time past.
If all time is eternally present
All time is unredeemable.
What might have been is an abstraction
Remaining a perpetual possibility
Only in a world of speculation.
What might have been and what has been
Point to one end, which is always present.
Footfalls echo in the memory
Down the passage which we did not take
Towards the door we never opened
Into the rose-garden.
(T. S. Eliot, *Four Quartets: Burnt Norton*)

I quote those words at the beginning for the sake of their relevance to what I'm going to be talking about this evening in the context of *Tom's Midnight Garden*, because if we had to say in one word what that novel was about, there's little doubt that the answer would be 'time'.

The book is a wonderfully wrought story, but it's more than that, though a good story is quite enough for anything to be; it's a lens through which we can see something more clearly, and the something in this case is that mysterious thing called time. The grandfather clock that strikes thirteen when it should strike midnight undoes our normal time, the time of wakefulness and the business of daily life, and allows us an hour of a different time from somewhere, or somewhen, else. It does this through the person of Tom, who experiences these different times, and through the calm, kindly voice of the narrator who tells us about him.

Original UK edition of
Tom's Midnight Garden

I read the book when I was young, and fell under its spell, as so many did, though I didn't remember it very accurately. When I was young I thought the daily life of Tom's own time was itself a long time ago, because of one or two little things that stuck in my mind: like the dreadfully serious way all the adults took measles, as if it were some deadly miasma before which medical science fled with its hands in the air. Tom's age isn't given, but to go by the date of publication, if he was a contemporary boy he must be more or less exactly my own age, living in my own time; and I'd had measles, and no fuss was made at all. But they obviously made a fuss in the old days, I thought. And there was the way people spoke. At one point Tom asks Aunt Gwen about the flowers she put in his bedroom: 'Had you to buy them?' he says. Elsewhere he also says, 'I wish I hadn't to go home tomorrow.' I registered those things with interest, as ways people must have spoken long ago. I certainly never heard anyone use either of those locutions when I was growing up.

So it was already a book set in the past, before the garden comes into the story with its even-further-back layers of time. Reading it recently, I saw that I must have been wrong about that, and Philippa Pearce in the 1950s was writing a contemporary story, though there were things about it that made it feel old-fashioned, as if the author herself were a little old-fashioned, a little more attached to and aware of the past than some other writers. I also saw a little more of how she was doing what she did, and therefore I found more to admire.

A quite extraordinary number of novels published these days, for adults as well as for children, use the present tense. I recently listened to a presentation by creative writing students at a certain university, and they had all written a novel or part of one, and by far the majority had written in the present tense. (When I asked their tutor why he thought they'd done this, he had to admit he hadn't even noticed). Fiction editors have told me that a large number of the books they receive from literary agents are told in the present tense, a good number of those in the first person as well. It's certainly true of the books they send me asking for a puff.

Something has happened to our understanding of fiction, or of the past, or something, to make the present tense the way in which young people, and adults as well, want to talk about something that can only be in the past, namely the events about which they're writing. It might be the influence of TV and film drama: drama, of course, happens *now* rather than *then*, and the present is the only appropriate tense for stage directions. It might be that, but in that case the turn to the present tense would have happened a lot earlier; this has been going on since the 1990s, as far as I can see. In the 1950s, when Philippa Pearce wrote *Tom's Midnight Garden* in the past tense that was conventional then, it was quite uncommon to use the present tense, though some writers had chosen to do so for perfectly good reasons. Dickens had done so, in parts of *Bleak House* and elsewhere. I've done so myself, though rarely. But now it's all over the place.

I make this point about the present tense to emphasise the contrast between what we often get now, the immediate, the up-close, the hectic of the incessant present tense, and what I might call the classical style of Pearce's writing, which has a great deal to do with how the narrator does her work. There's a coolness, a judicious calm about the way the story is told – a tone which more and more now seems itself to be old-fashioned, quite apart from the medical anxieties about measles and the way people speak. I like that classical tone very much, I admire it when I see it, I try to achieve it in my own work; and one of the aspects of that 'classical' tone is the voice of the narrator.

The technical term for the way she tells the story (and I'll come back to that 'she' in a minute) is free indirect style. This means that it's told from a point of view that takes in both what is happening and a particular character's thoughts and feelings about it. It seems to many readers a perfectly natural way of writing, but it hasn't had a very long history in comparison with the length of time people have been telling each other stories. Jane Austen is often put forward as the first consistent user of this point of view in English fiction: we're told what *happens* in *Emma* the book and also what Emma Woodhouse the character *thinks* about it.

The viewpoint isn't entirely limited to Emma's, though. The narrator can express a different point of view with great clarity. The voice that tells the story tells us more about Emma than she would necessarily like us to know:

> The real evils, indeed, of Emma's situation were the power
> of having rather too much her own way, and a disposition to
> think a little too well of herself.

This tart assessment of the young lady changes with the most natural air in the world into a view of Emma's own thoughts and feelings:

He had misinterpreted the feelings which had kept her face averted, and her tongue motionless. They were combined only of anger against herself, mortification, and deep concern. She had not been able to speak; and, on reaching the carriage sunk back for a moment overcome – then reproaching herself for having taken no leave, making no acknowledgement, parting in apparent sullenness.

It's such a swift and supple method of telling a story that most of us probably don't notice the way the point of view darts from one spot to another. We see the same process at work in *Tom's Midnight Garden*. Here's the voice from outside Tom:

Yes, you could hear it striking, very distinctly; you could count the strokes. Tom counted them, and smiled condescendingly: the clock was wrong again in its striking – senselessly wrong.

I don't think we'd find Tom using the word *condescendingly* about himself, even if he knew it. The narrator is making a judgement about him. This view from outside knows the world and how it works. On Tom's family – the Longs:

The Kitsons were better off than the Longs – there is all the difference, in expense, between having two children and having none at all.

Very occasionally we find ourselves neither in Tom's thoughts nor watching him from outside. Half a dozen or so times in the novel, the narrator finds herself needing to tell us something that was going on elsewhere:

Alan Kitson would have been disappointed if he had seen Mrs Bartholomew. She was lying tranquilly in bed: her false teeth, in a glass of water by the bedside, grinned unpleasantly in the moonlight, but her indrawn mouth was curved in a smile of easy, sweet-dreaming sleep. She was dreaming of the scenes of her childhood.

And here's Tom and Peter's mother, looking at Peter asleep:

Once he smiled, and then sighed; and once such a far-away look came into his face that his mother bent over him in an impulse to wake him and recall him to her. She restrained herself, and left him.

But for most of the time we, the readers, are with Tom – in fact, we're inside his head. We share so much of his awareness that an interesting little point in this passage, for example, doesn't snag at our attention in the least:

His thoughts ran on the garden, as they always did nowadays. He reflected how dangerously near he had been to betraying it, just now.

Whose *nowadays* is it? Whose *now*? A pedant would no doubt say that the sentences should read:

His thoughts ran on the garden, as they always did at that stage. He reflected how dangerously near he had been to betraying it, just then.

After all, it's Tom's time we're reading about, not ours; *now* and *nowadays* belong to us, in our time, not his. But that's not quite right either, because is it our time, in the twenty-first century, or the narrator's time, in 1958? Surely the word *nowadays* should really be referring to her time, not his, and not ours either.

But of course we don't read like that. We've drawn so close to Tom in the preceding part of the story that his time has become our time, at least for the time we spend reading the book. We're with him so closely that we share his thoughts, and his reflections are partly ours, and his *now* and *nowadays* are ours too.

And this is where it gets really interesting, because (as I said about *Emma* the book) if it's done well we hardly notice the moments when the point of view shifts from outside Tom to inside Tom, from Tom then to Tom now, from Tom him to Tom us. If we're not looking for it we don't notice it at all. The movement is performed so swiftly and lightly that it seems the most natural thing in the world, even though really it's a complicated psychological manoeuvre.

But who's making this manoeuvre?

Well, Philippa Pearce, of course, says Mr Common Sense, the Reader Who Will Not Be Fooled. But Mr Common Sense is deeply fooled if he thinks that. A moment ago I spoke about the narrator, and used a possessive pronoun to speak of the time in which something happened: *her* time, I said. Mr Common Sense was perfectly happy with that, because he thought I was referring to the author. But I wasn't. I was referring to the narrator, and I might just as correctly have said *his* time. (Why shouldn't the disembodied voice of the narrator be male?) In fact, I said *her* because I also had a *his* in the sentence, meaning Tom's, and I wanted to distinguish between them. 'Her time, not his, and not ours either,' was what I said.

But isn't the author the narrator? says Mr Common Sense, on the verge of being outraged.

No, is the answer. The narrator is a character invented by the author, just as much as Tom is, and Hatty is, and Uncle Alan and Aunt Gwen are, just as much as Mr Woodhouse and Emma and Mr Knightley and Miss Bates and every other character in a novel. The narrator is a very unusual character, mind you, only manifest as that disembodied voice. I believe that the narrator is not actually a human character at all, and his or her relationship to time is one of the ways in which his or her uncanny inhumanness is manifest.

Think what the narrator can do. He or she can flit between one mind and another, as we've seen. Human beings can't do that. He or she can dart backwards and forwards along the stream of time like a kingfisher. As I've said before, my favourite example of this kind of narration, the so-called omniscient sort, is the famous chapter in Thackeray's *Vanity Fair* about the panic in Brussels during the Battle of Waterloo. The narrator speeds over all the extent of the panorama, focusing now on this detail, now on that, sometimes looking a little ahead to the days after the battle and sometimes looking a little back to the days just before, and then looking both backwards and forwards along a whole length of time.

And finally in the wonderful last paragraph taking in the panorama of the whole landscape and then focusing closely on two of the main characters, one knowing nothing of the other, the other capable of knowing nothing about anyone any more:

> No more firing was heard at Brussels – the pursuit rolled miles away. Darkness came down on the field and the city; and Amelia was praying for George, who was lying on his face, dead, with a bullet through his heart.

This capacity of the narrator to move from here to there with the speed of thought, to see a whole panorama in one glance and then to fly down like a dragonfly and land with utter precision on the most important detail, to look ahead in time as well as to look behind, is one of the most extraordinary things we human beings have ever invented. We take it for granted, and I think we should applaud it a little more. I don't know if it makes anyone else rub their eyes in wonder, but it certainly makes me do so; and every time I read a book where the author is so miraculously in control of this ghostly being, the narrator, this voice so like a human's but so uncanny in its knowledge and so swift and sprite-like in its movement, I feel a delight in possibility and mystery and make-believe.

(A little side-note: a moment ago I referred to 'the so-called omniscient' narration, or narrator. We often hear it referred to as omniscient, but that isn't a very accurate name for it, because to demonstrate the narrator's omniscience we would need a text that did literally speak about everything, and that would take longer than the universe has been in existence. We haven't got time for that. The narrator clearly knows many things, though, and should really be called *multiscient* – a perfectly respectable word. I was curious to see whether my favourite dictionary had taken note of this, so I opened it: Chambers' revised edition of 1959, now much battered and mended, a handy size, and full of those little explosions of mischief among the definitions that delight all Chambers devotees. And there it was, in the form of '*multiscience*: knowledge of many things'. Wondering if the word was still current, I opened my latest Chambers, the 10th edition of 2006, the approximate dimensions of a microwave oven, and found that it had gone. On the way to it, though, I found this definition of *mullet*, which I recommend to you: 'a hairstyle that is short at the front, long at the back, and ridiculous all round'.)

I want to look briefly at two other forms of narration, both familiar in different settings.

One is the first-person way of telling a story:

> Whether I shall turn out to be the hero of my own life, or whether that station will be held by anybody else, these pages must show. To begin my life with the beginning of my life, I

record that I was born (as I have been informed and believe) on a Friday, at twelve o'clock at night. It was remarked that the clock began to strike, and I began to cry, simultaneously.

The opening of Dickens's *David Copperfield*. There are many advantages of telling a story like this. It seems natural: the witness to events is telling us about them directly. It's long-established: Daniel Defoe, sometimes referred to as the founder of the English novel, used it for *Robinson Crusoe*. It's still highly popular; one of its most comfortable forms of expression is the thriller, but it is flexible enough to serve the most literary of texts: 'For a long time I used to go to bed early …' It still satisfies readers, and more than satisfies: I heard of one American reader, the friend of a friend, a highly educated man, who refuses to read any fiction that is *not* written in the first person, on the grounds that he doesn't know where it's coming from, who's telling the story – he just can't trust any voice that isn't attached to a name.

There are disadvantages to the first-person method too. I've rarely used it myself, because I can't help asking why should this character who's telling this story sound so like me? Because he or she inevitably would, no matter how hard I tried. And there's the matter of plausibility. I have put down unfinished more children's novels than I could count because they purport to be told by a child or a teenager, and yet their main characteristic is a slick mastery of tone and structure that can only come from a practised adult with an eye on the marketplace. You have to be plausible about what knowledge is available to your narrator too. Conan Doyle solved that problem by making Dr Watson a bit slower and simpler than Sherlock Holmes, and as much in the dark as the reader is, until Holmes reveals exactly how the unfortunate Miss Stoner met her ghastly death – or whatever.

Could *Tom's Midnight Garden* work as a first-person narrative? Only with a great deal of strain. Tom himself is too young to make a plausible narrator – too young as he is in the book, anyway. You could have a grown-up Tom reflecting on this extraordinary passage from his child-hood – that would be plausible enough – but why bother, unless the real theme of that book were his adult life? But that would be a different story. *This* is the story: the story is the things that are happening to Tom now, not Tom thinking about them later.

Hatty could possibly do it, but that would mean breaking the story in two – the first part to tell about the strange ghost-like boy who haunts her childhood, and the second to tell of their meeting again after so many years. And that would mean losing the magic of Tom's encounters with the garden, which we encounter with him in that wonderful slow-devel-oping way, which works as well as it does because of the frustration and unhappiness before it, which we also encounter with him through the free indirect method that Pearce uses. So it would be no good asking Hatty to tell the story either. Furthermore, there are those little glimpses of other people elsewhere that wouldn't be available either to Tom or to Hatty. The story we have is told the only way – well, no: the *best* way it could be told.

The other form of narration I want to consider is what we get in fairy tales. I mean fairy tales of the Grimm variety, not the Andersen.

'Once there was a miller who had a beautiful daughter …'

'Once there was a king who had three sons …'

'There were once two brothers, one rich and the other poor …'

Once upon a time, in fact. A long time ago, not now. Of literary style in fairy tales there is not a smidgeon, because these are not literary works, they're oral ones. It doesn't matter precisely what words the story is told in – there is no authentic text: all we have are transcriptions of oral render-ings, sometimes faithful, sometimes bowdlerised, sometimes elaborated, renderings which themselves may differ greatly from one storyteller to another, even when telling the same story. The *words* don't matter; what matters is the sequence of events.

But that matters a great deal. If you read all the Brothers Grimm stories, as I've been doing recently, and you happen to be struck by the neatness and power of this one or that one, there's a good chance that you'll find, when you look it up, that the Grimms' source for it was a woman called Dorothea Viehmann. She was a seller of fruit and vegetables, the widow of a tailor, and altogether she contributed thirty-five of their stories, including some of the best, like *Faithful Johannes*, *The Devil with the Three Golden Hairs*, and *The Goose Girl*. She had the unusual power, according to the brothers Grimm, of not only being able to tell the tale swiftly and vigorously the first time, but also of then being able to go back and retell it slowly, passage by passage, not altering it a bit, so they could write it down accurately. Clearly she had worked the story over in her head many times, getting it just right, cutting out everything redundant, making sure everything necessary was in the right place and given its proper weight.

And not interposing anything *literary*. Modern literary fairy tales are almost universally ghastly, in my view, being affected, whimsical, putting on a show, nudging us, winking at us, showing us how clever they are, or how compassionate, or making sure we get the right political message – swanking or ingratiating or hectoring. Away with them! The great folk tales are interested in none of that sort of thing. In the words of the American poet James Merrill, the voice of the folk tale has 'a tone licked clean / Over the centuries by mild old tongues, / Grandam to cub, serene, anonymous.'

Here's a passage from Grimm in that sort of tone:

> At midnight everyone was asleep except for the nurse, who
> was sitting beside the cradle in the nursery. She saw the door

open and she saw the real queen come in. The queen took the baby out of the cradle, put it to her breast and suckled it. Then she plumped up the pillow, laid the child down again, and covered it up with its little quilt.

And she didn't forget the fawn. She went to the corner where he was lying and stroked his back. Then without a word she left the room.

In the morning the nurse asked the guards if anyone had come into the palace during the night, and they said, 'No, we haven't seen a soul.' After that the queen came many nights, and never said a word; the nurse always saw her but didn't dare mention it to anyone.

[*Little Brother and Little Sister*]

I could have opened Grimm almost anywhere and found a passage to quote, but I wanted one with 'midnight' in it, to go with David Copperfield and pay tribute to the grandfather clock in *Tom's Midnight Garden*.

Anyway, what that tone says, anonymously and serenely and beyond any doubt, is: 'These things happened.' The events are located firmly in the past, once upon a time. The narrating voice knows exactly what they were, and what order they happened in, and how best to make these events clear and unambiguous. (Ambiguity is, or can be, one of the virtues of a literary text: who can be sure *exactly* what Henry James is saying in some of his passages? Are the apparitions in *The Turn of the Screw* objectively there or the product of the unfortunate governess's disordered mind? No one knows; and how much less powerful the story would be if we did).

But there can be no ambiguity in the folk tale. The real queen in the passage I read just now from *Little Brother and Little Sister* is as dead as a doornail; we even know where her body is hidden. She's a ghost if ever there was one. Clarity is everything.

That has the corollary that the events of the folk tale, which are shown to us with such brilliant and uninflected clarity, must be interesting in themselves if the story is to work. They must be dramatic, violent, exterior and visible. Consider trying to tell *Emma* as a folk tale:

> *Once there was a rich man who had a beautiful daughter ...*

I think you'd get that far and then you'd have to stop and scratch your head. To try and tell the story of *Emma*, or of *Vanity Fair*, or of *Tom's Midnight Garden*, as a folk tale would be to create a kind of monster; the novel is a complex thing, and many of its events, compared with the ferocious melodrama of the folk tale, are interior and invisible.

The ferocious melodrama of the *events* of the folk tale, I should emphasise, because in the voice of the Brothers Grimm's best stories, or for that matter some of those assembled by Katharine Briggs or Italo Calvino or Aleksandr Afanasyev, or for the matter of that in ballads such as *Sir Patrick Spens*, a great folk tale can have something of the same quality I attributed to Philippa Pearce's style earlier on: a 'classical' quality, characterised by clarity and steadiness and coolness of tone.

But *Tom's Midnight Garden* isn't a folk tale, or anything like one; once again, the way it's told is the best way it could be told.

I want to finish my brief look at different aspects of this mysterious thing, the narrator, by looking in a little more detail at some aspects of the narrator's activity in the book itself.

The first thing we encounter, of course, is the opening, and anyone who's tried to write a story knows that the right opening is a very hard thing to get right. Where – at which point in the characters' lives – do you start? Consider the points in the stream of time where the story might just as well have begun. It could have opened with Tom and Peter planning to make their tree house, their project that's later frustrated. Or with the first symptoms of the measles that will separate the brothers for the summer. Or with Alan Kitson and Tom arriving at the Kitsons' flat in the big house crowded round with newer, smaller houses, the house with no visible garden, where Tom's adventure will take place. Or with Tom's mother writing to the Kitsons asking if they can take Tom in till Peter is better. All perfectly reasonable choices. So is the one we do have: the story opens with Tom about to leave in the car with Uncle Alan, and feeling bitter and resentful about having to do so. Why is that better than the others? Or is it? Might it have been better to go way back to Hatty, and have the story open with the little Victorian girl looking wide-eyed at the pyjama-clad boy whom nobody else sees?

Well, I think it would have been wrong to begin with Hatty, if only because this is Tom's story and not hers, and the character we see first is the one to whom we feel the story belongs, in some way. One of the characteristics of the classical style is that it's not afraid of the obvious, and it never tries to be original. This is a story about Tom and his adventure: why begin with anyone else? As for *when*, this moment is pivotal. We can see both Tom's background, where he comes from, the past, the people he's leaving behind, especially the brother he'll miss so much, *and* the car and the driver who are going to carry him into the future. In T. S. Eliot's words I quoted at the beginning,

> Time present and time past
> Are both perhaps present in time future –

– the future time when we shall be reading the story.

The opening of a book only occurs once, but that doesn't mean the problems are over when you've found the best opening. Every sentence that comes afterwards has to be thought over, an appropriate position and stance established for the narrator. How close to the characters is the narrator going to stand? Close enough to see them in detail, at least.

A book that begins 'All happy families are alike; every unhappy family is unhappy in its own way' had better quite quickly find a particular family to focus on, or the reader in search of a novel will take it for a work of sociology. A novel needs to look closely at people.

I'll finish with three examples of the narrator's looking closely, and of her perfect tact in doing so, by which I mean finding precisely the best spot to look from and the best moment to do it.

The first is where Tom is questioning Uncle Alan about Time. Uncle Alan, as the narrator never says but as we can see with perfect clarity, is an overbearing know-all who enjoys the domination he's established over his wife and which he'd like to establish over Tom.

> 'What *is* Time like, Uncle Alan?' asked Tom.
>
> His uncle put his book down altogether; and his aunt nervously put down her mending, too.
>
> 'Tom,' she said, 'you shouldn't always be asking such very odd questions of your uncle. He's tired after his day's work.'
>
> 'No, no, Gwen. A child's questions should certainly be answered. All I would object to Tom's questions is their lack of connexion, and sometimes of seriousness, too. Look at his first question: he asked whether it would be possible to go through a door – he actually asked *how* it would be possible!'
>
> 'Well!' cried Tom's aunt, with a relief that came from her not having paid attention to the earlier conversation. 'Well, that seems a very sensible idea – so sensible that it's almost silly!'
>
> Alan Kitson raised his eyebrows, and his wife went on hurriedly: 'You know what I mean – going through a door's such an everyday happening.'

The passage continues in the same vein, and there's plenty there to show us what the narrator is doing: showing us what a pompous bully Alan is by looking not at him but at Gwen, and her nervous reactions to everything he says or might say.

(Two other tiny points in the narrator's destruction of Alan Kitson: in the final section, where Tom wakes the household by crying out in distress when he finds the garden isn't there, Alan explains to the other tenant on their floor that *his wife's* nephew has been sleepwalking: deflecting some of the blame on to her. Tom is his own nephew as well, by marriage: it wouldn't have cost him much to say 'my nephew'.

Then next day when they learn that Mrs Bartholomew upstairs expects an apology for the noise in the night, when Aunt Gwen is ready to defend Tom and protest strongly, he shrinks back and says, 'Careful, Gwen! She is the landlady. If we upset her, she could be very awkward.'

It's the most delicate dissection of a bully, all done by looking in the right direction at the right moment.)

The second example of looking closely from the right spot comes at the end of Tom's series of encounters with Hatty, when they skate to Ely and climb the tower of the cathedral. We start with a glimpse from Hatty's point of view:

> From the other side of the leads, Hatty looked round to see where Tom had got to. She saw, instead of one boy, two: they were very much alike, and dressed identically in pyjamas. The second boy had the same insubstantial look that she had detected recently in Tom himself: she was almost sure that she could see the tower parapet through them both. She stared in wonderment.
>
> 'But, Tom, where's the garden?' Peter was saying, rather querulously. 'I thought you were with Hatty, in the garden.'
>
> Tom answered directly, because he felt in his bones that

time was short, and shortening. 'The garden's back there,' he said briefly, flinging his arm outwards, in the direction of Castleford. 'And Hatty's here.'

'Where? I can't see her,' said Peter.

Tom was pointing with his finger, and Peter was facing Hatty across the leads – she was the only one among the sightseers who had turned in his direction.

'There!' said Tom. 'Right opposite to you – the one carrying skates.'

'But that' – said Peter indignantly – 'that's not Hatty: that's a grown-up woman!'

Tom, staring at Hatty as though he were seeing her for the first time, opened his mouth to speak: but he could not.

'Time' – called the tower-keeper – 'time to go down again, if you please, ladies and gentlemen!'

At that point we the readers needed to see Hatty through other eyes than Tom's. Peter was the only other character who could both have seen her and expressed the meaning of what he saw, without knowing it himself, to Tom. And I can feel the delight that must have touched Philippa Pearce as she thought of the tower-keeper's intervention: 'Time!'

I shall end where the book ends, with that marvellous final paragraph (in the true meaning of that word: it's a marvel, a wonder, something miraculous).

Here it is:

Afterwards, Aunt Gwen tried to describe to her husband that second parting between them. 'He ran up to her, and they hugged each other as if they had known each other for years and years, instead of only having met for the first time this morning. There was something else, too, Alan, although

I know you'll say it sounds even more absurd…Of course, Mrs Bartholomew's such a shrunken little old woman, she's hardly bigger than Tom, anyway: but, you know, he put his arms right round her and he hugged her good-bye as if she were a little girl.'

Why does the narrator not tell us directly what happened, instead of giving the job to Aunt Gwen? And if we are to see it through Aunt Gwen's eyes, why not tell us what she sees at that moment, instead of skipping ahead to a time when she, the narrator, could say 'afterwards'?

To my mind that would be rather like asking, 'Why did Mozart write this note, and not that one?' The only answer is, 'Because he was Mozart.' When we see perfection we should acknowledge it and applaud. That famous last paragraph *is* perfect, and part of its perfection is its perfect tact, that very classical virtue.

Consider the consequences of finding the last line, 'he put his arms right round her and he hugged her goodbye as if she were a little girl', told in the voice of the narrator. How wrong that would seem! What a catastrophic error! In the narrator's voice those words would sound stridently sentimental, when what we need most is the warm depth of true feeling. The genius of this passage, of course, is that Gwen expresses the feeling without knowing what she's saying, and allows us to make the connection. It has to come *afterwards*, because we don't need the narrator telling us what Gwen was feeling as she was feeling it: we need her own words as she tells her husband what she's seen. In some ways Aunt Gwen, that kindly, nervous, occasionally silly woman who is much more courageous and infinitely more perceptive than her husband, is the heroine of this book. Like the gardener Abel – the only one from Hatty's time who can see Tom – she can see across time to the little girl that Mrs Bartholomew was, and she offers that vision to her husband, knowing, as she says, that he'll think it absurd.

Well, so much the worse for those who are clever enough to think things absurd and scoff at them on that account, and all praise to those who offer their visions to the clever ones, in spite of all disappointment.

There are many other things to say about this book, and about the mysterious and shadowy figure of the narrator, and about other figures as well. Author and narrator are not the only participants in the process of reading. There is the real reader, and there's that shadowy figure, the reader the book seems to expect. And then there's that other even more shadowy figure, the implied author (or as I prefer to say, the inferred author).

And then there's Mr Common Sense, the Reader Who Will Not Be Fooled. But he doesn't come to lectures, so we can forget about him, and in any case all my time is used up.

THIS TALK WAS DELIVERED AS THE PHILIPPA PEARCE LECTURE, HOMERTON COLLEGE, CAMBRIDGE UNIVERSITY, 2011.

After I'd given this lecture, a person in the audience – who turned out to be Philippa Pearce's daughter – came up to me and asked if I knew about the editing of that famous last chapter. I didn't, and she told me that there had originally been another chapter to follow it, but the editor had said to the author that that chapter was redundant: this ending was perfect as it was. Pearce was sensible enough to take that advice. I sometimes think each book should contain, as well as a little note about the typeface and the design, the name of the editor.

Reading in the Borderland

READING, BOOKS AND PICTURES

On the space between the reader's mind and the book
they are reading, and on some of the books with illustrations
in whose borderlands I have most enjoyed wandering

THE BORDERLAND, THE LAND ALONG THE FRONTIER, IS THE SPACE THAT opens up between the private mind of the reader and the book they're reading. It'll be different for every individual, because while parts of the borderland belong to the book, other parts belong only to that particular reader – to us: our own memories, the associations we have with this or that particular word or landscape, the aspects that resonate with our own individual temperament; so whereas many readers might be reading the same book, no two of them will read it in exactly the same way. However, we can come back and talk about it; we can tell others about our experiences of it, and compare our part of the borderland with other people's.

And it's a liminal thing – a matter of thresholds. Traversing this borderland is to find oneself between one state or condition of mind, one existential plane, if you like, and another. When I looked up liminality on Wikipedia (in 2010), I found this definition, which I think could scarcely be bettered: it's a state 'characterized by ambiguity, openness and indeterminacy. One's sense of identity dissolves to some extent… it's a period of transition where normal limits to thought, self-understanding, and behaviour are relaxed – a situation which can lead to new perspectives'.

The Convalescent by Gwen John (*see overleaf*) depicts this fluidity, this dissolving, ambiguous state of being, marvellously well. Gwen

259

The Convalescent by Gwen John

(*see also colour section*)

John had a perfect eye and a perfect hand, and she painted many pictures of women reading; it was almost her favourite subject. The expression on her reader's face is rapt, focused, calm, both attentive to the book and perfectly relaxed. The world around her seems to be dissolving into a state of pale ghostlike dreaminess. She might have been reading for five minutes, or five hours. The world in which she temporarily lives is invisible to us; she's in that borderland, and all we can see of her is the small closed circuit between her eyes and the book in her hand. She's alone, but not alone. She is perfectly content, like the man in the picture by Daumier.

There's something perfectly self-contained about a scene like this. The reader, the book, the setting; and we fellow-readers who look at it with pleasure and recognition. There's a perfect harmony here: activity and stillness, the interior of the borderland and the exterior of the sunshine and the orchard, relaxation and attentiveness. When we see someone reading like this, we see a fellow-lover of books, someone we

A Man Reading in the Garden

by Honoré-Victorin Daumier

The Living Room by Balthus

don't know at all and yet whom we have such a lot in common, someone whose pleasures and desires we share and understand and approve of. We too would be happy in that dappled shade, in that comfortable chair.

And we understand the ferocity too of the reader in this painting by Balthus (*above*). Stalking the book, almost, like a predator. The cat, which at the moment is sitting there so innocently, only seems innocent because it hasn't got a mouse to play with. This girl has her mouse: it's the book her hand is curled around, and she's not going to let it go. Like many of Balthus's paintings, this one is full of ambiguities and mysteries and sexual sub-texts, or not so sub-texts, and sinister implications: why is the other girl asleep with what looks like the head of a cello case resting on her lap? Why is there a jug standing perilously on the other end of the cello case? As far as the young reader on the floor is concerned, the other girl might as well be dead, actually.

261

Learning to Read and Write by Deng Shu

If you're reading like this, no one else matters at all. The obsessive, merciless, solitary, amoral, almost savage devouring of a text to the obliteration of everything else is something we all, if we're honest, have experienced at some point.

Last in this little sequence, a print from Communist China (*above*) showing a happy gathering of workers and peasants learning to read. This too is a picture of what reading looks like from the outside, but it's a very different kind of reading. Nothing solitary here; reading is a social imperative; it's your duty to the party; once you can read, you will be able to learn the correct line to take on every problem by studying the works of Mao Tse-tung, and the dictatorship of the proletariat will rise like the sun, from the east.

It's a collective thing. Which is why we're not surprised to learn that private reading, solitary reading of the Daumier, Gwen John, Balthus sort, is actively and forcefully discouraged under a regime like this. It would be anti-social; it would almost be an act of treason. It would be turning your back on the collective will. It would be betraying the party. Hence the power of such books as that wonderful novel *Balzac and the Little Chinese Seamstress*, by Dai Sijie, which celebrate that very privacy, secrecy almost, that the first three painters were celebrating in the act of reading.

All those pictures, the private ones and the collective one, look at reading from the outside. They show what is left in this world when someone, or some people, are travelling in the borderland. They leave their bodies here, but their imaginative sympathy, their consciousness, is partly elsewhere. We know what they're doing, these strange still figures holding books, because we too are readers, we too have travelled in the borderland; but we don't see exactly what they're seeing, because their part of the borderland is different from ours. To see what it looks like from the inside, we have to look at a different sort of picture altogether.

Wanderer above the Sea of Fog by Caspar David Friedrich (*see overleaf*), is almost the perfect image of that space I've called the borderland. The traveller is alone; what he surveys is being seen by no eyes except ours; he and he only has travelled to this mountain top, and what opens out in front of him now – this great range of further mountains above the clouds, this mighty prospect extending as far as the infinite edges of the sky – belongs only to him. It's an intensely romantic vision, and I acknowledge that. I'm perfectly happy to be romantic about my vision of reading, and education, and many things besides.

I think this is a good picture of reading because it depicts both the objective landscape that's visible to the traveller and his subjective reaction to it. And one is an analogue of the other. The rocky crags, half obscured by the mist below – they are the struggles and difficulties he's had to overcome to get here. Reading something worthwhile isn't always

Wanderer above the Sea of Fog by Caspar David Friedrich

an easy process; it does involve concentration and persistence. The tree
on the distant crag, which his crooked elbow is pointing to: that's almost
a mirror-image of himself, emphasising his identification with nature.
The tree looks at him as he looks at the tree; he is not only observing this

landscape, he is part of it, and being observed by it in turn. When we read great literature, we see people such as ourselves in a context that gives a perspective and a meaning to the situation we're in. The even higher mountains in the distance are a moral exhortation: there is further to go! There are greater tasks ahead, and greater visions to discover!

This is the borderland. And the real point here, the reason I chose this picture, is that the figure in it, the image of the reader, as I've called him, is solitary. We are each alone when we enter the borderland and go on to explore what lies in it and beyond it, in the book we're engaged with. True, we can come back and talk about it, and if we talk well and truthfully and interestingly enough we might entice other readers into it, and they too will explore it – but they too will be alone there until *they* in turn come back and tell us what *they* found there. And it may be that they will find treasures beyond compare that we've overlooked, or that the things that strike us as marvels will seem to them commonplace and not worth discussing.

This disjuncture between one reader and another happens quite often with children and their parents, the children demanding to be read the same book night after night, long after any remaining nourishment has been wrung out of it, the exhausted parent thinks.

'Look, dear, here's a wonderful book called *War and Peace* – shall we try that one instead tonight?'

'No! No! I want *Jolly Rabbit* again!'

There is some magic in the borderland that keeps calling to them.

I'm going to take a sudden swerve now off at a right-angle and talk about some books that have been important to me, or in whose border-lands I've loved to wander. Pictures are very important here. I'm not alone in lamenting the change that came over children's publishing, I suppose about thirty years ago, just when I was about to get going as a novelist, when it became no longer fashionable to illustrate children's novels.

Picture books, beautifully and richly printed in many colours, were becoming easier to publish and to print – there was a great flowering of picture books that began around then – but black and white illustrators such as Anthony Maitland, or Fritz Wegner, or Robin Jacques, or Charles Keeping, or Victor Ambrus were no longer required to draw the pictures that we used to see in the work of Leon Garfield, Philippa Pearce, Rosemary Sutcliff and others. A great loss, it seems to me.

Anyway, the pictures I've loved in the books that I've loved are wonderful images of the borderland. And of course they work differently from words. Specifically, in this case, they function like a window – we can look through it, we can lean on the windowsill and daydream, we can send our imagination out like a bird to fly over the landscape someone has so generously imagined for us, and make our own discoveries there.

This is the cover of one of my favourites among Leon Garfield's novels, *The Pleasure Garden*. The illustration is by the great Fritz Wegner, whose work I always wished would one day illustrate some words of mine. Anyway, because I'm talking about the borderland, which means the space the book or the illustration shares with me, I'm going to talk about my reaction to this picture – the things I enjoy about it – and be quite cheerfully subjective.

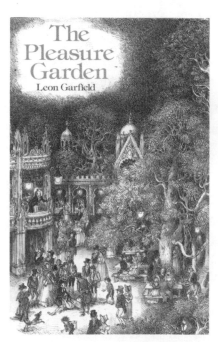

Cover of *The Pleasure Garden*, illustration by Fritz Wegner (*see also colour section*)

So what I love here, as well as the marvellously romantic atmosphere, the lights in the trees, the lovers on the benches, the orchestra on the bandstand – all that – what I love is the great command of technique that Wegner has at the tip of his pen. I love the immense range of different kinds of small movement that the pen has made. Look at the way he represents the leaves, both on the trees nearby and on the ones in the distance. Look at the row of little arbours in the background, where couples or larger groups are sitting around tables under little lights, and each table has a tablecloth – lovely detail – and look at the sort of criss-cross trellis-work outside each of the arbours, which is quite different from the sort of cross-hatching we see in the shadows or in the dark sky above. Look at the crockets and finials on the lovely mock-Gothic bandstand, the sort of faux-oriental archways over the arbours, the delightfully absurd crenellations above them; and look at the range of textures his pen can evoke – the muslin of the dresses, the velvet of the coats, the bark of the trees – we know what they'd feel like to our hand. And the way the characters themselves are moving about or standing to talk or listen to the music – the young dandies showing off their fine calves, especially.

Here's the opening paragraph of the novel:

> Eastward in Clerkenwell lies the Mulberry Pleasure Garden: six acres of leafy walks, colonnades, pavilions and arbours of box, briar and vine, walled in between Rag Street and New Prison Walk. When night falls, the garden opens its eyes: lamps hang glimmering in the trees and scores of moths flap and totter in the shadowy green, imagining themselves star-drunk...

Lucky illustrator, to have prose like that to play with! Lucky novelist, to have an illustrator whose talent was worthy of it!

The next picture (*see overleaf*) is by an artist with almost no talent at all – for drawing, that is. It just shows how well you can draw without much talent.

Arthur Ransome was a wonderful writer, whose stories from *Swallows and Amazons* onwards have an extraordinary consistency of quality; and that quality, it seems to me, would be markedly reduced if they'd been

Illustration from *The Picts and the Martyrs* by Arthur Ransome

illustrated by someone who could draw – someone like Fritz Wegner. Part of the charm of Ransome's books is this very amateurish, lumpish, clumsy drawing – they wouldn't be the same without it.

This, on the facing page, is from *The Picts and the Martyrs* – and while he had no idea of how shoulders worked, for instance, or what a tree looks like at the point where it joins the ground, there is a great integrity about what he depicts and the way he depicts it. And clearly he loves the landscapes he's drawing. His scratchy, laboured pictures have been part of *my* borderland for fifty years now, and I wouldn't change one scratch.

Tove Jansson, on the other hand, couldn't make an clumsy line if she tried. Tove Jansson is utterly unique: there is none like her, none. The peculiar, charming, disconcerting world she created out of the Finnish landscape and especially seascape is oddly both completely fantastical and realistically down-to-earth, or down-to-water. The thousands of little islands in the Gulf of Finland are exactly as she depicts them. I don't know whether you have to be inoculated with her atmosphere when you're young, as I was – I found her for myself on the shelves of the Battersea Public Library when I was nine years old – but once you've got it, it stays got. You have a free pass for life to the world of the Moomins.

Illustration from *The Exploits of Moominpapa*
by Tove Jansson

269

The next picture comes from a French novel for young readers called *A Hundred Million Francs*, by Paul Berna, which was published in the late fifties. The illustrations are not actually French – they're by Richard Kennedy for the UK Puffin edition – but I didn't know that when I first read the book, and I didn't care. I first came across it about the same time as I fell in love with the Moomins, or perhaps a year or two later, and as far as I was concerned it was about as French as anything could possibly be.

I found his vision of a working-class area of Paris – those crumbling walls, those shaky roofs, the torn posters, the cranes, the building sites, the railway sidings, the smoky skies, the air of semi-dereliction, patched-up buildings – utterly thrilling and exotic. I gazed again and again at these pictures of a world not all that unlike the world I knew, because the London I lived in then still bore the scars of wartime bombing, and there were patches of dereliction and improvisation, or corrugated iron

Illustration by Richard Kennedy for *A Hundred Million Francs*

and weed-choked mud not far from the streets I moved around in, but somehow this was richer and sexier and much more interesting.

And without being aware of why I liked looking at his drawings, why they bore looking at again and again, I did love Richard Kennedy's fluent and elegant line – scratchy, if you like, but scratchy in a quite different way from Arthur Ransome's painstakingness, scratchy with swiftness and confidence. I'm sure the girl in Kennedy's pictures turned up forty years later, called Lyra.

I've spoken about this book and its illustrations often, and just to show that it's worth enthusing about one's enthusiasms, someone once sent me a copy of the original French edition, which has a different title – *The Horse without a Head* – and a different look altogether.

These illustrations, by Pierre de Hey, are fine, but I don't think I'd ever have been captivated by them as I was by the Richard Kennedy pictures.

Illustration by Pierre de Hey for *Le Cheval Sans Tête* (*The Horse without a Head*)

Illustration from *The Little Grey Men* by 'B.B.'

Something utterly different now. Through the scraper-board pictures by Denys Watkins-Pitchford, otherwise known as 'B.B.', I came to know and love that part of my outlying regions where the last gnomes in England live. The one on the facing page is from *The Little Grey Men*.

'B.B.' was one of the great writers about nature in children's books; in *Brendon Chase*, for example, his descriptions of the woodland where his heroes spend a summer living wild are intensely lyrical. In some ways he was a limited writer, but the honesty and passion with which he talks about wild things and wild places suffuses his best passages with a love of landscape, and specifically the English landscape, that is irresistible.

And I'm beginning to see, as I continue this talk, something about my particular borderland which might not be true of every reader – it probably isn't. One more example of the sort of thing I respond to very strongly is *Rupert Bear*, illustrated overleaf.

Alfred Bestall, who started drawing and writing the Rupert stories in the 1930s, quite soon established a formula for the Rupert page that was unlike anything else and full of the most delicate and charming imaginary landscapes. It was a formula that was instantly recognisable – I should think every British adult who was a child when Bestall was still at work would recognise a Rupert page at once – and it worked very well, not least because of the redundancy of information.

There were so many ways to read the story that you could go over it again and again. But it was the landscapes that had me hooked. They were full of odd things; those strange constructions standing on posts in the sea in the bottom picture are prison cells. Bestall was full of *fancy*: I'm sure that's the word for the special quality of lightness, delicacy, charm that his landscapes, his stories, embody.

But as I was thinking about this borderland business and wondering which pictures to show you and talk about, I found that there were some children's books which, for all their great quality, for all the great quality of their illustrations, aren't interested in landscape at all. I didn't like

Rupert and the Whistlefish

RUPERT BOWS TO THE KING

At last, the old man comes to tell,
"My king, him wish to say farewell."

" I hope he means to let us go ! "
Sam whispers, as the friends bow low.

The aged man escorts the chums,
And bids them board the boat that comes.

" I'm still not sure they'll let us leave ! "
Sam whispers, clutching Rupert's sleeve.

The meal is over at last. " Now I wonder how we're going to get home again," says Sailor Sam. Seeing his guest wishes to speak, the king sends for his aged interpreter. " Ah, my king realise it time you return to your country," says the old man. " So now he make farewell, yes ? " And Rupert and Sam bow low while the little king waves and chatters as cheerfully as ever. " I hope he's not asking us to come and see him again," murmurs Sam under his breath. " I've se̶ ̶ ̶

enough of these parts ! " The soldiers and ser- vants of the king do not delay. Rupert and Sam are marched outside to the long causeway over the sea. The great gong is banged and a boat heads rapidly for them with its odd rattling noise. " Here, I say. I hope those men have had the right orders," says Sam, as they are hustled aboard. " This is the same sort of boat that took me to that sea-prison." However, it swings away from the prisons and towards the distant water city.

Rupert Bows to the King from *Rupert* by Alfred Bestall (*see also colour section*) them, or indeed love them, any less: it's just that they were different.

Richmal Crompton's William, whose literary life (in the course of which he grew not a day older) lasted even longer than Rupert's, was drawn from the beginning by Thomas Henry, and it's this scruffy, muddy-kneed schoolboy who is our image of William still and always. And while Henry, like Richmal Crompton, was very interested in human beings and delighted to represent the various comic types, both child and adult who impinged on the life of William and the Outlaws, the back-

"GOOD MORNING, LITTLE BOY," SAID THE VISITOR.
"UMPH!" REPLIED WILLIAM.
"WHAT'S YOUR NAME, DEAR?" SHE ASKED.
"PETER," SAID WILLIAM.

Illustration by Thomas Henry from *William Again*

grounds against which these comedies took place were very rudimentarily sketched. We seldom have any sense of a real place full of its own atmosphere, its own intense and pungent personality, like Richard Kennedy's Paris or Arthur Ransome's Lakeland.

Someone with nothing better to do and some time on their hands once tried to work out where in England William's family lived, going by whatever clues they could find in the stories – the sort of time Mr Brown arrived home from work, the range of shops there were in the village, that sort of thing; and the best guess they could make was that the Brown family lived in Bromley. It doesn't seem very likely to me, but then it could be anywhere really. It's just generic middle-class England. Crompton just wasn't that interested in landscape, and nor are her stories, and neither was Thomas Henry, and it doesn't matter; but it's true.

Another great favourite of mine, and very much part of my borderland, is *Emil and the Detectives*.

This is set, of course, very firmly in Berlin, but you wouldn't really know that from these wonderful drawings by Walter Trier. I've spoken about *line* before – Kennedy's line, Wegner's line, Jansson's line – Walter Trier's line is immediately recognisable as his, and wonderfully fluid and expressive. But they could be sitting anywhere, these children, there's no background at all, and the room they're in is completely invisible. They could be in Arizona. They could be on the moon. But just look at those lines! What economy! What versatility! What elegance and wit, how they rhyme with one

'Pony Hütchen went from one to the other pouring out delicious hot chocolate' by Walter Trier

another! Here they represent the children's hair – there they are the curve around the side of the jug of chocolate – somewhere else they are the struts in the back of the chairs – and down below they are the shadow under the table – just quick lines, to do all that! And every single figure is characterised differently, and he's got ten of them – ten! Sitting around a single small table. *And* a cake. Genius, really.

Just look at the journalists in the next picture, each one a complete individual. See how cleverly he's arranged them in the space, leading the eye from Emil back to the editor at his desk, cigar in hand; see how the room is suggested with the barest of means, the desk lamp, the suggestion of some kind of telephone, or it might be a typewriter or a teleprinter, it

'The newspaper men asked Emil a great number of questions' by Walter Trier

doesn't matter, because suggestion is all we need here to evoke the busy and important life of a great modern newspaper – modern for 1930, of course.

But for Walter Trier and his illustrations for *Emil*, just as for Thomas Henry and his pictures of William, the landscape wasn't interesting for its own sake. It was a place for something to happen in; it might as well have been a stage set. The *interest* of those stories lies not in the spaces they depict, the places, but in the people who move and act and talk in them. The little town of Bromley might as well have been Andover or Gerrard's Cross; the big city of Berlin might as well have been Vienna or Amsterdam. The work of Arthur Ransome, on the other hand, is quite inconceivable without its very specific and particular setting in the Lake District, the lakes, the fells, those great silent hills that he loved so much.

And I wonder whether there's a genuine difference here between two kinds of writer, two kinds of illustrator, two kinds of children's book. For one kind, action and character are the important things, and the setting is more or less incidental; for the other kind, setting and landscape are absolutely integral to the kind of story they want to write – to the only kind of story they *can* write.

I think C. S. Lewis was talking about something like this when he described two kinds of readers: the one who cared only for the action and the suspense and didn't care in the least whether the story was set in Camelot, or on Mars, or in Los Angeles; and the one like himself for whom such things as 'snowshoes, and deep forests, and Hiawatha sort of names' were an essential part of the pleasure – I couldn't find the essay in which he said this, or I'd quote his exact words, but I'm completely with him on the matter.

And as for the difference between one sort of book and the other, whether it's a deep difference or a superficial one I couldn't say, nor could I say whether or not it matters very much. It matters to me because I'm interested in it, but that's all I can claim.

Now I'm going to make another right-angled swerve and talk briefly about two more illustrators, one being the great Peter Bailey, who's done several books of mine.

These illustrations (*see facing page*) are both from *Northern Lights*, in an edition published by the Folio Society. The Folio Society, of course, has resolutely gone on publishing books with pictures in them when most commercial publishers, mainstream publishers, had long given up. When they proposed an edition of *His Dark Materials* I was delighted, not least because it would give me another chance to see my words illustrated by Peter Bailey. He'd done my four fairy tales beautifully, but this was a different scale of thing, and all I can say is that I'm very happy with it. First, Lyra in the opening scene, and then a little later on, trying to make sense of the alethiometer for the first time. What Peter does very

Lyra (left), *Lyra making sense of the alethiometer* (right)
by Peter Bailey for the Folio Society (*see also colour section*)

well, it seems to me, is get the sense of Lyra's character, as well as the setting she's in.

Last in the pictures I'm going to show are some of my own. When *Northern Lights* was in preparation, the editor suggested having a little decorative device at the opening of every chapter, and after some persuasion I managed to get him to agree to a different one for each chapter, and furthermore to let me draw them. They were going to be printed very small indeed, so my limited skills wouldn't ruin a

Illustration for Chapter 14 of
Northern Lights, by the author

279

whole page. After some experimenting I fixed on a size to draw them at – a square six centimetres by six – and a sort of style that depended on heavy blacks and solid whites, which wouldn't get lost in the printing – they were going to be about postage stamp size, and the paper was pretty cheap and coarse too, and couldn't take fine lines. This is the borderland between the book and its writer, you could say.

Illustration for Chapter 23 of
Northern Lights, by the author

The very last chapter decoration in *Northern Lights* was this one.

It took ages – I must have done hundreds till I got Lyra's face looking more or less right. She's looking up at the universe opening out above her, and wondering at the extraordinary spectacle while being daunted by the thought of what she now has to do, while simultaneously being absolutely determined to do it... I tried to get some of that into her expression, and I'm quite pleased with it. But as far as we're concerned here, the most significant thing is what's not there. Every one of the other pictures is in a box – it has a frame, a border around it. This one doesn't. All the barriers have been smashed, all the frontiers have been blown away, the whole universe is wide open; so there's nothing shutting her in.

And now the last picture of all. How could I represent the subject of the last chapter of *The Amber Spyglass*, in which Lyra and Will have to part? Their farewell takes place in the Botanic Garden in Oxford, and I went there and drew this bit and that bit but none of my

Illustration for Chapter 38 of
The Amber Spyglass, by the author

attempts worked. Finally I decided to abandon the idea of simple representation – the heart of that chapter isn't about a place or a space, really, it's about love and loss – so I thought it best to be kind of abstract about it and go for something entirely symbolic.

It could be more elegant – if Fritz Wegner had done it, it certainly would have been – but there we are. Will and Lyra are bound together by their love, but they have to face away from each other for ever. I think a sort of emblem rather than a picture was the only way of doing this, so that's what I ended the book with. And that seemed the right place to stop.

THIS TALK WAS DELIVERED AT EXETER UNIVERSITY, 21 JANUARY 2010.

If I'd learned to draw properly when I was young I might have gone straight into making comics, or illustrating books by other people. I love all the business of drawing, the pencils, the paper, the ink, all of it, but I know my limitations; and besides, if I had to do it for a living, instead of playing at it, I might not enjoy all the stuff that goes with it. Or not so much.

Oliver Twist

AN INTRODUCTION

On energy, murder, plausibility, melodrama and myth

ENERGY, PURE UNTRAMMELLED STRENGTH AND VIGOUR: AN ENERGY SO prodigious that it throws off vivid sparks of glee and gives out spontaneous flares of combustion. Dickens has many great qualities (and, to be sure, there are some qualities he lacks), but the ones he has in abundance are all aspects of that vast original energy.

Consider the young author in 1836, at the age of twenty-four. He is partway through his first great success, the serialisation of *The Pickwick Papers*. He is offered a contract to edit a new monthly magazine, *Bentley's Miscellany*. He agrees to supply sixteen pages of new material for each issue – no mention of what sort of material it is to be – although he is already committed to a three-volume novel for one publisher and two more of the same length for another, not to mention twelve more numbers of *Pickwick*, a further series of his *Sketches by Boz* and the libretto of a comic operetta called *The Village Coquettes*.

But what does that matter? Of course he can write sixteen extra pages a month. He signs the contract and sets to work. His first contribution is a farcical short story. But as it happens, the young author's first child is born in the same week as the first issue of *Bentley's Miscellany*, and perhaps that event ignites another flare of that exuberant energy. Suppose a child were born in mysterious circumstances... And suppose his mother, who had a secret, were to die at once... And suppose this were to happen *in a workhouse...*

It's not hard to see the attraction of this theme for the young Dickens.

Pickwick was comic, broadly and exuberantly so. This new long story could strike a quite different note: it could be grim and dark and melo-dramatic; it might even involve the most lurid and ghastly motif of all – murder. (When he was five, Dickens had been enthralled and terrified by the stories a maidservant told him about a cannibalistic villain called Captain Murderer. Some of the horrid thrill he felt then must have stayed with him for a long time, perhaps for the rest of his life.)

And a new subject for a writer is like a new colour for a painter. What can we do with it? What will it look like next to that other colour we discovered last time? Comedy *and* murder, side by side in the same story: will it work? There are few excitements comparable to that of sensing, not quite visible yet but nearby, very close, only an arm's length away, a new kind of story to tell. The twenty-four-year-old Dickens must have sensed the whole of his nature leaping to the idea like a magnet to a steel rod.

And so he began, in January 1837, and for some time the two novels were written turn and turnabout. For the first two weeks in the month, he wrote *Oliver Twist*, and for the other two, he worked on *The Pickwick Papers*. In November of that year *Pickwick* came to an end, and three months later, after various other short pieces, Dickens began his next novel, *Nicholas Nickleby*, writing that and *Oliver Twist* side by side in the same manner.

From then on, all his novels were to be written and published in serial form. Unlike some novelists, Dickens did not write the whole story before it came out in parts: he really did make it up as he went along. Six months before the serialisation of *Oliver Twist* came to an end, there were two separate adaptations of it already playing on the London stage, but Dickens said in a letter to one of the theatrical managers concerned that: 'Nobody can have heard what I mean to do with the different characters, inasmuch as I don't quite know, myself.'

Of course, there may have been something disingenuous in that remark, and we know that later in his career, at the time of *Bleak House*

(1852), for example, he did make extensive notes on the composition of his work in hand; but there is still an engaging air of youthful improvisation about *Oliver Twist*. His brother-in-law Henry Burnett tells of an evening when he and his wife called on Mrs Charles Dickens and sat talking with her. Dickens came to join them, but sat apart writing at a little table, and 'every now and then (the feather of his pen still moving rapidly from side to side) put in a cheerful interlude. It was interesting to watch, upon the sly, the mind and the muscles working (or, if you please, *playing*) in company, as new thoughts were being dropped upon the paper.'

Does it show in the finished text? Perhaps a more considered approach would have relied less on outrageous coincidence as a means of moving the plot along. Take Oliver's exercise in pocket-picking, or fogle-hunting, in the company of the Artful Dodger. How likely is it, really, that their very first victim should happen to be the oldest friend of Oliver's dead father?

Or take the house-breaking expedition to Chertsey. In a radius of thirty miles from London there must have been thousands of houses full of tempting silver plate. But this is the one Bill Sikes heads for, and this is where Oliver is shot and wounded, and where he's taken in and looked after by the kindly women who live there; and how likely is it that one of them should happen to be the sister of Oliver's dead mother?

The answer is, not in the very least. Coincidences do happen in real life, to be sure, but to offer them quite so blatantly is to stretch plausibility well past snapping-point. But more importantly: does it matter? There's an artistic pattern emerging here which might be worth the sacrifice of likelihood. With each crime Oliver is involved in, he struggles against it with all his strength, and each time it turns out that the victim is closely involved with his own unknown history – with himself, in fact. He is being led by the agents of wickedness into something damaging to his own integrity, and each time that very integrity fights back and saves him. Only later do we see what's going on underneath: his half-brother, the sinister Monks, is deliberately trying to corrupt him. It makes symbolic sense for the crimes he's involved in to be designed to harm those who represent his own background.

On the other hand, the coincidences don't end there. Take Chapter 42, when Noah Claypole and Charlotte re-enter the story. There are dozens of public houses nearby where they could stop for refreshment; so how likely is it that they should make their way to the very one where the villainous Fagin just happens to come by and find them? ('Of all the gin-joints in all the towns in all the world…')

But although that's the sort of thing that makes our eyebrows rise when we see it on the printed page, it would be quite different if we saw it inside a proscenium arch by the lurid gaslight of a theatre. I've already mentioned the early dramatic adaptations of *Oliver Twist*; and in this context, a remark that Dickens made twenty years after completing that novel illuminates much of his approach to storytelling. In a speech to the Royal General Theatrical Fund in 1858, he said, 'Every writer of fiction, though he may not adopt the dramatic form, writes in effect for the stage.'

Throughout his life, Dickens was powerfully attracted to the theatre. His involvement with amateur theatricals, his close association with pro-fessional actors, and not least his own public readings, which were pow-erfully dramatic – all testify to his great love of the stage. What matters here is the effect that passionate interest had on the way he told stories on the page. Again and again he comes up with scenes and characters whose brilliance and force (or, to be sure, whose exaggeration and sheer *noise*) seem to demand darkness and limelight, a proscenium, an auditorium, an audience, in order to achieve their full effects.

It's partly a matter of space and scale: in order to be seen clearly from a distance, effects have to be broad enough to seem coarse when close to. This, I'm sure, is part of the source of Dickens's particular melodramatic quality. His story was occupying a mental space that demanded vivid light and profound darkness and loud volume in order for the events and the characters to be perfectly clear to the furthest occupant of the highest seat in the gods, and that colossal energy of his was equal to the task. Hence the *dramatic* quality of such scenes as Oliver asking for more gruel; as the boys practising their pickpocketing under the direction of Fagin; as the murder of Nancy.

Later in Dickens's career, he was actually writing for a medium that didn't yet exist: I mean, the cinema. The opening chapter of *Bleak House*, for example, or the Veneerings' dinner party in *Our Mutual Friend*, are nothing less than shooting scripts complete with camera angles, and with stage directions in the appropriate present tense. One little thing makes it clear that we're in the realm of the cinematic, and not the theatrical: Dickens was a master of the close-up (the fog in the stem and bowl of the skipper's pipe in *Bleak House*; Mr Podsnap's large allowance of crumpled shirt-collar in *Our Mutual Friend*). There are no close-ups on the stage. As his command grew, so the dramatic effects became more rich and subtle; but they were always devoted to the end of making the reader see.

In *Oliver Twist*, for all the dramatic force, we can still find an occasional clumsiness when it comes to stage-management. There is an odd moment in Chapter 39, during the scene between Fagin and Nancy. Monks comes in, and wants to speak to Fagin privately, so the two of them withdraw upstairs. Nancy, fearful and anxious to penetrate the mystery, 'ascended the stairs with incredible softness and silence; and was lost in the gloom above'. Do we go with her? No. We're left with a bare stage: 'The room remained deserted for a quarter of an hour or more; the girl glided back with the same unearthly tread…' Why does the author make us stay in a deserted room when he could just as easily take us upstairs with Nancy and let us eavesdrop with her? Because it's not the best time for the reader to learn what she learns, that's why. But all the same, that empty room; that quarter of an hour! Perhaps Dickens's attention was momentarily elsewhere. Perhaps he was writing that passage when his brother-in-law called.

As well as illuminating the broad melodrama of the big effects, that incandescent energy of Dickens also shows up the tiny details of behaviour, the little incidents that he seems to find at the tip of his goose-quill, that spring into being the moment he writes them down. Mr Bumble, in his humiliation, absently and automatically boxing the ears of the boy who opens the gate for him; Sikes's dog wagging his tail, although he senses that Sikes wants to kill him; Nancy stooping to kiss the drugged lips of Sikes before she goes out to betray Monks to Rose; Sikes himself, after the murder, returning to Jacob's Island:

> He laid his hand upon a chair which stood in the middle of the room, but shuddering as he was about to drop into it, and seeming to glance over his shoulder, dragged it back close to the wall – as close as it would go – ground it against it – and sat down.

Sikes grinding the chair against the wall as if to obliterate Nancy's ghost – who could have worked that detail out beforehand, in cold blood? Scarcely anything could bring his horror more vividly to life; and such is the speed and vigour of the passage that Dickens seems to have found it there when he got to it.

When the first edition of a book to appear before the world happens to have illustrations, it's worth looking at them, since the text will have been written in the knowledge that there would be pictures as well as words on the page. In the case of *Oliver Twist*, the illustrator was George Cruikshank, who had already illustrated several of the *Sketches by Boz*, and who had become a friend of Dickens. Later in life they quarrelled, and the friendship faded; in fact, after Dickens died, Cruikshank claimed to have originated the story of *Oliver Twist* himself, the illustrator suggesting the plot and the characters to the author rather than the other way round. Whatever the truth of that (and it doesn't seem likely to me), Cruikshank certainly worked closely with Dickens as this story developed.

The result is a series of illustrations that almost matches the words for vividness and memorability. Cruikshank's wiry line scribbles in the darkness, bringing all kinds of grotesques into the half-light. He had the gift of selecting the most dramatic moments in the tale, and of staging them to bring out their fullest effects – which, just like the prose, are often matters of detail. Look at the eyes in the picture of Oliver asking for more gruel;

Oliver Asking for More by George Cruikshank

for example: the wide-eyed faces of the seven other boys watching (one has his back to us, and is desperately tilting back his bowl to get at the last of what's in it), the horrified pop-eyed look on the face of Mr Bumble, his head isolated against a lighter patch of wall.

Or the disposition of Fagin's body in the condemned cell: desperately chewing the fingers of one hand, he hugs the other arm to his breast, and his knees are pressed together while his heels seem to be lifted off the floor, as if he's helplessly rehearsing what's going to happen in the morning.

Fagin in the condemned Cell by George Cruikshank

Or Sikes's dog, unwilling to come and be drowned: was there ever a more abject creature than poor Bull's-eye? His tail is firmly tucked between his legs, but a front paw is lifted half in defence, half in appeasement, while Sikes tries to conceal the stone and the handkerchief.

The first readers of *Oliver Twist* would have experienced the pictures and the words together, and from the beginning the two must have been inseparable in the public mind. The film director Michael Powell (*The Red Shoes, A Matter of Life and Death*) recognised the importance of the conjunction of words and pictures in popular fiction; he maintained that 'the silent film, the sound film, the colour film, TV, videotape, all the audio-visual storytelling inventions of the next ninety years' had their origins in Sidney Paget's illustrations to Conan Doyle's Sherlock Holmes stories in the *Strand Magazine*. 'The pictures, as much as the text,' he said, 'created the immortal folk figure.'

I think that's true, but Doyle and Paget were not the first pair of creators to seize the public mind in that way. Sixty years before Sherlock Holmes, *Oliver Twist* was being brought to a double life by Dickens and his illustrator, and when we think of Bill Sikes, or Fagin, or Mr Bumble, or the Artful Dodger, it is Cruikshank's figures that emerge in the mind's eye, and Cruikshank who lies behind every adaptation of the story for stage or screen since then.

The success of the novel was immediate. It proved that the sensation the young author had made with *Pickwick* was not a flash in the pan, but that here was a writer whose range was wide, whose energy was formidable, whose inventiveness unlimited.

How lucky to be a reader at that time, when *Pickwick* was drawing to an end, and *Oliver Twist* was coming out month by month, and *Nicholas Nickleby* was just beginning! From then on, Dickens was as secure in the affections of the public as any writer has ever been, before or since.

And it is hardly too much to say that *Oliver Twist*, thirty years later, killed him. In the last few years of his life, Dickens turned more and more

Sikes attempting to destroy his dog by George Cruikshank

to performance: to the public reading of his works as a source not only of money (an abundance of it), but also of a sort of psychological reassurance. The applause, the laughter and the tears, the praise with which he was showered, and even the faintings and the cries of horror – all drew him back time and again to the platform and the limelight.

And in 1868, he devised a reading from *Oliver Twist*: Sikes's murder of Nancy. His son and some of his friends, seeing the alarming effect it had on Dickens's state of mind as well as his body, urged him not to do it, but he insisted on going ahead. Perhaps he was exorcising his childhood fear of Captain Murderer, or perhaps he was engaging with some subterranean passion whose origins no one can guess at now; but he acted out the scene with such an extremity of frenzy that, as well as terrifying his audiences, it seriously undermined his strength. Eighteen months later, he was dead.

But the book lives, and is as vigorous and healthy now as it ever was. In fact, it's more so; because like a very small handful of other figures from the history of the novel – Don Quixote tilting at the windmills, Heathcliff and Cathy on the moors, Captain Ahab in his mad quest for the white whale, Dr Jekyll drinking the potion that will turn him into Mr Hyde – little Oliver Twist asking the beadle for more gruel has passed beyond the limits of literature altogether, and entered the realm of myth.

THIS ESSAY WAS FIRST PUBLISHED AS THE INTRODUCTION TO THE MODERN LIBRARY EDITION OF *OLIVER TWIST* (RANDOM HOUSE, 2001)

I don't think any edition of Dickens ought to leave out the illustrations. The same goes for many nineteenth-century books, Vanity Fair *in particular, where the pictures are Thackeray's own work, and frequently undermine or comment subtly on what the words are saying. And any criticism that ignores the pictures is failing to do its work.*

Let's Pretend

NOVELS, FILMS AND THE THEATRE

On stories in different forms: the literal,
the metaphorical and the magical

I ONCE HEARD CHRISTOPHER HAMPTON MAKE A VERY INTERESTING
point about the novel, and the theatre, and cinema. He said that the
novel and the film have much more in common than either of them does
with the stage play, and the main reason for that is the close-up. The
narrator of a novel, and the director of a film, can look where they
like, and as close as they like, and we have to look with them; but each
member of the audience in a theatre is at a fixed distance from the action.
There are no close-ups on the stage.

And that makes a real difference in telling a story. It makes a difference to adaptations too. There's a sense in which novels adapt more
naturally to the screen than to the stage, especially novels written in the
past hundred years, ever since the cinema and its fluent, swift-moving,
swift-cutting narrative began to enrich our common understanding of
how stories can work.

But should we adapt stories from one medium to another in the first
place? Isn't there something a little second-hand about the process?

It's possible to become rather stern about this. Some critics, including
the estimable Michael Billington, theatre critic for the *Guardian* newspaper, somewhat disapprove of adaptations, and would prefer the theatre to
produce new plays rather than rework old books. The trouble with that
position is that the theatre itself is much less high-minded than those
who keep a watchful eye on its purity; the stage has always cheerfully

swiped whatever good stories were going. Dickens, for example, was a favourite source. As is well-known, two separate adaptations of *Oliver Twist* were playing on stage before the monthly serialisation of the novel came to an end.

Today we take it for granted that if a novel is successful, it must be followed in due course by the film. And various expectations and assumptions about fiction and cinema have now become commonplace – that the best films are often made of the least good books, for example, or that short stories make better films than novels, or that the Merchant-Ivory 'heritage' model is the only appropriate way of filming most English classics. In particular, there's the feeling that an adaptation of a well-loved novel will always be disappointing, because *she* doesn't look like that, and *he*'d never say that, and they've left out our favourite character, and they've set the story in San Francisco instead of Wolverhampton, and they've changed the ending. So we all know about films and books.

But because of the dominance of the cinema, it's become rather less common for novels to make it to the stage. Consequently, they are more conspicuous when they do, and the process is more closely questioned, especially when it happens in the subsidised theatre.

Part of this is no doubt sound social bookkeeping: is public money being sensibly spent? Shouldn't the taxpayer be supporting new work rather than recycling old? This is reinforced by the fact that novels are usually adapted for the stage when they are already popular and successful. No one is rushing to adapt stories that the public has clearly decided it doesn't like. The argument *against* presenting best-sellers on the subsidised stage is that the commercial theatre is the place for that sort of production; the last thing such books need is yet another chance to make their authors rich. The argument *for* it is that public money ought to be spent on stories the public actually likes, rather than arty stuff that's only of interest to a self-appointed elite. This is such a familiar debate that you could wind it up and it would go on by itself, indefinitely.

But the case of children's books is slightly different. A sort of *worthiness* argument sometimes comes into play here: it's *good* that children should know classic stories like *Treasure Island* and *The Lion, the Witch and the Wardrobe* and *The Secret Garden*, and so it's OK to adapt them for the stage, because if the children get a taste for the story they might read the books later on – or at least be able to display the sort of superficial familiarity that will help with homework and exams. It's educational. So the play in this case is not a destination, but a road sign: the real importance and value of the experience is not here but over there.

The *worthiness* argument also values theatre over film. It costs less to go to the cinema, and we do it more often. Visits to the theatre are expensive and infrequent; so, unconsciously, we feel theatre must be more valuable. Manners come into it too. People tend to behave more decorously in the theatre than in the cinema; they don't usually spread popcorn all over the place, or talk loudly, or sprawl with their legs over the back of the seats in front. If we accustom our children to the theatre, their manners will improve, perhaps.

Well, I'm all for improving children's manners, and I do think that they ought to be thoroughly educated. But the trouble with getting the theatre to bring these things about is that it isn't actually the theatre's job. I think the theatre should do what it does best, the thing that only it can do. To get to what that is, we have to touch on another point of difference between the stage and the screen, which is this: the screen is literal, the stage metaphorical. It may sound paradoxical in an age of computer-generated wizardry and special effects, but the cinema is essentially a realistic medium. When it comes to representing something with literal accuracy, the cinema will always trump the stage.

To take an example from *His Dark Materials*; if I describe in the novel a dæmon changing shape from a cat to a snake, or a gigantic bear wearing armour, or ten thousand witches flying through the Arctic skies, the cinema can show us that, exactly that, complete in every detail. The theatre can't.

But where the theatre scores over the cinema is in the power of metaphor and its engagement with the audience's own imagination. A puppet with a light inside it represents a dæmon that's alive; with imagination, we understand that the light fading and going out represents the dæmon's death. A puppet moves not by itself but because an operator moves it; dress the operator in black and hide their face behind a black mask, and with imagination we accept that the operator is not invisible but 'invisible'. A boat emerges from the darkness on a platform that slowly sinks towards the stage, turning as it does so we can see the boatman's face; with imagination, we accept that it's moving across a dark body of water towards us.

We have to pretend, and furthermore all of us have to pretend together. With video and DVD the experience of film is often, these days, not so much a joint experience in a big public space as a private experience in a small one. But there is no way of packaging the theatre up and taking it home; we have to go there, and share it with others. And once there, we have to agree to sit in the dark and be quiet at the same time and all imagine together.

In short, the thing that the theatre does best and most potently is to tell stories in a way that partakes of magic, of ritual, of enchantment. It doesn't always happen: sometimes a play just doesn't work; sometimes it might work in a smaller space, or a different space, but not the one it happens to be occupying; sometimes a cast is tired or discouraged, and performances are perfunctory; sometimes the audience doesn't play its part, and sits there radiating sullen hostility and giving nothing back to the performers.

But when everything is working well, something mysterious happens between an audience and a play that isn't just the sum of the component parts. It can spring from the obviously fantastical and from the most minutely described realism: Rostand makes it happen, and so does Shaw. It happens with original plays, and it happens with adaptations. But *some-*

thing happens, and everything is transformed. We could use a scientific term like emergence for this process, or we could use an older word and call it sorcery; but whatever we call it, there's no point in trying to explain it to those who insist on a functional justification for everything, those who can only see value in an activity if it brings in money from tourists, or helps children with their exams. They'll never understand. You have to find some other sort of language if you want to convince them.

But that strange and inexplicable thing is what the theatre is for. That's why we need it.

THIS ESSAY FIRST APPEARED AS AN ARTICLE IN THE *GUARDIAN*, 24 NOVEMBER 2004, WITH THE STAGE ADAPTATION OF *HIS DARK MATERIALS* IN REP AT THE NATIONAL THEATRE, LONDON, AND *THE FIREWORK-MAKER'S DAUGHTER* ABOUT TO OPEN AT THE LYRIC HAMMERSMITH, LONDON.

Schools must take children to the theatre. This activity must be subsidised. Children should be able to join a youth theatre near where they live, and learn how to take part in every aspect of putting on a play. Places like that should be subsidised too. These things are not luxuries: they're essential to our wellbeing.

The Firework-Maker's Daughter on Stage

THE STORY OF A STORY

How she became a play, then a book, and then another play

A VERY LONG TIME AGO, WHEN I WAS A TEACHER, I USED TO WRITE A
play every year to put on at my school. It was supposed to be for the
benefit of the pupils, but really it was for me. As the summer came to an
end I would start to write the script, and what I wrote would depend on
what kind of atmosphere I wanted to revel in at the end of the autumn
term. One year it was Gothic, with a demon huntsman and a gloomy
castle and caves in the snow-bound forest; another year it was a Victorian
penny dreadful, with fog-bound streets and opium dens and desperate
villainy; another year it was the atmosphere of the *Thousand and One
Nights* and a bird with a magic feather.

Each year I would add some new theatrical trick to my repertoire:
a shadow-puppet interlude, or a scene painted on a gauze that would
magically vanish when you raised the lights behind and lowered them in
front, or a wind machine and a thunderstorm. I had more fun fooling
about with those things than I've ever had before or since.

And one year I wanted to involve fireworks. Well, you can't really,
of course, not in a school play, not indoors; there are things called fire
regulations. Nevertheless, I wanted to. I wanted lots of bright lights and
blazing rockets and loud bangs, and I wanted… I wanted… gamelan
music! Gongs and xylophones and lots of dancing – and masks – and an
elephant! I was desperate to have an elephant.

So I did. My play wasn't called *The Firework-Maker's Daughter* to
begin with. In a library somewhere, a long time before, I had seen some

stage designs for a play called *The Elephant of Siam, or The Fire-Fiend*. It was by a dramatist called William Moncrieff, who lived in the early part of the nineteenth century. His greatest success was called *The Cataract of the Ganges*, which featured a real waterfall on stage (they knew how to put plays on in those days). I don't think *The Elephant of Siam* was ever published, because I've never managed to find the script; but I loved what I remembered of the stage designs – all flames and wild rocks and exotic dancers, and I suppose those pictures must have been at the back of my mind when I wanted a play full of fireworks and so on. So I wrote my play to fit that title – *The Elephant of Siam, or The Fire-Fiend*.

What I had to do, to start with, was find a plot that connected the elephant and the fire-fiend. And in turn that meant that I had to think what a fire-fiend might be, and what part he could play in the story; so I thought about that for a while, and then put it aside to think about the elephant. I'd heard of the famous white elephants of Siam, and the way the King would give such an elephant to someone he wanted to ruin, because those rare and important beasts would cost so much to feed and care for that the unfortunate victim would go bankrupt trying to look after them. A white elephant… what could I do on stage with a white elephant?

The idea came at once: *graffiti*. All that white space would be so tempting; and if there was a naughty boy in charge of the elephant, he could get other naughty boys to pay him to let them write BANGKOK WANDERERS FOR THE CUP or CHANG LOVES LOTUS BLOSSOM TRUE XXX on the elephant's flanks. And if the elephant was an artistic, sensitive soul, who was horribly embarrassed – so much the better!

Well, that was the elephant seen to. And as for the fire-fiend – who was now important enough to have capital letters: he was the Fire-Fiend – that was the point where I could have my dancing, and masks, and maybe some flame effects. (The man I hired the stage lights from every year was always keen to tell me about the latest effects he had in stock, and I was always keen to use them. I spent a lot of the play's budget with him. We got on very well). The Fire-Fiend would have to be the god of fire. And someone would have to go to his grotto and walk through the flames. Why did he have a grotto? Because I like the word grotto, and I like to use it as often as possible. Of course he had to have a grotto – in a volcano, naturally. And somehow that all suggested fireworks… someone needed something to make fireworks with… what? What *special* thing, that you could only get from the Fire-Fiend himself?

That was how the story began to put itself together. But my first Lila wasn't the daughter of a firework-maker; she was a princess. She was the daughter of the King, who had apprenticed herself to Lalchand the fire-work-maker, and this was a most deadly secret, because of course princesses weren't allowed to do interesting things like make fireworks, and if it was discovered, then both she and Lalchand would face death. (There was an executioner with an enormous axe, who was always complaining: 'I'm not doing all them,' he protested when he was told to see to Rambashi's gang at one point in the story.)

There was also a sub-plot involving an invasion masterminded by the Queen of China, as far as I remember, but it was only there to provide an excuse for a gigantic custard-pie fight at the end.

The music was very important. I wanted that full gamelan orchestra. Never mind the fact that gamelan music isn't Thai, or Siamese; white elephants can't speak, either. I wanted the sound of all those gongs and drums, and I was going to have it. A friend of mine called Tony Dixon, a brilliant engineer, made a mock-gamelan out of hubcaps and lengths of mild steel and copper tubing, and his wife Rachel, the music teacher at the school, wrote a score for it. It looked so good that we put it on the stage, and the musicians were costumed, and acted like a sort of Greek chorus, looking shocked or approving and cheering or booing as the story unfolded.

And masks… I didn't let anyone else make the masks. I wanted to have all the fun myself. I made the Goddess of the Emerald Lake out of papier-mâché, and the Fire-Fiend (who had now got a name: Razvani) out of book-cloth, or buckram stiffened with size, which I cut into small strips and soaked in Polycell and formed over a plasticine mould. You can build it up until it's as thick and tough as leather. And then you can paint it. The Razvani mask is still with me, sitting on the bookshelves just behind me in my study.

Well, that play came and went, as plays do. But I always thought the story deserved another lease of life, so in due course I made it into a book, and changed it somewhat. Lila became the firework-maker's daughter; the Queen of China disappeared entirely; and I introduced the fireworks contest instead of the custard-pie fight. It was better like this, because something real and important – in fact, desperate – hangs on the outcome.

And it was only when I was making it into a book that I realised the real meaning of the story. That's the way it happens with me: I never start with a theme and make up a story to exemplify it – I start with colours and noises and atmospheres, and gradually characters and incidents emerge and join together, and finally, last of all, come the theme and the meaning.

I realised I was telling a story about the making of art. Lila has to make the dangerous and terrifying journey to the Grotto of the Fire-Fiend in order to gain the Royal Sulphur, without which her fireworks will have little effect; and she doesn't know that she has to take three gifts with her to offer to Razvani. The three gifts are the three qualities every firework-maker, or every artist, has to have – and what they are she only finds out at the end, when she learns that she really does have them, and she really has dedicated them to Razvani; and in return he really has blessed her with the Royal Sulphur, which is… well, what *that* is, she learns at the end as well.

I think that that lesson is true. And I think that fairy tales, for this is a fairy tale, are ways of telling us true things without labouring the point. They begin in delight, and they end in truth. But if you start with what you think is truth, you'll seldom end up with delight – it doesn't work that way round. You have to start with fun.

And now it's come full circle, and it's a play again. I'm very happy indeed that my story, and Lila and Chulak, and Hamlet the elephant, and the Goddess of the Emerald Lake and Razvani the Fire-Fiend, are all going to be given life on the stage; and I like to think that the ghost of William Moncrieff will be there as well, to take a bow at the end. And of all the theatres in the world, where better to put it on than one named after a pot for melting ores and refining metals? At the heart of every firework-maker's workshop, after all, there is a Crucible.

THIS ESSAY WAS WRITTEN AS A PROGRAMME NOTE FOR THE PRODUCTION OF *THE FIREWORK MAKER'S DAUGHTER* PUT ON AT THE SHEFFIELD CRUCIBLE IN MARCH 2003.

I repeat: you have to start with fun.

Imaginary Friends

ARE STORIES ANTI-SCIENTIFIC?

*Answering Richard Dawkins's assertion that fairy tales may
have a pernicious effect on children, with reference to the author's
own experience of reading and imagining*

RICHARD DAWKINS'S BOOK, *THE MAGIC OF REALITY*, IS A TOUR DE FORCE IN which he tells a number of myths (about, for instance, the creation of the earth, or rainbows, or where animals came from) and then gives a scientific account of the phenomenon in question, showing how thrilling knowledge and scientific inquiry can be and what a profound sense of wonder they can give us. It's a book that I shall certainly give to my grandchildren in a year or two. I have never seen a better introduction to science for young readers.

But it reminded me of Dawkins's misgivings, expressed in a TV news interview two or three years ago, about such things as fairy tales in which frogs turn into princes. He said he would like to know of any evidence about the results of telling children stories like that: did it have a pernicious effect? In particular, he worried that it might lead to an anti-scientific cast of mind, in which people were prepared to believe that things could change into other things. And because I have been working on the tales of the Brothers Grimm recently, the matter of fairy tales and the way we read them has been much on my mind.

So, what evidence might there be to settle this question?

We believe different things in different ways and for different reasons. There's the rock-hard certainty of personal experience ('I put my finger in the fire and it hurt'), which is probably the earliest kind we learn. Then there's the logically convincing, which we probably come to through the maths we learn at school, in the context of Pythagoras's theorem or something similar, and which, if we first encounter it at the right moment, bursts on our minds like sunrise, with the whole universe playing a great chord of C major.

However, there are other ways of believing that things are true, such as the testimony of trusted friends ('I know him and he's not a liar'), the plausibility of likelihood based on experience ('It's exactly the sort of thing you'd expect to happen'), the blind conviction of the religious zealot ('It must be true, because God says so and His holy book doesn't lie'), the placid assent of those who like a quiet life ('If you say so, dear'), and so on. Some of these carry within them the possibility of quiet scepticism ('I know him and he's not a liar – but he might be mistaken').

There's not just one way of believing in things but a whole spectrum. We don't demand or require scientific proof of everything we believe, not only because it would be impossible to provide but because, in a lot of cases, it isn't necessary or appropriate.

How could we examine children's experience of fairy tales? Are there any models for examining children's experience of story in a reasonably objective way? As it happens, there are. A very interesting study was carried out some years ago by a team led by Gordon Wells and his colleagues at Bristol University and was described in a book called *The Meaning Makers: Children Learning Language and Using Language to Learn* (Hodder, 1986).

Wells and his team wanted to find out how children's language was influenced by what they heard around them. They selected a large number of families with children who were two or three years old, whom they followed right up to the end of their primary education, giving the children unobtrusive, lightweight radio microphones, to be worn under their clothes, which could pick up not only what the children said but also what was being said by parents or others nearby. The microphones were switched on at random intervals for ninety seconds at a time, the results were recorded and transcribed and then an enormous amount of analysis was done on the results.

In brief, they discovered that the more included children were in the conversation and chatter going on around them, the quicker and more fully they picked up every kind of language skill. One interesting discovery was that the most enriching experience of all was the open-ended exploratory talk that arises from the reading of stories. In *Language and Learning: an International Perspective* (1985), Wells and his colleague John Nicholls write: 'Several investigators have noted how much more complex, semantically and syntactically, is the language that occurs in this context... Furthermore, the frequency with which children are read to has been found to be a powerful predictor of later success at school.'

So, it's not impossible to set up experiments to test how children acquire various forms of understanding and to learn interesting things from them. But to go back to Dawkins and his question, how on earth would we set up an experiment to test the effect of fairy tales?

It would have to go on much longer than the Bristol study: it would have to last as long as childhood itself. And it would have to differ from that study in an important way, because it would need a control group. Whereas the scholars at Bristol were concerned with finding out what happens in the natural course of a child's life, this study would depend on having some children who were allowed fairy tales, fantasy and so on, and another group that wasn't.

To make it absolutely beyond question, it would have to be policed pretty rigorously. No *Harry Potter* under the bedclothes. No nursery rhymes either, which are full of impossible things, such as cows jumping over the moon. And we would follow the children all the way through their schooling, right up to leaving age, to see whether the ones who were kept away from magic and spells were thereby advantaged in their understanding of science.

Of course, we wouldn't do it. It would amount to child abuse. To make sure that our subjects never encountered fairy tales of any kind, we would have to keep them in a sort of prison camp. Dawkins knows this; he wouldn't ask for the unreasonable, or the impossible, or the cruel. When he says that he would like to see some evidence, I assume that he is prepared to be a little generous in his view of what evidence there could be.

And the only way we can know what is going on in the mind of someone who reads a story is to believe them when they tell us about it and compare it with our own experience of reading and see what we have in common. When it comes to the matter that Dawkins is concerned about, namely the question of children's belief in fairy tales and magic and spells, all we have to go by is belief and trust. It's that sort of evidence, and that's the only sort we've got – but then, we get by pretty well with that in most of our dealings with other people.

So, do children believe what they read in stories, or don't they? And if they do, in what way do they believe it? Well, this is what I think about it. I think that childhood reading is more like play than like anything else. Like pretending. When I was a boy of eight or nine, in Australia, we pretended to be figures from comics or films and we acted out stories based on the adventures we'd seen. Davy Crockett was very big at that time – every little boy in the western world had a Davy Crockett hat. I knew I wasn't really Davy Crockett but, at the same time, I liked imitating things that I'd seen Davy Crockett do on the cinema screen – say, at the Siege of the Alamo.

We fought with passion, and when we died we did so with heroic extravagance. My body was doing all that an eight-year-old body could do to run out from behind a wall, fire a musket, clutch my chest, stagger, crumple to the ground, slowly drag a revolver from a holster with a trembling hand and kill six Mexicans as I breathed my last.

Those were the things my body was doing. What was my mind doing? I think it was feeling a little scrap – a tiny, fluttering, tattered, cheaply printed, torn-off scrap – of heroism. I felt what it was like to be brave and to die facing overwhelming odds. That intensity of feeling is what both fuels and rewards childhood play and reading alike. When we children play at being characters we admire, doing things we value, we discover in doing so areas and depths of feeling it would be hard to reach otherwise. Exhilaration, heroism, despair, resolution, triumph, noble renunciation, sacrifice: in acting these out, we experience them in miniature or, as it were, in safety.

Yet at no time during the endless hours of play I spent as a child did I believe that I was anyone other than myself. Sometimes I was me and sometimes I was me pretending to be Davy Crockett. But now that I think about it carefully, I realise that it was a little more complicated than that. When I was playing with my brother and my friends, I was almost entirely Crockett, or Batman, or Dick Tracy, or whoever it was (and I remember games when there were about six different Batmans racing through the neighbourhood gardens). It was when I played alone that I found it possible to be myself, but a different myself, a myself who was Davy Crockett's close and valued friend, who sat with him beside a campfire in the wilderness or hunted bears in the trackless forests of suburban Adelaide. Sometimes I rescued him from danger and sometimes he rescued me, but we were both pretty laconic about it. In some ways, I was more myself at those times than at any other – a stronger and more certain myself, wittier, more clearly defined, a myself of accomplishment and renown, someone Davy Crockett could rely on in a tight spot.

What's more, he seemed to value me more than my friends and family did. He saw the qualities in me that their duller eyes failed to perceive. Davy Crockett wasn't alone in this superior perception; I remember that King Arthur had a high opinion of me, and so did Superman.

Now I think that those experiences were an important part of my moral education as well as the development of my imagination. By acting out stories of heroism and sacrifice and (to use a fine phrase that has become a cliché) grace under pressure, I was building patterns of behaviour and expectation into my moral understanding. I might fall short if ever I were really called on, but at least I'd know what was the right thing to do.

And that sort of play, the solitary play, perhaps, even more than the communal play, seems to me very similar to what we do when we read – at least when we read for no other purpose than our enjoyment, and especially when we read as children. I'm conscious that the way I read as an adult is a little different, because there's a part of my reading mind now that looks with critical attention at the way the story is told as well as at the events it relates.

What I thought mostly when I was a child was, 'I want to be in this story with them.' It was like the sort of game where I was by myself with Davy Crockett in the wilderness, because in a story I was able to be both myself here and myself there. I didn't want to stop being myself; I didn't want to be them; I wanted to put myself into the story and enjoy things happening to me. And in the sort of private, secret, inviolable space that opened out miraculously between the printed page and my young mind, that sort of thing happened all the time. It's the state of mind in which you can hear the voice of your dæmon. In fact, there are probably dæmon voices whispering to us all the time, and we've forgotten how to hear them.

I remember it happening especially powerfully with the Moomins. Little creatures who looked like miniature hippopotamuses and lived on an island in the Baltic Sea? Absurd. What I felt for the Moomin family and all their friends, however, was nothing less than love. In fact, I loved them so much that I would never have said to my friends, 'Let's pretend we're Moomins.' That would have been inconceivable. I would have had to make public something I felt private and secret about, something I could hardly voice even to myself, something if – were it ever discovered – I would have felt embarrassed by; and the shame of discovery, I'm sure, would have been followed quickly by the even greater and longer-lasting shame of betrayal. To save face, I'd have felt obliged to mock and scoff at those dear friends of mine, and at any kid who was so stupid and babyish as to like stories about them.

But when I was alone, with a Moomin book open in front of me and that great, secret space opening up between my mind and the pages, I could revel in their company and sail off in their floating theatre or travel to the mountains to see the great comet or rescue the Snork Maiden from the Groke and no one could possibly have told, from looking at me, what my mind was doing.

Here comes the test: did I believe that the Moomins were real? No, of course I didn't. I knew that they were made up. I was pretending they were real in order to enjoy being with them in imagination. I wasn't in the slightest danger of confusing them with real life. The delight of being with the Moomins was a complex kind of delight, made up partly of the sweetness of their characters, partly of the delicate, simple precision of the drawings, partly of the endless inventiveness of Tove Jansson, their creator, partly from the fascination I felt with the northern landscape in which they lived: a whole bundle of things, none of which depended on their being true or real.

Nor did I believe for a second that elephants' trunks were long because one of their ancestors had played a desperate tug of war with a crocodile, as Rudyard Kipling told me in the *Just So Stories*. If someone had asked me, in a serious kind of way, why I thought elephants had long trunks, I'd have scratched my head and said, 'I dunno.' I knew, even when I was very young, that 'because the crocodile got hold of the elephant's child's nose and pulled and pulled' was the wrong sort of answer.

I would have been just as fascinated, in a different kind of way, to hear the real answer; but that wouldn't have diminished my pleasure in the story, which included the delight that I felt in murmuring the sounds of the words: the 'satiable curtiosity' of the elephant's child, the 'great, grey-green, greasy Limpopo River, all set about with fever trees'. 1 knew these story things, these play things, weren't real, but that didn't matter, because I didn't want them to be real, I wanted them to be funny. Or delightful. Or exciting. Or moving. And they could be all those things and real as well, as some things were, or all those things and imaginary and I could tell the difference, and it didn't matter.

I agree that it would be a different question entirely if parents actually brought their children up to believe that frogs could change into princes. And some parents do bring their children up to believe that things can change into other things – bread into flesh and wine into blood, to be specific, and that they'll go to hell if they don't believe it. Some parents also bring their children up to believe that the world was created 6,000 years ago and that scientists are wrong when they tell us about evolution and shouldn't be allowed to teach it in schools. I fully agree with Dawkins when he says that this is pernicious and damaging.

Yet there's a world of difference between that sort of thing and offering a child a fairy tale. No one says, 'You must believe that the frog changed into a prince, because it's true and only wicked people don't believe it.' Children really do learn quite early on that there are different ways of believing in different kinds of story.

And when it comes to evidence, I think there's nothing for it: we just have to trust what people tell us and check it against our own experience. If what they say is that stories of every kind, from the most realistic to the most fanciful, have nourished their imagination and helped shape their moral understanding, then we have to accept the truth of that. My guess is that the kind of stories children are offered has far less effect on their development than whether they are given stories at all; and that children whose parents take the trouble to sit and read with them – and talk about the stories, not in a lecturing sort of way but genuinely conversing, in the way that Wells describes – will grow up to be much more fluent and confident not only with language, but with pretty well any kind of intellectual activity, including science. And children who are deprived of this contact, this interaction, the world of stories, are not likely to flourish at all.

What sort of evidence that is, I don't know, but I believe it.

THIS ARTICLE FIRST APPEARED IN THE *NEW STATESMAN*, 13 DECEMBER 2011.

There's probably a temperamental aspect to the way we believe things, too. Some people are simply inclined to believe things more literally than others do, and no doubt they suffer from continuous disappointment. Others don't believe anything, and very soon scepticism becomes cynicism, which can never be disappointed. As William Blake pointed out, you never know what is enough unless you know what is more than enough.

Maus

BEHIND THE MASKS

*On craftsmanship, emotion and truth in Art Spiegelman's
illustrated Holocaust history*

SINCE ITS FIRST PUBLICATION IN 1987, MAUS HAS ACHIEVED A CELEBRITY
that few other comics have ever done. And yet it's an extremely difficult
work to talk about. In the first place, what is it? Is it a comic? Is it biogra-
phy, or fiction? Is it a literary work, or a graphic one, or both? We use the
term graphic novel, but can anything that is literary, like a novel, ever really
work in graphic form? Words and pictures work differently: can they work
together without pulling in different directions?

In the preface to *The Western Canon*, his attempt to define 'The Books
and School of the Ages', Harold Bloom says: 'One mark of an originality
that can win canonical status for a literary work is a strangeness that we
either never altogether assimilate, or that becomes such a given that we
are blinded to its idiosyncrasies.'

This is an accurate description of my reaction to *Maus*. In one way
the work stands squarely in the comics tradition, observing many of the
conventions of the form: a story about anthropomorphically depicted
animals, told sequentially in a series of square panels six to a page, containing speech balloons and voice-over captions in which all the lettering
is in capitals, with onomatopoeic sound effects to represent rifle-fire, and
so on. So it looks very like a comic.

It also refers to earlier forms. The stark black-and-white drawings, the
lines so thick in places as almost to seem as if they belong in a woodcut,
hark back to the wordless novels of Frans Masereel, with their expression-

Page 125 from *The Complete Maus* by Art Spiegelman

ist woodcut prints; and those in turn take their place in an even older northern European tradition of printmaking that goes back to Holbein and Dürer. In telling a story about Germany, Spiegelman uses a very German technique.

Yet in other ways *Maus* does have a profound and unfailing 'strangeness', to use Bloom's term. Part of this is due to the depiction of Jews as mice, Germans as cats, Poles as pigs, and so forth. This is what jolts most people who come to it for the first time, and still jolts me after several readings. It is such a risky artistic strategy, because it implies a form of essentialism that many readers will find suspect. Cats kill mice because they are cats, and that's what cats do. But is it in the nature of Germans, as Germans, to kill Jews?

The question hangs over the whole work, and is never answered directly. Instead we are reminded by the plot itself that this classification into different species was precisely how the human race was then regarded by those who had the power to order things; and the question is finally dispelled by the gradual gentle insistence that these characters might look like mice, or cats, or pigs, but what they are is *people*. They have the complexity and the surprisingness of human beings, and human beings are capable of anything.

At the heart of the story is the tormented relationship between Art and his father Vladek, a survivor of Auschwitz, an obsessive, mean, doting, helpless, cantankerous, altogether impossible old man, whom we come to know in two different worlds: the present-day world of penny-pinching retirement in New York and the Catskill mountains (names signify), and the remembered world of occupied Poland and the extermination camps. The work as a whole takes the form of a memoir by Art in which he tells us of his interviews with his father about Vladek's experiences under the Nazis. As Vladek tells his story, the first-person-past-tense captions in Art's voice give way to those in Vladek's, so the bulk of the narrative is technically a flashback.

Names signify. Is the Art of the story the Art of the title page? Art Spiegelman is a man, but the Art in the story looks like a mouse. In one extraordinary passage about two-thirds of the way through, Art is worrying about art – about his art, and what it's doing to himself and to its subject matter.

But the Art shown at that point is not a mouse but a man in a mouse mask, and the journalists who come to pester and interview him are people in cat or dog masks, but men and women, not cats and dogs. This Art is the author, as distinct from the Art who is the narrator. So for six pages, as we follow the man-Art's anxiety about his art, we are in a different kind of world from either of the story-worlds, and in this sequence alone the words are not written in capitals.

What shape things have, and in what kind of letters the words are printed, and how a picture is set against its background, are matters we have to think about when we look at comics. A comic is not exactly a novel in pictures – it's something else.

But the presence of pictures is not a new thing in printed narrative: William Caxton included woodcuts in the first books he printed in English, and some of the greatest novels in the language were conceived from the beginning as being accompanied by pictures. *Vanity Fair* is incomplete without Thackeray's own illustrations, which often extend and comment on the implications of the text; and in a sense the entire career of Dickens as a novelist began when he was commissioned to provide a text for a series of engravings of Cockney sporting life by the artist Robert Seymour. This grew into *The Pickwick Papers*. Our experience of Dickens is also an experience of 'Phiz', his most prolific illustrator Hablot K. Browne, just as our sense of the world of Sherlock Holmes comes from the drawings by Sidney Paget as much as from the words by Conan Doyle.

So a criticism that was able to deal adequately with comics as a form would have to abandon the unspoken assumption that pictures aren't

quite grown-up, or that they're only for people who don't read properly, and that clever and serious people need only consider the words. In
order to have anything to say about comics, where the pictures generate
a large part of the meaning, it would have to take the shape of things
into account. For example, take the full-moon shape against which the
characters are silhouetted at important points in the story of *Maus*, as if
on a movie poster.

This echoes the claim old Vladek makes to young Vladek near the
very beginning of the story, that he was romantic and dashing; but we
know that movies are make-believe, and so the full-moon shape is bitter
as well as sweet. It indicates something wished-for, not something true.
There was no happy ever after; Anja was haunted by her experiences, and
committed suicide in 1968. The shape carries a charge of irony: we see it
and feel it in a glance.

Perhaps the most powerful moment comes very close to the end, and
it could only come by means of a picture. Vladek, after Auschwitz, is
making his way home to Anja, and one day Anja receives a letter telling
her that he's on his way. And in the envelope there's a photograph. Old
Vladek explains to Art: 'I passed once a photo place that had a camp
uniform – a new and clean one – to make souvenir photos ...'

And there is the photograph. Here on the page is the character we
have come, with Art, to hate and love and despair over in his old age
– not a mouse any longer, but a man: a handsome man, a strong man,
a proud and wary man in the prime of life who has survived appalling
suffering, and survived in part because of the very qualities that make
him so difficult to like and to live with. In short, a human being in all
his urgent and demanding complexity. As Anja says when she opens the
letter and finds the photograph, 'And here's a picture of him! My God –
Vladek is really alive!'

He's really alive. This story is really true. The impact of that photograph is astonishing.

ANJA WENT A FEW TIMES EACH DAY OVER TO THE JEWISH ORGANIZATION... BUT NO SIGN CAME OF ME.

SO SHE SAT HOME EVEN MORE DEPRESSED, UNTIL... KNOCK KNOCK KNOCK

ANJA! GUESS WHAT! A LETTER FROM YOUR HUSBAND JUST CAME!

HE'S IN GERMANY... HE'S HAD TYPHUS! IT'S JUST LIKE THE GYPSY SAID.

AND HERE'S A PICTURE OF HIM! MY GOD—VLADEK IS REALLY ALIVE!

I PASSED ONCE A PHOTO PLACE WHAT HAD A CAMP UNIFORM—A NEW AND CLEAN ONE—TO MAKE SOUVENIR PHOTOS...

ANJA KEPT THIS PICTURE ALWAYS. I HAVE IT STILL NOW IN MY DESK! HUH? WHERE DO YOU GO? I NEED THAT PHOTO IN MY BOOK!

Page 294 from *The Complete Maus* by Art Spiegelman

Comics are a modern form, but this story has ancient echoes. At one point early in the war, the young Vladek, having been drafted into the Polish army and then captured by the Germans, escapes and finds his way home, and when he tries to pick up his young son Richieu, the boy is frightened and cries out.

In the *Iliad*, Homer relates a little episode on the walls of Troy:

… Shining Hector reached down
for his son – but the boy recoiled
cringing against his nurse's full breast,
screaming out at the sight of his own father,
terrified by the flashing bronze, the horsehair crest…
(*translation by Robert Fagles*)

Men in uniform have been terrifying their own children for thousands of years.

At the very end, little Richieu's name appears again, although he died *forty* years before. Vladek, ill and near the end of his own life, is talking to Art, and he says: 'So… let's stop, please, your tape recorder… I'm tired from talking, Richieu, and it's enough stories for now …

Art stands by the bedside, silent, because art has been subsumed under a larger heading, namely life. There's nothing more for him to say.

I began with a series of questions, and I'm not sure they can ever be completely answered; *Maus* is a masterpiece, and it's in the nature of such things to generate mysteries, and pose more questions than they answer. But if the notion of a canon means anything, *Maus* is there at the heart of it. Like all great stories, it tells us more about ourselves than we could ever suspect.

THIS ESSAY IS AN EXPANDED VERSION OF PART OF PHILIP PULLMAN'S CHAPTER IN *CHILDREN'S BOOK PUBLISHING IN BRITAIN SINCE 1945* EDITED BY REYNOLDS AND TUCKER (SCOLAR PRESS, 1998), WHICH FIRST APPEARED IN THIS FORM IN THE *GUARDIAN* IN 2003.

Apart from anything else, Maus *is a lovely piece of book-making. It sits comfortably in the hand; the paper is heavy and opaque; the printing is strong and clear, with the blacks truly black, and that miraculous photograph sharp and brilliant. All books should be made like that.*

Balloon Debate

WHY FICTION IS VALUABLE

An argument for fiction to be kept in the balloon,
with special reference to its beguiling aspects

I'M HERE TO TALK ABOUT FICTION, AND TO TRY AND SHOW HOW VALUABLE it is, and why it ought to stay in the balloon. And the first thing to say is that I'm rather handicapped here by my own profession, because as a storyteller I don't set out to *persuade*; I'm not used to putting forward a case. Novels and stories are not arguments; they set out not to convince, but to beguile. When you write a story you're not trying to prove anything or demonstrate the merits of this case or the flaws in that. At its simplest, what you're doing is making up some interesting events, putting them in the best order to show the connections between them, and recounting them as clearly as you can; and your intention is to make the audience sufficiently delighted or moved to buy your next book when that comes out in due course.

But fiction doesn't merely entertain – as if entertaining were ever *mere*. Stories also teach. They teach in many ways: in one obvious way, they teach by showing how human character and action are intimately bound up together, and that actions both spring from character and help to shape it. Conrad's *Lord Jim* is a good example.

They also teach an attitude – a temperament. One writer's temperament might embody (for example) a passionate interest in the physical world, so that the narrator of the story notices the colours and smells and sounds of things, and makes them vividly present to the reader; while another writer's attitude will demonstrate a sort of sharp sardonic worldliness in the way the story describes behaviour, so that we learn what it's like to see people like that – and so on. I think this is inherent in the very nature of saying 'Once upon a time' and then choosing what to write next. It's the way narrative works.

And stories teach not only attitudes, but beliefs – not that such-and-such a belief is true, but what it feels like to hold it. For example, when we read a novel by G. K. Chesterton we can feel what it's like to see things from the point of view of someone who believes in God. When we read George Eliot, we can feel ourselves in a universe governed by moral relations but bereft of the certainties of belief.

And, most importantly, fiction can engage with questions of *meaning* – questions such as: 'Is there a purpose to life? Where do we come from? Why do we not feel at ease in the world?' The way it does this is to tell new stories, or re-tell old stories from a new angle, which explore these questions.

These are the sort of questions, of course, which religion claims to have special answers to. When it comes to that last question, 'Why don't we feel at ease in the world?', which is one that interests me greatly, as it interested that great psychologist William James – when it comes to that question, the answer from Christianity has to do with original sin. Apparently there is a flaw in the relationship between us and the universe, and it's our fault. We were created to be at one with nature without asking questions, but we were tempted to want more knowledge, and the result of giving in to that temptation is unhappiness, sin, death and so on. It's the myth of Adam and Eve in the garden of Eden.

Now I think that's a very interesting story, but unlike the Church, I strongly approve of original sin. I think that we should be celebrating Eve, not deploring her. What I was trying to do in my trilogy *His Dark Materials* was roughly that: to tell that story from a different moral angle, as it were – to tell a story in which Eve was the heroine, and to show a way in which it was possible to see that the knowledge that we gained as a result of Eve's curiosity – and of the generous, wise and self-less behaviour of the serpent, which risked the anger of God by passing on what it knew – was the beginning of all human wisdom.

And it did set us apart from nature: we are self-conscious. The first thing that happened to Adam and Eve was that they felt embarrassed: they noticed that they were naked. In self-consciousness lies the root of our ability to reflect on ourselves, on the shortness of our lives, on the profound mystery and the absolute beauty of the physical universe. And the Fall didn't take place just once, six thousand years ago, or thirty or forty or fifty thousand years ago when the first human beings thought about death and life and who they were, and made patterns and marks and images to register this thinking – the Fall happens in every human life, at adolescence. We leave the unselfconscious *grace* of childhood behind and take our first faltering steps through the complexity and mire of life towards whatever we can reach of wisdom, which it is our job to increase and pass on. If there was no purpose in evolution, there is a purpose in our individual lives, and that is it.

But I wouldn't keep fiction in the balloon myself if all it could do was *teach*. It's the *way* it teaches that reaches our hearts as well as our minds. And the way it works is through projection – we project the story we're told, the story we read, on to our own experience, our own situation, and understand it in all kinds of different ways. The way a young listener experiences *Little Red Riding Hood*, for example – the excitement, the shock, the dread, the triumph – is not the way that a parent, responds to it. A child thinks, 'That could happen to me!' A parent thinks, 'That could happen to my child! How can I keep her safe?' And the child thinks, 'There probably aren't any real wolves left, I hope, at least not round here,' and the parent thinks, 'That's not how wolves behave, but it's certainly how some men behave,' and so on. And the parent thinks, 'Perhaps it's too scary – I better not tell her that story again for a while,' and the child thinks, 'I hope they tell me that story again *tonight!*'

Because, most of all, stories give *delight*. That's the point I began with, and I'll come back to it to finish up: they *beguile*. They bewitch, they enchant, they cast a spell, they enthral; they hold children from their play, and old men from the chimney corner. The desire to know *what happened next*, or *whodunit*, or how Odysseus and his men escaped from the Cyclops' cave, or what is the meaning of the enigmatic words *The Speckled Band* or *The Black Spot*, or whether the single man in possession of a good fortune will, as we all hope, succeed in marrying Elizabeth Bennet, or what Mr Bumble will say when Oliver Twist asks for more, or what Achilles will do now that Hector has killed Patroclus.

The desire to know these things is passionate and universal. It transcends age and youth; it ignores education and the lack of it; it beguiles the simple and enchants the wise. It was as entrancing in the fire-lit cave as it is in the seminar room.

In one way fiction has no more strength than gossamer – it's only made of words, or the movement of air, of black marks on white paper – and yet it's immortal. You *couldn't* throw it out of the balloon even if you wanted to, because if you did, you'd only turn round to find it still there; you would be telling yourself the story of how it fell to earth, or grew wings and flew away, or got eaten by a bird that laid an egg that hatched and out came… another story. You couldn't help it. It's how you're made.

And finally, if an atheist may call a distinguished witness, I'd like to refer you to the example of Jesus himself, one of the greatest storytellers of all, who knew that if you want your listeners to remember what you say, tell them a story. *Thou shalt* and *Thou shalt not* are easily ignored and soon forgotten; but *Once upon a time* lasts for ever.

I commend the cause of fiction.

THIS BALLOON DEBATE HAPPENED AT THE SEA OF FAITH CONFERENCE IN LEICESTER 2002.

BALLOON DEBATE

In that debate I was opposed by Don Cupitt. I remember his pointing out that if I had used a slightly different argument I would have won outright and left him defenceless, but I now can't remember what that was.

The Anatomy of Melancholy

AN INTRODUCTION TO AN INDISPENSABLE BOOK

On the sparkling language, fantastical imagination,
sound good sense and vivifying personality of Robert Burton

THIS BOOK IS VERY LONG. WHAT'S MORE, LIKE THE BOOK ALICE'S SISTER was reading on that famous summer afternoon, it has no pictures or conversation in it. To add to the drawbacks, parts of it are in Latin. And finally, as if that wasn't bad enough, it is founded on totally outdated notions of anatomy, physiology, psychology, cosmology and just about every other -logy there ever was.

So what on earth makes it worth reading today? And not only worth reading, but a glorious and intoxicating and endlessly refreshing reward for reading?

The main reason I'm going to adduce is perhaps the least literary. It's that *The Anatomy of Melancholy* is the revelation of a personality, and that personality is so vivid and generous, so humorous, so humane, so tolerant and cranky and wise, so filled with bizarre knowledge and so rich in absurd and touching anecdotes, that an hour in his company is a stimulant to the soul.

Burton (or Democritus Junior, as he styled himself) may claim, in his brief hundred and six pages or so of introductory remarks, the writer's ventriloquial privilege: "Tis not I, but Democritus, *Democritus dixit*: you must consider what it is to speak in one's own or another's person, an assumed habit and name – a difference between him that affects or acts a prince's, a philosopher's, a magistrate's, a fool's part, and him that is so indeed' (*Democritus to the Reader*) – but even if we agree to pretend with him that the voice that speaks in these thirteen hundred or so pages is not Burton's own but that of a character of his invention, it is nevertheless the voice of a character it's very good to know.

Those readers who have some experience of the disorder of the mind we now call depression will know that the opposite of that dire state is not happiness but energy; and energy is contagious. We can catch it from others. They cheer us up. Burton's energy is as free and abounding as that of Rabelais, and its effect on the reader is similar: an invigorating of the natural spirits (created in the liver), causing a quickening of the vital spirits (produced in the heart), leading to a stimulation of the animal spirits (formed in the brain). In other words, a tonic.

That energy is visible in the way the great onward stream of his argument overflows into digressions of every kind – digressions that never settle into stagnation, but flow on to rejoin the main stream.

Burton is fully conscious of this habit of his, and defends it stoutly:

> Which manner of digression howsoever some dislike, as frivolous and impertinent, yet I am of Beroaldus his opinion, 'Such digressions do mightily delight and refresh a weary reader, they are like sauce to a bad stomach, and I do therefore most willingly use them.'
> (*1.2.3.2*)

The longest of these digressions is Partition 2, Section 2, Member 3, the great digression of the Air. And what an epic opening it has:

> As a long-winged hawk, when he is first whistled off the fist, mounts aloft, and for his pleasure fetcheth many a circuit in the air, still soaring higher and higher till he be come to his full pitch, and in the end when the game is sprung, comes down amain, and stoops upon a sudden: so will I, having

now come at last into these ample fields of air, wherein I may freely expatiate and exercise myself for my recreation, awhile rove, wander round about the world, mount aloft to those ethereal orbs and celestial spheres, and so descend to my former elements again.

And off he goes, for thirty-five pages, taking in 'that strange Cirknickzerksey lake in Carniola, whose waters gush so fast out of the ground that they will overtake a swift horseman, and by and by with as incredible celerity are supped up', the mystery of where birds go in winter and the possibility that they lie at the bottom of lakes holding their breath, a fossil ship with forty-eight carcasses on board discovered at Berne, showers of frogs, mice, rats, 'which they call lemmer in Norway', the likelihood of life on other planets, his certainty that Columbus did not discover America by chance, but because God willed it so, the similarity between the air in a region and the character of its inhabitants ('In Périgord in France the air is subtile, healthful, seldom any plague or contagious disease, but hilly and barren; the men sound, nimble and lusty; but in some parts of Guienne, full of moors and marshes, the people dull, heavy, and subject to many infirmities'), the desirability of building a house in a place 'free from putrefaction, fens, bogs, and muck-hills', the benefits to melancholy persons of juniper smoke, 'which is in great request with us at Oxford, to sweeten our chambers', and the importance of light and fellowship: 'wax candles in the night, neat chambers, good fires in winter, merry companions; for though melancholy persons love to be dark and alone, yet darkness is a great increaser of the humour'.

The point about Burton's digressions is not how far he roams but how firmly and certainly he comes back. He holds the whole argument in his mind, and every example or quotation or excursion grows from it organically. I mentioned the energy visible in his digressive impulses, but what keeps the whole book from bounding apart like a carelessly packed box of springs is an intellectual quality: a power of memory and comparison.

In this capacity of his, he reminds me of another great Englishman, John Constable. Paintings such as *Stratford Mill* of 1819–20, or *Wivenhoe Park, Essex* of 1816, display a complexity of light and shade in which every patch of clouded shadow on the grass, every glow of sunlight among foliage, every reflection of sky in water, has exactly the value and intensity it should have next to all the rest. Constable *remembered* the colour of the reeds at the water's edge in sunlight, and the glitter of the distant façade of that white house among the trees, and adjusted them precisely to the values they would have at one precise moment under the constantly changing light of an English summer afternoon. The painting took hours, days, weeks, to make; it shows one moment, exactly.

In just the same way, Burton remembers exactly where he is in his great argument, brings out precisely the right quotation, flourishes a curious story, offers a sardonic quip, and brings us back to the line of the discourse without seeming to make an effort.

And, like Constable, he does it with a dazzling quickness and dash. Close to, there is a *roughness* about each of them, which if it weren't for the marvellous intelligence in charge might even seem coarse-textured. But in fact, it's the outward and visible sign of an inward and intellectual certainty: the power of holding an immense complexity fully and consciously in mind, and of placing each detail instantly in the light of its relations to the whole. If Burton and Constable were computers, you'd say they had a great deal of RAM.

Part of this power of memory and reference is visible on every page in the overflowing abundance of quotations. Burton seems to have read everything, and remembered all of it. A wonderful example of this ability to bring out apposite examples comes early on in the Partition concerning Love-Melancholy. He begins a paragraph: 'Constantine, *de agric. Lib. 10, cap. 4*, gives an instance out of Florentius his Georgics, of a palm-tree that loved most fervently…' A palm-tree in love? It's impressive enough to know one example of this. But not content with citing this Constan-tine-who-cites-Florentius, Burton goes on to cite Ammianus Marcellinus, Philostratus, Galen, Jovianus Pontanus, Pierius, Melchior Guilandinus, Salmuth, Mizaldus, and Sandys, hardly any of whom the modern reader has heard of, but all of whom, apparently, have stories about amorous palm-trees. Burton defies us to disbelieve him:

> If any man think this which I say to be a tale, let him read that story of two palm-trees in Italy, the male growing at Brundisium, the female at Otranto... which were barren, and so continued a long time, till they came to see one another growing up higher, though many stadiums asunder. (*3.2.1.1*)

The story is so charming that this reader, at least, couldn't care less if Mizaldus and Salmuth and Melchior Guilandinus and the rest were figments of Burton's imagination, and didn't exist at all. Elsewhere (*1.2.1.4*) he anticipates a similar suspicion: if such examples, he says, 'may be held absurd and ridiculous, I am the bolder to insert, as not borrowed from circumforanean rogues and gipsies, but out of the writings of worthy philosophers and physicians, yet living some of them, and religious professors in famous universities, who are able to patronize that which they have said, and vindicate themselves from all cavillers and ignorant persons.'

Well, I shall never know any more about Melchior Guilandinus than I have read here; but I shall never forget the palm-trees in love. And I shall certainly use the word *circumforanean* when I next need to refer to rogues hanging around marketplaces.

Burton's power of finding examples doesn't stop with other authors. He's just as ready to find plenty of examples from life. In the Subsection from the First Partition where he's dealing with loss of liberty as a cause of melancholy, there's a passage that begins:

> And what calamity do they endure, that live with those
> hard taskmasters, in gold mines (like those 30,000 Indian
> slaves at Potosi, in Peru), tin-mines, lead-mines, stone-quar-
> ries, coal-pits, like so many mouldwarps underground,
> condemned to the galleys, to perpetual drudgery, hunger,
> thirst, and stripes, without all hope of delivery!

– and continues for a page or so with example after example of the
miseries of imprisonment, before concluding with that abruptness that
lovers of this book recognise like the quirks of an old friend:

> But this is as clear as the sun, and needs no further illustration.
> (*1.2.4.5*)

The examples he gives to illustrate his themes are often gross – some
so much so that they were kept, in many editions, in the sober obscurity
of Latin. Others remind us of the dangers of embarrassment, such as the
case of the unfortunate Dutchman, 'a grave and learned minister', who
was 'suddenly taken with a lask or looseness' while walking in the fields,
and compelled to retire to the next ditch to relieve himself; but being seen
by two gentlewomen of his parish, 'was so abashed, that he did never after
show his head in public, or come into the pulpit, but pined away with
melancholy.' (*1.2.3.6*)

As if ordinary human shame weren't enough, we have to contend with
diabolical possession as well, like the young maid who purged a live eel,
a foot and a half long, and afterwards 'vomited some twenty-four pounds
of fulsome stuff of all colours, twice a day for fourteen days,' before going
on to void great quantities of hair, wood, pigeon's dung, parchment, coal,
brass, etc. 'They could do no good on her by physic,' says Burton resign-

edly, 'but left her to the clergy.' (*1.2.1.2*)

That the supernatural should figure in Burton's great analysis is only to be expected; because although the first edition of *The Anatomy* was published in 1621, just seven years before William Harvey published his treatise on the circulation of the blood and revolutionised the study of medicine, and when Galileo had established the truth of the Copernican system, the world Burton describes is firmly pre-modern. He is not in the slightest doubt about the existence of a benevolent God (atheism is 'poisoned melancholy', he tells us in *3.4.2.1*), or about the power of evil spirits, as in the case of the poor maid with the eel; and he's careful to acknowledge the authority of experts in the matter of goblins and other devilish beings ('Paracelsus reckons up many places in Germany where they do usually walk in little coats, some two foot long' – *1.2.1.2*).

But on the whole, there is less of that sort of thing than we might expect. 'The stars incline, but not enforce,' as he says in *3.2.5.5*. The greatest current in Burton's interest and sympathy is not towards superstition ('that great torture, that infernal plague of mortal men' – , *3.4.1.3*), but towards real human life and human feelings. After all, this is why he wrote the book: 'The chief end of my discourse,' he says near the opening, is to make this great mass of material and knowledge 'more familiar and easy for every man's capacity, and the common good.' (*1.1.1.3*)

In fact, Burton is on the side of human nature. These days, the very existence of something called 'human nature' is the subject of passionate disputation, with the evolutionary psychologists on one side and the theorists of post-modernism on the other; and I'd like to hear what Democritus Junior might have had to say about that debate. But there's no doubt that he knew human appetites, fears, affections, and sufferings very well, and felt that the natural inclinations of men and women were to be dealt with kindly, and not suppressed:

How odious and abominable are those superstitious and rash vows of popish monasteries, so to bind and enforce men and women to vow virginity… to the prejudice of their souls' health, and good estate of body and mind!
(*1.3.2.4*)

The best evidence for his wide-ranging human sympathy comes in the great Third Partition, on love and jealousy. 'After a harsh and unpleasing discourse of melancholy, which hath hitherto molested your patience and tired the author,' he says in the preface, he is relieved to turn to love. ''Tis a comical subject,' he admits, and in hundreds of pages and thousands of examples, he proves it to us.

His very language sparkles. The famous passage demonstrating the blindness of love begins:

Every lover admires his mistress, though she be very deformed of herself, ill-favoured, wrinkled, pimpled, pale, red, yellow, tanned, tallow-faced, have a swollen juggler's platter face, or a thin, lean, chitty face…

and continues with over a hundred epithets, to conclude:

he would rather have her than any woman in the world.
(*3.2.3*)

You don't write a sentence like that without enjoying it. Men don't escape, either: the absurdities of aged lechery frequently move him to eloquence. 'How many decrepit, hoary, harsh, writhen, bursten-bellied, crooked, toothless, bald, bleary-eyed, impotent, rotten old men shall you see flickering still in every place?' he asks in *3.2.1.2*. I saw that very man myself in New York not long ago, being helped out of a limousine by a fair maid who was young enough to be his granddaughter, but probably wasn't.

On the other hand, love can work wonders with such unpromising material.

> Ancient men will dote in this kind sometimes as well as the rest; the heat of love will thaw their frozen affections, dissolve the ice of age, and so far enable them, though they be sixty years of age above the girdle, to be scarce thirty underneath. (3.2.3)

And honest love aroused by beauty wins his hearty approval:

> Great Alexander married Roxane, a poor man's child, only for her person. 'Twas well done of Alexander, and heroically done; I admire him for it. (3.2.2.2)

In fact, although *The Anatomy* shows us scoundrels in plenty, such as that oily rascal (*suave scelus*) Bishop Beventinus, who commends sodomy as a divine act, and says that tributes to Venus should be paid in no other way (3.2.1.2); and although it becomes positively Jonsonian in its dramatic power when depicting extremities of passion, as in 3.3.2, where an obsessed man, deranged by jealousy, is pictured in two or three pages of intensely imagined action – 'He pries into every corner, follows close, observes to a hair... Is't not a man in woman's apparel? Is not somebody in that great chest, or behind the door, or hangings, or in some of those barrels?... If a mouse do but stir, or the wind blow, or a casement clatter, that's the villain, there he is', etc. – the great sane balance of the book is in its sympathy with ordinary human affections and sorrows and happinesses. So we have the story of the honest country fellow in the kingdom of Naples, whose beloved wife was taken by pirates, and whose willingness to become a galley-slave in order to be near her so moved the

Moors that they set them both free and gave them a pension (*3.2.5.5*).

And this humanity of Burton's blows like a gale through the final section, on the melancholy caused by religious madness. This species of insanity, he says:

> ... more besots and infatuates men than any other above named whatsoever, doth more harm, works more disquietness to mankind, and hath more crucified the souls of mortal men (such hath been the devil's craft) than wars, plagues, sicknesses, dearth, famine, and all the rest.
> (*3.4.1.1*)

True, it's a Protestant gale, blowing from an Anglican quarter, but we can make allowances for that; and there are things he has to say about other religions that would give a living author no end of trouble if they were newly written today, but that fact simply bears out what he says about religious madness. Blind zeal, as he says, is religion's ape. Temperance, kindness and hope make up Burton's recipe for coping with the ravages of this variety of melancholy, as of many others; and I think it is a good one.

So finally: is the book in any sense a cure for melancholy? Because it is a dreadful condition still: 'if there be a hell upon earth, it is to be found in a melancholy man's heart' (*1.4.1*) is as true now as it was then. Our word 'depression' has always seemed to me far too genteel, too decorous for this savage and merciless torment. Anything that can palliate it is worth knowing; and certainly no disorder has ever had so rich, so funny, so subtle and so eccentric an anatomy.

We can learn much from his psychology, which is acute and wise: 'many dispositions produce an habit' (*1.2.4.7*) anticipates the American psychologist William James; his passage in *1.3.1.4* on the seductive pleasure of the early stages of melancholy looks ahead to some of the stories of Poe that so impressed Baudelaire, the first melancholic of modernism.

His recommendation of St John's Wort, whose 'divine virtue drives away devils', is taken seriously by some modern doctors, who see it as a mild but effective herbal version of Prozac; his advice to keep busy is honest good sense.

But perhaps the soundest testimony to the effectiveness of the *Anatomy* is the praise of that great melancholic Samuel Johnson, the only man to improve on Burton ('What is a ship but a prison?' *Anatomy, 2.3.4*; 'No man will be a sailor who has contrivance enough to get himself into a jail; for being in a ship is being in a jail, with the chance of being drowned,' Boswell's *Life*, 16 March 1759).

Burton ends his stupendous work with the excellent advice: 'Be not solitary; be not idle.' This is a great direction, says Johnson, but he would modify it thus: 'If you are idle, be not solitary; if you are solitary, be not idle.' There are many sufferers from melancholy who swear by the truth of that, and innumerable readers throughout nearly four centuries who agree with Johnson that 'there is a great spirit and great power in what Burton says'.

Nor would we wish the book a sentence shorter, or be without one of the thousands of anecdotes and quotations. This is one of the indispensable books; for my money, it is the best of all.

The essay was first published as the introduction to the Folio Society edition of Robert Burton's *The Anatomy of Melancholy* (2005).

I find Post-It notes indispensable. They really came into their own when I was preparing to write about this book. The pages of my paperback copy bristle with so many little yellow stickers that its thickness is almost doubled, and it wasn't a slender book to start with.

Soft Beulah's Night

WILLIAM BLAKE AND VISION

*On the influence and power of a poet who has inspired
and intoxicated me for fifty years*

SOMETIMES WE FIND A POET, OR A PAINTER, OR A MUSICIAN WHO
functions like a key that unlocks a part of ourselves we never knew was
there. The experience is not like learning to appreciate something that
we once found difficult or rebarbative, as we might conscientiously try
to appreciate the worth of *The Faerie Queene* and decide that yes, on
balance, it is full of interesting and admirable things. It's a more visceral,
physical sensation than that, and it comes most powerfully when we're
young. Something awakes that was asleep, doors open that were closed,
lights come on in all the windows of a palace inside us, the existence of
which we never suspected.

So it was with me in the early 1960s, at the age of sixteen, with
William Blake. I came to Blake through Allen Ginsberg, whose *Howl*
I read half aghast, half intoxicated. I knew who Blake was; I even had an
early poem of his by heart ('How Sweet I Roam'd from Field to Field');
I must have come across 'The Tyger' in some school anthology. But if
Blake could inspire the sort of hellish rapture celebrated and howled
about by Ginsberg, then he was the sort of poet I needed to read. Hellish
rapture was exactly what I most wanted.

Accordingly, I searched for Blake in the nearest bookshop, which was
W. H. Smith in Barmouth, in what used to be called Merionethshire.
There was no Blake there. The local library didn't help, either. It wasn't
until I went to London on a rare holiday visit that I found a *Selected Blake*

in a small American paperback, edited by Ruthven Todd and published by Dell in their Laurel poetry series. If I'd bought it in the USA it would have cost 35 cents; I can't remember what I paid for it in Foyles, but it must have been well under a pound.

It's on the table next to me now, battered, the cover coming apart, the cheap paper flimsy and yellowing. It's the most precious book I have. A couple of years later I acquired, as a school prize, Geoffrey Keynes's Nonesuch Press *Complete Prose and Poetry of William Blake*, a handsome hardback now almost as battered, almost as yellowed, almost as precious. But I could put the Dell *Blake* in my pocket, and for years I did.

Thanks to those books, and thanks to my encounter with Ginsberg, and thanks further back to the enlightened local education authority that sent a library van around to the secondary schools in Merionethshire so that I could choose from their shelves the anthology (Donald Allen's *The New American Poetry 1945–1960*: still in print, still irreplaceable) that contained *Howl* – thanks to those things, I discovered what I believed in. My mind and my body reacted to certain lines from the *Songs of Innocence and of Experience*, from *The Marriage of Heaven and Hell*, from *Auguries of Innocence*, from *Europe*, from *America* with joyful immediacy. What these things meant I didn't quite know then, and I'm not sure I fully know now. There was no sober period of reflection, consideration, comparison, analysis: I didn't have to work anything out. I knew they were true in the way I knew that I was alive. I had stumbled into a country in which I was not a stranger, whose language I spoke by instinct, whose habits and customs fitted me like my own skin.

That was fifty years ago. My opinions about many things have come and gone, changed and changed about, since then; I have believed in God, and then disbelieved; I have thought that certain writers and poets were incomparably great, and gradually found them less and less interesting, and finally commonplace; and the reverse has happened too – I have found wonderful things, unexpected depths of treasure, in books and poems I had no patience to read properly before.

But those first impulses of certainty about William Blake have never forsaken me, though I may have been untrue to them from time to time. Indeed, they have been joined by others, and I expect to go on reading Blake, and learning more, for as long as I live.

One such impulse of certainty concerns the nature of the world. Is it twofold, consisting of matter and spirit, or is it all one thing? Is dualism wrong, and if so, how do we account for consciousness? In the opening passage to *Europe: A Prophecy*, Blake recounts how he says to a fairy, 'Tell me, what is the material world, and is it dead?' In response the fairy promises to 'shew you all alive / The world, where every particle of dust breathes forth its joy'. This is close to the philosophical position known as panpsychism, or the belief that everything is conscious, which has been argued back and forth for thousands of years. Unless we deny that consciousness exists at all, it seems that we have to believe either in a thing called 'spirit' that does the consciousness, or that consciousness somehow emerges when matter reaches the sort of complexity we find in the human brain. Another possibility, which is what Blake's fairy is describing here, is that matter is conscious itself.

But why shouldn't it be? Why shouldn't consciousness be a normal property of matter, like mass? Let every particle of dust breathe forth its joy. I don't argue this; I perceive it.

Things that are living, whose bodies however small pulse with that same energy, are capable of even more joy than the particle of dust:

> How do you know but ev'ry Bird that cuts the airy way,
> Is an immense world of delight, clos'd by your senses five?
> (*The Marriage of Heaven and Hell*)

That perception carries a moral charge, which is most clearly expressed in *Auguries of Innocence*, a poem not published during Blake's lifetime.

I think it is one of the greatest political poems in the language, for the way it insists on the right to life and freedom without qualification, uniting large things and small, and showing the moral connections between them:

> A Robin Redbreast in a Cage
> Puts all Heaven in a Rage.
> A dove house fill'd with doves and pigeons
> Shudders Hell thro' all its regions.
> A dog starv'd at his Master's Gate
> Predicts the ruin of the State.
> Each outcry of the hunted Hare
> A fibre from the Brain does tear.
> The wanton Boy that kills the Fly
> Shall feel the Spider's enmity.

Each couplet is a hammer blow in the cause of a justice that includes all creatures, and tells the truth about power:

> Nought can deform the Human Race
> Like to the Armour's iron brace.

This is not a matter of arguing so much as of perceiving. It's a matter of vision. And when it comes to vision, we need to be able to see contrary things and believe them both true: 'Without Contraries is no progression' (*The Marriage of Heaven and Hell*), despite the scorn of rationalists whose single vision rejects anything that is not logically coherent.

Blake was hard on single vision:

> Now I a fourfold vision see
> And a fourfold vision is given to me;

Tis fourfold in my supreme delight
And threefold in soft Beulah's night
And twofold Always. May God us keep
From Single vision and Newton's sleep!
(*Letter to Thomas Butts*)

Fourfold vision is a state of ecstatic or mystical bliss.

Threefold vision arises naturally from Beulah, which, in Blake's mythology, is the place of poetic inspiration and dreams, 'where Contrarieties are equally True' (Blake, *Milton*).

Twofold vision is seeing not only with the eye, but through it, seeing contexts, associations, emotional meanings, connections.

Single vision is the literal, rational, dissociated, uninflected view of the world, characteristic – apparently – of the left hemisphere of the brain when the contextualising, empathetic, imaginative, emotionally involved right brain is disengaged or ignored. (I owe this observation to Roderick Tweedy's remarkable *The God of the Left Hemisphere* (2012), and through that to Iain McGilchrist's *The Master and His Emissary* (2009), a profound examination of the differences between the left hemisphere of the brain and the right.)

I believe this too. Single vision is deadly. Those who exalt reason over every other faculty, or who maintain that other ways of seeing (the imaginative, the poetic, etc.) are fine in their place but the scientific is the only true one, find this position ridiculous. But no symphony, no painting, no poem, no art at all was ever *reasoned* into existence, and I knew from my youth that art of some kind was going to be the preoccupation of my life. Single vision would not do. 'I will not Reason & Compare: my business is to Create.' (Blake, 'Jerusalem'.)

If I didn't know that from experience when I was young, I know it now. We find the truth of it most forcibly when twofold or threefold vision fails, and we fall into the state described by that great Blakeian

W. B. Yeats as 'the will trying to do the work of the imagination'. It's a condition, I dare say, in which most writers and artists have found themselves marooned from time to time. To get lost in that bleak state when inspiration fails is to find yourself only a step away from an even darker labyrinth, which goes by the entirely inadequate name of depression.

A savage deadly heaviness, a desolation of the spirits, an evil gnawing at the very roots of our life: if we're unlucky enough to feel that, we will know from experience that the opposite of that abominable condition is not happiness, but energy. 'Energy is the only life, and is from the Body; and Reason is the bound or outward circumference of Energy. Energy is Eternal Delight.' (*The Marriage of Heaven and Hell.*)

Blake's equation (Energy = Eternal Delight) is as profound and important as Einstein's $E = MC^2$. In the absence of energy, goodness, intellect, beauty – and reason too – are listless, useless phantoms pining for the blood of life. When I had the misfortune to fall under the oppression of melancholia (another inadequate word), one of the things to which I owed my escape was an edition of the letters of Bernard Shaw, where I found energy abounding. I have loved him ever since.

With twofold vision it's possible to see how contrary things could be believed. With threefold vision, with the inspiration that comes from the unconscious, from Beulah, it's possible to believe them. I have found over many years that my way of writing a story, from what used to be called the position of the omniscient narrator, allows me a freedom that writing in the first person doesn't permit. It means the telling voice can inhabit a multitude of different imaginative states. The voice that tells my stories is not that of a person like myself, but that of a being who is credulous and sceptical simultaneously, who is both male and female, sentimental and cynical, old and young, hopeful and fearful. It knows what has happened and what will happen, and it remains in pure ignorance of both. With all the passion in its heart it believes contrary things: it is equally overawed by science and by magic. To this being, logic and reason are pretty toys to play with, and invaluable tools to improve the construction of the castles and grottoes it creates in the air. It scoffs at ghosts, and fears them dreadfully, and loves to call them up at midnight, and then laughs at them. It knows that everything it does is folly, and loves it all the same.

And thanks to the genius of William Blake, it knows that 'All deities reside in the human breast', and that 'Eternity is in love with the productions of time' (*The Marriage of Heaven and Hell*). And it thinks that those things are worth knowing.

THIS ESSAY FIRST APPEARED IN THE *GUARDIAN*, 26 JANUARY 2015, TO COINCIDE WITH THE EXHIBITION *WILLIAM BLAKE: APPRENTICE & MASTER*, AT THE ASHMOLEAN MUSEUM, OXFORD (4 DECEMBER 2014 TO 1 MARCH 2015).

One test of poetry – not the only one by any means, but a good one all the same – is memorability. Blake's lyrics, especially those in Songs of Innocence and of Experience, *pass that test triumphantly. Has anything so simple and so profound been said so unforgettably as 'The Sick Rose'?*

> *Oh Rose, thou art sick!*
> *The invisible worm*
> *That flies in the night*
> *In the howling storm,*
>
> *Has found out thy bed*
> *Of crimson joy,*
> *And his dark secret love*
> *Does thy life destroy.*

I once had a student who translated that into Dutch. It seemed to go perfectly, almost word for word.

Writing Fantasy Realistically

FANTASY, REALISM AND FAITH

The view that fantasy is a load of old cobblers –
unless it serves the purposes of realism

THANK YOU FOR INVITING ME HERE, AND THANK YOU FOR DEMON-
STRATING my favourite virtue. The most *important* virtue is Charity, of
course; but the one whose company I most enjoy is Hope. Clearly, in
asking me to speak to a conference about religion, you're hoping that I
shall have something relevant to say. Well, I hope so too, of course, but in
my case the hope is tempered by experience, whereas yours is still fresh,
vigorous, undamaged. I shall try not to damage it too much.

The title of this conference – 'Faith and Fantasy' – refers to the third
great Christian virtue. Well, here comes the first disappointment: I have
to tell you that although I know something about fantasy, and a little
about charity and hope, I know almost nothing about faith. I can tell
you neither how to get it, nor what it feels like, once got. So I've been
looking for something to say which (a) doesn't repeat too much of what
I've said before; and (b) has at least something to do with your subject;
and (c) won't tread too heavily on what I've got in mind to write next. If
I talk about the things I'm supposed to be writing about, they disappear.
Talking about things I've already written about is much safer.

And while I was thinking about what I could say in this talk, it was
very helpful to read what Don Cupitt – the noted scholar of Christian
theology and philosopher of religion – has had to say about stories and
the part they play in helping us to understand the otherwise formless
flow of life. Even when he's chiding me for clinging to the apparatus of

supernaturalism, what he has to say is worth attending to.

But it's not just any sort of story that features in the title of your conference: it's *fantasy*. And the thing that bothers me is that I don't much care for fantasy. I've got into trouble for saying this; apparently, since what I write is labelled fantasy, I should be a champion of it. But I didn't begin to write fantasy because I was a great reader of it, a lifelong fan of orcs and elves and made-up languages. In fact, if you're a devotee of the works of J. R. R. Tolkien, I should warn you that I have some stern things to say about *The Lord of the Rings* later on. In my own case, I began writing *His Dark Materials* hesitantly, doubtfully, and it was a surprise, not altogether a flattering one, to find that my imagination was liberated when it found itself in a world where people have personal dæmons, and polar bears make armour, and spies three inches tall ride on dragonflies.

But liberated was exactly what it was. In fact (and it embarrasses me to admit it), I even felt that in some odd way I had come home. This was where I was connected with all the things that gave me strength; where the air I breathed was full of the scents I recognised and relished, where my feet were on soil where the bones of my ancestors were laid, and where the language I heard around me was the language I thought and spoke and dreamed in, and where manners and customs were familiar – you know everything I mean when I say the word *home*; well, this world was *home*, in a way that no other world that I've written about has ever been – not even late nineteenth-century London, which I know pretty well. It was *more* than home, actually. This caused me a great deal of surprise, as I say, and I felt taken aback. Embarrassed.

Embarrassment is often a sign that something important is happening: some revelation is taking place. For those of us with white skins, the revelation of a blush is signalled with red, the most alarming of colours. Darwin was fascinated by that: 'Blushing,' he said, 'is the most peculiar and the most human of all expressions.' He believed that it has a social function, that it signals to other people that the individual who blushes is not to be trusted, because he or she has violated the mores of the group, or has even committed some crime.

Now I was embarrassed to discover that I felt so much at home writing fantasy, because I'd previously thought that fantasy was a low kind of thing, a genre of limited interest and small potential. I had thought (and I do still think) that the most powerful, the most profound, the greatest novels I'd read were examples of realism, not of fantasy.

Take a supreme example of literary realism: George Eliot's *Middlemarch*, a great novel in which nothing in the slightest degree fantastical even flickers into existence. Everything that happens in *Middlemarch* could happen in real life, and what gives it a great deal of its power is the recognition of the similarities between the situations the author describes and the experiences we ourselves have lived through. I used to teach a course on Victorian fiction to student teachers, and the younger ones found *Middlemarch* pretty hard going; but the mature students, often women in their thirties and forties whose children were now at school, and who were able to come back into education themselves for the first time for twenty years or more, revelled in the book for what it showed them about the things that, by now, they'd had time to learn about: marriage, and incompatibility, and disappointment, and compromise, and just getting on with things, and thwarted ambition, and passionate hope, and tenderness, and so on. They enjoyed the book because of what they *recognised*: it was *realistic*, it was like *reality*. The writers we call the greatest of all – Shakespeare, Tolstoy, Proust, George Eliot herself – are those who have created the most lifelike simulacra of real human beings in real human situations. In fact, the more profound and powerful the imagination, the closer to reality are the forms it dreams up. Not the most *unlike* real things, but the most *like*.

That's what I thought, and that's what I think.

However, there I was, led by my imagination towards something quite different. So I couldn't help thinking about what I was doing, and wondering why I felt that way about fantasy, and what the difference was between fantasy and realism in the first place.

After all, the characters in *Middlemarch* never really existed, any more than Frodo Baggins did. There never was a Dorothea or a Casaubon; Dr Lydgate and Mr Brooke had no corporeal existence; Mary Garth and Fred Vincy are no more than phantoms. Like God, they are non-real.

But they *seem* real, because they have the sort of psychological complexity and depth and unpredictability that our friends do. So maybe *that* was the problem with fantasy: not that it was about elves, but that it was psychologically shallow. Because when I thought about – when I think about – the fantasy that I've read, the sort of stuff written by Tolkien and his thousand imitators, I have to say that it's pretty thin. There's not much nourishment there: 'There's no goodness in it,' as my granny used to say about tinned soup. Inventiveness a-plenty – no shortage of strange creatures and made-up languages and broad landscapes – 'prodigious noble wild prospects', in Dr Johnson's words – and the film of *The Lord of the Rings* was inventive in just the same way; but that kind of thing is not hard to make up, actually. Entities of that sort multiply themselves without much effort from the writer, because a lot of the details are purely arbitrary.

But there isn't a character in the whole of *The Lord of the Rings* who has a tenth of the complexity, the interest, the sheer fascination, of even a fairly minor character from *Middlemarch*, such as Mary Garth. Nothing in her is arbitrary; everything is necessary and organic, by which I mean that she really does seem to have grown into life, and not to have been assembled from a kit of parts. She's *surprising*.

It's not just character-drawing, either; it's moral truthfulness. I can't remember anything in *The Lord of the Rings*, in all that vast epic of heroic battles and ancient magic, that titanic struggle between good and evil, that even begins to approach the ethical power and the sheer moral *shock* of the scene in Jane Austen's *Emma* when Mr Knightley reproaches the heroine for her thoughtless treatment of poor Miss Bates. Emma's mortification is one of those eye-opening moments after which nothing is the same. Emma will grow up now, and if we pay attention to what's happening in the scene, so will we. That's what realistic fiction can do, and what fantasy of the Tolkien sort doesn't.

Well, *that* was what I was embarrassed about: that I might be writing stuff that would turn out to be mere invention, superficial, arbitrary, trivial, with nothing to distinguish it externally from a thousand other big fat books crowding the fantasy shelves, all with titles like *The Doomsword Chronicles, Volume 17* or *Runequest* or *Orcslayer*. But I was anxious that there'd be nothing to distinguish my work from that sort of thing *internally*, either. I feared that I'd find myself assembling *my* characters in an arbitrary way from a kit of parts, and finding nothing important to say about them.

What it boiled down to was that I was doing something I didn't quite *believe* in, because that's one of the things that embarrassment signifies: a lack of conviction – the self-consciousness that arises from being caught doing something unconvincing – you hesitate; the *belief* goes; to paraphrase Eliot, between the thought and the action falls a shadow.

Now I knew that *His Dark Materials* was going to be a long story. I guessed it would take over a thousand pages to tell it in full: not months of work, but years. And the thought of spending all those years – it was to take me seven years, in the end – doing something in which I didn't believe was horrible. We have to believe in our work; the only thing that lightens the burden of it, sometimes, is the sense that it *matters*, and that we've committed ourselves to something *valuable*, so that even if we don't succeed we'll have an honourable failure.

So there was my imagination, pulling me towards a world of talking bears and witches, and there was my embarrassment, or something, whispering, 'You don't believe in it. You don't think it's worthy of you. What's the point of working at something you're going to be ashamed of?'

However, if I know anything about writing stories, it's this: that you have to do what your imagination wants, not what your fastidious literary taste is inclined towards, not what your finely honed judgement feels comfortable with, not what your desire for the esteem of critics advises you to. Good intentions never wrote a story worth reading: only the imagination can do that. So the imagination was going to *win* here, if I had anything to do with it; and what I had to do to help it win was to neutralise my uneasiness about fantasy; and the way to do *that* was to find a way of making fantasy serve the purposes of realism.

Because when I thought about it, there was no reason why fantasy *shouldn't* be realistic, in a psychological sense – and it was the lack of that sort of realism that I objected to in the work of the big Tolkien and all the little Tolkiens. After all, when I looked at *Paradise Lost*, there was plenty of psychological realism going on there, and the fantastical elements – the angels and the devils, the landscapes of hell, Satan's encounter with Sin and Death, and so on – were all there to embody *states of mind*. They weren't unreal like Gandalf; they were non-real like Mary Garth – convincing and truthful in every way except actual existence.

I saw that it *was* possible to use fantasy to say something important, and clearly I'd have to do that, or try to, in order to get through the next seven years. I had to try to use all my various invented creatures – the dæmons, the armoured bears, the angels – to say something that I thought was true and important about us, about being human, about growing up and living and dying. My inventions were not real, but I hoped I could make them non-real, and not unreal.

This, finally, is what I think the value of fantasy is: that it's a great vehicle when it serves the purposes of realism, and a lot of old cobblers when it doesn't.

I must also say that while I'm perfectly happy to point out what I think are the good things in my own work, I'm not blind to its defects. There are things about my trilogy which I'd like to go back and change – shading down some of the starkness *here*, pointing up the contrasts a little more *there*. I can tell you what my biggest mistake was: I was wrong about the motivation of the President of the Consistorial Court of Discipline, Father MacPhail. In the book as it is now, he seems to be motivated mainly by the lust for power. I wish I'd seen, as I was writing it, that it would be much more effective if his motivation were love: that he does these terrible things out of sheer compassion. He's killing people in order to save their souls. If I'd written it like that, it would be easier to see that the struggle in the story is not one between good and evil – because that's easy; we all know whose side we're on; there's no doubt about it. We might as well be reading Tolkien. It's much more interesting, because much more realistic, when there's a struggle between different goods.

But there we are. No literary work much longer than a haiku is going to be entirely without faults. Even *Middlemarch* has its sunspots. But although we often end in disappointment, we can begin again in hope; as writers or readers, when we start a new book, we hope that this time it'll be good all the way through.

Thank you for inviting me here, and thank you for listening.

THIS TALK WAS DELIVERED AT THE SEA OF FAITH NATIONAL CONFERENCE IN LEICESTER ON 24 JULY 2002.

This was written for the same event as the balloon debate (p. 323). I'm always interested to listen to religious people, some for longer than others, perhaps. People with the religious position associated with the Sea of Faith, which is (roughly speaking) that God is non-real, are more inclined to listen in return than others, perhaps.

The Story of The Good Man Jesus and the Scoundrel Christ

A RESPONSE TO PUZZLED READERS

On telling a familiar story from a different angle

SOME WRITERS – APPARENTLY WILLIAM GOLDING WAS ONE – ARE FIRMLY of the opinion that there is a correct way to read their books, and they argue strongly with readers who, they think, have got them wrong. My view is exactly the opposite. Readers may interpret my work in any way they please, and people do. Some readers, indeed, have seen things – connections and patterns and implications – I had no idea were there. If such phenomena reflect well on me, of course, I claim to have put them there on purpose.

The problem with *my* telling people what I think such-and-such a story means is that my interpretation seems to have some extra authority, which shuts down debate: if the author himself has said it means X, then it can't mean Y. Believing as I do in the democracy of reading, I don't like the sort of totalitarian silence that descends when there is one authoritative reading of any text.

So in general I prefer not to discuss the meaning of my work. But *The Good Man Jesus and the Scoundrel Christ* is different from the sort of books I've published before. It isn't a novel, not exactly, and yet it's fiction, or seems to be, but it's fiction of a sort we don't often see these days: it's allegory, of a kind, but not straightforward allegory either. It has become apparent to me that there are readers who are failing to get it not only because they don't like it, but because they think it's one kind of thing, and it's another.

Moreover, the protagonist of this story belongs not just to me but to the history and the culture of the past 2,000 years, and the story about him is not just any story but the foundation story of the Christian religion. It is too important to too many people for me to take my usual line. This time I have to say something about what I've done with this story, and explain, so to speak, where I'm coming from.

Christianity formed my mind. I wasn't an unusually pious child, but I did firmly believe in the God I was told about, and I did believe everything I said in the Apostles' Creed every Sunday. I didn't question it for a moment; I assumed it to be true in the way I assumed there to be an equator and lines of latitude and longitude, which I could see on the map but never actually on the ground or on the water. I had crossed the equator four times by the age of nine, each time at sea, and each time the event was celebrated with a jolly ceremony involving sailors dressed up as King Neptune and people being ducked into the swimming pool.

So I knew that grown-ups behaved as if the equator certainly existed, although you couldn't actually see it; and they did so in serious ways as well as comical ones, because the ships I was on were navigated according to these invisible lines. Grown-ups believed that the equator existed, and so did latitude and longitude, and by acting on this belief they brought me safely to land. Why should I doubt them when they told me that God existed (though you couldn't see Him either), that various improbable events had taken place in the life of Jesus, and that I would go to Heaven if I believed it all and was a good boy? I believed every word of it.

A further reason for its hold on me was that Christianity was transmitted to us in those days in the language of the King James Bible, the *Book of Common Prayer*, and *Hymns Ancient and Modern*. I was always susceptible to the music of language; it was the rhythms of Kipling's *Just So Stories* that taught me to read, and I was never daunted by words I didn't understand as long as I could pronounce them. Indeed, singing or intoning or simply whispering words I didn't understand was a sensuous delight. I was perfectly comfortable with not understanding much of what I heard in church: 'In the beginning was the Word, and the Word was with God, and the Word was God' meant little, but resonated greatly; the line 'Lo, he abhors not the Virgin's womb' from the carol 'O come, all ye faithful' was utterly mysterious to me, but delightful to sing.

In fact, the traditions and the language of Christianity are so deeply embedded in my memory, in my nerves and my muscles, that not even a surgical operation could remove them.

I know nothing about other religions, by the way; if I tried to write about (say) Islam, I would make all kinds of blunders without even realising that they were blunders, because I'm not at home there. That is why (to answer one correspondent) I haven't written *The Good Man Muhammad and the Scoundrel Allah.*

As I say, I was formed by Christianity – but memories are not enough to sustain a faith. It was in my teenage years that believing finally became impossible; after I'd learned a little science, the meaning of creation in six days and conception by means of the Holy Ghost had to be understood metaphorically rather than literally, and once that was done, the miracles vanished and only God himself was left. Although I carried on a fairly anguished one-sided conversation with Him for some time, the silence on His part was complete.

Nowadays I'm as sure as I can be that there is nothing in that God-shaped space. I'm a thoroughgoing materialist. I think that matter is quite extraordinary and wonderful and mysterious enough, without adding something called spirit to it; in fact, any talk about *the spiritual* makes me feel a little uneasy. When I hear such utterances as 'My spiritual journey', or 'I'm spiritual but not religious', or 'So-and-so is a deeply spiritual person', or even phrases of a thoroughly respectable Platonic kind such as 'The eternal reality of a supreme goodness', my reaction is a visceral one. I pull back almost physically. I feel not so much puzzlement as vertigo, as if I'm leaning out over a void. There is just nothing there.

Consequently, the immense and complicated structures of Christian theology seem to me like the epicycles of Ptolemaic astronomy – preposterously elaborated methods of explaining away a basic mistake. When astronomers realised that the planets went round the sun, not the earth, the glorious simplicity of the truth blew away the epicycles like so many cobwebs: everything worked perfectly without them.

And as soon as you realise that God doesn't exist, the same sort of thing happens to all those doctrines such as atonement, the immaculate conception of the Blessed Virgin Mary, original sin, the Trinity, justification by faith, prevenient grace, and so on. Cobwebs, dusty bits of rag, frail scraps of faded cloth: they hide nothing, they decorate nothing, and for me they mean nothing.

'But look at the good work the churches have done!' I hear. 'Look at the hospitals, the orphanages, the schools! And look further, at the architecture, the art and music they have sponsored and inspired!'

Yes, and all those things are good, and we are better off for their existence. They go some way towards mitigating the evils the churches have done too: the Crusades, the witch-hunts, the heretic-burnings, the narrow fanatical zeal that comes so swiftly and naturally to some individuals in positions of power when faith gives them an excuse.

However, the people who use that argument seem to imply that until the church existed no one ever knew how to be good, or create a work of art, or do anything selflessly, and no one could do good nowadays unless they did it because of their faith. I simply don't believe that.

But I can't escape my Christian background. And I am a storyteller. We write out of what we are; and I thought it would be interesting to read the gospels again, and to see if I could tell the familiar story from a different angle. So I picked up the Bible again. Actually I picked up three: the Authorised Version, the New English Bible, whose publication I remembered causing great excitement when I was a child, and the

New Revised Standard Version. Having no Greek, I thought I should at least triangulate between different English versions to get the meaning clear in my mind.

I began there, because by far the most important sources for the life of Jesus are the four canonical gospels. The canon of scripture was settled in the fourth century, when the gospels of Matthew, Mark, Luke and John were chosen by a council of the church to form part of the New Testament. They are the basis for orthodox Christian belief.

But there are many other gospels, some of which have been known for centuries and some of which have been more recently discovered. I thought I should look at them too. One view of these other texts is that of M. R. James, the great writer of ghost stories, who published a translation of various apocryphal gospels in 1924. He wrote:

'People may still be heard to say, "After all, these Apocryphal Gospels and Acts, as you call them, are just as interesting as the old ones. It was only by accident or caprice that they were not put into the New Testament." The best answer to such loose talk has always been, and is now, to produce the writings and let them tell their own story. It will very quickly be seen that there is no question of anyone's having excluded them from the New Testament; they have excluded themselves.'

In other words, they're just not very good. And it's true. For the most part, the apocryphal gospels in James's selection have nothing like the clarity and force of Matthew, Mark and Luke, or the poetry of John. They include some remarkable fragments, but also a welter of undistinguished narratives, sayings, exhortations, and fairy tales that make pretty hard reading.

A different view of the value of the 'excluded' gospels comes from Elaine Pagels, whose *The Gnostic Gospels* (1979) introduced many readers to the texts that were found at Nag Hammadi in Egypt in 1945. With the knowledge of these new sources (which were, of course, not available to M. R. James) she implies that the excluded texts were left out of the canon for another reason: 'Why were these other writings excluded and banned as "heresy"? What made them so dangerous?'

Some of those other writings are fascinating indeed. But I wasn't interested in heresy and danger at this point so much as in narrative pure and simple, and I particularly wanted to revisit the stories that were known to me as a child, so I returned to Matthew, Mark, Luke and John.

I considered the gospels purely as stories, and I was struck by how unlike most other narratives they are. They're not biographies, because so much of the subject's life is left out: instead the focus is almost entirely on the last year or two of his life and deeds. They're not novels, with the novel's interest in psychology and feeling and emotional relationships; and furthermore there is no description. What did Jesus look like? We have no idea. There are no landscapes; there is a storm, but apart from that no weather to speak of, and novelists enjoy weather and use it a lot. In their spareness and urgency the gospel narratives resemble folk tales and ballads, except that they have a quite different purpose: to tell us what to believe.

The problem is that they seem to tell us to believe contradictory things.

John's gospel tells us that Jesus's expulsion of the money-changers from the Temple took place at the beginning of his ministry; the other gospels say that it happened just before his crucifixion. At one point Jesus seems to be telling his listeners to take no thought for the morrow, and at another he condemns those foolish girls who didn't think ahead and bring enough oil for their lamps; one day he blesses the peacemakers, and another he says he has come not to send peace, but a sword.

Of course, the church has had two thousand years to reconcile these contradictions and paradoxes, and there is no shortage of smooth and polished interpretations that make perfect sense, if you have a taste for that sort of thing.

What do I believe? I believe there was a man called Jesus who lived in what later became known as Palestine at the beginning of our era.

I believe he was a moral teacher of unusually clear perception and force, and besides that, a storyteller and phrase-maker of genius. To invent a story like that of the Good Samaritan, a story that anyone can tell after only hearing it once, a story that makes its moral point with unforgettable power, takes genius. To tell listeners to take the plank out of their own eye before they criticise the speck in someone else's takes a brilliant verbal inventiveness combined with an earthy sense of physical reality, a combination that is also a kind of genius. It seems that in the last couple of years of his life, Jesus wandered the roads of Galilee, Samaria and Judaea, preaching and gathering disciples until he was arrested and executed for political reasons by the Roman occupying power.

One of the main points of Jesus's teaching seems to have been that the arrival of the kingdom of God was imminent. I believe he was wrong about this; certainly there has been no sign of it yet, after two thousand years. If he had not been put to death, I think he would have had to explain its failure to turn up, and that might have been fatal to his claims about it.

There is something else I wondered about: something in the gospels that felt like fiction. Most of the gospel narratives describe events at which there were other people present as well as Jesus, who could testify to what had happened. Even strange and unlikely events, such as the Transfiguration, occur in the presence of witnesses. There is always someone who can vouch for the truth of the narrative.

But on two occasions, Jesus is represented as being alone. The first is during the temptation in the wilderness, where he encounters Satan, who tries unsuccessfully to tempt him. How did the gospel writers know what Jesus said and did on that occasion? Logically, they could only know if he told them; but does that feel likely? The Jesus we see elsewhere does not tell stories about himself.

The other occasion is when Jesus and three of the disciples, Peter, James and John, go to the garden of Gethsemane on the night of his arrest. He tells the disciples to remain where they are while he goes a little way off, a stone's throw away, and prays by himself. We are told the words of his prayer, and the Luke writer even says that his sweat became like great drops of blood falling on the ground: pretty much a close-up view. But in all three accounts, in Matthew, Mark and Luke, we are told that the disciples fell asleep and Jesus had to wake them up. If none of them was awake, there was no one to witness Jesus's prayer, no one to see those drops of sweat like blood, no one to see the angel who, according to the Luke writer, came down from heaven to give him strength. And there was no time afterwards for Jesus to have told the disciples what went on in those anguished minutes, because he is arrested and taken away almost at once, and they never speak to him again. So again: how do the gospel writers know these things?

Altogether, those two passages felt very like fiction to me. The first is school debating society knockabout and the second is profound and very moving psychological drama, but if they don't even pretend to produce any evidence or name any witnesses, I can only regard them as fiction.

And then there was the problem implicit in the very name Jesus Christ. Jesus and Christ, it seemed to me, were two quite separate beings. There was the man Jesus, whom the Gospels talked about, and there was the other sort of being, Christ, the Messiah, who featured more prominently in the Epistles. In the letters Paul wrote, he uses the term 'Christ' a hundred and fifty or so times, and 'Jesus' about thirty. Paul is clearly much more interested in Christ; by the time he wrote, a generation or so after the crucifixion, the myth was already overtaking the man.

Thinking of these problems and contradictions in the gospels, I wondered if they could originate in the idea of a man working out his own thoughts as he spoke. Could there have been another voice close by, 'correcting' what the first voice said so as to make it conform to an emerging 'line'? In effect, there would be two characters: Jesus, obviously a man and no more than a man; and Christ, a fiction. The idea began to intrigue me. How would the story work?

Needless to say, the second character – the Christ – could not be God. I can't write about things I don't, at some level, believe in. I'd have to find another way of representing him. At the same time, I wanted this Christ to embody as much as possible of what the church later did to alter, edit and ignore the words of Jesus, and to benefit from his death and his supposed resurrection.

What happened as I wrote and as the story appeared under my hands was something many writers will recognise: a character began to move, speak and think independently of my intentions. This Christ developed in a way I hadn't expected, and found himself with a human conscience, tempted and torn and compromised. And in the end what compels him to do what he does is the desire to tell a story, but he no longer thinks that his story will tell the truth; the Stranger has told him that truth is not the same as history. Truth is transcendent, eternal, above the vicissitudes of time and chance, and the job of the storyteller is to alter history, if necessary, so that it serves the cause of that greater truth. The Stranger himself, of course, expresses the view the church would express, if there were such a thing as a single church, and it could intervene in its own history, and it had a voice. I can't help it if from time to time he sounds like the Devil.

The story at the heart of Christianity leads to the cross, but it doesn't end there. The cross has a dramatic visual clarity that accounts for much of its success as a symbol (it's a triumphant piece of what would now be called branding), but no Christian would claim that the death on the cross was the climax of the Christian story. The climax is the resurrection. That's the part that everything else is leading up to.

And as to that resurrection, there's one supreme piece of narrative tact in all four Gospels. We never see the resurrection itself: we only see the consequences. An account of a dead body coming to life and walking out of a graveyard would be squalid, grotesque, bathetic. The confused, contradictory, almost breathless accounts of what happened on the morning after the sabbath when one woman, or two, or three, came to the empty tomb are vastly superior as storytelling – intensely realistic accounts of the confusions and contradictions on the morning when the grave was found to be empty, of a kind recognisable to anyone who's served on a jury and heard conflicting statements from witnesses. The realism of that quite magnificent storytelling has led some Christians to maintain that its very contradictions are testimony to the truth of the central claim, because if the disciples were making it up, wouldn't they at least try to make their accounts match? I believe that deserves praise for its chutzpah, but it doesn't outweigh the utter improbability of that central claim.

I believe the story of the resurrection in the way I believe the account in the *Iliad* of Priam's visit to the tent of Achilles. That is also moving and convincing – when I read it I feel that if that event had happened, it would have happened just like that.

But it's a story, and I think that's all it is. In his *The Resurrection* (2008), the great Jesus scholar Geza Vermes examines six possible explanations for the empty tomb, finding none of them entirely satisfactory; and concludes that the best way of understanding the event is to think of a 'resurrection in the hearts of men'. If only Christians had been wise enough to leave it at that!

Something, however, seems to have brought the disciples to a pitch of excitement following the death of Jesus and the disappearance of his body. They became convinced that he was alive, even if they couldn't actually see him, or that some of them had seen him, though they didn't recognise him at first, and that not long afterwards he ascended into heaven. This conviction – together with the extraordinary and growing notion that the man they had known was in fact the son of God himself – was enough to fire the disciples with the energy and courage to travel far and wide preaching, enduring every kind of hardship and persecution, organising groups of believers in every city and district, and developing the first complexities of Christian theology.

Here too, I believe Christians display a kind of impudence: how on earth, they say, could simple men and women, with no training or experience, create such a thing as the Christian church unless they really were inspired by God? Quite easily, is the answer. Creating a religion is not difficult in the least: look at Scientology; and we've seen in our own time how readily people can be induced to feel a state of ecstatic religious energy that can be turned to political ends.

I believe that the church that developed out of those early activities and grew to a peak of worldly power and wealth, that split into different factions, which then persecuted one another with vicious cruelty; that sponsored great art and music; that set up schools and hospitals; that looked after the poor and the dying; that for hundreds of years provided poor people with the only examples of artistic and musical and architectural beauty they would ever encounter; that supported dictators in many third-world countries and persecuted its own priests when they championed the rights of the poor; that hid evidence of childhood abuse by priests and nuns; that comforted the lonely and the sick; that discriminated against women and homosexuals; that encouraged great philosophical and scientific speculation with one hand while shutting it down with the other; in short that did all kinds of good and all kinds of evil – is an entity based on nothing but its own organisational momentum. It's entirely a human construction.

In this construction I believe that the imaginary figure of Christ was of much greater use to the church than the historical person of Jesus, and that when talking about him it would be an aid to clear thinking if we said which part of him we meant. Thus 'Jesus was born in Bethlehem', not 'Christ was born in Bethlehem'; 'Christ was the Son of God', not 'Jesus was the Son of God'. I dare say that Christians will claim they are one and the same, but they are not: they have different origins and different functions.

Human beings are inclined to look for causes and explanations where there are only mysteries; in the absence of any other cause, they will settle for a supernatural one rather than for no cause at all. I don't believe this makes them stupid or wicked; it's how they are. But the fact that they believe something, even intensely, doesn't make it true. In all its vast complexities and subtleties, Christian theology is a work of the human imagination, not an investigation of truth.

And what of Jesus?

I keep thinking of that man who, two thousand years ago, was betrayed and flogged and put to death.

And I imagine this: I imagine a procession of ghostly visitors to Jerusalem in that week before Passover – spirits from the future, ghosts of Pope and priest and prelate and preacher, cardinals and archbishops and elders and patriarchs, in all the panoply and splendour of their rank, the chasubles, the albs, the copes, the pectoral crosses, the jewelled rings, the mitres, the tailored suits and the Cadillacs, the gleaming teeth and the bouffant hair.

And I imagine that each of these ghosts has the power, should he wish to use it, to embrace Jesus, much as Judas did, but for a different purpose: their kiss will transport him magically at once to Alexandria, or Athens, or Baghdad, or Rome, and thus save his life. There would be no terrible death on the cross. Jesus would live on, perhaps to vanish into obscurity, perhaps to add to the extraordinary and wonderful words he had spoken, perhaps even to write a book; but at least be alive and safe from that appalling death.

And I imagine each of these ghosts looking at the man as he goes about his angry work, denouncing the money-changers, debating with the scribes and chief priests and lashing them with his wit and his scorn, and getting closer every day to the betrayal and the death that each of the ghosts has known about for so long.

And I imagine the ghosts whispering:

'After all, it's God's will...'

'He foretold it himself...'

'I can't stand in the way...'

'It's a painful and sorrowful thing, no doubt, but after all, three days later...'

'The entire current of human history from that day on would be turned aside, and would go in a different direction altogether. This is too great a responsibility for me to bear...'

'My grandeur! The magnificence of my cathedral! The splendour of the music in my choir! It is my duty not to give those things up...'

'Looking at it in all, taking an objective view, the church without Jesus is better than Jesus without the church. I shall let him die...'

'Without this death and the church that came after it, that little dying child I spoke to in the hospital will have no solace...'

They look at the man, they see his rough hands and dirty fingernails, they hear the rasp of his voice, they smell a sweet ointment mingled with the sweat from his body, they see the snap and flash of his eyes as he scoffs at the Pharisees; and any one of the ghosts could reach out and save him from the death that's two days, a day, a few hours away.

And for a thousand reasons, each of the ghosts holds back and turns aside; and proudly or fastidiously, humbly or uneasily, with diplomatic murmurs of regret or with passionate sorrow, they drift away and go back to their own time and the comforts and rituals of the church they know, and abandon the man to his death.

That's the thought-experiment I'd put to every believing Christian: if you could go back in time and save that man from the horrible death of crucifixion, would you or not? And if you think it would be better to let him die so that the church would live, how are you different from Judas?

THIS ESSAY ORIGINATES IN TWO PIECES: 'HOW TO READ THE GOOD MAN JESUS AND THE SCOUNDREL CHRIST', AND: 'AFTERWORD TO THE GOOD MAN JESUS AND THE SCOUNDREL CHRIST' FROM THE PAPERBACK EDITION OF *THE GOOD MAN JESUS AND THE SCOUNDREL CHRIST* (CANONGATE, 2011).

I wrote that book for a series called Myths, *published by Canongate. I liked the idea of telling a myth, and I tried several of them in my mind before realising that this was the natural home for my thoughts about the central figure of the Christian religion. It's been old hat now for well over a hundred years to talk of Jesus as a myth, but that didn't stop several dozen people writing to me when the book was announced to tell me that I was going to be summoned before the Great White Throne and condemned to hell. Oddly, the letters all stopped once the book was published. I suppose the writers thought it was too late then.*

The Cat, the Chisel and the Grave

DO WE NEED A THEORY OF HUMAN NATURE
TO TELL US HOW TO WRITE STORIES?

Considering how a writer might know when a story is going wrong,
suggesting that writing is best done by going with the grain, not against it,
and proposing storytelling as a great School of Morals

GENERALLY SPEAKING, I FIND THEORIES OF ANY KIND INIMICAL. Though I'll qualify that at once by saying that it's other people's theories that are inimical. My own are entirely congenial. I have a theory about science, for example: I think it far more likely than not that there are some statements that are true, and that much of what science tells us belongs in that category. I don't think it's at all likely that science is a culturally constructed way of thinking that is only true for us, and might not be true for someone in another place or another time.

So I believe in science. But I don't think scientifically when I write. When I'm writing a story, the only thing that matters is whether something helps, or whether it hinders. I welcome anything, any form of superstition, even, that will help me when I sit down with a pen in my hand; and I still use a pen, because I have a lucky one. What I need at that point is not a theory of human nature, or a theory of evolution, but a theory of ghosts, demons, spirits, hobgoblins, magic rituals and diabolical possession.

And since the only thing I know about with any authority is what it feels like to write a story, I'm going to focus on that, because I think that if you're looking closely at one thing, you can see other things faintly at the edge of your vision, which flee away if you try to look at them

371

directly. And there are a couple of things hovering there in the semi-darkness, which I think might have a bearing on this human nature business. I've got twenty minutes, I'm told, which is just time for one question, one observation, and one epitaph.

So here goes. The question is this: how is it that I know when a story's going wrong? If I'm making up something new from scratch, how can there be a right way and a wrong way of doing it, a right shape and a wrong shape? Because this sense is very clear and strong; there's no mistaking it. I can think of several origins for this feeling, and here are five of them.

Firstly, it might be that there is a sort of Platonic realm of absolute perfection for every story that could ever be told, and that in some mysterious way, when I write I can experience it directly, and sense when I'm getting warm or cold with regard to the 'pure' story, close to it or further away.

Secondly, it might be cultural conditioning – the experience of hearing and reading a lot of stories of a particular sort, and coming to think that that's the only natural way for a story to be, and feeling uncomfortable unless I'm with something familiar. In other words, what the *right shape* is could be purely arbitrary, and it's just that we're used to that sort of shape.

Thirdly, it might be the faint apprehension of something that's definitely below the level of conscious perception most of the time. We've heard about experiments that show how our muscles begin a movement before we consciously decide to do it. Maybe my writing hand has already decided what the story should be, and my satisfaction or unease with the way it's going is a result of either getting close to what's already been decided or it going away. So my sense of *the right shape* and *the wrong shape* might be an awareness that what I take to be my conscious decision-making life is an illusion, and that in fact I'm determined or programmed by something below my conscious perception.

Fourthly, as a variation on that, I might be being guided by a higher power. I was recently told by one person, expert in her field, that I was channelling truths from the spirit world, and then by someone else, equally expert in hers, that my work clearly showed evidence of the unconscious working out of Oedipal conflicts. In neither case, apparently, was I – the conscious I – greatly responsible for it. So the feeling I'm talking about, as I say, might come from the fact that I'm being guided.

Fifthly, it might be the fact that my own narrative nerves and muscles are wonderfully developed, that – like a football player who has practised and practised until he can kick a ball into the corner of the net every time – I am just good at what I do. So my sense of *No, that's wrong* and *Yes, that's right* are the sort of semi-automatic adjustments and reflections and calculations that any practitioner of any complex activity makes all the time, and that get better with practice.

Anyway, my sense that *something is going wrong* and, elsewhere, or later, my sense that *this is the right way to do it* could be due to any of those things. For reasons of amour propre I prefer some of them to others, naturally. I also think some of them are simply more *likely* than others.

But if I don't know where it comes from, I can describe roughly what it feels like. It feels like the satisfaction we get when we hang a picture in the best place on a wall. There are places that simply look better than others. There's a sort of harmony or balance about them, and often we sense that before we learn about such things as the Golden Section – a system of balances and ratios often called the Divine Proportion and noted by artists and architects since the days of the ancient Greeks. The interesting thing about learning how the Golden Section works is that it doesn't feel like learning something that might just as well be otherwise, such as the rules of the road. That *we* drive on the left is arbitrary; other countries drive just as successfully on the right. Learning about the Golden Section *feels different* from that: it feels like learning a *truth* that until now we had sensed but not clearly seen.

A similar thing happens with sound: when you learn to hear the beats that tell you that two strings are not perfectly in tune, or the harmonics that govern the intervals of a fourth, a fifth, and so on, you're not learning something arbitrary and then *imposing* it on otherwise unstructured or inchoate matter; you're learning how to perceive an order that already exists in nature. These things are *there*.

Well, my point about narrative is that it's like that. Some narrative shapes are better than others. The shape of classical tragedy – great hero rises to glory and then is brought low by fundamental flaw in character – is a case in point. It's a very good shape for a story. There might be a small number of these good shapes, and a much larger number of shapes that aren't so good, and you just get to know what they are. It *feels* like that. When you're actually *doing* it, it feels non-arbitrary.

But I still don't know where it comes from. However, that isn't the point. I've been sneaking up on the point while looking at something else. *This* is the point: I don't know where that sense comes from, but it doesn't matter, because I *like* being in the state in which I believe all of those things at once. I don't know if that's a state of mind in which you can write theories, but it's by far the best one in which to write a story. You have to learn how to be in several contradictory states of mind at the same time, *not this one for a while and then that one*, and *not this one a lot and that one just a bit*, but all of them, and many more, simultaneously, to the full, without judging between them. In fact, you have to be like Schrödinger's cat, which is both alive and dead until you look at it.

So what helps me most to write stories is the ability to be profoundly sceptical and profoundly credulous, to be in utterly contradictory states, at one and the same time. Whether or not that's a theory of human nature I have no idea, but cats can do it.

That was my question. Here's my observation: you should go with the grain and not against it.

You see, I spent a lot of time and effort when I was younger trying to write stories of a kind that I wasn't good at. I tried to write the sort of thing that's called literary fiction, and I didn't do it at all well.

It wasn't until I was teaching twelve- and thirteen-year-old children, and writing plays for them to act in, that I found something I could do with freedom and exhilaration. The sort of stories I wrote for them were melodramas and fairy tales and Gothic romances. And I loved it. Eventually I made one of them into a novel, and then another, and another, and I found I was a children's author, to my surprise.

But then I found myself in another corner of the same trap I'd been in before. I thought that I ought to write realism, because that was a higher sort of thing than the fairy tales and the melodrama. So I wrote a couple of novels of that sort, and they're still in print, but they were nothing special.

And it was hard work – a particular kind of hard work. Now I'm not going to pretend that writing novels is ever easy, but I wasn't enjoying it either. Nor do I want to give the impression that every moment of a novelist's life is a riot of happy fun; but something just wasn't right at a basic level.

I didn't realise what that was until I began to write *His Dark Materials*. Here was a story that – whether you call it fantasy or not – is at least non-everyday-realistic. And what I felt at that point was that I was coming home, that something in my nature leaped towards this way of imagining things, so that I felt a happy and confident ease when I wrote about dæmons and little people six inches high with poison spurs who ride on dragonflies. This was native to me in a way that realism, much as I'd have liked it to be, wasn't.

In fact, the way I felt was very similar to what I've felt when carving wood. The wood might be straight-grained and free from knots, the chisel might be as sharp as twenty minutes of dedicated honing can make it – but if you're going against the grain, you'll have an extra layer of difficulty to cope with. Turn the work-piece around and carve the other way, and the chisel will cut with nonchalant accuracy, and curls of smooth wood will obediently lift themselves from the surface.

It's a question of finding the grain of your own talent and going with it, not against it. You have to observe yourself closely and honestly, and see what you're good at, and what you enjoy, and what you can do with the imagination you have. Some writers are like boxwood; their talent has a tight and perfectly uniform grain that cuts as happily in one direction as another, so they can turn from history to comedy to tragedy without faltering. Others are like construction softwood, coarse-textured, incapable of taking fine carving, easily splintered. They can only do one kind of rough structure, which may be very large, it may be strong and robust; but we're talking about carpentry and nails rather than cabinet-making and dove-tailed joints.

But whatever your talent is, you have to discover its nature and go with the grain of it. Otherwise, not only will you be perpetually frustrated and dissatisfied, because making the will do the work of the imagination is a melancholy business; but the work you produce will not express the nature of what it's made of. A jewel-box made of deal will be a poor jewel-box, either too flimsy or too clumsy; and to make the rafters of a house out of ebony is to waste the beauty of the costly wood by putting it where it won't be seen.

I said I'd end with an epitaph. You'll find this one on a tomb in the church of St Peter Mancroft in Norwich, and whenever I go to that city I make a sentimental pilgrimage to see it. It's the tomb of a young woman. The inscription reads:

> *This Stone is dedicated to the Talents and Virtues of Sophia Ann Goddard, who died aged 25 March 1801 aged 25. The Former shone with superior Lustre and Effect in the great School of Morals, the THEATRE, while the Latter inform'd the private Circle of Life with Sentiment, Taste, and Manners that still live in the Memory of Friendship and Affection.*

I don't know any more about Sophia Goddard than her epitaph tells us, but clearly she was greatly loved and admired.

But you can see what I'm going to focus on. *The great School of Morals, the THEATRE* – it's not easy to imagine anyone using a phrase like that today. It belongs to a particular time in the history of the theatre, and by extension in the history of fiction and narrative generally. I think of Jane Austen's famous and exactly contemporary comment about the novel in *Northanger Abbey*: that it's a work in which you find 'the most thorough knowledge of human nature, the happiest delineation of its varieties', and so on. Audiences and readers at that period saw narrative as a proper vehicle for moral enlightenment, for instruction as well as delight. The Puritans who closed the theatres down a hundred and fifty years before Sophia Goddard died would have had a quite different view.

Or perhaps not all that different, after all; because both the Puritans who abhorred the immorality of the theatre, and the late eighteenth-century audiences who applauded Miss Goddard, took seriously the idea that narrative art had a true and meaningful connection with human life. They took for granted that the behaviour of human beings, in all its variety, could be depicted faithfully in stories, and that stories would have a moral effect – whether good or bad – and an emotional and intellectual effect, for that matter, on those who read them.

As a matter of fact, so do I. Together with pretty well everyone else who has ever read a book, I find that an entirely *natural* way of reading. As for *nature*, and what that means: I think that human nature is what we have made ourselves as well as what we were given to start with, and that culture, which includes both technology and narrative art, is the way we do the making. What we are now is partly a result of our remote ancestors' mastery of fire, for example, which meant that they could migrate into colder regions and evolve different body shapes and skin colours to cope with different climatic conditions, and adjust to different diets; and also partly the result of enjoying, and pondering on,

and emulating – or avoiding – the models of human behaviour set out
for us by Homer, Shakespeare, Austen, George Eliot, Dostoevsky, etc.
not to mention the great fairy tales, and passing on what wisdom we gain
from it to our children.

So, finally: do you need a theory of human nature in order to write
stories? I think you need a theory of your own nature. But that's not so
easy to come by as you might think. You can spend years, for instance,
thinking that you're interested in something, only to discover eventually
that you were never really interested; you just thought you should be.
Self-knowledge is hard-won.

And I think you need the capacity to take other people's theories very
lightly indeed. Steal what you need, play with them, fool around with
them, but don't whatever you do become a slave to them. Remember the
cat; sometimes in order to be freely and fully human we have to be a little
feline too.

THIS TALK WAS FIRST DELIVERED AT THE INSTITUTE OF CONTEMPORARY
ARTS ON 8 MAY 2004 IN THE SYMPOSIUM 'SCIENCE, LITERATURE, AND
HUMAN NATURE'.

Apart from anything else (and I still stand by everything I said in this piece)
The Cat, the Chisel and the Grave *is the best title I've ever thought of.*

I Must Create a System...

A MOTH'S-EYE VIEW OF WILLIAM BLAKE

*On 'systems' – religious, theoretical, mythological, scientific
and other sorts – and whether they are necessary*

I SEE THAT THE TITLE OF THIS LECTURE IS GIVEN AS 'BLAKE'S DARK Materials'. Now in the lecturer's handbook, the second rule says: 'You need take no obsessive notice of the title that has been announced in advance.' Whether Blake's materials are dark or not I couldn't really say, but I am going to talk about Blake, partly, and partly about religion.

Appropriate, perhaps, in a place like this, but you might think not appropriate from someone whose reputation is that of a scoffer or mocker or critic of religion; but I haven't come here to scoff or mock. Nor have I come here to recant, as a matter of fact. I'm profoundly interested in religion, and I think it's extremely important to understand it. I've been trying to understand it all my life, and every so often it's useful to put one's thoughts in order; but I shall never like God.

I should also say that I'm delighted to be giving this lecture for the Blake Society, which is an excellent organisation of which I am the entirely undeserving President. Having done nothing to justify my occupation of this exalted office, I was very glad to say yes when they asked me to come and give this lecture. William Blake, as we know, had such extraordinary and penetrating insights into the nature of religion, and expressed them with such force and clarity, that it's always worth looking at what he has to say on the question. So I'm going to flutter around Blake like a moth around a lamp, trying not to burn my wings, and trying to see with my moth-eyes what the lamp illuminates; because

379

this particular moth is like the drunk man who has lost his keys over *there*, but is looking over *here* because this is where the light is. This moth is also slightly like a butterfly, and slightly like a bee, but I shall come to his uncertain insect-hood at the end, when I describe what he believes, in the form of seven axioms.

But I'll start with an odd thing that happened to me a few years ago. At that time I was deep in writing the novel *The Amber Spyglass*, which is the final part of a trilogy called *His Dark Materials*. Because I'd stolen the name of the trilogy from *Paradise Lost*, and because the view I'd formed of Milton had been influenced by Blake's, I was naturally interested in anything that spoke about the two of them. So when I saw a new book called *The Alternative Trinity: Gnostic Heresy in Marlowe, Milton and Blake*, I bought it at once. It was the word Gnostic that attracted my attention as well. I thought I had the Gnostic thing clear in my mind, but it was always good to have a new point of view.

The book was by A. D. Nuttall, who was Professor of English and Fellow of New College, Oxford, and a very good book it was. It was so good that I began to read it at once and found myself fascinated. But as I read, I was conscious of a faint grinding sound from somewhere, a slight but distinctive shudder in the structure of something, an almost subliminal unease in that part of the ear that deals with balance. In fact, I felt as if I was on board a very large and massively moving vessel whose keel had encountered, on the sea bottom, an equally large and massively immovable rock.

What Nuttall does in this book is to look at his three authors and the tension displayed in their work between orthodox Christian doctrine and that tendency of thought called Gnosticism, especially the branch of it known as the Ophite heresy. The Ophites (the name comes from the Greek *ophis*, serpent) emerged in Egypt early in the Christian era, and according to an authority quoted by Nuttall, they believed that 'the *serpent* by which our first parents were deceived, was either CHRIST himself or *Sophia* [wisdom], concealed under the form of that animal'.

Well, that's the sort of thing I like to hear.

As a matter of fact, that was the very sort of thing I was writing. The scene with the serpent and the temptation was exactly what I was leading up to, but I hadn't got there yet. I stopped on the way to read Nuttall's book. And I found myself reading this fascinating account of the underground survival, as it were, of the Ophite serpent-wisdom idea as it manifested itself in Milton and in Blake. And that was when the grinding sound and the deep shuddering feeling and the uncertain loss of balance kicked in.

And very soon they all stopped together, giving way to another feeling – that of having stopped. I stopped writing the novel and I stopped reading the book. The vessel had succumbed to the rock.

I'll step away from that metaphor now. I'll abandon that ship for a minute. What had happened was that the more I read about Milton's use of the *felix culpa* idea, the happy sin, or Blake's complex transformation of the moral imperatives of orthodox doctrine by means of a form of the Ophite heresy – the more I was impressed by Nuttall's account of Blake and Milton, in short – the more perplexed I found myself to be with relation to my own novel. I worried that I'd got bits of it wrong, and I wasn't sure how to put them right. In fact, I found myself immobile, held down by a thousand tiny threads.

Putting it another way, I had felt my ankles sinking into a quicksand, and I knew that the only way to avoid sinking altogether was to keep as still as possible.

In other words, I was royally stuck. I was in real difficulties. It seemed that I was writing an examination paper rather than a story, and one that was going to be marked very severely, what's more, because I hadn't done nearly enough work in the library. It was a curious state to be in.

What freed me from it was remembering the well-known lines from plate 10 of *Jerusalem*:

I must Create a System, or be enslav'd by another Mans
I will not Reason & Compare: my business is to Create.

Those are the words of Los – Blake's fallen angel, the divine aspect of imagination: 'in fury & strength'.

Well, I seized on them with gratitude and relief, and repeated them to myself several times like an incantation. And I'd like to think that the delusion that had briefly enslav'd me behaved like the Spectre described in the lines that follow:

... in indignation & burning wrath
Shuddring the Spectre howls. His howlings terrify the night
He stamps around the Anvil, beating blows of stern despair
He curses Heaven & Earth, Day & Night & Sun & Moon
He curses Forest Spring & River, Desart & sandy Waste
Cities & Nations, Families & Peoples, Tongues & Laws
Driven to desperation by Los's terrors & threatning fears...

I'd like to think it did, as I say, but the delusion that had me in its coils didn't quite behave like that. Instead it softly and suddenly vanished away, just like the hunter of the Snark that turned out to be a Boojum. As soon as I realised that *of course* I was creating my own system, and *of course* my business was to create, and not reason and compare – with one bound I was free.

But it was a nasty moment.

Anyway, with a profound nod of thanks to William Blake, I went on and finished the book.

I should have remembered that Milton had saved me from a similar predicament at the very beginning, when I found myself inexorably – helplessly – bound into the writing of a fantasy, a genre of story I neither enjoyed nor approved of. I didn't think much of fantasy because most fantasy I'd read seemed to take no interest in human psychology, which for me was the central point of fiction. It was only when I realised that *Paradise Lost*, a poem I loved and admired more than any other, was itself a sort of fantasy, and that the angels were not simply big-people-with-wings but could also be understood as emblems of psychological states, that I felt free to go ahead with my ideas about dæmons and talking bears and alternative worlds and what have you. I could use the apparatus of fantasy to say something that I thought was truthful and hoped was interesting about what it was like to be a human being.

Milton had showed me that, and now Blake was showing me that I didn't need to creep around in somebody else's system trying not to knock things over or make too much noise. I could arrange things exactly as I needed them in my own story, because I was creating my own system.

The relief was immense. I felt rather like the freed slave in Blake's *America*:

> Let the slave grinding at the mill run out into the field,
> Let him look up into the heavens & laugh in the bright air;
> Let the inchained soul, shut up in darkness and in sighing,
> Whose face has never seen a smile in thirty weary years,
> Rise and look out; his chains are loose, his dungeon doors are
> open;
> And let his wife and children return from the oppressor's
> scourge.
> They look behind at every step & believe it is a dream.

Well, something like that.

But that disconcerting experience, and my rescue from it, raises a couple of questions, and I want to think about them now and see if I can come to any conclusion.

The first one is: what is a system?

The second one is: are the only two attitudes possible towards systems – to create them or to be enslav'd by someone else's?

And there is a third question too, which I'll come to later.

So, first of all, what do we mean by a system? One large and obvious meaning it could have, in the context of this discussion, is undoubtedly religion. To call oneself a Christian, for example, is to announce your allegiance to a system, and a fertile one too. The Christian religion, which is the one I know about, has provided a system – an account of what the universe means, and of our place in it – that underpins the greatest part of our cultural heritage, including, not least, *Paradise Lost*. Being a Christian used to mean that you believed certain things and behaved in certain ways, but these days we can't assume that we know exactly what those things are; any system that can claim the allegiance of both the Reverend Don Cupitt and the Reverend Jerry Falwell is a pretty accommodating one. Christianity, more than other religions perhaps, has been characterised by inveterate fissiparousness. Sect divides from sect, and the more closely they're related, the more they hate each other. But never mind; there are people who are supremely happy to know that they belong to the only true faith, the Reformed Independent Baptist Exclusive and Particular Redeemed Seventh-Day Rapturous Children of God. Everyone else will go to hell.

Another thing *system* might mean is theory. So, for example, you might feel yourself enslav'd by psychoanalytical theory and the need to interpret everything through the glass of infantile sexuality and the Oedipus complex, so you break free of it and create your own system that involves a collective unconscious and archetypes and images from alchemy and Eastern religion. You feel free in this new system; it fits the contours of your mind and your imagination and your temperament; it doesn't constrict any part of you. In other words, you are Jung breaking away from Freud, and your system is a psychological one.

Or else your system could take a political form. Casting around for a way to explain the injustices and cruelties that press on your consciousness daily, but which most of your fellow citizens don't even seem to notice, you discover feminist theory. At last! Suddenly a hundred things whose causes and relations were troubling and obscure become linked in a web of crystalline light. Everything is clear, from the smallest example of fatherly disapproval to the furthest reaches of tyranny and despotism. Or else you discover Marxism, with exactly the same result. Or else you become a devotee of the capitalist market system, with exactly the same result. A discovery of that sort would be an example of finding another man's system in which you felt perfectly at home, and not enslav'd at all; in fact, you could say, and many people do, that it was only through finding this system that you first tasted freedom itself, and the slaves are those who have not yet entered the system with you, and who languish in the ignorance and darkness outside.

Another meaning that system might have is mythology, with a set of stories about characters like Yahweh, or Zeus, or the giant Albion, or Jesus Christ. Mythologies deal with the creation of things, and the appearance of human beings in a world we did not create. I'm not aware of any mythology that says the universe was created by human beings; we always turn up afterwards, and the relation we have with the place we find ourselves in is part of what gives the system its emotional tone – determines whether it's tragic, or optimistic, or dramatic, or whatever. Sometimes we are the rebellious children of the great creator; sometimes we are the children made by a sub-creator who rebelled against the first creator, like the creatures of Prometheus; but our presence here is accounted for in the story. We are part of everything that's going on; even if we don't fully understand it, we have the sense of coherence somewhere.

Blake's mythology is a case in point, being endlessly complex and rich enough to sustain many an interpretation, with its gallery of enormous figures emerging from the clouds and the fires to howl their rage and defiance and disappear again into obscure darkness. What makes it great to a sympathetic reader is our awareness that although we can't always fully understand the precise relations between Los and Urizen, or Rintrah and Palamabron, Blake himself has a clear idea of it all. It's not like seeing part of a painted landscape through a window and guessing that if you moved a little to one side, you'd see the edge of the painting and the bare wall beyond it; it's like seeing part of a real landscape through a window, and knowing that however far you moved to one side or another, there would always be more landscape to see. The parts we can't see, the things we can't understand, are really there beyond the edge of our vision, and in a proper relationship to one another – it's just that they're not easily visible. In other words, Blake's system is a true system, and not the arbitrary ravings of a lunatic which it seemed to some of his early readers.

So *system* could mean religion, or it could mean theory, or it could mean mythology. Could it mean science? Or if not science itself, then an attitude to the world that accepts the value and importance of the scientific method, and the truth of what that method discloses?

Undoubtedly science does provide an explanatory narrative about the way things are, and that narrative includes ourselves. The difficulty for many people about the large-scale explanations that some scientists give is that these explanations reduce the importance of the part about us to insignificance. Some of them – the well-known book by Jacques Monod called *Chance and Necessity*, for example – paint a picture of a universe so bleak and pitiless, so empty of any meaning or consolation, that they demand an unusual degree of courage and resolution from us if we're to accept them as they stand.

Which raises the question: does a system *have* to console? Why should a system exist for our benefit? It might have its own meaning and purpose, which are too big and mysterious for us to understand. Nevertheless, I think we could live with that, because of the hope that one day we might understand it; and that would give us the purpose of trying to find out the bigger purpose. I think we could even live with a malign purpose. It might even be bearable to discover that we had been put here to be fattened and eaten by some immense greedy god, in the form of human *foie gras*, because then we would have the great and noble aim of rebellion and the overthrow of tyranny. But science doesn't seem to let us have even that savage purpose. The physicist Steven Weinberg says, 'The more we understand about the universe, the more it seems to be utterly pointless.' It seems that we need a certain amount of moral fortitude if we're to live our lives believing in nothing but science. It's a noble system, no doubt, if it is a system at all, but it's an austere and demanding one.

Well, I've looked at some of the things that might be meant by the word *system* in Blake's lines. I want to go on now to my second question, which was about the two alternatives he proposed. 'I must create a System, or be enslav'd by another man's,' he said. Are those the only two options, I wonder? Is there another attitude we could take? And remember, I'm talking about urgent practicalities here, about profound and vital questions. I'm not talking about adopting a system as one might take up a hobby, or choose a new tie or a new colour for the bathroom; I'm talking about something that will make it possible to write, or prevent it. I'm talking about what will allow life to flow through you, or what will choke it off and kill it. It's that important.

Well, the first option, to create your own system, certainly worked for Blake. And he wasn't the only writer to try that method. Another great poet who developed a private mythology was W. B. Yeats – a great admirer of Blake, of course. The use that a writer makes of a private mythology may be quite independent of its merit, by the way. As far as I can understand, Yeats's system is absolute bunkum; miscellaneous bits and pieces of occult symbolism, numerology, invented ritual from the Order of the Golden Dawn, rubbish about the phases of the moon, and the like. You wouldn't give tuppence for it if it were sold separately. But without it, Yeats wouldn't have written those great poems of his final period – some of the most thrilling poetry in our language. The greatness of the poems, though, lies in the language and not in the system that inspired them, and we might – though it is with the greatest possible tentativeness that I advance this view under the auspices of the Blake Society – we might think the same of some of Blake: that the greatness of the *Songs of Innocence and of Experience*, for example, is independent of their setting; even if we'd never heard of the rest of his system, even if we'd never seen his extraordinary illuminations. 'The Sick Rose' and 'The Tyger' and 'The Little Girl Lost' and so many others would work their enchantment over us because of the majestic and magical power of his language. The value of a writer's system, to the general reader, is not so much that it can be entered and enjoyed and lived in for its own sake, as that it gave rise to the work. No system, no work; or at any rate, much less interesting work.

The alternative to creating your own system – Blake's alternative – was, you remember, to be enslav'd by another man's. Well, I described earlier on, with reference to A. D. Nuttall's book, how I found myself inadvertently enslav'd for a brief spell by a system that I certainly didn't create; and it's a profoundly irksome thing. But thinking of this *slavery* image for a minute, and remembering Blake's famous words about Milton – that he 'wrote in fetters when he wrote of Angels & God, and at liberty when of Devils & Hell… because he was a true Poet and of the Devil's party without knowing it' – the implication of *the fetters* is that Milton was for some of the time enslav'd by a system that didn't suit his particular genius.

The sharpness of Blake's perception here is summed up, for me, in the last three words: Milton was of the Devil's Party *without knowing it*.

There have been plenty of writers who did not know where their true talent lay. It's perfectly possible to be enslav'd by a conception of *the right thing to do* which is totally at variance with the equipment you have to do it with. Sir Arthur Sullivan thought his duty was to write grand opera, and was impatient with that fellow Gilbert and his silly notions; and yet how many performances of the opera he did write, *Ivanhoe*, are there for every thousand of *The Mikado*?

If you're lucky, you find out where your talent lies before it's too late. It took me a long time to rid myself of the enslaving notion that the only proper sort of novel to write was a sternly realistic one. You can make yourself work in the shackles of duty for a certain amount of time, but it's hard and painful; slave's work, unredeemed, in a phrase of Ruskin's, or making the will do the work of the imagination, in a phrase of Yeats's. It's trying to make cobwebs out of clay. When you discover where your talent genuinely lies, it really does feel like being set free. The enslavement Blake speaks of isn't always imposed from outside. Mind-forg'd manacles are just as heavy as any other.

So when it comes to systems and our relation to them, you can create a system; you can find yourself enslav'd by one; and you can discover a system or a theory that you didn't create, but in which at last you feel free, as I described a few minutes ago in the case of the person who is set free by their discovery of feminism, or Marxism, or whatever. Those seem to be the three main options. But earlier on I mentioned two questions I had in mind about systems: what is a system, firstly, and secondly, what are the possible attitudes to take towards systems; and I said there was a third question I'd come to later. Well, here is the third question: does a writer need a system at all? Is it possible to have no system? What would it be like to have no system? To be committed to nothing, to be enslav'd by nothing, to be labelled by nothing, to be known as nothing, to be fixed and limited by nothing?

I have to say that of all the ways of being I've described so far, my own nature leaps towards that one like a lover. But, of course, it's not as simple as that.

Because we may be without a system, but we're certainly not without all sorts of other mental baggage. It might be delightful if we were. In Tove Jansson's *The Exploits of Moominpappa*, the young Moomin runs away from the Foundlings' Home. Having made his escape, he says, 'I had nothing to call my own. I knew nothing, but believed a lot. I did nothing by habit. I was extremely happy.' However much we might wish to be back in that condition, it doesn't last very long. Habits grow quickly; and no one is without a temperament that colours their perceptions of the world, and inclines them to joy or to melancholy, to irritability or to patience; and hazard or sickness or fortune soon begin to make their marks, and those marks are indelible, and they keep coming until our characters are a palimpsest of the graffiti of circumstance; and if all those weren't enough, we absorb the assumptions and prejudices of our parents and the social class we're born into so early that they come to seem the only natural way to think and feel; whereas if we'd been born a mile away, with a differently coloured skin, we might have a completely different view of everything around us.

So each one of us has a whole complex of attitudes and experiences which, if they're not as coherent as a worked-out system, function in a similar way. They provide the solid and unquestioned support for all the work we build on top of them. And not only the work. They function like an invisible armature shaping every action we take, every assumption we make, every view we form of society or politics or religion. They are there whether we know it or not. And sometimes we deny they're there at all. People who are successful in a worldly way, in administration or business or politics or journalism, for example, often claim that they see things clearly and they're not taken in by any fancy theories and they know what's what and they've got their feet on the ground. The system they have acquired by a thousand tiny chances doesn't seem to them like a system at all; it seems to be a perfectly designed edifice of truth – mighty, beautiful and flawless – which corresponds in every particular to the way things really are.

But it works. As long as they don't think about it, it stands. It might seem from the outside like a haphazardly acquired combination of prej-

udice, ignorance, random experience, scraps of cracker-barrel senten-
tiousness, things they were taught before they were seven, superstition,
sentimentality, wishful thinking and saloon-bar knowingness; a gim-
crack, jerry-built, patchwork thing, crawling with dry rot, with rats in
the basement and death-watch beetle in the attic, with staircases that lead
nowhere and corridors blocked off by fallen masonry, with broken windows banging in the wind and great holes in the roof letting in the rain.
Never mind. As long as the inhabitants don't question its absolute right-
ness and truthfulness, it'll stand. Plenty of people live their entire lives in
a state of boundless confidence, and die never once having doubted the
happy certainty of the things they know. Lucky them; this unquestioning
confidence is a source of great strength.

In literary work, which is my main concern, a system like that – the
one you don't know you've got – often only becomes clearly visible
a generation or two after the work was first published. As the sun moves
round, the shadows change; and popular fiction of the first half of the
twentieth century seems to a reader of today to be darkened by shadows
that readers then didn't notice. Anti-Semitism, for example. The attitude
many such stories embody is that Jews are not like *us*, somehow – the *us*
that is understood to include the reader that books of that sort seem to
expect. Jews may be very clever, they may be imaginative and artistic; but
somehow they are not like *us*; we unconsciously signal the difference by
referring to their Jewishness all the time. Better books reflect the same
social assumptions, but more subtly: in Graham Greene's *Stamboul Train*
of 1932, the author signals this all-pervasive awareness of difference by
locating it either in the words or the consciousness of the characters. The
purser on board a cross-Channel ferry is talking to a waiter. 'That Jew,' he
said, 'did he give you a good tip?' A young actress is coming round after
having fainted: 'She was aware of the heavy slow movement of the train.
Lights streamed through the window across the doctor's face and on to
the young Jew behind.'

I dare say that much work of the present day, including my own, will in time reveal some equally unfortunate attitudes, some ugly shadows, of which we're quite unconscious at the moment. The point is that we cannot be free of these things; to claim that we have no system, that we see things exactly as they are, that we write without any preconceptions or hidden ideology, is to deceive ourselves. We are already enslav'd.

When we first realise that, it comes as a terrible shock. And all that sunny confidence we had when we didn't think about it vanishes at once.

Blake in *The Auguries of Innocence*:

> If the Sun & Moon should doubt
> They'd immediately go out.

I'm going to follow this line for a minute, because it leads back at last to the other word I mentioned in the title of Nuttall's book, the word 'Gnostic', and I want to think about whether the Blake I love – that small corner of the great continent of all his work that I've wandered about in, and grown to know and revere – can truthfully be called Gnostic, and whether the Gnostic system is one in which I might feel free.

So: this business of doubt.

William James, in *The Varieties of Religious Experience*, has a name for people who have never doubted the assumptions they live by: he calls them once-born. And once you've doubted, once you've seen the arbitrary and contingent and contradictory nature of the system you didn't think was a system at all, you become as it were twice-born.

Not *born again*, in the modern phrase that comes originally, I suppose, from the Southern Baptists; being *born again* is a very different thing. It means conversion to a particularly shrill and enthusiastic form of Christianity. Born-again people have all the certainty of the once-born, with an added and obnoxious self-righteousness. But twice-born people are in a different condition.

William James describes the difference like this:

> In the religion of the once-born the world is a sort of
> rectilinear or one-storied affair, whose accounts are kept in
> one denomination, whose parts have just those values which
> naturally they appear to have, and of which a simple alge-
> braic sum of pluses and minuses will give the total worth.
> Happiness and religious peace consist in living on the plus
> side of the account. In the religion of the twice-born, on
> the other hand, the world is a double-storied mystery. Peace
> cannot be reached by the simple addition of pluses and
> elimination of minuses from life.
>
> Natural good is not simply insufficient in amount and
> transient, there lurks a falsity in its very being... it gives no
> final balance, and can never be the thing intended for our
> lasting worship.

James doesn't mention Gnosticism directly in *The Varieties of Religious
Experience*, but in that last couple of sentences, he perfectly summed
up the attitude that fuels it. Gnosticism is a perennial system of radical
existential scepticism that flares up in times of millennial crisis such as
the present. It's an extraordinarily intoxicating system, because it tells
a thrilling story that's exactly like a conspiracy theory, involving our very
deepest selves.

The idea is that the real God is nowhere to be found in this universe,
but is infinitely distant. Our souls (it's a little more complicated than
that, but *souls* will do) belong with Him, the distant unknowable God,
and not here in this world, because each soul is a spark of divinity that was
stolen and imprisoned here by the evil creator of the material universe,
the Demiurge or false God who is worshipped by all those who aren't in
the secret. Only those who *know* can pass on the secret knowledge of how
to find our way back to our true home.

What could be more thrilling than to feel ourselves in possession of knowledge like that, and of a fate so grand and all-encompassing? To feel our own lives bound up so intimately with the origins and the destiny of the universe itself? It's no wonder that the Gnostic impulse keeps flaring up again like an underground fire that can't be put out. It lies behind a lot of popular narrative art of the sort that deals with the questions of who we are and why we're here and why those in authority are deceiving us: *the truth* about Jesus, or God, or our own deepest identity, is not what we have been told up till now. *The truth* is something radically different, which is in the possession of a few initiates, and if only people knew what it was, it would change their view of everything.

Anyway, Gnosticism forms a natural refuge for the twice-born. It accounts for all kinds of things, not least for the existence of evil in a world that was supposedly created by a good God – because the world was created by a *bad* God, and the real God is somewhere else. It accounts for the mysterious feeling of alienation that the twice-born suffer – because it's natural to feel alienated from a world where you don't belong, a world where you are yourself an alien. It accounts for the power of the Christ story – because Christ was not a man at all, but an emissary from the distant Godhead sent to show us the way back home. There are secret gospels, and secret ways of reading the familiar gospels, that make this clear to those in the know. Everything we have taken for granted is wrong, and must be re-interpreted in order to be understood in a new way.

Now there are passages in Blake that sound very like this. In *The Marriage of Heaven and Hell*, the Devil, in conversation with an Angel, speaks about Jesus Christ: 'Now hear how he has given his sanction to the law of ten commandments: did he not mock at the sabbath and so mock the sabbath's God? murder those who were murder'd because of him? turn away the law from the woman taken in adultery? steal the labour of others to support him? bear false witness when he omitted making a defence against Pilate? covet when he pray'd for his disciples, and when he bid them shake off the dust of their feet against those who refus'd to lodge them? I tell you, no virtue can exist without breaking these ten commandments. Jesus was all virtue, and acted from impulse, not from rules.'

The Angel who's being addressed, says the narrator of *The Marriage of Heaven and Hell*, 'is my particular friend; we often read the Bible together in its infernal or diabolical sense, which the world shall have if they behave well.'

So far, so Gnostic. *The Marriage of Heaven and Hell* is one of the most radically troubling and exhilarating works that has ever been written, and a great deal of it seems to support a sort of antinomian reversal of conventional morality ('Sooner murder an infant in its cradle than nurse unacted desires') which has formed a strong part of the Gnostic tradition. A. D. Nuttall's reading of Blake demonstrates that although that is certainly there, it's far from the whole of it, and that Blake's Gnosticism is seen even more vividly in the opposition he depicts between the aged father-tyrant and the revolutionary, life-bringing son.

Well, possibly. Blake's genius was so protean that it's possible to find support for all kinds of theories about it in the teeming riches of his verse.

But for me, although Nuttall doesn't agree with this, the tendency of the poetry points the other way. The Blake I love was not a Gnostic. The defining mark of Gnosticism is its mistrust and hatred of the natural world, its contempt for bodily experience, and that is why, for all the intoxicating excitement of the conspiracy theory of creation, I could never be a Gnostic, and I could never love Blake if I thought that he hated the physical world.

But remember, I'm seeing this with the eyes not of a scholar but of a moth, as I mentioned at the start. All I can do is tell you what I see with those eyes. I say moth; I might as well say butterfly. I admitted in the afterword at the end of *The Amber Spyglass* that my principle was to 'read like a butterfly, write like a bee', and what I meant was that

I read unsystematically, carried from place to place by the impulse of the moment. I sample dozens of flowers every morning; if a strong wind comes along, I'm lifted helplessly and deposited a hundred miles away; whatever attracts me can have my attention for as long as it can keep it, and then I'm off. That's how I read.

But there are some flowers I return to again and again for the quality of their nectar, as a butterfly, or there are some lights I can't help fluttering back to, as a moth. And this tiny insect-brain or insect-instinct knows what's good for it and what's bad; and little by little it's been gathering drops of nectar from *here*, and beams of light from *there*, and making them into something which, if it isn't as grand and all-embracing as a system, is at least a series of Axioms, if you like, which make it possible for the moth-butterfly, when he returns to his little hexagonal cell and becomes a bee, to write with a sort of coherence.

So here, to end with, are seven of the drops of nectar and beams of light that this unstable insect has gathered from Blake. They are engraved on the walls of the cell under the title *The Republic of Heaven*.

> Axiom number one: the moth-butterfly-bee believes that this physical world, this matter of which we are made, is amorous by nature. Matter rejoices in matter, and each atom of it falls in love with other atoms and delights to join up with them to form complex and even more delightful structures: '… and shew you all alive This world, where every particle of dust breathes forth its joy.'

> Axiom number two: things arise from matter-in-love-with-matter that are not themselves matter. Thoughts emerge from the unimaginable, the non-disentangle-able complexity of the brain, thoughts that are not material, though they have analogues in material processes, and you can't say where

one ends and the other begins, because each is an aspect of the other. 'Man has no Body distinct from his Soul; for that call'd Body is a portion of Soul discern'd by the five senses.'

Axiom number three: the consciousness inherent in matter demonstrates that consciousness is a normal property of the physical world and much more widely diffused than human beings think. 'How do you know but ev'ry Bird that cuts the airy way, Is an immense World of delight, clos'd by your senses five?'

Axiom number four: bodily experience underlies, sustains, feeds, inspires, and cherishes mental experience. 'Energy is the only life, and is from the Body; and Reason is the bound or outward circumference of Energy. Energy is Eternal Delight'.

Axiom number five: we should use what works. And if invoking ghosts, demons, spirits, gods, demigods, nymphs or hobgoblins helps us to write, then we should banish the superstition about not being superstitious and invoke them without embarrassment or hesitation. 'All deities reside in the human breast.'

Axiom number six: the true object of our study and our work is human nature and its relationship to the universe. 'God Appears & God is Light To those poor Souls who dwell in Night, But does a Human Form Display To those who Dwell in Realms of day.'

Axiom number seven: the work we do is infinitely worth doing. 'Eternity is in love with the productions of time.'

Well, those are some of the things that this moth-butterfly has learned from Blake. These are the axioms he lives by. Whether it amounts to a system he couldn't say; but he's still young; he's not sixty yet. He will continue to visit the flowers in the garden of Blake – and elsewhere too, and not only the flowers of poetry, but the flowers of music and painting and philosophy and science and those that occur naturally in the landscapes of the sky and the earth and the sea – and gather nectar of all kinds until his wings grow too old to fly with.

And from time to time, as I say, he goes back to his cell and becomes a bee and begins the long silent contemplative process of turning the nectar into words. But that's another story.

This talk was delivered to The Blake Society at St James's Church, Piccadilly, on 25 October 2005.

William James's The Varieties of Religious Experience *is one of the most interesting and enlightening books I've ever read. What makes it particularly valuable is that he's not pushing a particular view of the truth of religion: instead he's examining, with a wealth of examples and a great depth of psychological insight, what it feels like to be religious. It's never a waste of time to look honestly at human experience.*

Talents and Virtues

ANOTHER VISIT TO MISS GODDARD'S GRAVE

Considering the delight and wisdom to be had from stories, and contrasting two ways of reading them, which might be called 'democratic' and 'theocratic'

THANK YOU FOR INVITING ME TO SPEAK HERE IN THIS DISTINGUISHED series of lectures. Quite what prompted you to ask me to talk about religious education I can't immediately see; you must have been desperate. As I'm not an academic, nor a member of the clergy, nor a teacher, whatever I say about the subject will be the observations of an amateur with no standing in the field. Furthermore, given that I've voiced some criticisms of religion in the past, and that various Christian groups have expressed their criticisms of me, it might be that whatever I said on the subject would be hostile in any case.

Well, I hope it won't be that. But we shall see. I'll begin by taking you to the churchyard of St Peter Mancroft overlooking the marketplace in Norwich. Not far from the door of this church there's a tomb – a finely carved family sort of tomb, one of those big boxshaped ones. At one end there is an oval cartouche, and inside it the inscription:

> *This Stone is dedicated to the Talents and Virtues of Sophia Ann Goddard, who died 25 March 1801 aged 25. The Former shone with superior Lustre and Effect in the great School of Morals, the THEATRE, while the Latter inform'd the private Circle of Life with Sentiment, Taste, and Manners that still live in the Memory of Friendship and Affection.*

I've been fond of that tomb, and this inscription, and by extension of Miss Goddard herself, for most of my life. I know nothing about her; if I had the time I'd spend a few hours in the county archives to see if there was any record of an actress called Sophia Goddard in Norwich at the end of the eighteenth century. Clearly she was greatly loved and widely admired. There must have been a portrait made at some stage; people have always liked looking at pictures of young actresses; they still do. Perhaps it's still hanging in a house somewhere in the city, or at the back of an antique shop, with the title 'Unknown young woman, late 18th century'. There's a story there; in fact, there are several.

But what I'm concerned about tonight is the relevance of her epitaph to the theme of my lecture. I don't profess any religion; I don't think it's possible that there is a God; I have the greatest difficulty in understanding what is meant by the words 'spiritual', or 'spirituality'; but I think I can say something about moral education, and I think it has something to do with the way we understand stories, which is why I've begun with Miss Goddard's grave.

Sophia Goddard's tomb

'The great school of morals, the theatre' – it was possible in 1801 to use a phrase like that and not be misunderstood, not be suspected of irony. The people who patronised Miss Goddard's performances would really have believed that the theatre was indeed a place to which we might go and find instruction or enlightenment about matters of morality.

So when the monumental mason cut the words 'the great School of Morals, the THEATRE' on Miss Goddard's tombstone, there would not have been a scandal. Few people would have disagreed with the idea that the theatre could teach us about moral questions. You might not go to see a play specifically in order to become a more moral person; the latest Harlequinade or pantomime might be stronger on farcical slapstick and transformation scenes than on ethical instruction; but taking it by and large, the audiences would have felt that the experience over a season's or a life's theatre-going of seeing many different stories, some full of sentimental pathos, others bristling with martial bravado, some tragic, some comic – that wide mixed experience would tend to give the audience a moral education. That was the assumption. People would come to see that some kinds of behaviour – such as generosity and forgiveness – led to happy outcomes, and were praiseworthy; other kinds of behaviour – such as greed or deceitfulness – led to unhappy outcomes, and were disapproved of. Yet other kinds of behaviour – such as renunciation or noble self-sacrifice – led to sad outcomes in the short run, but were highly praised, because they led to happy outcomes for others in the long run. There would be degrees of subtlety, of course; both a violent melodrama and *Macbeth* would tell the audience that murder was not a good thing, but the Scottish play would do it by showing the effect Duncan's murder has on the murderer himself. We learn from Macbeth's fate that killing is horrible for the killer as well as the victim. And these things were all felt to be part of an education in the great school of morals.

But it wasn't only the theatre that was felt to have this educative effect. At around the same time, Jane Austen was writing these famous words in *Northanger Abbey*:

> 'Oh! It is only a novel!... Only Cecilia, or Camilla, or Belinda;' or, in short, only some work in which the most thorough knowledge of human nature, the happiest delineation of its varieties, the liveliest effusions of wit and humour are conveyed to the world in the best chosen language.

And Jane Austen's own novels, of course, do exactly that. Think what happens in *Emma*, especially in the passage where Emma is thoughtlessly rude to poor elderly Miss Bates, and especially this exchange that follows it. Mr Knightley is older than Emma, and she admires him without knowing yet that the feeling that's growing in her is love. She is quite profoundly taken aback when he says this:

> 'Were she your equal in situation – but, Emma, consider how far this is from being the case. She is poor; she has sunk from the comforts she was born to; and, if she live to old age, must probably sink more. Her situation should secure your compassion. It was badly done, indeed! You, whom she had known from an infant, whom she had seen grow up from a period when her notice was an honour, to have you now, in thoughtless spirits, and the pride of the moment, laugh at her, humble her – and before her niece, too – and before others, many of whom (certainly *some*) would be entirely guided by *your* treatment of her. This is not pleasant to you, Emma, and it is very far from pleasant to me; but I must, I will, tell you truths while I can, satisfied with proving myself your friend by very faithful counsel, and trusting that you will

some time or other do me more justice than you can now.'

While they talked, they were advancing towards the carriage; it was ready; and before she could speak again, he had handed her in. He had misinterpreted the feelings which had kept her face averted, and her tongue motionless. They were combined only of anger against herself, mortification, and deep concern. She had not been able to speak; and, on entering the carriage, sunk back for a moment overcome – then reproaching herself for taking no leave, making no acknowledgement, parting in apparent sullenness, she looked out with voice and hand eager to show a difference; but it was just too late. He had turned away, and the horses were in motion. She continued to look back, but in vain; and soon, with what appeared unusual speed, they were half way down the hill, and every thing left far behind. She was vexed beyond what could have been expressed – almost beyond what she could conceal. Never had she felt so agitated, mortified, grieved, at any circumstance in her life. She was most forcibly struck. The truth of his representation there was no denying. She felt it at her heart. How could she have been so brutal, so cruel to Miss Bates! How could she have exposed herself to such ill opinion in any one she valued! And how suffer him to leave her without saying one word of gratitude, of concurrence, of common kindness!

I quote that passage in full because we need to see the whole progress of her shame and mortification and grief, grief that she has done wrong, mixed, to be sure, with grief that it has been noticed by someone whose good opinion she especially values; but genuine sorrow too, that she has hurt someone thoughtlessly. The movement of the passage from Mr Knightley's reproof to Emma's self-reproach, her regret for appearing to be sullen, and not speaking to him, when in fact she was deeply ashamed, is the school of morals fully at work. Emma is being educated all right, and so are we.

You won't be surprised to hear, then, that I endorse this 'school of morals' view wholeheartedly. I think we can learn what's good and what's bad, what's generous and unselfish, what's cruel and mean, from fiction. In one way, this is so obvious that it's hardly worth saying; except that I think that from time to time it needs re-stating, or stating in terms that take account of the currents that have flowed through cultural life, through public discourse, since it was last stated. And I think that there are two such currents that have been flowing strongly in recent years, and I'll look at each of them in turn.

One is 'theory', and the whole project of theory, including post-structuralism, post-colonialism, post-modernism, and so on. As it affects this argument, it takes the form of saying that the connection between literary texts and the rest of life is characterised by contradictions and fractures and disjunctions and subversions and an endlessly regressive series of dialectical readings. A text is not, as we had innocently thought, a transparent window through which ideas or things or events or characters are visible with perfect clarity. As a matter of fact it's problematical to talk as if there were a difference between texts and the rest of life in any case, because '*il n'y a pas dehors-texte*', there is nothing outside the text. When I asked a leading practitioner of post-structuralism what that actually meant, she said, 'Ah, but Derrida didn't mean it in that sense,' which confirmed what I thought when I asked the question, namely that this was a mystery too profound for my feeble understanding to plumb.

This intellectual endeavour, or if you prefer mystery-cult, is a source of great fascination and enormous fun and considerable professional advantage to those who know how to play it. But to the non-academic reader it does seem to undercut a certain moral idea, namely responsibility. You seem to be able to say things without consequences, because whatever you say will automatically deny and subvert its own claims to truth. When 'theory' was at its height, the idea that novels or plays reflected more or less faithfully what human life was like and taught us how to behave by showing what happened when you did this or that seemed ridiculously old-fashioned and out of touch. In fact, some things that traditional readers and writers took for granted, like the thing Jane Austen called human nature, were scoffed at, and their very existence denied.

I'll come back to theory later in this lecture, because first of all I want to look at the other cultural force bearing on the school of morals, which is quite different. I suppose you could call it theocratic absolutism. I've written about it before, but I think what I said bears re-stating. Theocratic absolutism has been around for longer than theory, and its effects have been far more deadly. But first I'll have to clarify what I mean by theocratic, because I don't think you need to believe in God to have a theocracy; some theocracies are atheist. I mean a system that has these characteristics:

There is a holy book, a scripture whose word is inerrant and may not be doubted, which has such absolute authority that it trumps every other. Everything, even the discoveries of science, has to be judged against what the scripture says, and if there is a contradiction, the scripture wins. This scripture might be the Bible, it might be the Koran, it might be the works of Karl Marx.

There are doctors of the church, who interpret the holy book and pronounce on its meaning: it might be St Augustine, it might be the Ayatollahs, it might be Lenin.

There is a priesthood with special powers and privileges, which can confer blessings on the laity, or withdraw them. Entry into the priesthood is an honour; it's not for everyone; and the authority of the priesthood tends to concentrate in the hands of elderly men: as it might be, the Vatican, or the politburo in the Kremlin.

There is close control of the news media, and ferocious censorship of books. It was the Catholic Church of the Counter-Reformation that invented the word propaganda, and the Soviet Union that took it up with enthusiasm and incorporated it into their term *agitprop*.

And there are many more characteristics of this sort of system, which we can find parallels for in both religious and atheist forms of totalitarianism:

There is the concept of heresy and its punishment.

There is the concept of apostasy.

There is an Inquisition with the powers of a secret police force, or a secret police force with the powers of an Inquisition.

There is a complex procedural apparatus of betrayal, denunciation, confession, trial and execution.

There is a teleological view of history, according to which human society is moving inexorably towards a millennial fulfilment in a golden age.

There is a fear and hatred of external unbelievers.

There is a fear and hatred of internal demons and witches.

There is the notion of pilgrimage to sacred places and holy relics – the Turin Shroud, Red Square, the birthplace of Chairman Mao.

And so on, ad nauseam. In fact, as far as the way they behaved in practice is concerned, there are remarkable similarities between the Spain of Philip II, the Iran of Ayatollah Khomeini, and the Soviet Union under Stalin. We might see some parallels with the United States in the time of McCarthy. We might even see some resemblances to the present time. So when I say 'theocracy' in the context of what I'm saying tonight, I'm not limiting the term to those states that base their authority on the existence of a supernatural creator. What I'm talking about is the tendency of human beings to gather power to themselves in the name of something that may not be questioned, and to justify what they do in terms of absolutes: absolute truth; absolute goodness; absolute evil; absolute hatred; if you're not with us, you're against us.

Now, remembering where we began, with the idea that stories can offer a moral education, I want to look briefly at how theocracies regard literature – how they read stories and poems and plays.

The first thing is that people with this cast of mind have low expectations of literature. They think that literature has only one purpose, which is ideological, and so its worth can be judged by how well it fulfils that ideological purpose. There's a very good description of this cast of mind at work in *Reading Lolita in Tehran,* by the professor of literature Azar Nafisi. She recounts how difficult it became to teach the sort of books she most wanted to teach – namely the subtle, the complex, the ambiguous – in the atmosphere in Iran after the Khomeini revolution. She says:

> Unable to decipher or understand complications or irregularities… the officials were forced to impose their simple formulas on fiction as they did on life. Just as they censored the colours and tones of reality to suit their black-and-white world, they censored any form of interiority in fiction; ironically, for them as for their ideological opponents, works of imagination that did not carry a political message were deemed dangerous. Thus, in a writer such as (Jane) Austen, for example, whether they knew it or not, they found a natural adversary.

So the Muslim activists had that view of fiction, but so did their opponents, the activists on the left. Unlike the people in charge, the leftists felt – and I quote Azar Nafisi's words again – they felt that:

> … we needed to read fiction like *The Great Gatsby* because we needed to know about the immorality of American culture. They felt we should read more revolutionary material, but we should read books like this as well, to understand the enemy.

The theocratic cast of mind is always reductive whether it's in power or not. Another example – a famous one – from an atheist theocracy is the criticism of the poetry of Anna Akhmatova by the Central Committee of the All-Union Communist Party in 1946:

> Akhmatova is a typical exponent of empty, frivolous poetry that is alien to our people. Permeated by the scent of pessimism and decay, redolent of old-fashioned salon poetry, frozen in the positions of bourgeois-aristocratic aestheticism and decadence – 'art for art's sake' – not wanting to progress forward with our people, her verses cause damage to the upbringing of our youth and cannot be tolerated in Soviet literature.

So reading one sort of stuff will damage; reading another sort of stuff will improve. And we shall decide which is which.

Well, needless to say, I think there's a vast difference between that view and the view I'm proposing tonight. And a large part of the difference lies not only in *what* theocratic or totalitarian societies choose to read, but in the *way* they read. A word that's emblematic of this attitude is the word *correct*. We've become used to it in the cliché *politically correct*, which is a right-wing caricature of a left-wing tendency to emphasise one approved kind of language we should use, one single attitude we should to adopt to social questions, one approved way we should behave in every situation, and so on. *Correct* is a word you find again and again in works of communist apologetics, such as a book I've just been looking at about the Cultural Revolution in China. 'The fundamental question has been and always will be whether the correct line is being followed or not... Education must promote revolutionary aims in the spirit of Mao Tse-tung Thought... Then, with victory for the correct line, things right themselves again', and so on.

This is really a form of fundamentalism. Karen Armstrong, in her book *The Battle for God* (Knopf, 2000), explains the nature of fundamentalism very well. She sets out the difference between 'mythos' and 'logos', different ways of apprehending the reality of the world. Mythos deals with meaning, with the timeless and constant, with the intuitive, with what can only be fully expressed in art or music or ritual. Logos, by contrast, is the rational, the scientific, the practical; that which is susceptible to logical explanation.

Her argument is that in modern times, because of the astonishing progress of science and technology, people in the Western world 'began to think that logos was the only means to truth, and began to discount mythos as false and superstitious'. This resulted in the phenomenon of fundamentalism, which, despite its own claims to be a return to the old true ways of understanding the holy book, is not a return of any kind, but something entirely new: 'Protestant fundamentalists read the Bible in a literal, rational way that is quite different from the more mystical, allegorical approach of pre-modern spirituality.'

This way of reading, in which everything is taken literally, doesn't allow for ambiguity, or mystery, or subtlety, or what Azar Nafisi called interiority of any kind. Everything is black or white, true or false, good or bad, right or wrong. There is no scope for interpretation, except the kind which is taught in the official schools, and approved by the authorities.

There is one way of reading and understanding a text, and only one: the correct way.

Now then: I said a few minutes ago that this way, the 'correct', the 'fundamentalist' style of reading that characterises theocratic absolutism, was one of the currents that had been swirling around the old-fashioned idea of the 'school of morals' in recent times. Has it had any effect? Does it place the school of morals in any danger? Is it a threat, or something we can ignore?

Well, this nation isn't yet a theocracy. There is still a certain amount of democratic back-and-forthness at work. But I'm worried by a couple of straws in the wind. I'm worried, firstly, by this government's willingness to endorse and support schools that teach so-called creationism. I'm thinking of the city academies that they put up for sale. If you're a rich person and you can afford £2 million, you can start a school and the government will fund the rest of it with ten times that amount of money, and give you control of the curriculum. Then if you want to teach the children that Darwin was wrong and that God created the world in six days, you are allowed to. This is an extraordinary development, and the government ought to be called to account for it. Science isn't a body of knowledge: science is a method of inquiry. And this closes down inquiry by stating in advance what is to be discovered. Our government is colluding in this, and it's wrong.

The second straw in the wind is the increasing tendency among people to describe their primary identity not in terms of ethnic or geographical origin, but in terms of the religion they profess. They don't say, 'I'm Asian,' or, 'I'm British Bangladeshi,' they say, 'I'm a Muslim.' Now of course people are surely allowed to describe themselves in any way they like, and for those of us who are British it's a fluid kind of thing anyway, because we constantly find ourselves shifting between British and English, or British and Scottish, or British and Afro-Caribbean, depending which part of our identity is salient at any moment. During the Ryder Cup golf tournament, many of us discover that we're European.

But this way of labelling ourselves by our religion is a new thing, and it worries me because it ties in with the third straw in the wind, which is the Serious and Organised Crime and Police Bill. This is the 'incitement to religious hatred' law. It's intended to protect people from being exposed to hatred or contempt because of their religion.

The ostensible cause for it was the practice of loathsome people such as the British National Party to avoid being criticised for making racist statements, which are illegal, by making religious ones instead: they don't say, 'Kick out the filthy Asians,' they say, 'Islam is an evil religion,' and their horrible followers know they mean 'Kick out the filthy Asians.'

As I say, that was the ostensible cause. A cynic might say that the real cause was the Labour Party's desire to regain the Muslim vote, which they used to be able to rely on, but which has been leaking away alarmingly. But whatever the cause, the result will be that people who identify themselves by their religion will be able to claim that anyone who criticises their beliefs is exposing them personally to hatred and contempt, because their religion is their identity.

This Bill has been widely and strongly criticised by those who care about freedom of speech. The Prime Minister has said that actually it won't be any threat to free speech, because in practice every complaint will come before the Crown Prosecution Service, and in most cases they won't prosecute. In fact, that will just make things worse. People will be invited to feel aggrieved by the invention of an offence that didn't exist before, and then denied the likelihood of satisfaction through the courts. Are the zealots going to say, 'Oh well, fair enough, we tried'? Are they hell.

So to ward off trouble before it begins, theatres and publishers will turn more and more to lawyers. A local authority that licenses and subsidises a theatre will insist on a legal opinion before they let a new play go on; a publisher with a risky novel will have it read by my learned friends; and of course they will advise against the risk, because – as the

Home Office minister Hazel Blears (who held this post during 2003–2006) has said – if such a case comes to court, 'It is difficult for me to say what a court would decide in those circumstances.' They won't take the risk; and books or plays that question or criticise religious belief will quietly vanish from sight.

And in case anyone thinks I'm exclusively criticising Muslims here, there's a new group called Christian Voice of which you might have heard. They were the people who demonstrated against the broadcast of *Jerry Springer, the Opera* on BBC, and disseminated the private phone numbers and addresses of BBC staff so they could be harassed at home. Only last week these champions of Christian virtue triumphantly announced that they had bullied a cancer charity into turning down the money raised during a benefit performance of that show, because it was 'tainted'. Well, of course they have the right to be heard; but when this law comes in, obnoxiously superstitious and self-righteous people like them will have the right to stop opinions they don't like from being heard.

So the cultural current I've called theocratic absolutism is alive and well and beginning to stir, and if we're not careful it could easily sweep away a basic and priceless freedom. And we would be very foolish to think that this couldn't happen here: it has happened here. Only a hundred and fifty years before Miss Goddard exhibited her lustre and effect on the stage of the great school of morals, the Puritan revolution closed the theatres down entirely.

Before I go on, and before we lose sight of what I mean by the school of morals, just to re-state it: it's the assumption that stories, in whatever form they come – drama, the novel, fairy tales, films – show us human beings like ourselves acting in recognisably human ways, and they affect our emotions and our intelligence as life itself affects us; that the stories we call the greatest are great because they are most like life, and the ones we think not so good are correspondingly less so – the characters in one are rich and complex and unpredictable, like real people; those in the other are two-dimensional and cardboard-like, stereotypes – that sort of thing. And our moral understanding is deepened and enriched by the awakening of our imaginative sympathy. I gave the example of *Macbeth* and murder earlier on: there's no need to list the great works that draw us in, imaginatively, into the experience of jealousy, or sexual obsession, or the lifelong consequences of a moment of thoughtless cowardice, or the folly of putting high-minded principle before human affection – and so on, and so on, and so on.

Now I can't *prove* this numerically. I can't show you statistics to demonstrate a twenty-three per cent increase in moral awareness among twelve- to fourteen-year-olds who have been exposed to fiction as opposed to those who have been kept without it; I can't point to studies demonstrating that murderers who have read Dostoevsky go about their business more thoughtfully than murderers who haven't; I can't quote official reports on the decline in adultery among reading groups discussing *Anna Karenina*. I don't think that's the way it works. I think the moral education that stories provide is a more subtle, fluid, all-pervasive thing, without a precise one-to-one correspondence in any place, and that it often works most effectively when it doesn't seem to be taking place at all.

As I say, there is no one-to-one correspondence. But here is an account by a Welsh miner called Robert Morgan about two friends of his, a collier and an engine driver, who, having educated themselves, did their best to awaken their friends to the delights of literature and music:

'At such times we did not feel we were colliers doing menial and dangerous jobs in the bowels of the earth, but privileged human beings doing something extraordinary. Most of us were badly or barely educated, but such young men as Ted and Jeff who, alone and without encouragement, educated themselves... seemed to glow with pride. The work they were engaged in, lowly as it was, never depressed them. They nei-

413

ther grumbled about the work they did, nor did they envy others in better positions on the surface of the pit. These characteristics I noticed about men such as Ted and Jeff, and from the examples of such men I was able to develop my own pride, my own search for knowledge… These two characters, their attitudes, their personalities, their cheerfulness, their honesty and their kindness, I am sure made the rest of us feel that culture had done much to make them better men.'

That was quoted in Jonathan Rose's extraordinary work *The Intellectual Life of the British Working Classes* (2001), which I recommend without reservation. Perhaps the only evidence for the existence of the 'school of morals' is anecdotal, but it's powerful; and there's a lot of it.

However, if you remember, I said earlier on that before I finished I'd come back to theory. I showed it out of the door, but here it is seeping up through the floorboards.

Because haven't I made a basic mistake early on in this approach? Isn't what I've been talking about not so much a school of morals as a school of manners? Robert Morgan's account of Ted and Jeff seems to be a description of good behaviour as much as of goodness; and as for Emma's cruelty to Miss Bates – wasn't that just a failure of politeness? Is this morality I've been talking about really little more than a matter of etiquette? And isn't that in turn a means of reinforcing the dominance of one social class, which knows how to behave, over another that doesn't?

Let's go back to Miss Goddard for a moment, and consider the audience in the great School of Morals, the Theatre. The sort of moral views that might be inculcated or polished there would be those that everyone *who could pay for a ticket* – everyone with a stake in society, the local clergy, the local gentry, the Lord Mayor and the prosperous citizens of Norwich – would share and approve of. Any moral views at variance with the inevitably conservative consensus wouldn't last long on the stage, full stop.

Then there's the fact that moral views change with time: they aren't eternal. If Miss Goddard's audiences could see our society today, they would be shocked at some things that we take for granted: the acceptability of sexual freedom, for example, and the frequency with which, these days, people bear and bring up children outside marriage without social disapproval. And the patrons of the Theatre Royal in 1801 would have viewed with incredulity the fervour – the moral fervour – that characterised the recent debate about fox-hunting. To spend 250 hours of Parliamentary time on this subject would have seemed to them insane; they would have thought our society was morally deranged.

Then there's the difference between this culture, ours – the Western liberal humane culture that has created all the literature I've mentioned so far – and the other cultures that exist in the world today. What does the world of the secular European intellectual have in common with the world of the mullahs and the ayatollahs? Are the moral teachings of one kind of literature universally valid, or are they contingent on culture? What do the novels of Thomas Hardy, what does the world of a poor shepherd in Dorset have in common with that of a poor black youth in Detroit? Does the word 'poor' mean anything like the same thing in both contexts?

And as for the implication that Jane Austen's novels did not carry a political message – well, post-colonial theory has helped us see that her work is saturated in political meanings and assumptions. Take the most famous example, *Mansfield Park*. Where does Sir Thomas Bertram's money come from? What is the source of the wealth that underpins the leisured way of life of these people who are so high-minded that they can fall into agonies of doubt and guilt over whether it's OK to indulge in amateur theatricals during their father's absence? The answer involves slavery. Sir Thomas is away in Antigua inspecting his plantations. And that fact, never questioned or examined in the novel, throws a different sort of light on the exquisite moral refinement of the protagonists.

So I don't think the discoveries of literary theory are easily dismissed.

There are things it tells us that are true and helpful, and others that are discouraging and deceptive, and we need to tell the difference.

To sum up the argument then, between what I've called the school of morals, and theocratic absolutism: that latter tendency in cultural life says that meanings are fixed and simple and determined by authority; whereas the school of morals sees them as ambiguous, complex, subject to development, and arrived at by experience and by imaginative sympathy.

As for the argument that the school of morals has with 'theory': theory says that truth is provisional and there is no such thing as human nature, that meanings shift and are contingent; whereas the school of morals says that there are some truths that endure long enough to be as good as permanent, and that human nature is certainly constant enough to be worth talking about – that even if we and the people of 1801 disagree about whether fox-hunting is good or bad, we would certainly agree that there *are* good things and bad things, that generosity is good and meanness is bad, that children should be looked after, that there is such a thing as empathy, that there are ways of dealing with conflict and disagreement, and so on, and so on.

Furthermore, the 'theory' line on language, that it's constitutive and not transparent, not only undercuts the responsibility of the writer; it contradicts the experience of the reader. That's just not what it feels like when we read. We feel fond of this character, we feel exasperated with that one; we feel pity for their predicaments, we cheer when they overcome them. *Of course* George Orwell was right when he wanted his prose to be a window through which we see and not a surface on which meanings contradict themselves in an endlessly playful dialectic.

But it's time I said something about how I think the school of morals actually works.

Well, the reading we do in the school of morals isn't like taking notes in a lesson, learning the correct line and parroting it back: it's like a conversation. There's a democracy about it. The book proposes, the reader questions; the book responds, the reader considers. We bring our own preconceptions and expectations, our own intellectual qualities, and our limitations too, our own previous experiences of reading, our own temperament, to the encounter.

And we are active about the process. The school of morals doesn't force us to read in a way determined by someone else – even by the author. We can skim, or we can read it slowly; we can read every word, or we can skip long passages; we can read it in the order in which it presents itself, or we can read it in any order we please; we can put the book down and reflect, or we can go to the library or, nowadays, to Wikipedia and the like, and check what it claims to be fact against another authority; we can assent, or we can disagree.

But when we disagree, or when we think we've caught the text disagreeing with itself, we don't lose faith altogether in the possibility of meaning. We know that our understanding of this meaning might be superseded by another in due course, but while it lasts, the school of morals encourages us to take it as being solid ground, and see how we get on.

And, little by little, as we grow up in the school of morals, we become better readers: we learn different ways to read. We learn to distinguish degrees of irony or implication; we pick up references and allusions we might have missed before; we learn to judge the most fruitful way to read this text (as myth, perhaps) or that (as factual record); we become familiar with the strengths and duplicities of metaphor, we know a joke when we see one, we can tell poetry from political history, we can suspend our certainties and learn to tolerate the vertigo of difference.

So the relationship with books and plays and stories we develop in the school of morals is a profoundly, intensely, essentially democratic one, and it's characterised by mutual responsibility. It places demands on the reader, because that is the nature of a democracy: citizens have to play their part. If we don't bring our own best qualities to the encounter, we will take little away. Furthermore, it isn't static: there is no final, unquestionable, unchanging authority. It's dynamic. It changes and develops as our understanding grows, as our experience of reading – and of life itself – increases. Books we once thought great come to seem shallow and meretricious; books we once thought boring reveal their subtle treasures of wit, their unsuspected shafts of perception. And this progress is real progress; it's not the endless regression of shifting sand underfoot and the shimmering falsity of a mirage endlessly retreating ahead, it's solid stepping stones, and clear understanding.

And it's *voluntary*.

Because this is the thing I really want to get across: the school of morals works best when it doesn't work like a school. The way real reading happens, the way in to the school of morals, goes through the gateway of delight.

Let me quote a little from Dickens to show the sort of thing I mean. This is from *Bleak House*. The Smallweed family are moneylenders; they have a strong and profound understanding of Compound Interest, and of very little else.

> The house of Smallweed, always early to go out and late to marry, has strengthened itself in its practical character, has discarded all amusements, discountenanced all story-books, fairy tales, fictions and fables, and banished all levities whatsoever. Hence the gratifying fact, that it has had no child born to it, and that the complete little men and women whom it has produced, have been observed to bear a likeness to old monkeys with something depressing on their minds.

There is a pair of young twins, and this is what they're like:

> Judy never owned a doll, never heard of Cinderella, never played at any game. She once or twice fell into children's company when she was about ten years old, but the children

couldn't get on with Judy, and Judy couldn't get on with them. She seemed like an animal of another species, and there was instinctive repugnance on both sides. It is very doubtful whether Judy knows how to laugh. She has so rarely seen the thing done, that the probabilities are strong the other way... Such is Judy.

And her twin brother couldn't wind up a top for his life. He knows no more of Jack the Giant Killer, or of Sinbad the Sailor, than he knows of the people in the stars. He could as soon play at leap-frog, or at cricket, as change into a cricket or a frog himself.

What he's talking about, what the Smallweeds have never known, is joy. Pleasure. The almost sensuous bliss, the intoxicating blend of excitement and surrender we feel when someone says: 'Once upon a time...'

Any education that neglects this dimension of experience will be a dry and tasteless diet with no nourishment in it. People – children especially – *need* this experience of delight. It isn't something you give them as a reward; it's something they will perish if they don't have. Some part of them will perish. Just look at a flower dying for lack of water, and then water it; it's like that. Look at children's faces as you tell them a story, or as they sit in the theatre. Look at the rapt flushed expression on the face of a child involved, lost, in a well-loved book.

That's the look of someone entering the school of morals.

Now I'm going to close by saying something that might sound strange, given what's come before, which is this: I think this is a theme that is possibly tragic. It's a very fine balance; it's 51/49; perhaps it's the other way.

Because I haven't by any means listed all the forces bearing on the school of morals, this little shaded pool of delight, beside which goodness and, in the thoughts of Emma weeping in her carriage, 'gratitude, concurrence, and common kindness' take root and blossom.

I've talked in detail about two of these forces, but I haven't mentioned, for example, the sheer relentless *busyness* of modern life – the *crowdedness*, the incessant thumping music and braying voices, the near impossibility of finding solitude and silence and time to reflect.

I haven't mentioned the commercial pressures, the forces urging us to buy and discard and buy again. When everything in public life has a logo attached to it, when every public space is disfigured with advertisements, when nothing of public value and importance can take place without commercial sponsorship, when schools and hospitals have to act as if their guiding principle were market forces rather than human need, when adults and children alike are tempted to wear T-shirts with obscene words on them by the smirking little device of spelling the words wrongly, when citizens become consumers and clients, patients, guests, students and pas-sengers are all flattened into customers, what price the school of morals? The answer is: what it would fetch in the market, and not a penny more.

I haven't mentioned the obsession with targets and testing and league tables, the management-driven and politics-corrupted and jargon-clotted rubbish that so deforms the true work of schools.

I haven't mentioned something that might seem trivial; but I think its importance is profound and barely understood. That's the difference between reading a story in a book, and watching a story on a screen. It's a psychological difference, not just a technical one. We need to take account of it, and we're not doing it, and I fear the school of morals is suffering as a result.

I haven't mentioned simple human wickedness. Or laziness, or greed, or fear, or the strongest regiment of all in the army of darkness: stupidity. Any of those can bring down the school of morals in a day.

I haven't mentioned death. I haven't mentioned hazard, or the environ-mental recklessness that will do for us all if we don't change our way of life.

These are mighty forces, and I think they will defeat the school of morals, in the end. But that doesn't mean we should give up and surrender. Nor does it mean we should turn the school of morals into a fortress, and surround it with rules and systems and procedures, and look out over the ramparts with suspicion and hostility. That would be a different kind of surrender.

I think we should act *as if*.

I think we should read books, and tell children stories, and take them to the theatre, and learn poems, and play music, as if it would make a difference.

I think that while believing that the school of morals is probably doomed, we should act as if it were not. We should act as if the universe were listening to us and responding; we should act as if life were going to win. We should act as if we were celebrating a wedding: we should act as if we were attending the marriage of responsibility and delight.

That's what I think they do, in the school of morals. And Miss Goddard's portrait hangs on the classroom wall.

THIS LECTURE WAS GIVEN AT THE UNIVERSITY OF EAST ANGLIA IN 2005.

God and Dust

On not believing in the existence of God, on good and evil, on reading His
Dark Materials, *the meaning of Dust and the Republic of Heaven*

Morning session

The first thing to say about the Bishop's arguments in his book (Richard
Harries: *God Outside the Box*, SPCK, 2002) is that I agree with every
word of them, except the words I don't understand; and that the words
I don't understand are those such as *spirit*, *spiritual* and *God*.

It may seem disingenuous to say I don't understand them – surely
I know what they mean? Take the words involving spirit: of course I
know what my dictionary says:-

Spirit: the animating or life-giving principle in a person or animal; the
intelligent non-physical part of a person; a prevailing mental or moral
condition or attitude, a mood, a tendency; the real meaning as opposed
to lip-service or verbal expression; an immaterial principle formerly
thought to govern vital phenomena, etc.

Spiritual: of or concerning the spirit as opposed to matter; concerned
with sacred or religious things; holy; divine; refined, sensitive; concerned
with the soul or spirit etc, not with external reality.

Soul: the spiritual or immaterial part of a human being, often regarded
as immortal; the moral or emotional or intellectual nature of a person…

And so on. I know how others use these words, and I know how
I would use them myself, and I have no difficulty understanding sen-

tences containing them – I can manipulate them like coins or counters in a game and not break any rules and achieve a meaningful result within the context of the game.

Nevertheless, it's not a game I choose to enter. I would never begin to talk of a person's spiritual life, or refer to someone's profound spirituality, or anything of that sort, because it doesn't make sense to me. I don't talk about that sort of thing at all, because when other people talk about spirituality I can see nothing in it, *in reality*, except a sense of vague uplift combined at one end with genuine goodness and modesty, and at the other with self-righteousness and pride. That's what they're *displaying*. That's what seems to be on offer when they interact with the world. And to my mind it's easier, clearer, and more truthful just to talk about the goodness and modesty, or about the self-righteousness and pride, without going into the other stuff at all. So the good qualities that the word 'spiritual' implies can be perfectly well covered, and more honestly covered, it seems to me, by other positive words, and we don't need 'spiritual' at all.

But in fact my reaction to the word 'spiritual' is even a little more strongly felt than that; I even feel a slight revulsion. I'm thinking of those portraits of saints and martyrs by painters of the Baroque period and the Counter-Reformation: horrible grubby-looking old men with rotten teeth wearing dark dusty robes and gazing upwards with an expression of fanatical fervour; or beautiful young women in sumptuous clothes with wide eyes and parted lips gazing upwards with an expression of fanatical fervour; or martyrs having the flesh ripped from their bones gazing upwards with an expression of fanatical fervour – gazing at the Virgin Mary, or a vision of the Cross, or something else that's hovering in the air just above them. And you know that what they're seeing isn't really there; that if you were there in front of them, *you* wouldn't see the Virgin sitting on a little cloud six feet above the floor – all you'd see would be the rotten teeth or the sumptuous clothes or the torture and the expression of fanatical fervour. They're seeing things. They're deluded, in fact.

So the word *spiritual*, for me, has overtones that are entirely negative. It seems to me that whenever anyone uses the word, it's a sign that either they're deluding themselves, or they're pulling the wool over the eyes of others. And when I hear it, or see it in print, my reaction is one of immediate scepticism.

This is a problem for *me* to deal with, no doubt, because I know people of obvious honesty and sincerity and intelligence who use the word without embarrassment; but for someone to talk openly about 'my spiritual life', for example, is rather like someone talking about their sexual life – isn't it private? Isn't it something you ought to keep to yourself?

Another word I have difficulty in using sensibly – to put it no more bluntly than that – is the word *God*. I don't believe there is such a being, and I don't think you can say anything true or useful about a being who doesn't exist, and I don't think it makes any sense to say, for example, 'God loves each one of us as though we were the only person in the world.'

This strikes me as being an assertion entirely unsupported by anything verifiable.

Furthermore, I think that the argument put forward in the chapter of 'The Silence of God' in *God Outside the Box*, that – in the quoted words of R. S. Thomas – 'It is this great absence which is like a presence', is an attempt to have your cake and eat it; it's cheek on a colossal scale. Simone Weil: 'Absence is the form in which God is present.'

Presumably we're talking about serious things here – as serious as the talk in a court of law, for example; and yet if you were being cross-examined and you said, 'It's the very fact that I did it that proves I didn't,' I think you'd be lucky to escape a charge of contempt of court. The argument seems to run: 'God is nowhere to be seen, nowhere to be heard; there is nothing to show he exists at all; and yet to believe in him is evidence not of mental derangement but of profound spirituality.'

God comes into *God Outside the Box* all the time, and that's precisely the difficulty I've had with it. Paragraph after paragraph of good human sense, all of which I agree with, and suddenly up pops a sentence that says, 'It is part of God's love for us that he has such a glorious vocation and destiny in mind for us.'

I want to say: how do you *know* that? As soon as you say that, you leave me completely. There's no *need* for it, I find myself thinking; it doesn't add anything to the truth of what you've just said; it's as if you were talking to someone who seemed level-headed and sensible, and suddenly heard them saying, 'The fairies want us all to be kind to the flowers.' And then you said, 'But there aren't any fairies!' And the other person said, 'Oh yes, the garden's full of fairies. It's the fact that you can't see them that *proves* they're there.'

At some point you have to shrug and move on to talk about something else, such as the football results. You will never make intellectual contact on the subject of fairies with someone who is convinced that they exist. Similarly with God. I say, 'He doesn't exist,' and you say, 'Oh, but he does,' and I say, 'Oh, no he doesn't,' and you say, 'Oh, yes, he does ...'

And we get nowhere.

The believer has to explain the lack of evidence for God in terms that become more and more ingenious. One such example is that offered on p.153: we are not close to God physically, because we couldn't be: the material world serves as a necessary sort of screen between us and him. If we were too close to him, we'd be drawn in like moths to a candle flame, unable to resist his goodness, beauty, splendour, etc. So as an act of mercy, God has put the screen of the material world between us, and given us freedom of thought and movement.

Well, it's ingenious.

So were the epicycles.

In the Ptolemaic system of astronomy, the Earth was imagined to be the centre of the universe, and everything revolved around it. The trouble was that the sun and the moon and the planets didn't seem to move regularly, as you'd think they should. They'd go a bit too fast or a bit too slow, and sometimes they'd even seem to go backwards for a bit, and altogether it was very hard to see the *perfection* up there that there should be.

But astronomers realised that they could interpret the actual movement they saw by saying that the planets moved not in perfect circles but in epicycles – little loops along the big circle of their orbit. That took care of the irregular movement; everything made sense again.

Until the better instruments and closer observation that came with time showed that the epicycles didn't explain everything. There were still movements that didn't make sense, that couldn't be understood in terms of orbits and epicycles.

So they invented epicycles on epicycles: not only loops in the orbit, but loops around the loops around the orbit. Once more everything was explained. It was complicated, to be sure, but God was wonderful, after all, and how much more wonderful that he had created the ingenious brain of mankind in order to understand and glorify the complexity of his work!

But the instruments got better and better and the observations kept on piling up, and yet more irregularities appeared. It began to look as if an infinite regression of ingenuity would be required to deal with the complexity of the whole thing.

Until the simple notion came from the mind of Copernicus: if we interpreted the evidence differently, the ingenuities were unnecessary. Suppose that everything went round the sun instead of going round the Earth: at once everything became gloriously clear, and simple too. No need for epicycles at all!

So it is with those who have to explain why, given that God exists, we have no evidence for him. The explanations become more and more complicated, more and more ridiculous, like P. H. Gosse and his explanation for fossils: naturally, God wouldn't have created an imperfect world, and a world without a history would have been imperfect; so he put the fossils there at the same time as he created everything else, to give it the appearance of a history.

These epicyclic explanations are all unnecessary; all the futile clutter of complexity upon complexity, ingenuity upon ingenuity, paradox upon dazzling paradox – it's all swept away at once, it all becomes gloriously clear and simple, once we realise that there is no God and never was. We don't have to go into fits of distorted logic, or to insist that nonsensical things are true (but true in a *deep* way, not like ordinary truth) if we just accept that God is not there. The absence is really an absence, and means no more than that: there's no one there.

Evil is one of those things that makes sense when it's an adjective, but which raises difficult questions when you use it as a noun. We can say, 'That is an evil deed' or even, 'He was an evil man', though I think someone has to be dead before you can sum them up and say for certain – but it is a step too far to go from that to saying that there is something, a quality, a presence, a force of *evil* in the abstract.

Because that sort of objectifies it, personifies it, reifies it. It doesn't mean *it* exists.

Nevertheless when we look at some historical phenomena, and some not so far in the past, we can seem to see people caught up in a sort of vortex of emotion and activity that leads to deeds so evil, so grotesquely far beyond anything we can see ourselves doing, that we feel unable to explain except by appealing to some power beyond the rational, the normal, the everyday. I mean, of course, the Nazi regime, or the massacres in Rwanda, as well as the sort of *folie à deux* murders committed by the Wests, the Moors murderers, and so on. I don't mean individual psychopaths for a moment; we can sort of grasp the notion that some people just don't have a sense of right and wrong – I mean the sort of thing when people seem to be *possessed* by a power greater than themselves. When others are drawn in too, and they seem to surrender their conscience. What's the explanation of that?

One explanation would be that there *is* a power of evil, a sort of disembodied power, which floats around freely until it enters into human beings and makes them behave like this. It would be a good explanation if it were possible to believe in it, but it isn't, for me. I don't think there's any such thing. I think a better explanation is Bishop Richard Holloway's: that when human beings come together, in a crowd or a mass movement or a body with one sort of aim, their psychologies can *resonate* together and *reinforce* each other. If you looked into it scientifically you'd probably find it was a matter of very small subliminal clues of behaviour which are picked up under the level of conscious awareness, and mimicked, which in turn are picked up by the people who send the clues out, thus modifying *their* behaviour, and so it resonates back and forth, getting amplified as it does. The same sort of thing probably happens when flocks of birds seem to wheel and turn as one, as if they're controlled by a sort of super-mind. They're not, but they look as if they are. In the end it really does probably feel as if this force is bigger than you are as an individual, and you have no choice but to go along with it, and you're not to blame for whatever happens.

This is the sort of thing that was probably meant by the phrase 'institutional racism' with reference to the police, after the Stephen Lawrence inquiry. A lot of the criticism of *that* came from people who thought that every police officer was thus being called racist, but it was different from that, I think.

It would be easier to understand if you looked at a positive example of this seemingly disembodied thing instead of a negative one, and called it *esprit de corps*. *Esprit de corps* is the sort of positive, good, beneficial, praiseworthy form of this psychological resonance and amplification; soldiers in a regiment are imbued with a sort of invisible armature of decent and brave behaviour by this feeling, which again is picked up by a hundred little examples, some too small to see consciously, of pride in one another and in the regiment's history and in all the little daily traditions of courtesy and fellowship as well as great examples of honour and courage in battle.

I think we can understand *that* without having recourse to the supernatural.

And 'institutional racism' is probably an example of exactly the same psychological process, but working in a negative way, morally speaking: young officers see and hear their elders and superiors using language or making jokes, or overlooking remarks that *they* make, which have a racist tendency. The *general assumption* is that that's the way we, the force, the canteen, the people in uniform – *us* – that's the way we see things. It all resonates and gets amplified.

And because a lot of this is subliminal and unconscious and never actually put into 'racist' words – it might be there in the slightest sigh or eye-rolling when anyone objects, or a lapse into false jocularity in the presence of a black officer, or that sort of thing – it's easy to deny that it exists, and it's even easy to believe that it doesn't.

I think these examples of psychological resonance and amplification are quite enough by themselves to explain how human beings can seem to be possessed by 'evil'. We don't need a devil. We don't need a 'force of evil'.

Similarly, I personally don't feel the need to evoke any supernatural power when trying to explain examples of great human goodness. Human beings are perfectly capable both of the most appalling wickedness *and* of great and incomprehensible goodness and self-sacrifice. I particularly dislike that sort of cynical view of things that says human beings are evil all through, selfish by nature and design, incapable of doing anything generous or good except for some hidden selfish motive. Christians are supposed to believe this, because of Original Sin. Nothing that a human being can do unaided is any good at all, and the only way you can get anything decent or good out of a human being is by the grace of God. So we are to blame for our defects, but we're not allowed any credit for our merits. My view is that we are responsible for both.

Actually, many Christians today don't seem to believe in Original Sin anyway. A lot of them are getting very New Agey about the whole business, tolerating all kinds of behaviour – especially in the sexual field

– which their sterner Christian ancestors never would.

It's when you use the word 'evil' as a noun that it seems to have some external, objective existence. You *reify* it – you make it into a thing by giving it a name, although it isn't really a thing at all. *Evil* is an adjective that we apply to deeds, or sometimes to people, and it seems to have intention attached to it. The destruction of the World Trade Centre was an evil deed, but if the same number of people were killed in an earthquake, we wouldn't call that evil.

We can talk in a sort of flippant or exaggerated way about the *evils* of modern life – mobile phones, and so on; but we don't mean evil, we mean nuisance. It's a kind of figure of speech – there's probably some technical term – overstatement of some kind.

Afternoon session

I'm here because I wrote a book – *His Dark Materials* – and because it's thought that I can argue about the position put forward in that book and defend it or persuade you of its merits.

But the transaction isn't as simple as that. When someone reads a book, there are not just two people involved, the writer and the reader; there are several others hanging about.

Firstly, there is the actual reader – the person who buys the book, or borrows it from the library, who carries it home, who sits down, whose eyes actually move over the page.

Secondly, there is the figure known to literary theory as the implied reader – the person the text seems to be addressing. It can't address the real reader, because of course no one knows who that will be; but to take an obvious example, the implied reader of the *Beano* is a young child, whereas the implied reader of a work of abstruse philosophy is probably someone academically and professionally interested in the subject. An academic philosopher could be the actual reader of a copy of the *Beano*, but the *Beano* doesn't seem to expect that, somehow.

Thirdly, there is the author – the actual author – the person who thought up the sentences and wrote them down.

Fourthly, there is a figure called the implied author. He or she is the hardest of all these shadows to grasp; the difference between the real reader and the implied reader is easy to understand, but the implied author, though his or her function is real, isn't quite so easy to get at. It might be more easily called the *inferred* author, because it's the figure felt by the reader to lie behind the book – the combination of all the attitudes, experience, literary skill and so forth that seems to have gone into its production.

Fifthly, there is the narrator. This is the voice that is doing the storytelling. I used to teach English literature to students who were going to be teachers, and one of the things these young people used to find hard to grasp at first was that the third-person storytelling voice in (say) a novel like *Vanity Fair* wasn't actually Thackeray's own voice, but the narrator's, and that the narrator was just as much an invented character as Becky Sharp or Rawdon Crawley.

So the narrator of *His Dark Materials* is the voice you seem to hear or see on the page; and behind that is the implied author, the imaginary me whose presence is inferred by the reader, and who seems to be manipulating the narrator and to be responsible for the attitudes and conclusions of the whole work; and behind that is the real me, who finished writing that book a long time ago and is now busy doing something else entirely.

And the implied reader, the reader the text – that particular text – seems to expect, is, I suppose, an intelligent person of either sex and any age, who is interested in many things, quick to feel sympathy, but perhaps inclined to be a little impatient with long passages of explanation or discursive material not directly related to the story; and the actual reader is – well, who knows? Perhaps you; perhaps your son or daughter, perhaps your mother or father; but someone with a life and a history and a personality and set of beliefs and attitudes entirely unknown to the real author, the implied author and the narrator.

Furthermore: the act of reading itself is not a simple thing, either. It's far from being the simple transmission of an idea, or an image, or the narrative of a set of events, unchanged, from one mind to another. Postman Pat or Federal Express work like that – delivering something from one place to another without interfering with it en route – but the human mind doesn't. Think for a moment of the different ways we know we read: the quick skim of the newspaper; the deep lingering involvement we have with a novel we're enjoying; the close interrogation we make of a text we're studying, constantly stopping to make notes, to look things up, to compare this text with others.

And think of the things that make it harder or easier to read in the way we want to, and the effect they have. To take a small example, the *Guardian* a few years ago changed its policy on capital letters. They no longer use capitals for things like Prime Minister, or Home Office, or even organisations like Royal Society for the Prevention of Cruelty to Animals. They write them out in full without capital letters, and it's extremely annoying, because the capital letters are one thing that actively help you to skim. Their current policy forces you to read the paper in a way you don't want to in order to make sense of it. Similarly with a novel that's printed in too small a typeface with not enough leading between the lines: it's just hard to read. These things make a difference; they affect the things that go on in our heads.

And then there are the different things we as readers *bring* to a text – our different expectations, our varying intellectual limitations or gifts, our experiences of previous texts, our predictions about this one. These are necessary things; without them we wouldn't begin to make sense of any text at all; and they're also inevitable: we can't look at any text in a state of nature, as it were, and pretend we know nothing, and come to it as complete virgins. We have to bring something to the text, and put something into it, in order to get anything out. This is the great democracy of reading and writing – it makes the reader a true partner in the making of meaning.

But it all makes it a little more difficult to talk about than it might seem at first.

Now I'm not beginning like this in order to disclaim responsibility for what I've written; I'm doing it to remind all of us, myself as well as you, that my book doesn't have a single meaning, and that my relation to it is complex, and that my interpretation of what I wrote is likely to be as partial as anybody else's, and that anything I say about it has not much more authority than a reader's. Maybe a *little* bit more, if for no other reason than that I know the text fairly closely; but no *final* authority.

So all I'm trying to do, to start with, is clarify some of the difficulties that stand in the way of the real author of a novel when he is talking to real readers. Which one of me is talking to which one of you?

One final thing: in talking about a novel, about what it means and what it says. Well, we can talk about what the characters are saying, what the narrator is saying, and what the implied (or inferred) author seems to be saying. We can also talk about what the book *as a whole*, as distinct from those parts and their sum, seems to be saying.

Now: having made that long proviso, let me talk briefly about what I think the book, as a whole, is saying.

I think it's saying that the world is a rich and beautiful place of unimaginable complexity; that our consciousness is one of the greatest treasures we possess – perhaps the very greatest of all; that promoting understanding and knowledge is our most important task, and worth living for. It is saying that trying to stifle understanding is wrong; that knowledge comes to us not only through the rational part of our minds, but through our emotions and our bodies as well; that there is no need to invoke the supernatural either to account for the existence of the universe in the first place or to help us understand it now; that, in fact, the invocation of supernatural causes and supernatural powers, the need to placate and obey them, has brought about a great deal of terrible cruelty and suffering, and that we would be better off without it. It is also saying that evolution might have brought us to this point entirely by chance and accident, and that there has been no purpose in it, but because we are conscious, there *is* a purpose now, and that purpose is to work towards bringing about a Republic of Heaven – namely, a state of affairs in this world, in this life, which is as full and free and rich and joyous as we can make it, for everyone.

Of course, the term '*The Republic of Heaven*' is a metaphor. People who ask, for instance, 'Who's going to be the President of the Republic of Heaven?' are asking the same sort of question as 'How long is God's beard?' One thing this book is *not* doing is asking you to read it literally. The Republic of Heaven is a metaphor for a state of being that's already partly present wherever human beings are treating each other with kindness and approaching the universe with curiosity and wonder.

One thing that plays an important part in the story is the mysterious entity I call Dust. It seems to be connected with human growth and understanding; it might even have a connection with Original Sin, which is why the theologians in the book are so agitated about it. It seems to be everywhere, to permeate the universe, but at the same time it gathers more thickly around adults than around children.

Dust lies behind many of the motivations of the different characters. At the end of the first part, Lyra, who has witnessed terrible things done by adults against children, reasons that if the people who do terrible things think Dust is bad, then Dust must be good. And in the course of the last book, the scientist Mary Malone, who's been investigating Dust with the help of the amber spyglass of the title, discovers that Dust is leaving the universe in a terrible flood, as if a great catastrophe had happened. The loss of Dust would be a disaster beyond imagining, because Dust seems to be a visible analogy or picture or metaphor (not a literal description,

I have to say again) of human consciousness.

Dust is everywhere, in our hearts and in between the stars; it nurtures us, and it delights in the facts of human love and understanding. In some ways it's not unlike God. But there's an important difference: Dust, unlike the traditional idea of God, depends on us. We depend on Dust in order to live to our full potential, but it depends on us too: if we don't strive to promote knowledge and understanding, if we turn away from compassion and towards fanatical hatred, then Dust will wither and die.

So it sets up a new kind of relationship between us and God – mutually dependent instead of being hierarchical. He didn't create us: we create each other. Instead of just being subordinate to a king, as we were under the old dispensation, we have an important part to play in keeping God alive. And that's part of what I mean by the Republic of Heaven: we are *responsible*, we are citizens, this is a democracy; and if we give up on our responsibilities, then tyranny could easily arise again.

I'm going to read a passage from the story which I think has a bearing on this discussion. Mary Malone is observing the Dust, when she feels a sense of being pulled away from her body:

> She flung a mental lifeline to that physical self, and tried to recall the feeling of being in it: all the sensations that made up being alive. The exact touch of her friend Atal's soft-tipped trunk caressing her neck. The taste of bacon and eggs. The triumphant strain in her muscles as she pulled herself up a rock face. The delicate dancing of her fingers on a computer keyboard. The smell of roasting coffee. The warmth of her bed on a winter night.
>
> And gradually she stopped moving; the lifeline held fast, and she felt the weight and strength of the current pushing against her as she hung there in the sky.
>
> And then a strange thing happened. Little by little (as

she reinforced those sense-memories, adding others: tasting
an iced Margarita in California, sitting under the lemon
trees outside a restaurant in Lisbon, scraping the frost off the
windscreen of her car) she felt the Dust-wind easing. The
pressure was lessening.

But only on *her*: all around, above and below, the great
flood was streaming as fast as ever. Somehow there was a
little patch of stillness around her, where the particles were
resisting the flow.

They *were* conscious! They felt her anxiety, and responded
to it. And they began to carry her back to her deserted body,
and when she was close enough to see it once more, so heavy,
so warm, so safe, a silent sob convulsed her heart.

And then she sank back into her body, and awoke.

She took in a deep shuddering breath. She pressed her
hands and her legs against the rough planks of the platform,
and having a minute ago nearly gone mad with fear, she was
now suffused with a deep slow ecstasy at being one with her
body and the earth and everything that was matter.
(*TAS*, 368)

The sense that the whole universe is alive, not just inanimate, but alive
and conscious of meaning, is one that I've felt on two or three occasions,
and they made such a deep impression on me that I shall never forget
them. One happened during a stormy late afternoon on the coast of
north Wales, where I grew up as a teenager. Another happened on a winter evening in London when I was in my middle twenties, just coming
home to our flat in Barnes from the library in Charing Cross Road where
I worked. I've never taken any drug stronger than alcohol or cannabis,
and not much of that, so I can't compare it to a drug-induced trance; and
there was nothing trance-like about it – I was intensely and ecstatically

awake, if anything. I just saw connections between things, similarities, parallels; it was like rhyme, but instead of sounds rhyming, it was meanings that rhymed, and there were endless series of them, and they went on for ever in every direction. The whole universe was connected by lines and chains and fields of meaning, and I was part of it. It lasted about half an hour in each case and then faded.

I've hardly ever talked about it, because it seems like something whose significance is private, but I found some of the intensity of it coming through in Mary's experience as I described it in the passage I've just read. I mention it now because it seems to me that this is the sort of experience that someone might call spiritual, or even mystical; but my whole being shies away from those words like a nervous horse at a firework.

Such words seem to imply some sort of contrast between the material and the spiritual; they seem to suggest an experience in which the material world is being transcended, or penetrated, or lifted aside like a curtain to show us something different, or much better, beyond it. But that wasn't what I felt at all. It was the physical world itself which was full of meaning – the precise grey of the clouds streaming over the sea and the white of the spray, the exact angle the wake of that barge made with the railing of Hammersmith Bridge as I walked across the Thames. There was no sense of the supernatural; I didn't feel at one with God; I felt at one with the physical world, and I saw what it *meant*, and what it meant was that I belonged in it.

So: very briefly summing up.

Atheist or agnostic? The difference is one of perspective. Seen from one perspective, the total amount of things-I-know is the tiniest conceivable speck of light, so small it's hardly there at all, against a vast and encircling and illimitable darkness which is all the things I don't know. There well may be a God out there in the dark; but I don't know, because I can't see that far.

But now let's come in closer and closer, bit by bit, to that little speck of light, and see what happens. As we come closer like a cine camera zooming in, it slowly gets bigger and bigger, and grows to fill the screen, and grows out wider still, until we're there in the middle of the speck of light and it's not a speck at all any more: from horizon to horizon, it's filled with light and things to see by it. I mean not only the things I know, but also the conclusions I've drawn from the things I know, and the guesses I make based on them.

And in all that wide horizon, I can see no evidence for God, not a bit. Everything I can see is perfectly well explained by purely natural things: by the way matter reacts to other matter. I see no intellectual need for the existence of God; I see no moral need for him; and I feel no emotional need. There is not a God-shaped hole in my life.

But when I look at the history and the present behaviour of the human race, I see a story of infamy, folly, cruelty and wickedness carried out in the name of a God who is not there. Steven Weinberg: 'Good people have done good things, and evil people have done evil things, without the help of religion; but for good people to do evil – that takes religion.'

And when the Bishop talks about human relations and human life, I applaud his good sense, I relish his wisdom, and I admire his good works; but when he speaks of God, he seems to me to be speaking a foreign language, or to be like the person who insists that the fairies *are* there in the garden, and the very fact that you can't see them proves it beyond all doubt. But if we are to continue talking at all, and I think we must, because conversation is an important part of the Republic of Heaven – if, as I say, we are to continue talking at all, then those are the points at which we have to change the conversation and speak of other things.

THIS TALK WAS GIVEN AT A STUDY DAY WITH THE BISHOP OF OXFORD AT THE OXFORD UNIVERSITY DEPARTMENT FOR CONTINUING EDUCATION, REWLEY HOUSE, OXFORD, ON 5 OCTOBER, 2002.

The Bishop of Oxford at the time was Richard Harries, a good and wise man, with whom I very much enjoyed debating.

The Republic of Heaven

GOD IS DEAD, LONG LIVE THE REPUBLIC!

Making a case for a 'Republic of Heaven' on earth, and drawing on children's literature for signs of what it might look like

WHAT I'M GOING TO SAY THIS EVENING IS NOT IN ANY WAY AN ACADEMIC examination of children's books and religion. I'm delighted that children's literature is at last beginning to receive the proper academic attention it deserves in this country. But I'm also glad that it's come too late for me to feel it necessary to go and study it.

I read English at Oxford in the belief that it would help me do what I most wanted to do, which was write books. It didn't help at all. If I were younger today, I'd probably feel that I ought to go and study children's literature and learn what the proper approach to the subject should be, before I dared to get up and speak about it. But I've learned by this time that that wouldn't work for me; it's no good, I can't do academic stuff, so I have to speak in the only way I can; and my approach this evening is going to be quite unacademic and highly improper. I'm not even going to mention didacticism, despite what it says in the programme.

My starting point is the question of what happens to the Kingdom of Heaven when the King dies. The idea that God is dead has been a central part of the understanding of many of us for over a century now. A. N. Wilson's book *God's Funeral* (John Murray, 1999) examines the idea in detail by looking at some representative figures in the argument, and Ludovic Kennedy's *All in the Mind: A Farewell to God* (Hodder and Stoughton, 1999) shows that the matter is still very much alive, even if God isn't.

So it's nothing new to say that God is dead. I take it that he is, and that since there is no king any more, there is no Kingdom either; but that we need heaven none the less. I'm proposing that we look for evidence of a Republic of Heaven. I think I *can* see evidence for it, in books that children read among other places; I think I can catch a glimpse of it here and there.

I can also see vestiges of the Kingdom, and I'm going to point out the difference. What I'm not going to do is draw up a short and narrow list of approved republican books or writers, and condemn the rest to the flames. That would be a thoroughly Kingdom-like thing to do. I was condemned to be burnt myself recently, or my books were. An article in the *Catholic Herald* said that my *His Dark Materials* was 'far more worthy of the bonfire than Harry [Potter]'; it was 'a million times more sinister'. Naturally, I'm very proud of this distinction, and I asked the publishers to print it in the paperback of *The Subtle Knife*. But I'm even more pleased to be living in a country and at a time when no one is actually going to go out and gather wood to set me alight, though I'm well aware that in some parts of our world today, the Kingdom is alive and flourishing. This is still a battle we have to fight.

No, what I'm going to do is point out, from the books I know, some moments or some qualities that are characteristic of what I call a republican attitude to the great questions of religion, which are the great questions of life. I make no claim to have read everything; I freely acknowledge that I may not have read very much. But if I describe this republican attitude clearly enough, then others may be able to see it too in the books they know.

To begin with, though, we must take account of some of the consequences of the death of God. What happens when we realise there's nothing there to believe in? The answer varies according to temperament, as much as anything else. G. K. Chesterton, for example, is reputed to have said something to the effect that when people stop believing in God, they don't believe in nothing, they believe in anything. This was a warning against astrology and the occult and fashionable religions, especially those from that sinister place, 'the East'. A powerful aphoristic style like Chesterton's can easily magnify a childish fear or prejudice into the appearance of a universal truth; it's worth remembering that we don't have to believe something just because it's well said.

A different temperament finds a different sort of expression. The melancholy long withdrawing roar that Matthew Arnold heard near Dover Beach, the sea of Faith going out, is more affecting – at least until we realise that, as A. N. Wilson points out, the metaphor isn't thought through: tides have a habit of coming back in again if you wait for long enough. Nevertheless, if we don't think too clearly about it, it sort of works. But Arnold's suggestion as to how we might put up with the loss of faith, 'Ah, love, let us be true / To one another,' is not a remedy: it's a palliative. It assuages the condition without curing it. If he was anxious about the death of God, an honest lover even in his beloved's arms would have to admit, as he looked at the universe over her shoulder, that the stars were cold and the night was empty and God was nowhere to be seen.

Chesterton's self-induced penny dreadful shivers over the sinister horridness of foreign gods (he once wrote about seeing 'evil shapes' in the pattern of a Turkish carpet, an odd idea that turns up in C. S. Lewis's Narnia too, where the Witch kills Aslan with a knife of 'a strange and evil shape' – what is an *evil shape*? Nonsense, that's what it is) and Matthew Arnold's mournful inability to read the tides are largely emotional. Altogether more thoughtful is the famous and utterly serious comment of George Eliot, talking about *God*, *Immortality*, and *Duty*: 'How inconceivable the first, how unbelievable the second, and yet how peremptory and absolute the third.' I like that earnestness. I admire it a great deal. And I think it leads to one of the most important consequences of the death of God, because something's lacking: if Duty is peremptory and absolute, so (given our nature) is the necessity for something else, which one might call joy. George Eliot's universe of duty is a bleak place, and human beings need more than that.

Now it's not legitimate, I know, to argue from the *want* of something to the necessity that that something must exist. It's very poor logic. But as I said a minute ago, I'm not being academic, and I'm with the young Jane Eyre on this: 'You think I have no feelings,' she says to her cold-hearted guardian Mrs Reed, 'and that I can do without one bit of love or kindness; but I cannot live so.' She demands love, because of her passionate need of it, and lo and behold, in due course love appears, though not before Jane Eyre the girl has grown and suffered. If we need something, says *Jane Eyre* the book, we must search for it, or create it. I think that the book is right, and I think we need this thing which I've called joy. I might also have called it *meaning*. What I'm referring to is a sense that things are right and good, and we are part of everything that's right and good.

Putting it another way, we need a sense that we're connected to the universe. This *connectedness* to things is what we mean by meaning. The meaning of one thing is its connection with another; the meaning of our lives is their connection with something other than ourselves. Religion, the religion that's now dead, did give us that, in full measure: we were part of a huge cosmic drama, involving a Creation and a Fall and a Redemption, and Heaven and Hell, and (not least) a Millennium. What we did *mattered*, because God saw everything, even the fall of a sparrow. And one of the most deadly and oppressive consequences of the death of God and his religion is this sense of meaninglessness or alienation that so many of us have felt in the past century or more. We're bereft of that connection with the universe as a whole which makes suffering bearable: 'Man can put up with any *what* as long as he has a *why*,' as someone said.

However, there is one religion that I want to look at briefly, because it seems to speak very directly to precisely this psychological condition. Spiritual condition, if you like. I'm talking about Gnosticism – a subject which has fascinated me for years. This has become the subject of a number of books and commentaries in the past half-century, as Gnostic texts from the beginning of the Christian era have gradually been discovered and translated, and as the peculiar and intense flavour of the religion they describe seems to meet our taste at the end of the second millennium.

The Gnostic religion, like the Christian one, tells us a story that involves ourselves. Some characters we know from Christianity appear in the Gnostic story too, but they have a very different aspect. To sum it up briefly and crudely, the Gnostic myth says that this world – the material universe we live in – was created not by a good God but by an evil Demiurge, who made it as a kind of prison for the sparks of divinity that had fallen, or been stolen, from the inconceivably distant true God who was their real source. These little sparks of god-ness are known as the *pneuma*, or soul, and each of us has a portion inside us. It's the duty of the Gnostics, the knowing ones, to try and escape from this world, out of the clutches of the Demiurge and his angelic archons, and find a way back to that original and unknown and far-off God.

Now whatever else this is, it's a very good story, and what's more it has an immense explanatory power: it offers to explain why we feel, as so many of us do, *exiled* in this world, *alienated* from joy and meaningfulness and the true connection we feel we must have with the universe, as Jane Eyre feels that she must have love and kindness.

So Gnosticism fits the temper of the times. It lends itself to all kinds of contemporary variations: a feminist one, for example, partly because of the important role it assigns to the figure of the Sophia, or Wisdom, the youngest and paradoxically the rashest of the emanations of the divine being. Somehow we're not surprised to learn that it was all her fault that the material universe came about in the first place.

And Gnosticism appeals powerfully too to the sense of being *in the know*, of having access to a truth not available to most people. And not least, it appeals because the story it tells is all about a massive conspiracy, and we love massive conspiracies. *The X-Files*, for example, is pure

Gnosticism. 'The truth is out there,' says Mulder: not *in here*, because *in here* is permeated by evil conspiracies that reach right to the heart of the Pentagon and the FBI and the White House and every other centre of power in the world. The Demiurge is in charge, *in here*. But *out there* somewhere is that distant unknowable God, the source of all truth, and we belong to him – not to the corrupt and dishonest and evil empire that rules this world.

So it's a powerfully dramatic myth, and it has the great advantage of putting us human beings and our predicament right at the heart of it. No wonder it appeals. The trouble is, it's not true. If we can't believe the story about the shepherds and the angels and the wise men and the star and the manger and so on, then it's even harder to believe in Demiurges and archons and emanations and so on. It certainly explains, and it certainly makes us feel important, but it isn't true.

And it has the terrible defect of libelling – one might almost say blaspheming against, if the notion had any republican meaning – the physical universe; of saying that this world is just a clumsy copy of a perfect original which we can't see because it's somewhere else. In the eyes of some Christian writers, of course, this sort of Platonism is a great merit. C. S. Lewis, at the end of the last book in the Narnia series, has his character the wise old professor explaining: 'Our world, England and all, is only a shadow or copy of something in Aslan's real world...' In fact, the two things are 'as different as a real thing is from a shadow or as waking life is from a dream.' And then he goes on to add under his breath 'It's all in Plato, all in Plato: bless me, what do they teach them in these schools!'

This notion that the world we know with our senses is a crude and imperfect copy of something much better somewhere else is one of the most striking and powerful inventions of the human mind. It's also one of the most perverse and pernicious. In the Gnostic world-view, it encourages a thorough-going rejection of the physical universe in favour of an unfortunately entirely imaginary world inhabited by evil powers, archons, aeons, emanations, angels and demons of every sort. Tremendously exciting stuff, but all utter nonsense. Just like *The X-Files*.

Why do I say it's pernicious? It's pernicious because it encourages us to disbelieve the evidence of our senses, and allows us to suspect everything of being false. It leads to a state of mind that's hostile to experience. It encourages us to see a toad lurking beneath every flower, and if we can't see one, it's because the toads now are extra cunning and have learned to become invisible. It's a state of mind that leads to a hatred of the physical world. The Gnostic would say that the beauty and solace and pleasure that can be found in the physical world are exactly why we should avoid it: they are the very things with which the Demiurge traps our souls.

Of course, the Puritanism that so poisoned the human mind later on said just the same sort of thing. I'd say that that position is an unhealthy and distorted one which can only be maintained at the cost of common sense, and of that love and kindness that Jane Eyre demanded, and finally of sanity itself. The Gnostic situation is a *dramatic* one to be in – it's intensely *exciting* – but it's the sort of paranoid excitement felt by those American militias who collect guns and hide in the hills and watch out for the black helicopters of the evil New World Order as they prepare for Armageddon. It's nuts, basically.

So the challenge remains to be answered: to reclaim a vision of heaven from the wreck of religion; to realise that our human nature demands meaning and joy just as Jane Eyre demanded love and kindness ('You think we can live without them, but we cannot live so'); to accept that this meaning and joy will involve a passionate love of the physical world, this world, of food and drink and sex and music and laughter, and not a suspicion and hatred of it; to understand that it will both grow out of and add to the achievements of the human mind such as science and art. Finally, we must find a way of believing that we are not subservient creatures dependent on the whim of some celestial monarch, but free citizens of the Republic of Heaven.

(A brief word at this point on the teleology of evolution. Evolution has no aim, we're told. We human beings are not in any way higher up some sort of ladder than our fellow creatures; we're not the product of a sort of Shavian creative evolution any more than we're the divinely created sons and daughters of God. Life has no purpose and evolution is blind and the universe is indifferent to our presence. I'll just note that view here, because it seems to be the only honest alternative to the Kingdom, and I'll put a marker down so I can come back to it later.)

Now then: is there anywhere we can get a glimpse of the Republic of Heaven? And is there anywhere we should look to see what the Republic of Heaven is *not* like?

To take the latter question first: Christian writers whose faith informs their work are not, of course, describing the republic. The most notable Christian storyteller for children has been C. S. Lewis, who in the Narnia books is so far from being a republican that you could take a line on pretty well anything in the republic by seeing what he says about it and then believing the opposite.

Take the exclusion of Susan from the stable, which represents salvation, near the end of the final Narnia book, *The Last Battle*. Susan is cast out because, as the prim Peter says, 'My sister is no longer a friend of Narnia.' 'Oh, Susan!' says Jill. 'She's interested in nothing nowadays except nylons and lipstick and invitations. She always was a jolly sight too keen on being grown-up.' In other words, normal human development, which includes a growing awareness of your body and its effect on the opposite sex, is something from which Lewis's narrative, and what he would like us to think is the Kingdom of Heaven, turns with horror.

I'm going to focus on those nylons for a moment. (Do people still call them nylons? He means stockings, of course.) Here's a passage from William Mayne's novel *The Midnight Fair*. (I must add that William Mayne's conviction for the sexual abuse of young girls in 2004, after I gave this talk, raises a different question entirely, which I discuss in my afterword.)

Paul, a boy of twelve or so, has found his attention increasingly absorbed by Victoria, a strange and solitary girl. He's just summoned up the courage to write a Christmas card for her. They've been in church, and he watches as she leaves with her mother.

> The service ended for the rest of the congregation. For Paul it had not begun, and he would have liked an instant replay, but that was not in prayer books old or new.
>
> He stood up. The girl came along the aisle, nearing him. He would follow her out, catch up in the porch, and present the card... The girl came past. Paul wanted to jump out and give her a hundred cards.
>
> She did not see him. Why should she? She walked with her mother. In a brown skirt, stockings with a small white hole beside one ankle, brown leather shoes with a frilled flap on the instep, a green sweater, and a bronze coat. She was quite plain, but unearthly beautiful; there was nothing else like her, and her uniqueness was the reason for all creation.

Lewis's nylons were not real stockings; they were Platonic stockings, if you like, and their function was simply to carry a symbolic charge. What they mean is that if you give them too much of your attention, you're shut out from the Kingdom of Heaven. In the republic, stockings work differently. They're real stockings, for a start; they sometimes have holes in them. That little white hole beside her ankle is one of the things that make Victoria 'quite plain, but unearthly beautiful'; and of course Paul *can't* give too much attention to her stockings, and her shoes, and her coat, and everything about her. She is real, and he is in love.

As a matter of fact, Lewis's position as a whole wasn't at all consistent. Whereas the Narnia books illustrate the very antithesis of the Republic of Heaven, his critical writing – as I have pointed out elsewhere – often shows a more generous and sensible spirit. For example, talking about this very business of growing up in his essay *On Three Ways of Writing for Children*, he says: 'surely arrested development consists not in refusing to lose old things but in failing to add new things? I now like hock, which I am sure I should not have liked as a child. But I still like lemon-squash. I call this growth or development because I have been enriched: where I formerly had only one pleasure, I now have two.'

There's nothing there which a republican would have any quarrel with; but the sensible Lewis who wrote that was thrust aside in Narnia by the paranoid bigot who proclaimed that an interest in lipstick and nylons was not an addition to the pleasures of life but an absolute disqualification for the joys of heaven.

The ending of *The Last Battle* makes this position even clearer. 'The term is over: the holidays have begun,' says Aslan to the children, having just let them know that: 'There *was* a real railway accident. Your father and mother and all of you are – as you used to call it in the Shadowlands – dead.'

Using Narnia as our moral compass, we can take it as axiomatic that in the Republic of Heaven, people do not regard life in this world as so worthless and contemptible that they leave it with pleasure and relief, and a railway accident is not an end-of-term treat. Jane Eyre, as so often, got it right and gave the true republican answer when the pious Mr Brockle-hurst asks what she thinks she must do to avoid going to hell: 'I must keep in good health, and not die,' she says.

This world is where the things are that matter. If the Narnia stories had been composed in that spirit, the children who have passed through all these adventures and presumably learned great truths from them would be free to live and grow up in the world, even at the price of engaging with the lipstick and the nylons, and *use* what they'd learned for the benefit of others. If you're wiser and stronger as the result of your experiences, then do something useful with that strength and wisdom – make the world a bit better. That would be the republican thing to do. That's why Lewis doesn't let his characters do it, and why the Narnia books are such an invaluable guide to what is wrong and cruel and selfish.

No, the first requirement for the Republic of Heaven is that it should exist nowhere but on this earth, in the physical universe we know, not in some gaseous realm far away. That takes care of most fantasy of the Tolkien sort: closed fantasy, as John Goldthwaite calls it in his invaluable study, *The Natural History of Make-Believe* (OUP, 1996). No story in which there's an absolute gulf between our world and the story-world can depict the Republic of Heaven, because the republic can be nowhere but here.

The great fairy tales, on the other hand, are profoundly republican; so much *here* that the characters have everyday names like Jack and do everyday tasks like taking baskets of food to their grandmothers or working in the kitchen. It's a great pity that with the passing of time it's become less easy to see the difference between the truthful world of Jack and the Beanstalk or the peasant life of Italo Calvino's great collection of Italian folk tales, on the one hand, and the entirely artificial world of Tolkien's Shire on the other; the latter is no more real than the horse-brasses and the posthorns in an Olde English theme-pub – a place called *The Hobbit and Firkin*, perhaps. It wasn't even real when he wrote it. But both the real and the fake now look equally quaint to the uninformed eye.

Am I saying that there is no fantasy in the Republic of Heaven? That everything must be sober and drab, with a sort of earnest sociological realism? Not at all. If the republic doesn't include fantasy, it won't be worth living in. It won't be heaven of any sort. But *inclusiveness* is the whole point: the fantasy and the realism must connect. *Jack and the Beanstalk* is a republican story because the magic grows out of the most common and everyday thing – a handful of beans – and the beanstalk grows right outside the kitchen window. *The Lord of the Rings* is not a republican story, because there is no point at which it connects with our life. Middle Earth is a place that never existed in a past that never was, and there's no way we could ever get there. Nor do the people there behave like people, unlike those concerned with another Ring; the world depicted in Wagner's *Ring* cycle never existed either, but the *Ring* is a republican work because Wagner's gods and heroes are exactly like human beings, on a grand scale: every human virtue and every human temptation is there. Tolkien leaves a good half of them out. No one in Middle Earth has any sexual relations at all. I think their children must be delivered by post.

No, the Republic of Heaven must be a place where the people behave like us, with the full range of human feelings, even when they don't look like us, even when they look like beings that have never existed, like Tove Jansson's Moomins, or Sylvia Waugh's Mennyms, or Mary Norton's Borrowers. The people in the republic are people like us – even when they're dead. The republic is thronged with ghosts, and they have full democratic rights. A marvellous creepy little tale, Jan Mark's 'Who's a Pretty Boy, Then?' exemplifies what I mean: on the patch in the garden where nothing will grow, Dad builds an aviary. But the budgerigars don't thrive, and mysteriously they begin to speak:

> 'Oh, I'm so cold,' said one.
> 'I shall always be very cold,' said another, 'cold as clay.'
> 'I shall always be here,' said a third.
> 'I shall never go away,' said the white bird.
> 'Pity me.'
> 'Pity me.'

Ghosts that come only to scare us, ghosts that are only special effects, ghosts that might as well be aliens or prehistoric monsters have nothing to tell us about the Republic of Heaven. But ghosts that remind us of our own mortality are citizens like ourselves. In the republic, we honour the dead and maintain a conversation with them, in order to learn more about how to live. In short, the people in the republic are people we could have as friends, people on whose behaviour we can model our own and whom we'd be glad to be compared with; people with whom it's conceivable that we could fall in love. People like us.

The next essential quality of the Republic of Heaven is that what happens there *matters*, and what the characters do *makes a difference*.

Matters to *whom*, though? Makes a difference to *what*? The God who noted the fall of a sparrow is no longer around. It makes no difference to him. The important thing, I think, is that the actions of the protagonists make a difference to themselves. The republic is a place where you can change things; as H. G. Wells's Mr Polly discovers: 'If you don't like your life, you can change it.'

I'm talking this evening mostly about books that are read by children, and the situations such books deal with aren't necessarily what a grown-up would be thrown by; it's a question of scale, of course. What matters is the attitude the protagonists take to the problems they face, and the attitude the book takes to that.

A good example is the two books that Erich Kästner wrote about Emil Tischbein in the thirties: *Emil and the Detectives* and its sequel *Emil and the Three Twins*. In the first book, young Emil goes from the little country town of Neustadt to visit his relatives in the great city of Berlin. On the train he falls asleep, and a thief steals the money Emil's widowed mother has given him to take to his grandmother. Not much money, because they are far from rich, but that's the point: they can't afford to lose it, and Emil feels terribly responsible.

But once he arrives in the city, he finds that he's not alone. Some other boys, strangers at first, quickly join forces to track down and denounce the thief, and the story ends happily, with the money restored. The republican point here is that the children find the solution themselves, out of the everyday qualities they share: resourcefulness, quick wits, determination, and not least access to a telephone.

In the sequel, Emil is trying to come to terms with the fact that his widowed mother wants to marry again. He likes his potential stepfather, Herr Jeschke, but that isn't the point, as every stepchild knows. Emil would much rather she stayed alone with him, but he hasn't told her that. In a remarkable passage, unfortunately too long to quote in full, he and his grandmother talk through all the consequences of this, and he learns from her that his mother feels just the same as he does – she would really rather remain alone with Emil; but she's afraid of the future, because Emil will grow up one day, and leave home; and after all, Herr Jeschke is a good man. Emil says:

> 'What am I to do, Granny?'
> 'One of two things, Emil. When you get home you can ask her not to marry. Then you'll kiss and the thing will be settled.'
> 'Or?'
> 'Or you can keep silence, but the silence must last till the end of your days, and you must be cheerful in your silence and not go round with a face like a mourner at a funeral. You alone can choose which course to pursue.'

He chooses the right way, for Emil is a hero of the republic, which is a place where children learn to grow up, and where cheerfulness and courage do make a difference.

Another work I admire for similar reasons is Edward Ardizzone's *Little Tim and the Brave Sea Captain*. Tim has run away to sea, and has a fine time till a great storm comes up and the ship begins to sink. He and the captain are standing on the bridge.

> 'Come,' says the captain, 'stop crying and be a brave boy. We are bound for Davy Jones's locker and tears won't help us now.'

So Tim dried his eyes and tried not to be too frightened. He felt he would not mind going anywhere with the captain, even to Davy Jones's locker.

They stood hand in hand and waited for the end.

Little Tim is a picture book for young children, and sure enough, on the next page arrives the lifeboat; but Tim and the captain don't know that when they stand hand in hand waiting for the end. You're never too young to become a citizen of the Republic of Heaven.

So part of this *meaning* that I've suggested we need, this *connection* with a wider universe, the sense that we belong and matter, comes from the moral and social dimension that the Republic of Heaven must embody. In the republic, we're connected in a moral way to one another, to other human beings. We have responsibilities to them, and they to us. We're not isolated units of self-interest in a world where there is no such thing as society; we cannot live so.

But part of the sense of wider meaningfulness that we need also comes from seeing that we have a connection with nature and the universe around us, with everything that is *not* human as well. So the Republic of Heaven is also characterised by another quality: it enables us to see this real world, our world, as a place of infinite delight, so intensely beautiful and intoxicating that if we saw it clearly then we would want nothing more, ever. We would know that this earth is our true home, and nowhere else is. In the words of William Blake, one of the founding fathers of the Republic of Heaven, 'If the doors of perception were cleansed everything would appear to man as it is, infinite.'

Despite Aldous Huxley, we do not need drugs to cleanse the doors of perception: stepping aside from habit is often enough on its own. In what I take to be one of the central texts of the Republic of Heaven – the works of Tove Jansson – the little creature who one day is going to be Moominpappa escapes from the Foundlings' Home and sets out to explore the world. He says: 'I had nothing to call my own. I knew nothing, but believed a lot. I did nothing by habit. I was extremely happy.'

Blake again:

> How do you know but ev'ry Bird that cuts the airy way
> Is an immense world of delight, clos'd by your senses five?

Lesser writers than Blake have also caught the true tone of this immense world of delight, and made their contribution to the republic. For example, D. J. Watkins-Pitchford, who wrote under the name of B.B.: his books about the Little Grey Men will be familiar to some older readers. He belongs in a tradition of observing and writing about nature which includes, I suppose, Gilbert White of Selborne, as well as Dorothy Wordsworth. B.B. was far from being a graceful writer of prose, but in his novel *Brendon Chase* (1944) he does evoke the kind of delight that Blake speaks of. The three brothers Robin, John, and Harold run away to the forest and live wild for most of a year.

Here is the fifteen-year-old Robin alone in the forest:

> He would sometimes come upon some specially lovely tree, an oak, or a birch, and he would sit down and feast his eyes upon it, just as he would go to the Blind Pool to watch the water and the floating leaves. There was something about the birches which was extremely attractive – their white bark was the colour and texture of kid – sometimes there was a beautiful golden flush on the smooth trunks which felt so soft to the touch… Or perhaps it was another oak which took his fancy, bare and gaunt with each little twig and branch naked to the winds… He would listen to the low hiss of the winter wind among the intricate network, which sang like wires in every passing gust… He would put his ear to the kindly grey

trunk and hear that wild song much magnified, the whole tree would be pulsing, almost as though a heart beat there inside its rough body.

'All in Plato, all in Plato?' What utter nonsense.

At the furthest extent, this sense of delight in the physical world can blend into a sort of ecstatic identification with it. Here's a poem by Emily Brontë:

> High waving heather, 'neath stormy blasts bending,
> Midnight and moonlight and bright shining stars;
> Darkness and glory rejoicingly blending,
> Earth rising to heaven and heaven descending,
> Man's spirit away from its drear dongeon sending,
> Bursting the fetters and breaking the bars.

The Van Gogh who painted cypress trees like live green flames against a sky swirling with blazing stars would have recognised that state of mind. The point is not only to understand its origins in psychological terms, or to criticise its expression in formal terms, or to analyse its social implications in political terms; the point is to share it. To do that, we have to realise that that intensity of feeling, that perception of the connectedness of things, is not a delusion. It's true. The world, the republic of Heaven, really is like that. Emily Brontë wasn't making it up; she was seeing it. The high waving heather and the cypress trees and the starry night are not so far from Thomas Traherne's visionary sentence:

> You never enjoy the world aright, till the sea itself floweth in your veins, till you are clothed with the heavens, and crowned with the stars; and perceive yourself to be the sole heir of the whole world.

And never forget that it's *this* sea, *this* heather, *these* cypress trees, in *this* world; not elsewhere, in the Kingdom, but here in the republic.

So far I've been talking about various aspects of the Republic of Heaven as I see them, and not in any particular order; but they are glimpses, little windows opening into it here and there. What we need now is something more coherent and solid. We need a story; we need a myth. ('You think we can live without a myth, but we cannot live so.') Details of narrative don't matter at this stage; what I'm concerned with here is the function of the myth: what such an underpinning story needs to do.

First, it must do what the traditional religious stories did: it must *explain*. It must tell a story about how the world came about; about what we are doing here; about how things came to be as they are. It must satisfy that hunger for a *Why*. Why does the world exist? Why are we here?

Of course, there are two kinds of *Why*, and a myth must deal with both. There's the one that asks *What brought us here?* and the other that asks *What is our purpose?* One looks back, and the other looks forward, perhaps.

And in offering an answer to the first *why*, a republican myth must accept the overwhelmingly powerful evidence for evolution by natural selection. There's no room for a divine Creator in the republic. The neo-Darwinians are probably right: we have come here by chance, and we might not have come here at all. There was no purpose in that. But here I'll come back to the marker I put down earlier, when I described that view of evolution in terms which I think were reasonably fair. The processes of life are blind and automatic; there is no rising on stepping stones of our dead selves to higher things; there is no goal; there has been no purpose in our coming here.

Well, I think a republican answer to that would be: *there is now*. We are conscious, and conscious of our own consciousness. We might have arrived at this point by a series of accidents, but from now on we have to take charge of our fate. Now we are here, now we are conscious, we make a difference. Our presence changes everything.

So a myth of the Republic of Heaven would explain both how we came about, in terms that are as true as they can be to what we know of the facts, the facts of biology and physics and history; and it would explain what our true purpose is. Our purpose is to understand and to help others to understand, to explore, to speculate, to imagine – to increase the amount of consciousness in the universe. And that purpose has a moral force. It means that it is wrong, it is wicked, to embrace ignorance and to foster stupidity.

Talking of morality brings in the next task for our republican myth: it must provide a sort of framework for understanding why some things are good and others are bad. It's no good to say, 'X is good and Y is bad because God says they are'; the King is dead, and that argument won't do for free citizens of the republic. Of course, the myth must deal with human beings as they are, which includes recognising that there is a depth of human meanness and wickedness which not even the imagination can fully plumb. But it's no good putting the responsibility for that on a pantomime demon, and calling him Satan; he's dead too.

If we're so undermined by despair at the sight of evil that we have to ascribe it to some extra-human force, some dark power from somewhere else, then we have to give up the Republic too and go back to the Kingdom. There's no one responsible but us. Goodness and evil have always had a human origin. The myth must account for that. Nor would a republican myth endorse the view that human beings themselves are fundamentally worthless or contemptible, without any resources of courage or kindness or hope.

But as well as the traditional good things and wicked things (and there has never been much disagreement about those in all human history: dishonesty is bad and truthfulness is good, selfishness is wrong and generosity is right – we can all agree about those) I think we need to reinforce another element of a republican morality. We must make it clear that if an action seeks to restrict understanding and put knowledge in chains, then that is bad too. We haven't always understood that; that's a relatively new development in human history, and it's thanks to the great republicans, to Galileo and Milton and those like them, that it's been added to our understanding. We must keep it there, and keep it watered and fed so that it grows ever more strongly: what shuts out knowledge and nourishes stupidity is wrong; what increases understanding and deepens understanding is right.

The Christian Heaven used to be where we went when we died, if we did what we were told. If the Republic of Heaven is here, on this earth, in our lives, then what happens when we die? Is that all? Is that the end of everything for us? That's hard to accept; for some people it's the hardest thing of all. Well, our myth must talk about death in terms that are as true as they can be to what we know of the facts, and it must do what the Christian myth did, and provide some sort of hope. The myth must give us a way of accepting death, when it comes, of seeing what it means and accepting it; not shrinking from it with terror, or pretending that it'll be like the school holidays. We cannot live so; we cannot die so.

We need a myth – we need a story – because it's no good persuading people to commit themselves to an idea on the grounds that it's *reasonable*. We can learn from religion: Christians, for example, have always known the importance of emotional, imaginative engagement. The phrase *the leap of faith* catches exactly what happens. It's the leap itself which commits us; what involves the whole heart is the *risk*. A republic that's only believed in because it *makes more sense* or it's *more reasonable* than the alternative would be a pallid place indeed, and it wouldn't last for long. What induces that leap of commitment is an emotional thing – a story. How much effect would the Bible have had for generations and generations if it had just been a collection of laws and logical propositions? What seized the mind and captured the heart were the *stories* it contains.

So if we are to see what a Republic of Heaven might look like we must look for evidence of it, as I've been suggesting, in the realm of stories. And I've said before (so I won't spend too long on it here) that one place we can be certain of finding stories these days is in books that are read by children. One example of the kind of thing I mean is Peter Dickinson's book *The Kin* (1998). There's a myth of our origins which does a lot of what I've been suggesting is necessary.

Almost finally, a short warning. This myth I've been talking about, and these glimpses of the Republic of Heaven I've been trying to point out, are not luxuries. They're not just a sort of intellectual plaything that jaded people can turn to for half an hour's amusement. If we're not deadly serious about the republic, we might remember that there are plenty of other people who are deadly serious about the Kingdom. Of all the dangers that threaten us at the beginning of the third millennium – the degradation of the environment, the increasing undemocratic power of the great corporations, the continuing threats to peace in regions full of decaying nuclear weapons, and so on – one of the biggest dangers of all comes from fundamentalist religion.

Matthew Arnold's tide of Faith is coming back in, bringing all kinds of monsters with it. From the Christian conservatives in the USA to the Taliban in Afghanistan or the so-called Islamic State – these people are servants of the King, and they want to extend the Kingdom. Those of us who believe in the republic can't afford to be half-hearted about it, because we have a fight on our hands.

But I'll end by coming back to the children's literature which I should have been talking about all the way through. Literature, or... whatever this is, anyway: a nursery rhyme. If the Republic of Heaven were to have an anthem, I can't think of a better one than this:

> Boys and girls come out to play,
> The moon doth shine as bright as day.

This is a republic where we live by the imagination. Things are upside down and back to front and inside out, and still all right.

> Leave your supper and leave your sleep,
> And join your playfellows in the street –

Not in a private playground with security guards where some of us are let in and others are kept out, not in the park that closes its gates before the moon comes out, but in the street, the common place that belongs to everyone.

> Come with a whoop or come with a call,
> Come with a good will or not at all.

Like Emil, we must be cheerful and not go round with a face like a mourner at a funeral. It's difficult sometimes, but good will is not a luxury – it's an absolute necessity. It's a moral imperative.

> Up the ladder and down the wall,
> A halfpenny loaf will serve us all;
> You find milk, and I'll find flour,
> And we'll have a pudding in half an hour.

We can do it. That's the way it happens in the Republic of Heaven; we provide for ourselves. We'll have a pudding, and a good nourishing one it'll be too; milk and flour are full of goodness. And then we can play together in the bright moonlight till we all fall asleep.

THE REPUBLIC OF HEAVEN

This lecture was delivered in March 2000. A version of it appeared in *The Horn Book*, 1 November 2001.

The case of William Mayne raises the same sort of questions as the career of Eric Gill. Can we enjoy in any way at all the art or literature produced by a man who exploited children in a sexual way? I think we can, but our experience of it will be shadowed and complicated. Once we know about it, we can't ignore it and we shouldn't forget it. It's one of the things we know.

About the Author & Editor

PHILIP PULLMAN is one of the most acclaimed writers working today. He is best known for the *His Dark Materials* trilogy (*Northern Lights*, *The Subtle Knife*, *The Amber Spyglass*), which has been named one of the top 100 novels of all time by *Newsweek*. He has also won many distinguished prizes, including the Carnegie Medal for *Northern Lights* (and the reader-voted 'Carnegie of Carnegies' for the best children's book of the past seventy years); the Whitbread (now Costa) Award for *The Amber Spyglass*; and the Astrid Lindgren Memorial Award, in honour of his body of work. The first volume of Philip Pullman's long-awaited trilogy *The Book of Dust*, set in the same world as *His Dark Materials*, published in 2017.

Philip Pullman lives in Oxford, England. To learn more, please visit www.philip-pullman.com or follow him on Twitter at @PhilipPullman.

SIMON MASON writes books for both children and adults. His first adult novel won the Betty Trask First Novel award, while *Moon Pie*, a novel for young adults, was shortlisted for the Guardian Children's Fiction prize. *Running Girl*, his first Garvie Smith mystery novel, was shortlisted for the Costa Children's Book award. *Kid got Shot*, the second, won Crimefest's best Crime Novel for YA in 2017. Simon lives in Oxford, England.

Acknowledgements

By the Author

I am grateful to all the organisations that invited me to speak to them, and thus sponsored the pieces in this collection that were given as lectures or talks, and to the editors of the newspapers, journals and books where some of the other pieces were first published. My particular thanks go to David Fickling, whose generous insistence that it would be worth publishing them again overcame my idleness and reluctance to lift a finger and search them out, and especially to Simon Mason, whose skill, tact and industry vastly improved the raw material I found for him—some of it very raw indeed. What he did is a model of good and unobtrusive editing at its very best. My most long-standing gratitude goes to my readers, and to the publishers, booksellers, librarians and teachers who have brought my books to them over the years.

By the Editor

All books are collaborative. This book exists because of cover and interior design by Laurence Denmark of Webb and Webb, an original concept by Ness Wood, cover art by John Lawrence, copyediting by Sue Cook, proofreading by Julia Bruce, picture permissions arranged by Jane Smith, text permissions arranged by Connie Robertson, index by Christine Shuttleworth, additional image scanning and balancing by Paul Duffield, production and design management by Alison Gadsby and production control by Rachel Woodforde. Special thanks go to Anthony Hinton, who, as the in-house editor, has liaised with all the above, solving problems along the way, and has kept the book to its schedule with wonderful efficiency. David Fickling has been the book's guiding spirit from the beginning. But, above all, my thanks go to Philip for the essays themselves, and for the opportunity to work with him on them, a hugely enjoyable and stimulating experience.

Permissions

We are very grateful to all of Philip Pullman's publishers, including but not limited to Scholastic, Penguin Random House, Canongate, and Oxford University Press for their kind permission to reproduce extracts from his own work, both text and images, within the essays in this collection.

We are also grateful to the following for their kind permission to reproduce copyright material used within these essays:

Magic Carpets

Leon Garfield: extract from *The Pleasure Garden* (Kestrel, 1976), used by permission of the Estate of Leon Garfield c/o Johnson & Alcock Ltd.

The Writing of Stories

Robert Frost: lines from 'The Road Not Taken' from *The Collected Poems of Robert Frost* edited by Edward Connery Lathem (Vintage, 2013), used by permission of The Random House Group Ltd. Mark Turner: extract from 'Image Schemas' in *The Literary Mind: the origins of thought and language* (OUP, 1998), used by permission of Oxford University Press.

P G Wodehouse: extract from *Aunts Aren't Gentlemen* (Barrie & Jenkins, 1974), copyright © P G Wodehouse 1974, used by permission of the Estate of P G Wodehouse c/o Rogers, Coleridge & White Ltd, 20 Powis Mews, London W11 1JN.

Heinrich von Kleist

Heinrich von Kleist: extract from 'On the Marionette Theatre' from *Hand to Mouth and Other Essays* introduced and translated by Idris Parry (Carcanet, 1981), used by permission of Carcanet Press Ltd.

Paradise Lost

Michael Burgesse after John Baptist Medina, for Book XII of *Paradise Lost* – Image provided by kind permission of the Master and Fellows of Christ's College, Cambridge

The Origin of the Universe

George Orwell: extract from *Animal Farm* (Penguin Classics, 2000) copyright © George Orwell 1945, used by permission of Bill Hamilton as the Literary Executor of the Estate of the Late Sonia Brownell Orwell, c/o A M Heath & Co Ltd.

The Path through the Wood

Mulefa Visualization © Eric Dubois

Robert Frost: lines from 'The Road Not Taken' from *The Collected Poems of Robert Frost* edited by Edward Connery Lathem (Vintage, 2013), used by permission of The Random House Group Ltd

Children's Literature Without Borders

Richmal Crompton: extract from *Still William,* Book 5 in the William series (Macmillan Children's Books, 2016), copyright © Richmal

Belshazzar's Feast by Rembrandt – Belshazzar's Feast c.1636-38 (oil on canvas), Rembrandt Harmensz. Van Rijn (1606-69) / National Gallery, London, UK / Bridgeman Images. (Also refers to the image in the colour section)

A Scene from 'The Forcibly Bewitched' by Francisco Goya – Alamy/Artepics/Francisco de Goya The Bewitched Man 1798

The Baptism of Christ by Piero della Francesca – Alamy/FineArt/ Piero della Francesca/ Baptism of Christ 1450. (Also refers to the image in the colour section)

Embleme for the Month of May by George Wither – Housed at: Internet Archive/University of Illinois at Urbana-Champaign/Digital Copy: No Additional Rights

Allegory of Grammar by Laurent de La Hyre – Alamy/Painting/ Laurent De la Hyre/ Allegorical Figure of Grammar 1650

La Source by Jean Auguste Dominique Ingres – The Source, 1856 (oil on canvas), Ingres, Jean Auguste Dominique (1780-1867) / Musee d'Orsay, Paris, France / Bridgeman Images

Detail of *The Milkmaid* by Johannes Vermeer – Johannes Vermeer/Milkmaid 1657-1658/ Google Art Project/ Rijksmuseum

T S Eliot: lines from 'The Waste Land', *Collected Poems 1909-1962* (Faber, 1974), used by permission of Faber & Faber Ltd.

The Classical Tone

Original UK edition cover of *Tom's Midnight Garden* – Philippa Pearce/ By permission of Oxford University Press

T S Eliot: lines from 'Four Quartets: Burnt Norton', *Collected Poems 1909-1962* (Faber, 1974) used by permission of Faber & Faber Ltd.

Philippa Pearce: extracts from *Tom's Midnight Garden* (OUP, 2000), copyright © Oxford University Press 1958, used by permission of Oxford University Press.

Reading in the Borderland

The Convalescent by Gwen John – The Precious Book, c. 1916-1926 (oil on canvas laid on panel), John, Gwen (1876-1939) / Private Collection / Photo © Christie's Images / Bridgeman Images. (Also refers to the image in the colour section)

A Man Reading in the Garden by Honoré-Victorin Daumier – The Metropolitan Museum of Art, New York /Art Resource/Scala/Honoré-Victorin Daumier 1866

The Living Room by Balthus – Balthus, Le salon (The Living Room), 1942, oil on canvas, Digital image, The Museum of Modern Art, New York/ Scala, Florence, 114.8x146.9cm

Learning to Read and Write by Deng Shu – Ashmolean Museum, University of Oxford/Deng Shu

Wanderer above the Sea of Fog by Caspar David Friedrich – Alamy/Pictorial Press Ltd/Caspar David Friedrich 1818

Cover of *The Pleasure Garden*, illustration by Fritz Wegner – Viking Press/PenguinRandomHouse/ Leon Garfield 1976. (Also refers to the image in the colour section)

Illustration from *The Picts and the Martyrs* by Arthur Ransome – From 'The Picts & the Martyrs: Not Welcome at All', first published by Jonathan Cape. Reprinted by permission of the Random House Group Ltd and in the US by permission of David R. Godine Inc. ©Arthur Ransome 1943

Illustration from *The Exploits of Moominpapa* by Tove Jansson – ©Tove Jansson, 1968, Moomin Characters™

PERMISSIONS

Illustration by Richard Kennedy for *A Hundred Million Francs* – Penguin Random House by Paul Berna/Illustration by Richard Kennedy c/o daughter Rachel Ansari

Illustration from the original French edition of *Le Cheval Sans Tête* (*The Horse without a Head*) – Bodley Head/Illustrator Pierre Dehay/Penguin Random House

Illustration from *The Little Grey Men* by 'B.B.' – David Higham/BB (Denys Watkins-Pitchford)/ Oxford University Press

Rupert Bows to the King from *Rupert* by Alfred Bestall – Rupert Bear/ Alfred Bestall/Classic media now NBC Universal/DreamWorks group & Express Newspapers (Also refers to the image in the colour section)

Illustration by Thomas Henry for *William Again* – William Again/ Richmal Crompton /Illustration by Thomas Henry/ Published by George Newnes Ltd.

'Pony Hütchen went from one to the other pouring out delicious hot chocolate' by Walter Trier – Atrium Verlag, Zürich 1935/Walter Trier

'The newspaper men asked Emil a great number of questions' by Walter Trier – Atrium Verlag, Zürich 1935/Walter Trier

Lyra by Peter Bailey for the Folio Society – Illustration from The Folio Society edition of *Northern Lights/His Dark Materials* © Peter Bailey 2008 www.foliosociety.com

Lyra making sense of the alethiometer by Peter Bailey for the Folio Society – Illustration from The Folio Society edition of *Northern Lights/His Dark Materials* © Peter Bailey 2008 www.foliosociety.com

Leon Garfield: extract from *The Pleasure Garden* (Kestrel, 1976), used by permission of the Estate of Leon Garfield c/o Johnson & Alcock Ltd.

Oliver Twist

Oliver Asking for More by George Cruikshank – Alamy/Lebrecht Music and Arts Photo Library/ Illustration by George Cruikshank

Fagin in the condemned Cell by George Cruikshank – Alamy/ART Collection/ Illustration by George Cruikshank

Sikes attempting to destroy his dog by George Cruikshank – Alamy/Bookworm Classics / Illustration by George Cruikshank

Maus

Excerpt from MAUS: A Survivor's Tale: My Father Bleeds History by Art Spiegelman THE COMPLETE MAUS by Art Spiegelman (Penguin Books, 2003). Copyright © Art Spiegelman, 1973, 1980, 1981, 1982, 1983, 1984, 1985, 1986, 1989, 1990, 1991. All rights reserved

Excerpts from THE COMPLETE MAUS by Art Spiegelman (Penguin Books, 2003). Copyright © Art Spiegelman, 1973, 1980, 1981, 1982, 1983, 1984, 1985, 1986, 1989, 1990, 1991. All rights reserved

Homer: lines from *The Illiad* translated by Robert Fagles (Penguin, 1999), translation copyright © Robert Fagles 1990, used by permission of Viking Books, an imprint of Penguin Publishing Group, a division of Penguin Random House LLC. All rights reserved.

Talents and Virtues

Photograph of Sophia Goddard's tomb © David White Photography/ www.davidwhitephotography.co.uk

Azar Nafisi: extracts from *Reading Lolita in Tehran: a memoir in books* (Penguin, 2015), copyright © Azar Nafisi 2003, used by permission of I B Tauris and Company Ltd via PLSclear.

Index